Rock Climbing
COLORADO

Stewart M. Green

FALCON®

GUILFORD, CONNECTICUT
HELENA, MONTANA

AN IMPRINT OF THE GLOBE PEQUOT PRESS

Cover photo: Ian and Brett Spencer-Green climbing on Turkey Tail.
Back cover photo: Ian Spencer-Green on *Bullet the Blue Sky.*
Section front photos: Ted Steiner collection.

Library of Congress Cataloging-in-Publication Data

Green, Stewart M.
   Rock climbing Colorado / by Stewart Green.
      p.   cm.
   ISBN 1-56044-334-0
   1. Rock climbing—Colorado—Guidebooks. 2. Colorado—Guidebooks. I. Title.
   GV199.42.C6G74 1995   95-40241
   796.5'223'09788—dc20   CIP

Printed in Canada
First Edition/Seventh Printing

CAUTION

Outdoor recreation activities are by their very nature potentially hazardous. All participants in such activities must assume the responsibility for their own actions and safety. The information contained in this guidebook cannot replace sound judgment and good decision-making skills, which help reduce risk exposure, nor does the scope of this book allow for disclosure of all the potential hazards and risks involved in such activities.

Learn as much as possible about the outdoor recreation activities you participate in, prepare for the unexpected, and be safe and cautious. The reward will be a safer and more enjoyable experience.

CONTENTS

SOUTHERN FRONT RANGE

SOUTH PLATTE AREA

COLORADO SPRINGS AREA

CAÑON CITY AREA

CENTRAL COLORADO

ASPEN AREA

BUENA VISTA AREA

VI

ACKNOWLEDGMENTS

Colorado is a special place to climb. So it was with some trepidation that I approached this book after Falcon Press initially asked me to write it. A guide tends to bring more people to your favorite areas; people who, unfortunately, might not care as much as I do for these fragile areas. A lot of friends, however, encouraged me to do this book. It was something needed in Colorado climbing, and it was a chance to begin to educate all the new people coming into our sport. Guidebook writers have a serious responsibility to address environmental concerns and abuses, to interpret our tangled ethics and traditions, and to bring sensitivity to the crags. By educating and sensitizing climbers to our crags, they can appreciate both the beauty and fragility of Colorado's climbing areas and in turn help preserve them.

After I did my first technical route, a terrifying 5.6 on The Pinnacle in North Cheyenne Canyon in 1965 with my brother Mark, I was hooked on Colorado climbing. This book has its roots in all my forays around the state in the last 30 years with numerous friends and partners. To them I'm thankful for lasting experiences and friendships.

A book like this is a massive research project. You spend lots more time researching, writing, and photographing than actually going climbing. I traveled the entire state for 18 months, climbed at every area, scoped out almost every route, and talked with many climbers about their local areas and routes. My sincere thanks first to Bill Schneider, publisher at Falcon Press, and Randall Green, my editor, for the foresight to see the need for a Colorado climbing guide. Thanks also to Falcon's able staff who copy-edited and produced this stunning guide.

Thanks to the many climbers who gave me invaluable information and read, commented, and corrected parts of the manuscript, including Bob D'Antonio, Ed Webster, Jim Dunn, Charlie Fowler, K.C. Baum, Craig Luebben, Mark Rolofson, Larry Floyd, Mark Van Horn, Mark Hesse at The American Mountain Foundation, Jeff Achey at *Climbing* magazine, Allen Pattie, Antoine Savelli, Mike Covington, Bob Finch at Castlewood Canyon State Park, Pete Gallagher, Steve Landin, Mike Pont, Colin Lantz, Dennis Jackson, Martha Morris, and Ian Spencer-Green. Kudos and muchas gracias to Ian Spencer-Green, Brett Spencer-Green, Josh Morris, and Bob D'Antonio for traveling around with me, dragging my butt up numerous routes, and posing for photos. I'm indebted to you guys. Let's do it again—like next weekend. Also, many thanks to Nancy Spencer-Green for untiring support, holding down the homefront, and putting up with my gallivanting all over the damn place.

COLORADO'S ROCK CLIMBING AREAS

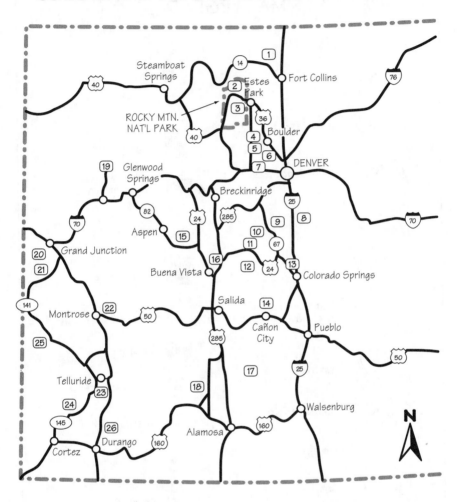

1. Greyrock
2. Lumpy Ridge
3. Rocky Mtn. Nat'l Park
4. Boulder Canyon
5. The Flatirons
6. Eldorado Canyon
7. Clear Creek Canyon
8. Castlewood Canyon
9. Bucksnort Slab
10. Turkey Rocks
11. Big Rock Candy Mtn.
12. Elevenmile Canyon
13. Garden of the Gods
14. Shelf Road
15. Independence Pass
16. Buena Vista Crags
17. Crestone Needle
18. Penitente Canyon
19. Rifle Mountain Park
20. Colorado Nat'l Monument
21. Unaweep Canyon
22. Black Canyon of the Gunnison
23. Ophir Wall
24. Lizard Head
25. Naturita Crags
26. Golf Wall

MAP LEGEND

 Trail

 Interstate

 Paved Road

 Gravel Road

 Unimproved Road

 State Line, Forest, Park, or Wilderness Boundary

 Waterway

 Lake/Reservoir

 Building

 Camping

 Gate

 Mile Marker

 Town

 City

 Climbing Area

 Crag/Boulder

 Cliff Edge

 Mountain Peak

 Trailhead

 Parking

 Interstate

 U.S. Highway

 State Highway

 County Road

Forest Road

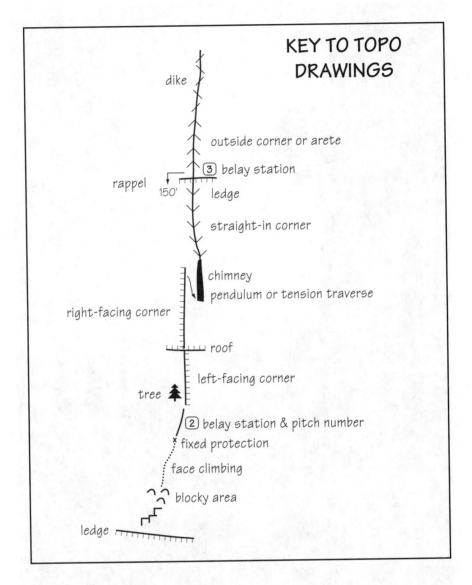

KEY TO TOPO DRAWINGS

dike

outside corner or arete

③ belay station

rappel

150'

ledge

straight-in corner

chimney

pendulum or tension traverse

right-facing corner

roof

left-facing corner

tree

② belay station & pitch number

fixed protection

face climbing

blocky area

ledge

lb.	lieback	thin	thin crack(to 1 ½")
chim.	chimney	3rd	class 3
ow	off-width	4th	class 4
HB, RP	very small chocks	KB	knife blade
TCU	small cramming devices	LA	lost arrow

Leonard Coyne on the classic *North Ridge* of White Spire at the Garden of the Gods. *Photo by Stewart M. Green.*

INTRODUCTION

Colorado—it's a magnificent landscape of stunning primeval beauty. Soaring mountain peaks lift snowcapped summits into the azure sky. Deep gorges carved by roaring rivers slice downward through ancient bedrock. Wide open prairies floor the limitless sky. Dark evergreen forests and gilded aspen groves spread across ridges and valleys. And cliffs of every rock type and size adorn Colorado's peaks and plateaus, offering the rock climber a spectacular arena to pursue the vertical craft.

With the possible exception of California, Colorado gives the climber a greater variety of rock and routes than any other American state. And Colorado, with its pioneering ascents on the Flatirons outside Boulder and Albert Ellingwood's early roped routes up Crestone Needle, Lizard Head, and The Garden of the Gods, can be properly called the birthplace of American rock climbing. It was here that climbers began venturing out into the mountains, exploring the intriguing possibilities offered by abrupt alpine faces and steep ice-filled couloirs. The high peaks in turn led early climbers to smaller, lower elevation crags where rope and piton techniques and hand and foot work could be practiced and perfected. It was on these practice crags that rock climbing as a sport developed. It was here that the quiet revolution took place. Budding hardmen pursued their bold ascents on the vertical walls of places like colorful Eldorado Canyon. They found grace, beauty, and purity in the climb itself. They discovered that the style of ascent was perhaps a more worthy goal than merely reaching the top. The upward movements became more important than the summit—a case of the means becoming themselves the end.

Colorado offers rock climbers a savage arena to challenge their abilities and test their nerves. The big cliffs, such as The Diamond on Longs Peak and The Painted Wall and North Chasm View Wall in the Black Canyon of the Gunnison, are remote places filled with solitude and wild nature. Here the adventure climber must be competent to handle every situation that arises and filled with the fortitude necessary to overcome the inertia of everyday living. Smaller crags like the limestone escarpments at Rifle and Shelf Road or the granite outcrops in Boulder and Elevenmile canyons offer different tests. Climbers at these areas chase the elusive hard numbers, finding joy and satisfaction in rock gymnastics unimagined 30 years ago. Colorado, with literally thousands of crags and

Layton Kor edges up the last slab pitch on the first ascent of *Wheel of Life* in the Black Canyon of the Gunnison. *Photo by Ed Webster.*

cliffs scattered across its 104,091-square-mile rectangle, yields every type of climbing experience from big-wall aid routes and long, multi-pitch free climbs to short overhung limestone testpieces and fiercely difficult boulder problems.

Rock Climbing Colorado locates and describes the best of Colorado's numerous climbing areas. Hundreds of routes are found on the following 40 crags and areas, sampling the state's immense diversity of rock. Climbers can discover and explore both popular and off-the-beaten-track places, finding the routes and rocks that appeal to their sensibilities. They're all out there waiting to be discovered, waiting for the human touch. Head down the open road and find the hidden granite heart of some secret canyon or watch the morning alpenglow spread across a mountain wall above a chilly bivouac. Climbers live on the edge with an awareness of the fragility and tenderness of both life and the world itself. The rock teaches that life itself is a cup that must be fully drunk from to understand, appreciate, and love its essential joys and sorrows. Climb Colorado's rocks then—learn their hard lessons, love their simple grace, and above all, take care of them.

GEOLOGY

Colorado, like the other mountain states, offers a complicated geology that is far beyond the scope of this introduction. To begin to understand today's geography, consider Colorado's three provinces: the Great Plains on the east, the Rocky Mountains straddling the mid-section, and the edge of the Colorado Plateau covering the western slope. Geology clearly defines each province.

The Great Plains, a vast sweep of horizontal and gently tilted sedimentary rock layers, cover the eastern third of the state. This rolling landscape is traversed by two major rivers, the Arkansas and South Platte. Few cliffs are exposed on the prairie. Those that are tend to be short bands of Dakota sandstone that rim sharp canyons in the state's southeastern corner.

Colorado's Rocky Mountains, part of the longest mountain chain in the world, dominate the state's geography. The sierra is divided into more than 50 separate ranges, including the Front, Sawatch, Sangre de Cristo, Elk, and San Juan ranges, and these are topped by 54 peaks over 14,000 feet, including Mount Elbert, the state's 14,433-foot high point. More than 830 peaks top 11,000 feet in elevation. The Continental Divide, twisting down the state's alpine spine, separates the Atlantic and Pacific watersheds. Much of the Rockies' core is composed of ancient Precambrian igneous and metamorphic bedrock. More recent rock formations of Paleozoic and Mesozoic age drape across the older rock. Some ranges, such as the Spanish Peaks and San Juan Range, were formed by fiery volcanism while others, including the Sangre de Cristo Range, are composed of sedimentary rock.

Many of Colorado's mountain cragging areas, including the Flatirons and Eldorado Canyon near Boulder, the Garden of the Gods in Colorado Springs,

A storm breaks over the Black Canyon of the Gunnison upstream from South Chasm View Wall. *Photo by Stewart M. Green.*

and Shelf Road outside Canon City, are formed from tilted and uplifted sedimentary formations that lie along the mountain edge in the interstice between prairie and peak. Other areas were sculpted by water and ice from giant granite batholiths or vast underground reservoirs of molten rock that slowly cooled. These areas include Elevenmile Canyon, the domes above the South Platte River, and the crystalline granite at Lumpy Ridge. Most of the rock found in the high mountains is unsuitable for climbing, being loose and rotten. Exceptions are the high granite and metamorphic peaks in Rocky Mountain National Park and the hard conglomerate of Crestone Needle in the Sangre de Cristo Range. The volcanic San Juan mountains, covering some 10,000 square miles of the state's southwestern corner, are composed of layers of sand, basalt, and ash. Most of this rock is loose and almost unclimbable, including Lizard Head, the erosion-resistant neck of an ancient volcano.

The Colorado Plateau region encompasses the state's western quarter. This is an austere region of horizontal sedimentary layers deeply incised by rivers and streams. Folding, faulting, and uplifting created high tablelands like Mesa Verde and the basalt-capped White River Plateau. Deep canyons slice through the layered rocks, exposing millions of years of geologic history at a glance. The sandstone canyon rims form most of western Colorado's climbing areas, including the pinnacles and walls at Colorado National Monument and the short cliffs at Naturita and Durango.

CLIMBING DANGERS AND SAFETY

Let's face it—climbing is a dangerous activity. Remember that every time you rope up, put on your climbing shoes and harness, and step onto the rock, you or your partner can be killed. Rock climbing is serious business—no matter how much fun you're having. My friend Jim Dunn, a guy who did the first solo ascent of a new route on El Capitan and put up numerous desperate Black Canyon and desert freeclimbs, says that every climber, no matter what their level of experience, will make stupid, unthinking mistakes. Everyone who has climbed for any length of time has had a friend killed while rock climbing or mountaineering.

It's up to you to minimize the risks of climbing. Always be safety conscious. This book is not a substitute for experience or sound judgment. Do not depend or totally rely on information in this book to get you safely to the top of a crag and back down. Guidebook writing is by necessity a compilation of information obtained by the author and other climbers. Errors will creep into route descriptions, topos, gear lists, fixed gear notes, and descent routes. You must rely only on your own experience and judgment to ensure your own personal safety and that of your partners.

Climbing experience is obtained by getting out and doing lots of routes. If you do not have the experience, it is prudent not to attempt serious routes in places like the Black Canyon or Rocky Mountain National Park. Many climbing areas are served by local guides and personal climbing instructors. Their invaluable services will help you develop the techniques and wise judgment required to successfully ascend many rock climbs. Guide services and schools are listed for each area in this book (see Appendix C for a complete list of addresses). Before committing to a guide service, ask about the guides' experience, their accident rates, safety procedures, and class or group sizes. If you have any question about a particular route, take the time to seek out a local and ask for his or her advice. Most local climbers are happy to give updated ratings, gear lists, and topos to their routes.

When using this book you may find possible misleading information or errors in route descriptions. Use your judgment to decide what is the safest way to go. Every effort has been made to ensure complete accuracy, but in the real world things change. The fixed protection or rappel anchors noted may not be there anymore. Ratings are subjective. Use them with a grain of salt. Many climbing moves are subject to the climber's experience and technique, body type, and strength. Some climbs may be harder for you than are indicated in this book. Again, use your judgment and don't let the rating fool you into thinking a route is easier than it really is. Every effort has been made to designate climbs with protection ratings. If there is no rating, then that route should be safe for anyone with experience in properly finding and placing gear. Both R and X ratings indicate more serious routes with possible serious injury, groundfall, or death as the result of a fall. Remember that every route can have the X rating if equipment is improperly used, if fixed protection including bolts and pitons fails, or if you fail to place safe gear.

Climbers who have learned their techniques in climbing gyms should take special notice of their limitations. Climbing inside a rock gym is not a substitute for real rock climbing experience. Climbing in a gym is safe. Climbing outside is not safe. Climbing outside requires rope handling, placing protection, setting up equalized belay anchors, properly rigging rappel anchors and lines, and doing all the other little things that keep you and your partner safe on the rock. Beginning climbers and gym climbers should take special note of ratings. Rated gym climbs do not accurately reflect real outdoor ratings. Just because can you climb 5.12 in the gym doesn't mean you can climb 5.9 outside. Every climbing route is serious, no matter what the grade is. Every experienced climber can relate a horror story from a seemingly innocuous moderate or easy route.

Keep safe by using common sense. Most accidents happen due to bad judgment and improper decisions, rather than an act of God. Use the following reminders to avoid accidents.

• Do not climb beneath other parties.
• Do not solo routes.

Pascal Robert free-solos the excellent *East Slab* on The Dome in Boulder Canyon. A fall while free-solo climbing can result in death or severe injury. *Photo by Stewart M. Green.*

- Do not climb beyond your skill level without appropriate safety and protection devices.
- Place protection wherever possible to protect yourself.
- Rope up on wet, snowy, or dark descent routes.
- Tie a knot in the end of your ropes to avoid rappelling off the end of the rope.
- Tie in after completing a sport pitch and double check your knot before climbing or lowering.
- Remember that belaying is an important part of the safety link. Belayers need to be anchored, competent, and alert.
- Tie a knot in the end of the rope to avoid being dropped by inattentive belayers when they're lowering you.

OBJECTIVE DANGERS

Something bad can happen every time you go climbing. Always keep that thought in mind. Numerous objective dangers are found walking to the crag, ascending your chosen line, and on the descent. It's wise to remember that you are not off a climb until you're safely back at your car. Many accidents happen on descent routes due to carelessness, loose rock, bad weather conditions, and darkness. Always rope up on a descent if you have any uneasiness about the situation.

Use all fixed protection with caution. Bolts, especially older 1/4" bolts, can shear off from the force of a fall. Fixed pitons often become loose due to rock weathering and expansion caused by freezing and thawing. In high-altitude or cold weather areas pay particular attention to unsafe fixed pitons. Metal fatigue and the age of the gear also affects its useful life. It might appear perfectly safe, but is, in fact, a sitting time bomb. Always backup fixed pro whenever possible, but always back them up at a belay stance or rappel station. Never rely for your safety or your partner's safety on a single piece of gear. Always build redundancy into the system so the failure of one part will not affect the overall safety of the system. Never rappel or toprope off a single anchor. Don't be so cheap that you're unwilling to leave gear to safeguard your life.

Loose rock is found on all of Colorado's crags. It's a fact of life. Get used to testing blocks and wedged chockstones to make sure they're safe and secure. Use extreme caution on belay ledges where rubble is precariously piled and on the top of cliffs where loose blocks perch on the edge. Warn your belayer if you feel a block or flake is unstable so they can be prepared for it to possibly fall by or on them. Winter's freezing and thawing cycles loosen blocks and boulders on rock walls. Watch for loose rock when climbing in the springtime. The movement of the climbing rope can also dislodge loose rock. Use care when pulling rappel ropes not to pull down loose rock. Wear a helmet while climbing and belaying to greatly reduce the risk of serious injury and death due to rockfall or falling. It may not be fashionable, but it can save your life.

Poison ivy, bee and wasp nests, ticks, and rattlesnakes are found at many of Colorado's climbing areas. Poison ivy can cause a severe itching rash that takes weeks to heal. Look for three shiny leaves and white berries on its short stalk. It is usually found in dense thickets along cliff bases in lower elevation areas like Eldorado Canyon, Shelf Road, The Black Canyon, Rifle, Castlewood Canyon, and Penitente Canyon. Bees and wasps live on many cliffs. Take note of any possible beehives and avoid climbing in those areas. Ticks are nasty little blood-sucking arachnids that are fairly common in lower elevation areas with lots of brush and woods. They're generally active in late spring and early summer. All can carry tick fever, the more serious Rocky Mountain spotted fever, or Lyme disease, a bacterial infection. Avoid tick-infested areas if possible. Otherwise use generous amounts of bug spray, wear clothing that is tight-fitting around the ankles, waist, wrists, and neck, and always check your clothing and yourself either at the crag or before getting into your vehicle. Ticks tend to crawl around on their potential hosts before settling down for a feast, so they can usually be found before the party begins. Ways to remove an imbedded tick include poking its rear-end with a hot match tip or coating it with fingernail polish. If the tick doesn't let go, use tweezers to pinch a tiny chunk of skin around its head (to make sure you get all of the tick), and pull it out. Try not to squeeze its body as this increases the risk of infection. Clean the wound with antiseptic. Ticks are extremely common at several Colorado areas including Rifle Mountain Park and the Black Canyon.

Rattlesnakes are common in many climbing areas below 7,000 feet. Snakes live in warm habitats that include dense tree thickets, underbrush, and boulder fields. They will usually be seen between May and October. Western diamond-back and prairie rattlers are the most common species encountered, typically between May and October. Rattlers have broad, triangular heads and a pit above each eye. The buzz of a rattler's tail is unmistakable, but sometimes the rattle is missing or the snake may strike without warning if surprised. Watch for them along access paths. Rattlesnakes will sun themselves on trails and open ledges on cliffs, or escape the day's heat by crawling under boulders or climbing into bushes. They usually blend in very well with grass, leaves, and cobbles. Watch where you put your hands and feet when scrambling. If you do encounter a rattlesnake, don't kill it. They don't see you as prey, but only as a large oaf that has stumbled onto their territory. They will usually strike only when they're cornered. Most bites occur when they're picked up. If you are bitten, get to a hospital as soon as possible. A snakebite is a major medical emergency. In about 25 percent of bites no venom is injected and in another 25 percent so little venom is injected that no antivenom is needed. Of the 8,000 or so bites each year in the United States, only 8 to 15 result in death. Do not attempt any first aid to a bite. Do not apply a tourniquet or ice and do not use a snakebite kit. The wrong treatment could result in the loss of a limb or life. Get the victim as quickly as possible to the nearest medical help, treating for shock as needed.

Keep an eye on the weather when climbing. Severe summer thunderstorms build up and move in very rapidly. Many of Colorado's climbing areas lie in mountainous regions subject to fickle, unpredictable weather. Torrential rain and hail storms can quickly drop temperatures. Be prepared for wet weather by packing appropriate rain gear and dressing in layers. Stay dry to avoid hypothermia, the lowering of the body's core temperature, and possible death. Temperatures do not need to be at the freezing point for hypothermia to occur. Most cases happen at temperatures between 40 and 50 degrees Fahrenheit. Hypothermia can cause disorientation and loss of judgment.

Exposure to hot temperatures in summer can cause heatstroke and heat exhaustion. Carry and drink lots of water to stay properly hydrated. A hat will keep your head cool in summer heat. Sit in the shade and have a drink if you're feeling too hot. Carry at least two quarts of water per person, per day in summer. Use sunscreen to avoid severe sunburns. The sun quickly burns exposed skin at Colorado's high altitudes.

Lightning causes more than 300 deaths in the United States annually and is a serious and common hazard on Colorado's crags. The state, along with Florida and Arizona, is a national leader in lightning strikes. Climbers and lightning are usually drawn to the same high points. Be constantly vigilant for lightning, especially on exposed mountain peaks and cliffs. Avoid becoming a lightning target by keeping a wary eye on the weather. Retreat if possible at the first sign of possible lightning. Lightning usually accompanies afternoon thunderstorms. Look for dark, towering clouds with high winds. Lightning can also occur before the onset of the storm. Avoid sitting under tall trees, overhangs, or near the mouths of caves. Lightning often travels down crack systems. If you're caught on a cliff face in a storm, tie yourself off away from your metal gear and nearby cracks. Avoid being on exposed ridges or summits. A sure sign of an impending lightning strike is St. Elmo's fire and the buzzing of static electricity in your hair. If you are trapped, flatten yourself as much as possible. Avoid rappelling during lightning storms. The electricity can travel down your rope. Most lightning strikes can be avoided by common sense and prudence. Don't hesitate to sound retreat in the face of a severe storm.

ACCESS AND ENVIRONMENTAL CONSIDERATIONS

Climbers in the 1990s have a growing ethical responsibility to minimize their impact on the crags and the surrounding lands. The natural world is a fragile place that is rapidly being damaged by insensitive and unthinking use by miners, loggers, ranchers, mountainbikers, horseback riders, rafters, and, yes, rock climbers. We need to focus more on preserving and protecting our precious climbing resources than we do on putting up new routes or debating old ethical concerns. The increasing number of rock climbers in the United States has begun to put numerous areas at risk. Environmental organizations like The Wilderness Society and Sierra Club and land management agencies like the Bureau of Land Management, Forest Service, and National Park Service are evaluating the uses of public lands. Many rock climbing practices—such as bolting and aid climbing—are viewed by these groups as a high-impact activities. Land managers are required by law to protect the areas that they manage; accordingly they are designing management plans for climbing and other outdoor uses to minimize human impact and to preserve the resource.

Rock climbers have traditionally been a maverick bunch, going their separate ways and doing their own things. That will change in the future. Various groups, including The American Mountain Foundation and The Access Fund, are working with governmental agencies to ensure continued access to our cherished areas and the least amount of red-tape regulations. To keep our climbing freedom, climbers need to adopt a new environmental ethic that shows concern for our crags. We need to be more sensitive to our impact on the rock environment as well as the greater ecosystems. We need to establish a partnership with land managers and agencies to actively preserve our rock resources. We need to serve as active stewards of the areas in which we climb by investing in what Mark Hesse of The American Mountain Foundation calls "sweat equity." Devote some of your climbing time to restoration and mitigation efforts by working on access paths, picking up trash, and removing unsightly colored slings. Educate yourself about the areas where you climb. Many parklands are set aside to preserve specific geological, biological, or cultural resources. Preservation of these values often takes precedence over recreational uses, and continued access depends on our sensitivity to them. We need to make the important decisions regarding our sport, rather than allow the politicians and political appointees in Washington to decide our future freedoms.

We can start the process by doing the little things that can make a difference. Notice the impacts climbers have on a crag and change your habits and style to begin to mitigate those impacts. Some suggestions include:

• Pick up your trash, including cigarette butts, tape, soda cans, and candy wrappers. If you carry it in, carry it back out.

Climbers edge up the precarious *North Ridge* of Montezuma Tower in the Garden of the Gods. *Photo by Stewart M. Green.*

• Bury human waste away from the cliff base or leave it in the open where it will rapidly deteriorate. Burn your toilet paper wherever possible. Don't leave human feces on access trails or at belay stances below routes. Use established toilets if they are nearby.

• Stay on approach and descent paths. Avoid shortcutting and causing extra erosion. Stay off loose scree and talus slopes. Soil erosion destroys plants and ground cover, leading to more resource degradation. Try to belay off a boulder instead of the lush grass ledge at the wall base. Do not chop down trees or tear off limbs that might interfere with the first few feet of a route. Use a longer approach or descent route to protect sensitive ecological areas.

• Do not leave cheater slings on routes or brightly colored rappel slings. Instead, use colors that match the rock's hue. Camouflage bolt hangers with matching paint.

• Respect wildlife closures. Many Colorado cliffs host nesting eagles, falcons, and hawks. Respect their right to live and proliferate. Climbing near active nests can cause raptors to abandon the site. If you are unsure of the closure area and dates, contact the Colorado Division of Wildlife for complete details.

• Practice a clean camping ethic when staying overnight. Don't tear down local trees for firewood; bring you own or do without. Put your fire out cold before leaving. Do not build rock fire rings; scatter the rocks from existing fire rings. Use a stove for cooking. Pick up all your trash. Use only sites that show signs of previous use. Use existing tent pads.

• Join and contribute money to worthwhile organizations like The Access Fund and The American Mountain Foundation. They are working to keep our climbing areas open. The Access Fund has purchased climbing land in Colorado including parcels in Unaweep Canyon, and has funded trails, parking areas, and facilities at other areas. The American Mountain Foundation works closely with state and federal agencies at areas that include Penitente Canyon, Shelf Road, and Eldorado Canyon to protect and preserve their natural resources as well as restore impacted sites.

ETHICS

As John Sherman so aptly points out in his Hueco Tanks guidebook, "Topping out on a climb means nothing. How you get to the top means everything." These statements lie at the heart of the ethical debate. Climbers have long promoted their individual and area ethics. But we need to agree to disagree only to the point where the rock itself does not become an unwilling and innocent victim to our own callous egos. Bolt wars have damaged numerous Colorado crags. Neither side won the war; only the rock lost. This growing trend of us versus them, of sport climbers against trad climbers, is inane. There are only rock climbers. Best to enjoy all the types of climbing and leave petty grievances behind.

The style in which a climb is accomplished is a personal choice. There is purity and beauty in the ground-up tradition, of accepting on-sight what the rock offers for both protection and technique. Most of Colorado's classic lines were established in this fashion. Keep in mind that before the clean climbing ethic of the 1970s, climbers used whatever means necessary to accomplish an ascent. It didn't matter if gear was pulled on or sections were aided. Modern gymnastic climbs require hang-dogging or toprope rehearsal. Each strenuous sequence of moves must be worked out and memorized for the climber to eventually succeed on the red-point ascent. Toproping is a legitimate ascent of many hard routes and boulder problems. It not only saves the climber from serious falls, but also saves the rock from unnecessary fixed protection.

Bolting offers a serious ethical dilemma. Permanently placed bolts have opened numerous new climbing areas and crags in Colorado, places with no prior tradition of rock climbing. Bolts have expanded the range and difficulty of modern climbing, allowing for unprecedented safety. But bolts have also been misused. Some modern crags have become a gridwork of bolted lines. These eyesores anger land managers and other users. Other traditional crags have been subjected to bolt wars, with the opposing factions either placing or chopping the offending bolt. Both placing and chopping bolts, in the end, affects only the rock—forever. A little common sense and a civilized decorum could go a long way to solving this conflict. Also check with area managers before placing any bolts to learn about any land-use concerns. Bolting is prohibited in any Colorado state park that does not have a specific climbing management plan.

Those who place bolts should seriously consider each and every placement. Toprope the proposed line and see if it is indeed worth the bolting effort and potential damage. If it is, place the bolts with sensitivity. Do not place bolts next to cracks that will accept gear placements. Use the natural line the rock gives, don't force it up the hardest way. End the route at natural stances or ledges. If this means running it out on 40 feet of easy climbing, then so be it. Don't just plug in a couple of anchors at the end of the stiff part. In the end, it doesn't really matter if a route is put in ground-up or on rappel. The important thing is the worthiness of the route and the safety of the fixed pro. And don't let the rappel-down style lead to over-bolting a line. Do not add bolts to existing routes. Respect the style used by the first ascent party. If you're too scared to do the line as is, then perhaps you should leave it until you're ready for the challenge.

Chipping and manufacturing holds and routes is a growing problem in American rock climbing. As climbers push standards higher, they desire harder routes to satisfy their quest for higher numbers. As gym climbers, usually newcomers to rock climbing, expand outward from their insular indoor plywood worlds, they see the natural rock as a malleable form ready for sculpting. They bring a gym ethic—that every hold and route is removable—to the outside world. Do not chip or chisel holds on any route or boulder problem. If you cannot do it with what's there, then you're not good enough to climb it yet or maybe that piece of rock was never meant to be climbed.

Chipping destroys the future of climbing. It takes hard routes away from the upcoming young climbers. If you can't do it as is, then leave it for a better climber and a better style. Chipped and manufactured routes are omitted from this guide. Publishing their names and grades would only validate their style of ascent. Unfortunately chipped routes are found at several Colorado areas, including Clear Creek Canyon, Shelf Road, Penitente Canyon, Rifle Mountain Park, and Elevenmile Canyon. One open 5.13+ project at The Gym at Shelf Road was chipped in the summer of 1994, leaving one of the area's potentially most difficult routes at a 5.12a grade. This selfishness and rampant egoism should not be tolerated.

Remember, in the end, neither the rock nor the route belong to you. You are only a traveler across the vertical terrain. Don't let egotism, ignorance, and arrogance dictate your ascent style and climbing ethic. Rather be sensitive to the rock and the environment, and consider each route a gift for everyone.

Using this Guide

Rock Climbing Colorado is, by necessity, a select guide to technical climbing routes at select crags and areas. Almost 1,500 routes are described here with words, photographs, and topos. A locator map at the front of the book shows the general locations of the main climbing areas.

Each area write-up includes: an **overview**, which may include a brief summary of the **climbing history** and ethics; **trip planning information,** which includes condensed summaries of specific information on each area; **directions** and **maps** to find the areas; and specific **climbing route descriptions,** which in many cases are accompanied by photos with overlays and maps identifying routes and showing the locations.

The **area overviews** describe the setting, the type of rock and climbing. Also included are recommendations for climbing equipment as well as some discussions of the local climbing history and ethics.

Trip Planning Information: A brief synopsis of the following categories.

- **General description:** A brief summary of the area.

- **Location:** Reference to largest nearby towns, major roads, or natural landmarks.

- **Camping:** Information on developed campgrounds and suggestions for camping in undeveloped locations.

- **Climbing season:** Description of when is the best time of year to visit an area.

- **Restrictions and access issues:** Important issues to be aware of, such as private land, parking, safety, and land use.

- **Guidebooks:** Published sources of information for that area.

- **Nearby retail mountain shops, guide services, and gyms:** Names of each are listed by town. A full listing of addresses and phone numbers is given, by town, in Appendix C.

Area write-ups include:

• **Finding the crag:** Description and how-to-get-there map with directions starting at nearest major road and town.

• **The cliff name:** Detailed discussion of location, special information pertaining to equipment, approaches, and descents.

• **Route descriptions:** Routes are listed numerically (for those climbers who can count beyond the number of their remaining fingers and toes), showing name and rating followed by a brief discussion of the location and nature of the climb, special equipment recommendations, length, and descent information. An overview map of each climbing area and photos—showing cliffs and route locations—accompanies the descriptions. Some of the more intricate and difficult routes on the big faces have route topo maps, detailing the climb.

The road map legend and key to topo map symbols are located at the front of the book on pages viii and ix.

Appendices offer further reading (**Appendix A**), rating comparison charts (**Appendix B**), and a listing of climbing equipment retail shops and clubs (**Appendix C**).

An index in the back of the book lists all proper names (names of areas, people, and climbs) alphabetically.

A book of this magnitude requires a wide selection of routes of all difficulties and lengths. Errors will creep into route descriptions due simply to the sheer diversity and number of routes detailed here. The area and crag descriptions have been carefully checked and double-checked by a wide range of active Colorado climbers to maximize the book's accuracy. Be forewarned, however, that things on paper aren't always as they are in reality. Take every route description with a grain of salt. This book is not intended to get you up any rock route. It will get you to the base of the cliff and point you in the right direction, but the rest is up to you and your sound decisions. This book is not a substitute for your own experience and judgment.

Almost all the routes included in this guide are worth climbing. No quality or star ratings are included here. Some climbers will not be happy about not having a "tick list" of starred routes to chase. Folks just want to rely on someone else's definition of quality, rather than finding their own happy medium. Make up your own mind about a route's possible value. Look at a line. If it looks good—go for it. Quality ratings tend to highlight certain routes, usually classics, leaving crowded queues at the route base, polished holds, trampled vegetation, and a degenerated experience for everyone.

RATING SYSTEM

This book uses the Yosemite Decimal System, the usual American grading scale, to identify the technical difficulty of the routes. Remember that ratings are totally subjective and vary from area to area. This book has tried to bring a consensus to the grades, but a Table Mountain 5.10 is still easier than a Turkey Rock 5.10. Most climbers give a fair estimation of a route's grade, but there are still a lot of variables. Some routes are height-dependent, with short climbers finding the moves harder than their taller brothers and sisters. Most routes are graded here for an on-sight attempt with little prior knowledge or beta of particular moves or protection. Top-roping or yo-yoing a route will lessen the grade as moves become familiar.

When you get out on the sharp end of the rope, ratings, says Colorado climber Charlie Fowler, "don't mean shit." Don't be lulled into thinking that an "easy" route is actually easy. A lot of good climbers have killed themselves on "easy" routes. *The Standard Route* up the east face of the Third Flatiron above Boulder is a prime example. While it's technically rated 5.4, it's a long and serious route that is potentially dangerous and has claimed many lives. Many routes listed also have protection or danger ratings. These routes generally have little or no protection and a climber who falls could sustain serious injuries or death. R-rated climbs have serious injury potential. X-rated climbs have groundfall and death potential. Remember, however, that every route is a possible R- or X-rated climb.

Mountain travel is typically classified as follows:

Class 1—Trail hiking.

Class 2—Hiking over rough ground such as scree and talus; may include the use of hands for stability.

Class 3—Scrambling that requires the use of hands and careful foot placement.

Class 4—Scrambling over steep and exposed terrain; a rope may be used for safety on exposed areas.

Class 5—Technical "free" climbing where terrain is steep and exposed, requiring the use of ropes, protection hardware, and related techniques.

The decimal rating system fails to follow mathematical logic. It is an open ended scale where the 5 denotes the class, and the difficulty rating is tacked on behind the decimal point, with 5.0 being the easiest and 5.14 (read five-fourteen) being the hardest (to date). When a route has had too few ascents for a consensus or the estimated difficulty rating is unclear, a plus (+) or minus (-) subgrade may be employed (5.8- or 5.9+ or 5.11- or 5.12+ for example). Where there is a consensus of opinion, additional subgrades of a, b, c, and d are used on climbs rated 5.10 and harder. To further complicate the matter, where the subgrade is uncertain, two letters may be used such as 5.11a/b. These subgrades represent a finer comparison of technical difficulty than the more general + and - signs. A climb rated 5.10a is considered to be harder than 5.9+ but easier than 5.10d, which is approaching the 5.11- standard. Thoroughly confused now?

More often than not, routes are rated according to the most difficult move. Some climbs may be continuously difficult, seeming more difficult than other routes rated the same but with only one or two hard moves. In some instances, routes will be described as "sustained" or "pumpy" to give an indication of the continuous nature of the climbing. Also, differences in strength and reach as well as distance between protection points may be factors contributing to rating variations. Where these factors seem significant, they may be pointed out in the written descriptions.

Aid climbing—using artificial means to progress up the rock—has a different set of ratings.

Class 6—Aid climbing; climbing equipment is used for balance, rest, or progress; denoted with a capital letter A followed by numbers progressing from 0.

A0—Equipment may have been placed to rest on or to pull on for upward progress.

A1—Solid equipment placements that can hold a fall; aid slings (etriers) are used.

A2—Placements are more difficult to position, and they support less weight than an A1 placement.

A3—Progressively weaker placements; may not hold a short fall.

A4—Placements can support body weight only; long falls can occur (this grade and the next one [A5] are only practiced by individuals not afraid of flying).

A5—Enough A4 placements to risk falls of 50-feet or longer.

A pitch or rope-length of technical climbing may have a combination "free" and aid rating such as 5.9/A3, meaning the free climbing difficulties are up to 5.9 with an aid section of A3 difficulty. On the route "topo" drawings or marked photos in this guide, the crux (most difficult section) often is marked with the difficulty rating.

An additional "overall seriousness" grade, referring to the level of commitment, overall technical difficulty, ease of escape, and length of route has been given to some of the longer routes. A Roman numeral from I to V may appear in front of the free/aid rating. Grade I typically is represented by Class 4 scrambles and easy Class 5 climbs that take only a few hours to complete. At the upper end of the scale, a Grade VI climb may take several days with a great deal of commitment in regard to technical difficulties, weather, and other objective hazards such as rockfall or avalanche danger. In this guide, the seriousness grades are only included on routes of Grade IV or more.

An additional "danger" rating may be tacked on to some climbs. Where the protection may not hold and a fall could result in injury or death, an R or X may be added. A route rated 5.9 R may mean that the protection is sparse or "runout" or that some placements may not hold a fall. X-rated (read skull and cross bones) routes have a fall potential that can be fatal, unless one has the confidence and ability to solo a route safely with absolutely no protection and without falling.

See Appendix B for table comparing the American system (Yosemite Decimal System) to the British, French, and Australian systems.

Injuries sustained from falls are always possible, even on routes that can be well protected. This guide does not give a protection rating nor does it provide detailed information on how, when, or where to place protective hardware. Suggested "standard" gear racks are described in the overview for each area, and some recommendations are made on types and sizes of protection that may be useful on some climbs. But safety and the level of risk assumed are the responsibility of the climber.

Certainly no standard equipment rack exists for the broad variety of Colorado rock climbing. Almost every area offers its own protection nuances. If a standard Colorado free climbing rack does exist, it should include: a set of RPs, a set of wired stoppers, a few hexentric nuts or Tri-cams, a selection of TCUs, a set of Friends or other camming devices, an off-width piece or two like a #4 or #5 Camalot, 10 or so quick draws, a few free carabiners, 4 to 6 runners of various lengths, and a 165-foot rope. An extra rope is necessary on many long routes for two-rope rappels, while some routes are more easily climbed using double-rope technique. Suggestions are occasionally given for a rack, but it's ultimately up to you to scope out the line and decide what to bring. It's always best to carry a few extra pieces of gear. Sport climbers should also eye their prospective route and count the number of bolts. Bolt counts are given for many routes, but things change on the real rock. Bolts get added or subtracted. Rockfall obliterates fixed protection. Again, it's up to you to decide what gear is needed. All that said—let's go climbing!

Northern Front Range

REGION

Brett Spencer-Green cruises up *Slab Happy* on Greyrock's South Slabs.
Photo by Stewart M. Green.

FORT COLLINS AREA

GREYROCK

OVERVIEW

Greyrock, a 7,613-foot granite peak, lifts its ragged outline above the low Front Range mountains northwest of Fort Collins. This little known and remote slabby dome, reached only after a stiff hour's walk uphill on a very popular hiking trail, yields a surprising number of excellent climbing routes from 1 to 4 pitches in length. More than 125 routes ascend Greyrock and its surrounding satellite crags, scaling crystals and edges up slabs and incipient cracks, and jamming excellent cracks that range from finger-size to off-width. The best parts of the Greyrock climbing experience are the numerous beginner and moderate routes that lace the crag and the spirit of adventure that still pervades this quiet, off-the-beaten-track area.

Climbing history: For years Greyrock has remained a quiet footnote in Colorado climbing, a place little known outside the Fort Collins area. The first reported climbers visited the crag in the 1950s. By the mid-1970s most of the moderate crack lines were done, many by Steve Allen and friends. The first ascensionists and their names for many routes are unknown, and subsequent parties rated and renamed them. The 1980s brought new interest and talent to the rock. New sections of the cliffs were explored and excellent routes established by climbers including Craig Luebben, who wrote the definitive guide to Greyrock, Don Braddy, Jeff Bassett, Jim Brink, and Steve Drake.

Greyrock is a traditional climbing area, with many crack routes that offer excellent protection. The bolted slab routes, put up on the lead, tend to be sparsely protected with bolts at the crux sections and creative pro placements in incipient cracks and thin flakes. Beware of long runouts on the slabs, especially on easier climbing, which tends to be toward the tops of the pitches. Some of the routes have serious fall and injury potential, some with groundfall possibilities. Use your best judgment when climbing, and don't be afraid to back off a serious pitch if you feel at all unsure of your abilities. Remember that climbing at any grade is serious business. Beefier 3/8" bolts protect most of the newer routes. Some of the older ones, however, still sport 1/4" bolts that may or may not hold a serious fall.

Rack: For most routes bring a rack that includes lots of small pro like RPs, wired stoppers, Tri-cams, Lowe Balls, TCUs, and small flexible Friends. A set of Friends is needed on the multi-pitch lines.

Trip Planning Information

General description: A slabby granite peak high above Poudre Canyon yields a diversity of excellent climbs on slabs, steep faces, and cracks.

Location: About 20 miles northeast of Fort Collins above the Cache La Poudre.

Camping: Public camping is found along Colorado Highway 14 a few miles west of the trailhead in Roosevelt National Forest, including Ansel Watrous, Stove Prairie Landing, Narrows, Mountain Park, and Kelly Flats campgrounds. All are fee areas located along the river and popular in summer. Camping is also found at Horsetooth Reservoir west of Fort Collins. Backpackers can camp in the forest around Greyrock for free.

Climbing season: Year-round. Summer days can be hot on the south-facing slab. Bring lots of water in summer. Afternoons, however, can be cloudy with severe thunderstorms. Avoid the top of the rock during lightning storms. Fall and spring offer good climbing weather. The crag's southern exposure also gives a surprising number of good climbing days in winter, although the access trail can be icy and snowbound.

Restrictions and access issues: Greyrock is in Roosevelt National Forest. There are no current climbing restrictions or access problems.

Guidebooks: *Greyrock* by Craig Luebben details the entire crag with excellent topos and descriptions. It's available at Fort Collins mountain shops.

Nearby mountain shops, guide services, and gyms: Adventure Outfitters, The Mountain Shop, Inner Strength Rock Gym, Desert Ice Mountain Guides (Fort Collins).

Services: All services in Fort Collins.

Emergency services: Call 911. Poudre Valley Hospital, 1024 Lemay Ave., Fort Collins, CO 80524, (970) 482-4111.

Nearby climbing areas: Poudre Canyon, Horsetooth Reservoir Boulders, Combat Rock, Lumpy Ridge, Hallet Peak, Petit Grepon, Notchtop, Spearhead, Chiefs Head, The Diamond, Longs Peak, Estes Valley crags, Big Thompson Canyon, Carter Lake boulders, Button Rock Reservoir crags, Lory State Park.

Nearby attractions: Cache La Poudre Wild and Scenic River, Cache La Poudre Wilderness Area, Comanche Wilderness Area, Rawah Wilderness Area, Poudre Canyon, Colorado State Forest, Roosevelt National Forest, Lory State Park, Rocky Mountain National Park, Trail Ridge Road, Longs Peak, Estes Park, Big Thompson Canyon, Pawnee National Grasslands, Pawnee Buttes.

Finding the crag: From Interstate 25 take Exit 269 and drive west into Fort

Collins on Colorado 14. Turn north on U.S. Highway 287/North College Avenue. Drive northwest on US 287 about 10 miles, then turn west and continue 8.5 miles on CO 14 to a parking area on the south side of the road for Greyrock National Recreation Trail. Cross the river on a footbridge and follow the steep trail (Trail 947) up a dry, rocky canyon, keeping right at the fork. Continue up a canyon to a high ridge below Greyrock. Allow about an hour of stiff hiking to the crag base. The South Slabs lie directly ahead; the Southeast Face is to the right; and the Northwest Slabs sit on the opposite side of the rock. The South Slabs and Southeast Face are easily accessed from the Greyrock Trail, which

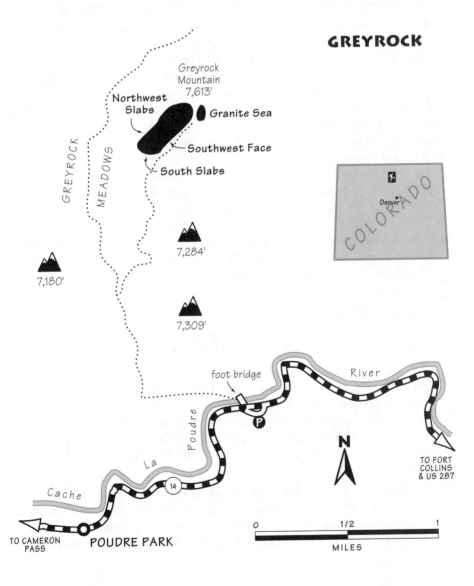

swings under the faces and works around the rock's northeast flank to its summit. The Northwest Slabs, not included in this guide, are reached by walking around the left, or west side, of the rock from the trail. A few small crags and walls lie northeast of Greyrock, including Granite Breakers and The Granite Sea. Numerous fine 1-pitch cracks and most of Greyrock's harder routes ascend these cliffs.

THE SOUTH SLABS

The South Slabs are a broad, south-facing wall broken by ledges and ramps into three cliff tiers. The easily accessible slab offers many excellent slab routes from 1 to 3 pitches in length. Most are done as single pitches, although link-ups on the different tiers are possible. Many of the routes are bolt-protected. Some have rappel or lowering anchors. **Descent:** The easiest descent from the upper tier is to follow a system of 3rd-class ramps and ledges that lead southwest between the middle and upper tiers. Fixed rappel anchors—a bolt and a slung chockstone—are atop *Cornercopia*. Bring 2 ropes for the 150' rappel and an extra sling in case one is missing. A large ledge/ramp, dividing the lower and middle tiers, is easily accessed from the base of the slabs. Approach The South Slab by continuing north on Greyrock Trail from an obvious trail junction to a point under the face. Look for a large trailside boulder with a small pine in it. A climber access path winds faintly up the hillside above the boulder. Routes are listed from left to right on the lower and middle tiers.

1. **Fun Flake** (5.6) A superb moderate line up the left side of the lower slab. Work left and then lieback and face climb straight up an excellent flake crack to a belay on the ramp above.

2. **2 Minds Meet** (5.7) Follow an angling crack up left to a long, easy groove.

3. **Between Nothingness and Eternity** (5.12a) Begin just left of the large trees at the base of the lower wall. Climb up right on paper-thin edges and dicey smears past 5 bolts to a runout easy slab. Belay from boulders on the ramp above.

4. **Bad Boys Bolt** (5.11b/c) Start in the shade behind the trees. Climb up left past 2 bolts and join BETWEEN NOTHINGNESS AND ETERNITY at its fourth bolt. Continue upward on easier climbing. **Black Market** (5.11b) is immediately to the right. Work up the thin slab past 2 bolts and angle up left (5.7 X) to the 5th bolt of BETWEEN NOTHINGNESS AND ETERNITY.

5. **Birdland** (5.9 R) A brilliant but runout route up the right side of the slab. Begin just right of the trees. Edge straight up to a bolt and work left into a crystal-studded water groove. Climb the groove and work left to a crack that takes large stoppers and small Friends. Run it out to the belay ramp.

6. **Jazzman** (5.10a) More good face climbing reminiscent of the South Platte domes. Climb to the 1st bolt of BIRDLAND and then face climb up just left of a blunt edge. **Rack:** Bring some large wires and small cams for pro.

7. **Testicle Traverse** (5.11a or 5.9) Excellent climbing up the bulbous testicle on the left side of the middle slab. Face climb up to the right side of the large roof and hand traverse/undercling left under some small roofs to a steep slab. Climb straight up past a bolt (5.11a) or swing right. Either way work up left to a stance at a horizontal crack; rap from here (1 bolt and a fixed piton) or continue up the 5.6 slab above. **Rack:** Bring some small and medium Friends and long runners for the traverse.

8. **Dirty Love** (5.10d) Begin under the TESTICLE TRAVERSE roof. Climb up under the roof to a fixed piton and undercling right (5.10c) into an obvious right-facing corner. Jam, chimney, and stem up the corner. Continue right up an easy slab from the top of the corner to a sloping belay ledge.

9. **Flirty Dove** (5.9) Begin as for TESTICLE TRAVERSE, only work up right from the roof onto a steep slab. Edge up to a bolt and climb incipient cracks (5.9) up to the right side of a small overhang. Traverse up left above the roof to the DIRTY LOVE dihedral and finish up it.

10. **Roofus Dickus** (5.11c) Begin just left of a large right-facing dihedral on the left side of the middle slab. Climb a shallow corner up right to an obvious finger crack over a roof. Strenuous jams lead over the roof (5.11c) to a headwall. Continue straight up (5.8) past a diagonal crack and onto an easier unprotected slab.

11. **Cornercopia** (5.7) A fun moderate route up the right-facing dihedral. Belay and rap with 2 ropes from anchors atop the corner.

12. **Slab Happy** (5.7) A superb slab route that arcs up and right past 4 bolts. It's a little scary getting to the anchors if you don't bring a large Tri-cam for the final traverse. Lower or rappel 70' from chains, or continue up left with decent pro to the anchors atop CORNERCOPIA.

13. **Slip** (5.6 R) Follow a thin ramp and seam arching right to anchors on a ledge below the huge roof. Protection is scant and far between.

14. **Climb On My Face** (5.10a) Thin edging (5.10a) leads to 1st bolt. Continue up left on fun face climbing past 2 more bolts to SLAB HAPPY'S anchors. Rap here or continue straight up past 2 more bolts (5.10a) and angle right to a leaning headwall. Jam a 5.9 crack up the wall to a good belay ledge. A great long pitch. **Descent:** Downclimb south along ramps.

15. **Wigs on Fire** (5.10b) A newer route that angles up right past 3 bolts and finishes with easy but runout climbing at ledge anchors.

16. **Wildstreak** (5.10d R) Boulder up to 1 bolt right of a pronounced black streak on thin face climbing (5.10d). Head up runout 5.6 rock with groundfall potential. End at good anchors on a ledge. **Descent:** Rap 70'.

17. **Beer for Breakfast** (5.8 R) Climb an unprotected groove to a narrow, pointed roof. Step over the roof and end at anchors. **Pitch 1** (5.9) begins right of JAZZMAN on the lower tier and follows a right-facing corner to the slab right of JAZZMAN.

18. **Grey Rat Rocksicle** (5.8 R) Begin on the upper part of the ramp. Work up left (5.8) into a flared crack, exit right and climb devious corners and discontinuous cracks to the right side of the huge roof. End on a ledge above the roof. **Descent:** Walk off southwest to down ramps. **Rack:** Bring small pro and be prepared to dice it up.

19. **Sugar Mountain** (5.5 R) One of the best beginner routes here. **Pitch 1** begins at the top of the lower ramp and climbs grooves, cracks, and slabs right of a water streak (not a lot of pro). Belay on a ledge at a horizontal break. **Pitch 2** tackles a left-facing corner to a roof, traverses right around the roof, and follows cracks up left to a good ledge. **Descent:** Downclimb southwest.

GREYROCK
SOUTHEAST FACE

THE SOUTHEAST FACE

This slabby wall offers some excellent multi-pitch crack and slab lines up to 500' long. **Descent:** Downclimb north from the top of the routes to the trail. Some routes have rappel anchors; bring 2 ropes if you plan any rappels. Approach the face by walking up the Greyrock Trail until directly below. Scramble up through the trees to the base.

A good problem for the off-width master is Craig Luebben's *Go Spuds Go* (5.12a) on a large boulder at the lowest point of rock between the South Slabs and the Southeast Face. This 15' problem, still awaiting a second ascent, jams an obvious 5" to 8", overhanging, nasty-looking roof crack. Luebben calls it "hard but really cool and atypical of Greyrock. It's one of the better trick off-widths around."

20. **Toolin' Woody** (5.10a) This 100' route is on the left side of the face on a steep buttress that ends below some large ledges. Climb thin cracks and slabs to anchors on a ledge by a small tree.

21. **The Woody Tool** (5.10a) Follow a left-angling seam up a steep slab to anchors. **Descent:** Rap 150'. **Rack:** Bring some thin pro for incipient cracks.

22. **Prints of Darkness** (5.8) Climb over the left side of a narrow roof and head up a black streak past 2 bolts to a good belay ledge. Traverse down right to THE WOODY TOOL'S anchors to rap. **Rack:** Bring a standard rack with an emphasis on small gear.

23. **Pretty Face** (5.8) A pretty face route with 3 bolts. **Descent:** Rap 150' from anchors.

24. **Theodore** (5.6) A fun moderate done in 4 to 5 pitches. **Pitch 1** jams a good hand crack (5.6) to a ledge. The crack is the middle of 3 distinct cracks, (Alvin is the 5.6 crack to the left and is a good alternate start). **Pitch 2** diagonals left up a lower-angle crack to a stance under a large jutting roof. **Pitch 3** jams easy cracks around a block to good ledges. **Pitches 4 and 5** continue angling up left to the summit in easy cracks and corners. **Rack:** Bring a standard rack.

25. **Simon** (5.8+) A companion route to THEODORE. **Pitch 1** jams the right crack (5.8 hands) to a good ledge. **Pitch 2** scales an easy, grassy crack to a stance at a horizontal dike under and right of the big roof. **Pitch 3** climbs a steep hand and fist crack right of the roof to a good ledge shared with THEODORE. **Pitches 4 and 5** angle up right in intermittent cracks, corners, and slabs to the final headwall cracks. **Rack:** Bring a standard rack with a large piece like a #4 Camalot.

26. **Mr. Gone** (5.10a R) Begin in the center of the wall beneath a prominent prow. **Pitch 1** follows thin face climbing (5.10a) past 3 bolts to a superb finger crack up a steep slab. Belay from anchors at an angling break. **Pitch 2** is short and climbs a moderate, unprotected slab to a stance under the prow. **Pitch 3** edges straight up the prow (5.10a) to a bolt. Go right to easier cracks or continue straight up (5.10a R) to a bolted stance left of a stepped roof band. **Descent:** 2 rappels lead to the ground from here; first rap is 100' to the 1st pitch anchors, second rap is 150' to the ground. **Pitch 4** stems up an easy, large, left-facing dihedral to the summit. Walk off.

27. **The Greatest Route at Greyrock** (5.8) It just might be the greatest line here with its good pro and fun jamming. Begin below a left-facing corner topped with a roof. **Pitch 1** moves left and climbs the face above the corner. Skirt right below the roof. Then step left and wander up incipient cracks to a small belay shelf at a horizontal break. **Pitch 2** climbs a long, narrow left-facing corner to an obvious roof. Pull over on jugs (5.8) and belay above. **Pitch 3** climbs a crack left of the belay to an easy left-facing dihedral. Belay on the right after 165'. **Pitch 4** face climbs and jams the final headwall to the top.

28. **Barfy's Favorite** (5.7) Begin atop a boulder just right of a large left-facing dihedral. **Pitch 1** face climbs a bulge to a good 5.7 hand crack. Belay at a tree. **Pitch 2** steps left and jams to another tree. Climb a good corner above to a belay stance at a horizontal dike. **Pitch 3** follows cracks and corners above to a stance left of a small roof. **Pitch 4** ascends to a short right-facing corner at the left end of a long roof. Pull left above the corner and roof and run up the slab above.

COMBAT ROCK

OVERVIEW

Combat Rock perches on the north side of Bobcat Gulch, a steep side canyon that drops south to the narrow valley of the North Fork of the Big Thompson River in the rugged Front Range mountains between Loveland and Estes Park. The south-facing crag, a spectacular shield of resistant granite, yields numerous excellent one- and two-pitch climbs that edge up its steep slabs, jam discontinuous crack systems, and swing over blocky roofs. The easily accessible cliff, approached via a short trail, receives lots of sunshine on its sheltered face making it an ideal day's outing in late fall or early spring.

Rack: While most of the routes are now bolted, carry a small rack with wired stoppers and small flexible Friends or TCUs to supplement the fixed protection. Thin horizontal seams and shallow flared cracks offer lots of opportunities for creative nutting and additional security.

Descend by either rappelling from chained anchors or hiking down the east or west flank of the crag. Double ropes are needed for any rappels from the cliff-top. Single-rope rappels are the rule on most one-pitch routes. Two 150-foot rappels from fixed anchors are on *Pearl Harbor* on the cliff's west side, while an 85-foot rappel and 150-foot rappel reach the ground from atop *Blood for Oil* on the cliff's center wall.

Climbing history: The crag's climbing history is short. Most of the gear routes went up in the 1980s, many by Scott Kimball, Randy Joseph, and Gary Sapp. Craig Luebben bolted most of the other lines on the lead in the early 1990s. A few other routes have since been squeezed in, but hopefully this brilliant little cliff won't become another trashy Euro-crag, gridlocked by inconsiderate bolts.

Trip Planning Information

General description: A compact 250-foot face with a diverse assortment of both bolted and crack routes on its steep, south-facing granite cliff.

Location: In the Front Range west of Fort Collins.

Camping: No public camping in the immediate vicinity of Combat Rock. The nearest campgrounds are in Rocky Mountain National Park 20 miles to the west.

Climbing season: Year-round. Summer days can be hot on the south-facing slab. Afternoons, however, are often cloudy with thunderstorms. Fall and spring offers good climbing weather. The crag's relatively low elevation and southern exposure give a surprising number of good climbing days in winter.

Restrictions and access issues: Within Roosevelt National Forest; no current restrictions.

Guidebooks: *Rocky Mountain National Park: The Climber's Guide* by Bernard Gillet, Earthbound Sports, 1993; and *Colorado Front Range Crags* by

COMBAT ROCK

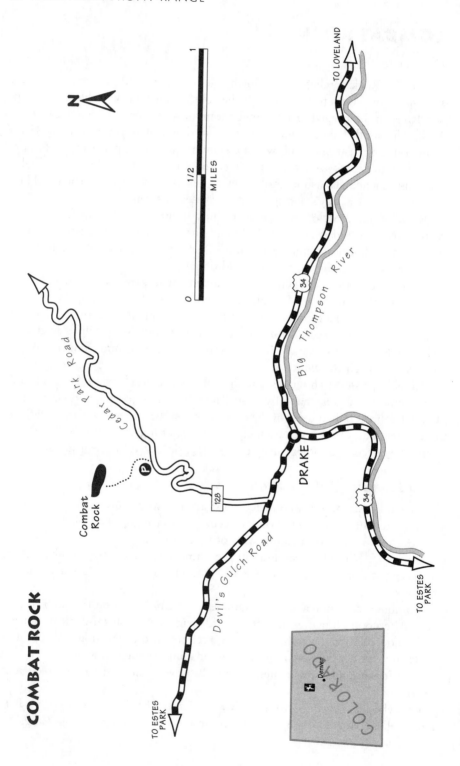

Peter Hubbel, Chockstone Press, 1994. Both cover Combat Rock with route descriptions and a cliff topo. *Rock & Ice,* issue 54, includes an excellent topo and beta by Craig Luebben.

Nearby mountain shops, guide services, and gyms: Wilderness Sports, Komito Boots, Colorado Mountain School (Estes Park); Desert Ice Mountain Guides, holds a permit to guide/teach at Combat Rock (Fort Collins).

Services: Limited services in Drake, including gas and groceries. Full services— lodging, dining, gas, groceries, beer, and espresso—in Estes Park and Loveland.

Emergency services: Call 911. Estes Park Medical Center, 555 Prospect, Estes Park, CO 80517, (970) 586-2317. McKee Medical Center, 2000 Boise Ave., Loveland, CO 80538, (970) 669-4640.

Nearby climbing areas: Lumpy Ridge, Hallet Peak, Petit Grepon, Notchtop, Spearhead, Chiefs Head, The Diamond, Longs Peak, Estes Valley crags, Big Thompson Canyon, Carter Lake boulders, Button Rock Reservoir crags, Boulder Canyon, The Flatirons, Eldorado Canyon State Park.

Nearby attractions: Rocky Mountain National Park, Trail Ridge Road, Longs Peak, Enos Mills Cabin, Big Thompson Canyon, Round Mountain National Recreation Trail, Indian Peaks Wilderness Area, Peak to Peak Highway.

Finding the crag: Combat Rock is easily reached from Loveland and Interstate 25 or Estes Park via U.S. Highway 34. From Loveland, drive west 17 miles on US 34 through scenic Big Thompson Canyon to Drake, or from Estes Park drive 13 miles east on US 34 to Drake. Turn west in Drake on Devils Gulch Road and follow it 0.5 mile to Cedar Park Road (Forest Road 128). It's the first dirt road on the right or north and is labeled "Forest Access." Follow the steepening road up a series of switchbacks for 0.8 mile and park in a large pulloff on the north side of the road just past a roadcut. Combat Rock sits immediately north. The 10-minute approach follows a rough trail that begins at the parking area. Drop down across Bobcat Gulch and meander up the opposite canyon wall to the cliff base.

1. **Arkansas Patriot** (5.9+) An excellent warm-up route on Combat's far west edge. Climb the steep slab past 3 bolts and a dike to chained anchors 75' up. **Rack:** Bring stoppers to supplement the bolts.

2. **Rambo Santa** (5.7) A popular 165' pitch up a long slab to double anchors. **Descend:** Rappel the route or walk off west.

3. **Pop Off Route** (5.7 R) This 2-pitch route offers good climbing up the west slab past funky 1/4" bolts. Begin on the left side of the diagonal band of roofs and ascend to the DIAGONAL belay below the upper roofs. Continue left and up on easy rock to a tree belay.

4. **Tree Roof** (5.8 R) Climb an easy slab to the obvious roof, pull over on buckets, and belay at a tree 40' up. Rappel or continue on mostly unprotected 5.6 rock to the upper DIAGONAL belay.

5. **Pearl Harbor** (5.10d) An excellent 2-pitch outing up a steep slab. Creative protection and 2 bolts protect thin slab climbing on the first pitch. Belay at chains. 6 bolts lead up the upper headwall to a 5.10d crux below the upper belay. **Descend** the route with 2 double rope rappels. **Rack:** Bring some small cams for an additional placement on this pitch.

6. **Eight Clicks to Saigon** (5.10d) A great route right of PEARL HARBOR. Climb the bolted slab with a mid-height 5.10d crux (harder for short people) over a small roof and either belay in the DIAGONAL crack above or continue up and left to PEARL HARBOR'S first belay. **Pitch 2** goes up and right, with some 5.9, to PEARL HARBOR'S upper belay. A good, well-protected combo climbs EIGHT CLICKS TO SAIGON'S 1st pitch and PEARL HARBOR'S 2nd. **Descent:** Rappel PEARL HARBOR or downclimb to the west.

7. **Ain't Nobody Here But Us Chickens** (5.11d) Scale a fun, moderate left-facing corner to a thin slab. End at anchors to the right on PEACENIK LEDGE.

8. **Across Enemy Lines** (5.11b) Delicate slab climb past 3 bolts, cross a dike and the DIAGONAL crack, and head up and right over an interesting bulge crux past 3 more bolts to anchors on PEACENIK LEDGE. **Rack:** A #2 Friend is helpful.

9. **Diagonal** (5.9) A classic route that follows the obvious left-diagonaling crack system that slices up the lower face. Jam the leaning hand crack in 1 long or 2 short pitches to a belay on the upper wall. Traverse back right under a roof to a right-leaning dihedral with a nice 5.9 crack. **Rack:** Friends, wires, and TCUs.

10. **Blood For Oil** (5.12b/c) The best hard route on Combat. Thin face climbing and edging between the first and second bolts leads to easier terrain and a ledge system. Continue up the steep slab above past another 5.12a crux and 5 bolts to a chained anchor. The spectacular second lead threads through the overhangs above with a third 5.12a crux and 5 bolts to chains. **Descent:** Rap 85' to the first belay and 150' to the ground. Bring flexible cams and Friends to #1.5. A partially bolted project goes up the initial slab from the ground a few feet to the east. Craig Luebben says it's "way desperate thin face to start, then four 5.12 cruxes to a belay 170' up."

11. **No More War** (5.10a R) Jam a flared 5.8 hand crack right of BLOOD FOR OIL to a tree. Rap from here or continue on face climbing (1 bolt) to BLOOD FOR OIL'S belay chains. The first crack alone is a popular route.

12. **Front Lines** (5.10a) A classic route with some devious but good protection. **Pitch 1** climbs thin offset 5.9 cracks past a bolt to a roof, goes right and up to a belay stance below a wide crack. **Pitch 2** steps right to a hand crack, surmounts the roof above with a strenuous finger crack (5.10a) and continues up a corner system to the summit.

13. **Lizzard Warrior** (5.11b) A superb bolted line that wanders up the lower slab on the east wall. A direct start to the first bolt offers 5.11 edging, or ease up to the bolt from the right for a 5.10 start. Either way climb the steep slab above on excellent edges and smears. Good route-finding skills keep you on line, otherwise it's easy to get sidetracked. Rappel or lower 80' from chains or continue up the steep bolted wall above on an A1 bolt ladder.

14. **GI Joe Does Barbie** (5.9+) Excellent climbing on sharp edges to a 2-bolt rap station under the big roof. Harder start for short climbers.

15. **Nuclear Polka** (5.10a) 2 pitches ascend the clean left-facing corner on Combat's east side. Two cruxes on the first pitch offer thin, well-protected climbing. **Pitch 2** slabs up and left to a 5.9 hand crack over a small roof.

ROCKY MOUNTAIN NATIONAL PARK AREA

THE HIGH PEAKS

OVERVIEW

Rocky Mountain National Park straddles the Continental Divide in northern Colorado, preserving a pristine swath of high country. This is a rugged and diverse landscape of abrupt canyons and wide, glacier-carved valleys, dark evergreen forests, sunny aspen groves, broad meadows, upland tundra, meandering rivers, and rushing creeks. Herds of bighorn sheep, elk, and deer roam the park. But mountains, first and foremost, define the 414 square miles within the park's boundaries.

Lofty, ragged peaks, chiseled and sculpted by ancient glaciers, lord over the lower valleys. The park includes 113 named mountain peaks above 10,000 feet, 71 over 12,000 feet, and Longs Peak, the park's high point at 14,256 feet above sea level. The park is also a mother of rivers. Four major rivers—the Cache la Poudre, Big Thompson, and St. Vrain on the eastern slope and the Colorado River on the western slope—spring from the Divide's snowfields. Fully one-third of the park is in the alpine zone above timberline. Snow plasters the high, windswept ridges and peaks for most of the year, and summer makes only a brief two-month visit in July and August.

Rocky Mountain National Park offers some of the best alpine climbing in the United States on its glaciated peaks. This vertical sanctuary hosts myriad classic multi-pitch routes, yielding superb challenges on excellent rock in an alpine environment. Renowned cliffs include the Diamond on the East Face of Longs Peak; the Northeast Face of Spearhead; the Northwest Face of Chiefshead; the spired summits of Sharkstooth, the Petit Grepon, and Zowie; the three buttresses on the North Face of Hallett Peak; and the South Face of Notchtop. These cliffs have long tantalized and attracted climbers with their sublime rock and purity of ascent.

Climbing history: Indians were the park's earliest climbers. The Arapahoes captured eagles from a skin-covered trap atop Longs Peak, while lofty Trail Ridge was traversed by a 15-mile Ute trail called *Taieonbaa* or "Child's Trail"

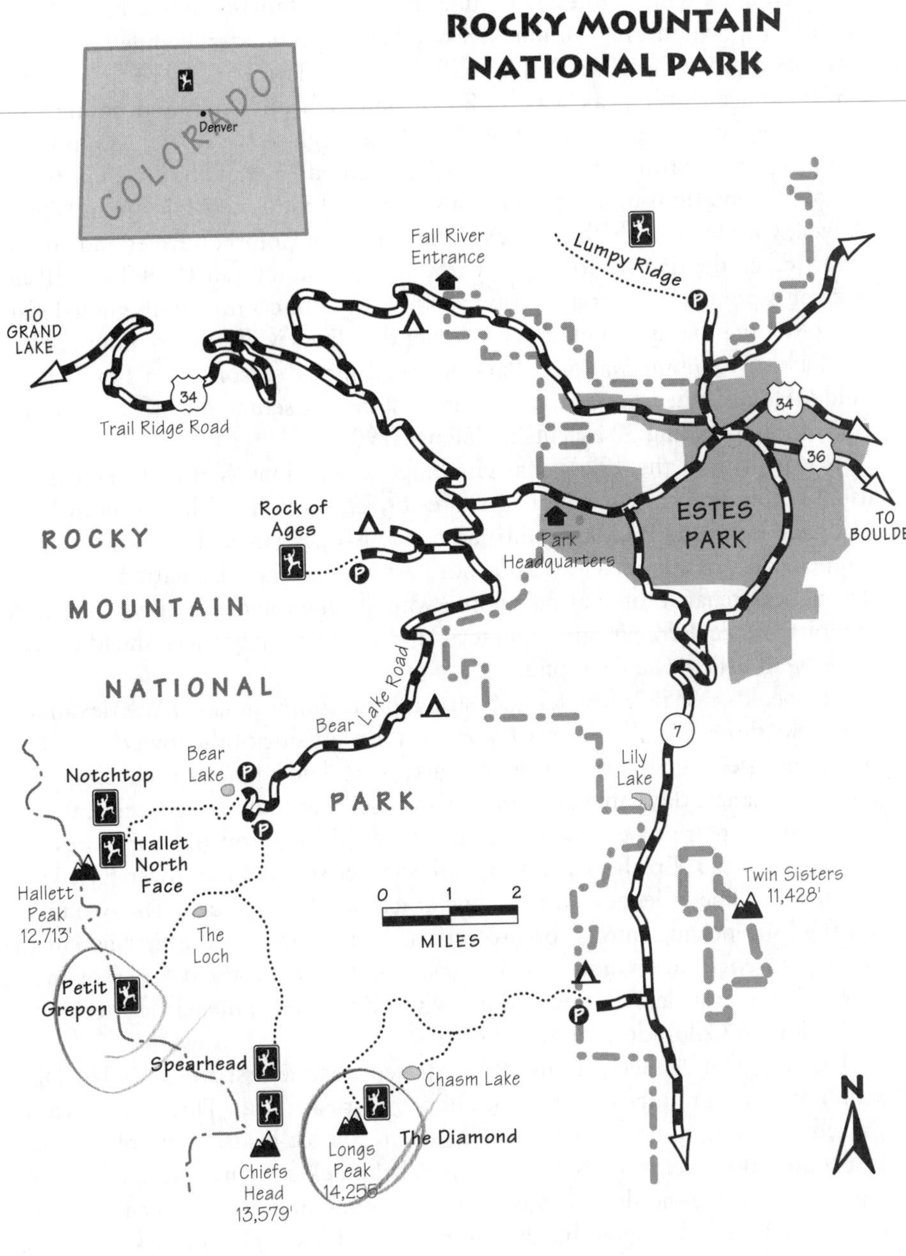

ROCKY MOUNTAIN NATIONAL PARK

COLORADO

Denver

Fall River Entrance

Lumpy Ridge

P

TO GRAND LAKE

34

Trail Ridge Road

34

36

TO BOULDER

ROCKY

Rock of Ages

P

Park Headquarters

ESTES PARK

MOUNTAIN

NATIONAL

Bear Lake Road

7

Lily Lake

Notchtop

Bear Lake

P

P

Hallet North Face

Hallett Peak 12,713'

The Loch

PARK

Petit Grepon

Twin Sisters 11,428'

Spearhead

Chasm Lake

0   1   2

MILES

The Diamond

Chiefs Head 13,579'

Longs Peak 14,255'

N

that was used by paleo-hunters 12,000 years ago. Ancient Clovis points found atop the ridge testify to their early passage.

Longs Peak, it's flat-topped summit dominating Colorado's northern Rockies, attracted the attention of early mountaineers. The Indians called the peak, together with neighboring Mount Meeker, "The Two Guides," while French fur trappers dubbed them Les Deux Oreilles or "The Two Ears." The first American reference to the peak was by Edwin James, a physician and botanist on Major Stephen Long's "Expedition from Pittsburgh to the Rocky Mountains" in 1820. James wrote that the great peak presented "a grand outline, imprinted in bold indentations upon the luminous margin of the sky." Major John Wesley Powell, who later made the first exploration of the Colorado River and Grand Canyon, led the first recorded party to the peak's summit in 1868. Longs Peak became a popular tourist attraction by the late 19th century, with guided visitors plodding to the summit every summer day. Enos Mills, the founding father of Rocky Mountain National Park, worked many seasons as a Longs Peak guide. He ascended the peak via today's standard scrambling Keyhole route 297 times, including 32 ascents in August, 1906.

It wasn't until the 1920s that climbing explorations ventured beyond the usual hiking and rock scrambling routes on Longs Peak, although both Enos Mills and Reverend Elkanah Lamb had previously descended ramps and icefields on the peak's East Face. The 1,700-foot East Face offers a dramatic and intimidating countenance of soaring granite walls broken and fractured by frozen couloirs, vertical cracks and chimneys, and an amazingly sheer shield on the upper wall called The Diamond.

The peak's east face first fell to visiting Princeton professor J.W. Alexander, who soloed the 5.5 *Alexander Chimney* on the left side of the lower wall. The professor aced out a strong Denver party who had planned their climb for Labor Day, three days after Alexander's success. The next major ascent came in 1927 when a pair of German immigrants from Chicago rode their motorcycles out to Colorado. Brothers Joe and Paul Stettner scouted the lower East Face and found a line of ledges, corners, and cracks angling upward. The two tackled the line, placing pitons for protection, and completed the first ascent of *Stettner's Ledges* in six hours. This classic 5-pitch route, rated 5.7, remains a Rocky Mountain classic. It was, along with Lizard Head, the hardest technical rock climb in Colorado until the 1940s.

The last great challenge Longs Peak offered was the first ascent of The Diamond, the abrupt, imposing 900-foot upper East Face wall. This 18-acre vertical expanse of granite is, at first sight, seems almost insurmountable. Closer inspection, however, reveals a web of parallel crack systems and hard granite studded with incut holds and convenient knobs and nubbins. Most early climbers deemed the face impossible due to the precipitous angle, the lack of ledges, and the quick, fierce storms that swept across the peak on summer afternoons.

Park Service regulations reflected this opinion, prohibiting any attempt on The Diamond in the 1950s. In 1959 Park Service Director Conrad Wirth specifically barred "stunt and daring trick climbing" with The Diamond in mind. By 1960 a chorus of Colorado climbers prodded the park into approving new regulations with stringent requirements, including proven competency and an able support/rescue team ready to pluck victims from the wall. Applications were sent to all climbers who had previously requested permission to attempt the face. Colorado climbers were unable to put together a team on short notice, so the first approved application fell to a pair of Californians, David Rearick and Bob Kamps. They picked out the obvious directissima line of cracks and chimneys up The Diamond's center, and began their ascent on August 1. The pair aided and free-climbed up the wall, emerging on the summit three days and 11 rope-lengths later, finding themselves conquering heroes in the national media.

Meanwhile the park's other great rock walls were being ascended. The Third Buttress of Hallett Peak fell in 1956 to a pair of Colorado climbers on their fourth attempt in three years. The first ascensionists, Ray Northcutt and H. Carter, talked their 5.7 nordwand route up as being one of America's most difficult rock climbs. The rumor was dispelled in 1959 after the second ascent party, Californians Yvon Chouinard and Ken Weeks, strolled up the reportedly formidable route in a mere four hours. The pointed spire of the Petit Grepon was first climbed in the late 1950s via its 5.6 *Standard Route,* while the coveted white wall of Spearhead was climbed by David Rearick, Richard Sykes, David Isles, and John Wharton via the now-classic *Sykes' Sickle* in 1958.

Legendary Boulder climber Layton Kor dominated the park's first ascent scene in the 1960s, doing not only the second ascent of The Diamond via *The Yellow Wall,* but making the first ascent of the *Northwest Face* of Chiefshead with Bob Culp in 1961. This intimidating route, renamed *Path of Elders* after its 1975 second ascent by Bill Westbay and Dan McClure, yielded 8 hard pitches with runout 5.10 face climbing and questionable belay anchors. Culp later noted that the route offered "consistently difficult climbing on good but small holds with little protection." Culp recalled the 3rd pitch: "As I approached him, Kor began getting me ready for the next pitch. He always preferred to lead and had been known to psych out his partners so he could get all the pitches. 'You're gonna love this next part.' I could hear him gloating. 'Perfectly smooth. No holds at all. You might get some protection about 50 feet up.' On and on. As I started off, it dawned upon me that his predictions were absolutely accurate....Kor was getting restless. After all we were wasting time with most of the wall above us. 'OK Layton, you give it a try,' I relented. Moments later I was trying to get tied onto the belay anchor with Kor already half-way to my high point and climbing rapidly. Without hesitation he pulled up on the small edge, shot an incredibly long arm to the high nubbin, and stepped neatly up. 'Good holds up here,' he remarked."

Bryan Becker makes the long traverse on the *Casual Route* on The Diamond in Rocky Mountain National Park. *Photo by Ed Webster.*

ROCKY MOUNTAIN NATIONAL PARK
THE HIGH PEAKS

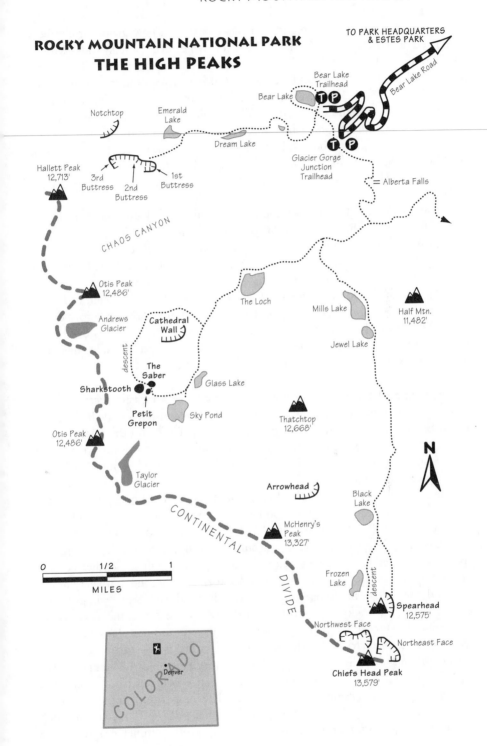

TO PARK HEADQUARTERS
& ESTES PARK

Bear Lake Road

Bear Lake
Trailhead

Bear Lake

Notchtop

Emerald
Lake

Dream Lake

Glacier Gorge
Junction
Trailhead

= Alberta Falls

Hallett Peak
12,713'

3rd
Buttress

2nd
Buttress

1st
Buttress

CHAOS CANYON

Otis Peak
12,486'

The Loch

Mills Lake

Half Mtn.
11,482'

Andrews
Glacier

Cathedral
Wall

Jewel Lake

descent

The
Saber

Sharkstooth

Glass Lake

Petit
Grepon

Sky Pond

Thatchtop
12,668'

Otis Peak
12,486'

Taylor
Glacier

Arrowhead

Black
Lake

N

CONTINENTAL

McHenry's
Peak
13,327'

Frozen
Lake

descent

Spearhead
12,575'

DIVIDE

Northwest Face

Northeast Face

Chiefs Head Peak
13,579'

0   1/2   1

MILES

COLORADO

Denver

This golden age was supplanted in the 1970s by a new group of climbers that lived in Estes Park, working for Michael Covington at Fantasy Ridge Mountain Guides and cobbler Steve Komito. These climbers, including Bill Westbay, Dan McClure, Jim Dunn, and Doug Snively along with a Boulder contingent of Roger Briggs, Mark Hesse, Duncan Ferguson, and Chris Reveley, brought a clean climbing ethic and impeccable style to their first ascents. New prizes were sought and gained, including first ascents on The Diamond and first free ascents of older aid lines. The first free ascent of The Diamond itself came in July, 1975 when Wayne Goss and Jim Logan freed a line up *D7* and *Black Dagger*. Jim Dunn and Chris Wood free-climbed an independent line near the *Yellow Wall* a couple of days later.

Climbers pushed the limits of free climbing on the park's alpine walls in the 1980s and 1990s. This new breed of rock jock, skilled at placing pro and adept at rock gymnastics, included Jeff Achey, Leonard Coyne, Ed Webster, Charlie Fowler, Pat Adams, Chip Chace, Mark Wilford, Alan Lester, Steve Levin, and Roger Briggs. Their achievements include the first free-solo of The Diamond via *The Casual Route* by Fowler in 1978; Webster's 1984 solo ascent of *Bright Star* on The Diamond; a one-day park tour by Lester and Dave Crawford of the Yellow Wall on The Diamond, *The Barb* on Spearhead, and *Birds of Fire* on Chiefshead in 1991; the late Derek Hersey's three Diamond free-solos in a day; and Briggs' sustained 5.12b Diamond route *Eroica* in 1987.

The high peaks of Rocky Mountain National Park are easily accessed from Denver and Boulder. U.S. Highways 34 and 36 both climb from the high plains up to Estes Park, the gateway to the park. Longs Peak and the Diamond lie south of Estes Park off Colorado Highway 7, while the other peaks are reached from Bear Lake Road west of Estes Park. Walking approaches are reasonable; the longest is six miles.

The climbing season runs June through September, although May and October both offer occasional spells of good weather. Winter's heavy snowpack melts in May and June. Watch for wet cracks and chimneys, and blocks loosened by frost-wedging. The park's brief alpine summer brings a mixture of warm, dry spells punctuated by cool, wet weather. Rainy periods will sometimes last for one to two weeks. Expect afternoon thunderstorms, sometimes with very heavy rain and corn snow. Be prepared for bad weather—always bring rain gear and extra clothes. Storms often build west of the Divide and can quickly move in. Be prepared to retreat from your chosen route or to alter your plans. One good way to avoid the park's notoriously severe weather is by starting early and getting off the route by noon. Lightning is a very real objective danger in the high mountains. Keep off high points and distance yourself from cracks and hardware. Alpine temperatures are also cold. The temperature at the summit of Longs Peak is usually 30 degrees colder than that in Estes Park, and freezing temperatures and measurable snowfall occur in every summer month. Other objective dangers include loose rock. It occurs on every wall and particularly on descent routes. Wear a helmet for maximum protection.

Rack: Standard equipment for most of the park's alpine climbs includes a rack with complete sets of wired nuts and cams, a few medium hexes, a dozen or so quick draws, and a few free carabiners. Bring a 165-foot rope and a light haul-line for bringing up a pack or rappelling. Extra clothes and rain gear will help ward off hypothermia if you are caught in a storm. Don't drink water from area streams; they all have Giardia. Instead, bring your own water or purify it before drinking. Park rules prohibit the use of power drills. Remember that the park's high peaks lie within a designated wilderness area. Abide by a wilderness ethic and don't add unnecessary bolts to routes.

Climbers must obtain a free permit to bivouac on or near their intended route. This permit system allows the Park Service to maintain crowd control and keep fragile ecological areas from being overused. Bivy permits can be obtained at the Longs Peak Ranger Station from 8 a.m. to 5 p.m. or at the main Backcountry Ranger Station at Park Headquarters from 7 a.m. to 7 p.m. Permits are issued in summer only from June 1 to September 30. Permits are issued if the site is more that 3.5 miles from the trailhead and the climb is more than 4 pitches long. Please obey the park's bivy rules: sleep on rock or snow (not vegetation); bivy 100 feet from water in a site clear of rockfall; party is limited to a maximum of four climbers; and use only stoves. Climbers with bivy permits must not camp below timberline, use tents, or build fires. Restricted sites, including Broadway, Chasm View, Notchtop, and Sky Pond, are heavily used areas that have exhibited environmental damage. Human waste is a serious problem at many bivy sites. Burn your toilet paper, bury waste beneath 4 to 6 inches of soil, and heed the call of nature well away from water sources.

Trip Planning Information

General description: A dramatic and varied selection of both long and short routes on lofty mountain peaks, including The Diamond on Longs Peak, the Northeast Face of Spearhead, the Petit Grepon, and Hallett Peak.

Location: Northwest of Boulder, straddling the Continental Divide.

Camping: There are four campgrounds on the east side of the park. Moraine Park Campground (250 sites) is 3 miles west of the Headquarters Visitor Center off Bear Lake Road. Glacier Basin Campground (152 sites) is 9 miles west of Estes Park off Bear Lake Road. Aspenglen Campground is 5 miles northwest of Estes Park near the park's Fall River entrance off US 34. Longs Peak Campground (30 tents-only campsites) is 11 miles south of Estes Park and 1 mile west of Colorado 7. Stays at Longs Peak CG are limited to 3 days from June through September. Camping in the park is limited to 7 days from June through September. Aspenglen and Longs Peak campgrounds operate on a first-come, first-served basis. Moraine Park and Glacier Basin campgrounds operate on an advance reservation system in summer. Contact the park for more info. Several commercial campgrounds are found in the Estes Park area. Longer term and cheaper public camping is found in Roosevelt National Forest south of Estes Park along Colorado 7, including Olive Ridge Campground near Allenspark.

Climbing season: June through September. The park's high peaks all rise above timberline or 11,500 feet. Summers are short and brisk. June is characterized by snowmelt. The rock is often wet and seeping, and approaches and descents often require crossing snowfields. July and August have sunny mornings, cloudy afternoons, and cool, clear nights. Expect heavy afternoon thunderstorms and downpours. Get an early start and bring appropriately warm clothing and raingear to avoid hypothermia. Lightning is an almost daily hazard somewhere in the park. September days are generally dry and warm, with occasional rainy periods. Snow can and will fall in any summer month here. Climbing is sometimes possible in October, depending on weather and snow conditions.

Restrictions and access issues: Regulations pertaining to rock climbing include: the use of motorized drills is prohibited, however, bolts can be placed by hand; it is illegal to remove vegetation from cracks; don't bother wildlife; no littering; dogs are not allowed in the backcountry and must be leashed in the parking areas and campgrounds; bivouac permits are required for overnight bivouacs in the backcountry (call the Backcountry Station at (970) 586-1242 for info and permits).

Guidebooks: *Rocky Mountain National Park: The Climber's Guide* by Bernard Gillet, Earthbound Sports, 1993. An excellent overall guide to the park's high peaks with complete topos and descriptions of most of the faces. Clay Wadman's Diamond topo poster offers lots of info on all the Diamond's routes and variations. Richard Rossiter's complete guide to all of Rocky Mountain National Park will be published in late 1995 by Chockstone Press.

Nearby mountain shops, guide services, and gyms: Wilderness Sports, Komito Boots, Colorado Mountain School (Estes Park); Neptune Mountaineering, Boulder Mountaineer, Basecamp Mountain Sports, Boulder Rock Club, (Boulder); Desert Ice Mountain Guides (Fort Collins).

Services: Full services—lodging, dining, gas, groceries, beer, fast food, campgrounds, and showers—in Estes Park.

Emergency services: For rescues and emergency situations call 911 or (970) 586-2371. Estes Park Medical Center, 555 Prospect, Estes Park, CO 80517, (970) 586-2317. McKee Medical Center, 2000 Boise Ave., Loveland, CO 80538, (970) 669-4640.

Nearby climbing areas: Lumpy Ridge, Estes Valley crags, Combat Rock, Big Thompson Canyon, South St. Vrain Canyon, Carter Lake boulders, Button Rock Reservoir crags, Boulder Canyon, The Flatirons, Eldorado Canyon State Park.

Nearby attractions: Trail Ridge Road, Longs Peak, Enos Mills Cabin, Big Thompson Canyon, Indian Peaks Wilderness Area, Peak to Peak Highway.

Finding the crags: From Interstate 25 east of Loveland travel west on US 34 for 34 miles to Estes Park. From Denver and Boulder drive north on US 36 to Lyons and continue 19 miles west on US 36 to Estes Park. A system of park roads branch out from Estes Park to reach parking areas and trailheads for all the routes detailed here. Rocky Mountain National Park is a fee area. Daily and long-term passes are purchased at the park entrance stations. For more park info contact: Rocky Mountain National Park, Estes Park, CO 80517, (970) 586-2371.

THE DIAMOND

The Diamond, sitting entirely above 13,000 feet, is perhaps the most spectacular alpine wall in the United States. It's a steep, diamond-shaped wall perched atop the massive, glacier-excavated East Face of Longs Peak. The 900' wall is a climber's paradise, with superb granite split by vertical crack systems and studded with incut handholds. More than 35 climbing routes and variations thread across The Diamond today. The left side of the wall yields some spectacular free climbs such as *Ariana, D7, Yellow Wall,* and *Casual Route.* The wet, overhanging right side hosts some serious nailing routes including *Diamond Star Halo, Steep is Flat,* and the *Dunn-Westbay* Route.

Climbing The Diamond is serious business. Don't expect a stroll up a sport climbing route, but rather a climbing adventure or a possible epic. The approach is long, circuitous, loose, and somewhat dangerous. The routes are vertical, exposed, and subject to severe weather. The descent via the North Face or Keyhole Route is hard to find in the dark, bordered by dangerous snowfields, and covered with loose gravel and boulders. Use your best judgment, and consider retreat an honorable option. The northeast-facing Diamond receives only morning sun, and shadows steal over the wall by 12:30 p.m. on the longest days of the year.

Approach The Diamond by driving 7 miles south from Estes Park on Colorado 7 to the Longs Peak Ranger Station and Longs Peak Campground at 9,500 feet on the west side of the highway. Park here and hike west through forest on the Longs Peak Trail. A major fork in the trail is reached after about 3 miles. The left fork continues up the valley to Chasm Lake, while the right fork swings around Mount Lady Washington to Chasm View and the Keyhole Route up Longs Peak. The Diamond can be reached via either trail.

The fastest way to Broadway, a large ledge at The Diamond's base, is via Chasm Lake. Continue up the valley to Chasm Lake at 11,800'; scramble around the north side of the lake; cross a large boulder field and part of Mills Glacier; and finish up 500' *North Chimney,* a large, wet gully directly below *D1. North Chimney* is a dangerous 4th and 5th class approach. Most parties rope up for a least 1 pitch, a 5.4 section. Exercise caution when climbing and watch for wet rock, loose blocks, and any parties above. Snow fills the gully in June. **Descent**

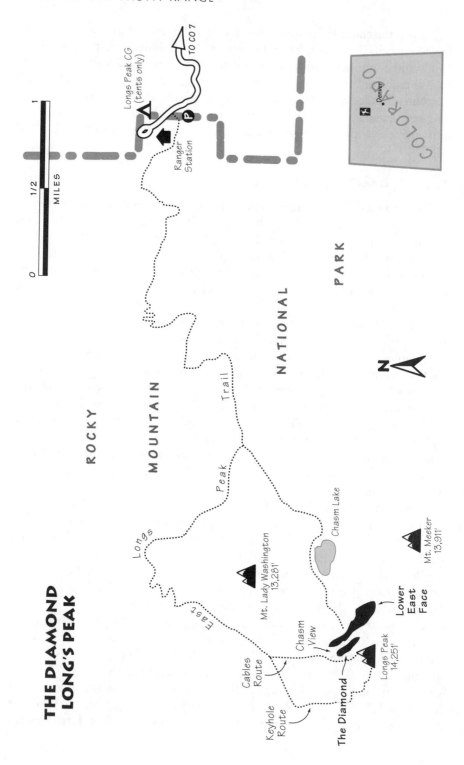

down *North Chimney* is accomplished in three double-rope rappels from numerous fixed anchors and tied-off blocks.

The other trail approaches The Diamond from the north. Follow the trail for several miles around Mount Lady Washington and across the boulder field to Chasm View. Chasm View is an airy overlook that perches directly north of The Diamond and above Chasm View Wall. Make three double-rope rappels from fixed anchors to Broadway. A quick party can reach the base of The Diamond in two to three hours from the parking lot. Allow a few hours extra if you're carrying heavy packs.

All of The Diamond's routes begin on Broadway, a large sloping ledge that slices across the East Face below the Diamond. Use caution when traversing Broadway above North Chimney. Several fatalities and accidents have occurred to unroped climbers on this exposed traverse. There are a limited number of excellent bivouac sites on Broadway, with a limit on the number of climbers permitted to stay overnight. A free bivy permit is obtained at the Longs Peak Ranger Station. No water, other than snowmelt, is found on Broadway.

Descent: All of the routes described here, except *The Yellow Wall,* end on Table Ledge, a prominent horizontal crack/ledge system that slices across the upper quarter of the wall. Exit off the routes by traversing left on Table Ledge to *Kiener's Route.* Scramble up 3rd class rock, gullies, boulders, and ledges on *Kiener's* to the summit of Longs Peak. A quick but dangerous descent route goes down the peak's North Face along the old Cables Route. Prudently descend scree slopes, boulder fields, and snowfields on the North Face above The Diamond's north flank. Be extremely careful. People have slipped and plummeted over the wall here. At the cliff-band, locate large eye-bolts that once anchored the cables and make two single-rope rappels down some wet, slabby dihedrals to the boulder field above Chasm View.

Besides the few Diamond routes detailed here, numerous other excellent lines ascend The Diamond, The Lower East Face left of North Chimney, and Chasm View Wall below Chasm View on the north side of the face. Other fine Diamond routes are *The Obelisk* (5.11a), *Black Dagger* (5.10c), *Eroica* (5.12b), and *King of Swords* (5.12a). The best Lower East Face routes include *Stettner's Ledges* (III 5.7), *Diagonal Direct* (V 5.11d R), and *The Diagonal* (V 5.11b AO). The Diagonal routes, following the prominent left-diagonaling crack system that slashes across the wall, can be combined with a Diamond route for a Grade VI ascent. The Chasm View Walls hosts two very good Grade IIIs—*Red Wall* (5.10a) and *Directissima* (5.10a). Detailed topos and descriptions of these and other routes are found in area guides.

1. **Pervertical Sanctuary** (IV 5.10c) This excellent free climb, first aided by Ron Olevsky and Bob Dodds in 1974 and freed by Bruce Adams and Tobin Sorenson the following year, is the second easiest free route on The Dia-

mond. The 6-pitch route follows a long crack system on the far left side of the wall. Approach the route's start by heading south on Broadway, carefully scrambling past a small snowfield below the wall's far left margin. Set the first belay out right from the snowpatch on a ledge below a broken crack system. **Pitch 1** traverses right and up to the left side of the Mitten formation. Continue up the left-facing 5.9 dihedral on the Mitten to a good belay ledge atop a long pitch. **Pitch 2** climbs a blocky, left-facing 5.9 corner to a stance. **Pitch 3** heads up the crack system to a small roof. Work left on 5.9 face climbing past an old bolt, then move right up a flake to a ledge just right of the Obelisk, an immense dihedral on the south edge of The Diamond. **Pitch 4** begins on the right side of the ledge. Jam the strenuous 1.5" 5.10c crack (route crux) for 50'; continue 50' more up the exposed splitter crack to a perch atop a wedged block. **Pitch 5** continues up the widening, sustained 5.9/.10- crack with hand and fist jams, enters a left-facing 5.8 corner, and ends on a spacious ledge. **Pitch 6** climbs a 5.9 finger crack in a corner to a belay on Table Ledge. Head up and left on easy rock to KIENER'S ROUTE. **Rack:** Bring a rack that includes small wired nuts to a #4 Camalot for the upper crack and doubles of Friends from #1.5 up.

2. **Ariana** (V 5.12a) This stunning 6-pitch route, The Diamond's first 5.12, was freed by Roger and Bill Briggs in 1985. It was first ascended by George Hurley and R. Bliss in 1975. The line follows a crack system just right of the left edge of the Obelisk Column. Begin down and right of the snowpatch

THE DIAMOND/LONG'S PEAK

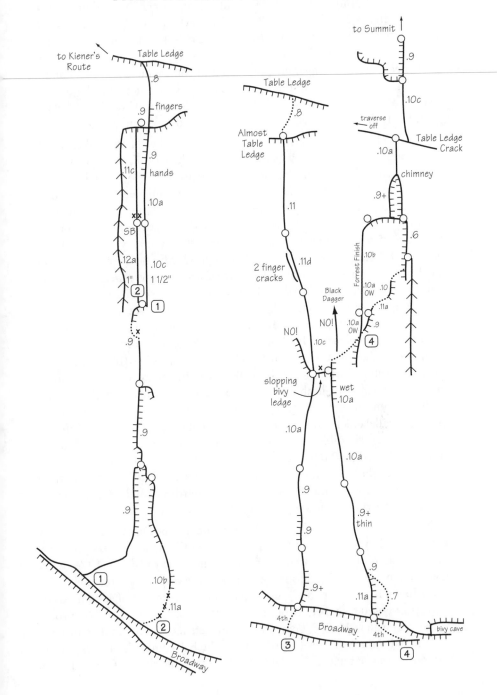

on a ledge above the south end of Broadway. **Pitch 1** climbs the 5.11a face above past 3 bolts, ascends a narrow corner to the bottom right-hand side of the Mitten, and finishes up the right-facing corner to the thumb of the Mitten. **Pitches 2 and 3** ascend PERVERTICAL SANCTUARY (5.9) to the belay stance opposite the Obelisk's base. **Pitch 4** is directly above—a 1" crack that lies a scant 5' from the left edge of The Diamond. Jam the well-protected, sustained finger crack (5.12a and continuous 5.11) to a hanging belay stance. **Pitch 5** continues up the steep 5.11 crack to a large belay platform. **Pitch 6** finishes up PERVERTICAL SANCTUARY'S last 5.9 lead to Table Ledge. **Rack:** Bring plenty of wired stoppers and pro to 3".

3. **D7** (V 5.11d) This route, first climbed in 1966 by Larry Dalke, Wayne Goss, and George Hurley, was the easiest and busiest route on the wall for years. Traffic slacked off after Richard Harrison and John Bacher's 1977 free ascent. D7, however, is still a superb clean aid line (5.7 C2) and is unmatched as an excellent but very difficult free climb. Begin down and right of ARIANA on a ledge/ramp (4th class) below an obvious, thin left-facing corner. This corner is 150' left or south of the bivy cave on Broadway. **Pitch 1** climbs the 5.9 corner 70' to a good ledge on the right; continue up the crack above to a belay ledge. **Pitch 2** ascends a left-facing corner 40' and follows corners and cracks above to a belay ledge. **Pitch 3** follows the system up widening cracks. The wide crack is often wet and can be face-climbed to the left at 5.10a. Belay on a sloping ledge on the right. Pay attention to the start of **Pitch 4** to avoid taking the wrong crack system. Don't go straight up the obvious crack above. This is D MINOR 7. Pitch 4 properly begins 5' right of D MINOR 7 and the belay ledge in a shallow right-facing corner. Climb and stem up the steep corner to a belay stance below 2 thin, left-leaning cracks. **Pitch 5**, the route crux, climbs the exposed, parallel cracks for about 130' to a small stance. **Pitch 6** continues up a thin 5.11 crack, which widens and leads to easier rock and spacious Almost Table Ledge. **Pitch 7** goes up and left for about 40' on 5.8 rock to Table Ledge. Follow Table Ledge left to KIENER'S ROUTE and continue on to the peak's summit. **Rack:** Bring a standard rack with extra stoppers for the upper thin pitches as well as a #4 Friend.

4. **Yellow Wall** (V 5.11a) This is the classic route up The Diamond. It was first climbed by Layton Kor and Charlie Roskosz in 1962 as the second ascent of The Diamond. Roger Briggs and Rob Candelaria freed it in 1976, while Charlie Fowler and Dan Stone free-climbed the original 1st pitch in 1978. The 8-pitch route offers fine, sustained climbing with lots of solid holds on a steep, exposed face. Begin about 60' south of the Bivouac Cave on Broadway on a 3rd class ramp below a narrow, left-facing corner. The original start aided up this corner (A3 or 5.11a). **Pitch 1** climbs 5.7 flakes for 70' right of the corner and works left to a ledge atop the corner. Continue up a

thin 5.9 finger crack for another 60' to a belay stance. **Pitch 2** goes up and left along a thin crack (5.9+) for another 130' or so to a small ledge. **Pitch 3** continues up the thin 5.10a crack to a hard 5.10a corner that is often wet. Belay on a narrow ledge on the left that the route shares with neighboring D7. **Pitch 4** laybacks a shallow left-facing corner above the right side of the ledge. Continue up and right under the obvious BLACK DAGGER off-width crack system, past the FORREST FINISH system, and into a thin, right-facing 5.9 red dihedral. Set a sling belay above. **Pitch 5** is the route's free and aid crux. An airy, hard-to-protect 5.11a traverse leads up and right on flakes to a thin 5.10 corner. Climb the corner to its intersection with the CASUAL ROUTE'S large dihedral. Belay here or continue 40' up the dihedral (5.6) to the spacious 4' x 20' Yellow Wall Bivy Ledge. This is a sustained, exciting pitch with good exposure, and requires creative use of RPs and small wires for pro. To avoid this pitch, climb 2 pitches up the FORREST FINISH to the bivy ledge. First is a 5.10a off-width, second is more 5.10 off-width to a steep hand crack. **Pitch 6** is shared with the CASUAL ROUTE. Stem up between two opposing corners (5.9+) above the right side of the ledge and enter a 5.8 chimney. Climb up and left past a fixed piton in a thin crack, over a 5.10a bulge, and belay at Table Ledge crack. Exit left here to avoid the upper 2 pitches. **Pitch 7** traverses right on Table Ledge crack for 15' and then climbs very exposed cracks to the foot of a large, obvious right-facing dihedral. Belay on a small ledge on the right side of the large, blocky overhang. This 5.10c pitch is adequately protected but very airy and scary. **Pitch 8** climbs the 5.9 chimney up the dihedral to a good belay. Scramble on easy rock to the top of the wall just below the peak's summit. **Rack:** Bring a generous rack with sets of RPs, wired nuts, and Friends to #3.5 along with a few hexes and TCUs.

5. **Casual Route** (IV 5.10a) This 8-pitch route, sharing parts of three other lines, is the easiest and most traveled route up The Diamond. It sees so many ascents that locals nicknamed it the "Cattle Route." The route was first climbed in 1977 by Duncan Ferguson and Chris Reveley. THE CASUAL ROUTE offers excellent moderate climbing with all the hard spots well-protected and is climbed in 6 to 8 pitches. Pitches 4 and 5 are usually wet early in the season. Watch for loose rock knocked off by parties above on busy days. Begin on Broadway just a few paces south of the upper rappel anchors for North Chimney. **Pitch 1** initially scales a 5.5 left-facing corner in the middle of the D1 Pillar, a large finger-like pillar below D1's obvious crack system, and then continues up cracks on the buttress face. An alcove is reached after 140' on the left side of the pillar. **Pitch 2** is short. Climb up and left to a belay stance below a crack just left of the pillar's top. **Pitch 3**, the flakes traverse, is the route's troublesome lead. Although not hard, it offers some route-finding problems. Numerous parties have begun the in-

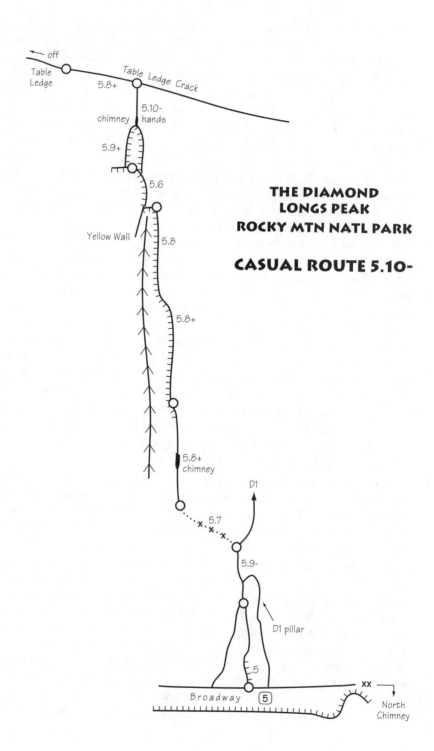

Table Ledge

Table Ledge Crack

5.8+

5.10- hands

chimney

5.9+

5.6

Yellow Wall

5.8

**THE DIAMOND
LONGS PEAK
ROCKY MTN NATL PARK**

CASUAL ROUTE 5.10-

5.8+

5.8+ chimney

D1

5.7

5.9-

D1 pillar

.5

Broadway ⑤

XX

North Chimney

famous traverse too low and found themselves on hard 5.10 face climbing with no protection and serious fall potential. Jam the 5.9 finger to hand crack above the belay to a small stance with a fixed peg. Climb up and left on a long, rising traverse up flakes and edges (5.6 and 5.7 climbing) and past several fixed pitons to a semi-hanging belay beneath the huge right-facing dihedral. Climbers have been injured in long, pendulum falls on this pitch. The fixed pegs certainly ease the mind, but climb cautiously. This is a long pitch. **Pitch 4** climbs a 5.8 chimney, jams cracks past a sloping ledge, and continues up cracks on the dihedral's left wall to a small belay ledge. **Pitch 5** continues up the 5.8 dihedral for almost a full rope-length to a belay niche near the top of the dihedral. **Pitch 6** is a short 5.6 lead up the dihedral to the Yellow Wall Bivy Ledge on the left. **Pitch 7**, the route's technical crux, stems up opposing corners above the right side of the ledge (5.9+), squeezes up a 5.8 chimney, jams a thin 5.10a crack over a bulge, and ends at an airy belay at Table Ledge crack. This pitch is shared with THE YELLOW WALL. **Pitch 8** hand-traverses left (5.8) along the horizontal crack. After about 30' the crack begins to widen. Climb aboard and continue traversing up and left along Table Ledge to KIENER'S ROUTE. **Rack:** Bring a good selection of gear, including some large RPs, a set of wired nuts, a couple of medium hexes, some TCUs, and a set of Friends. Many fixed pitons dot the route. Use them with caution; the severe alpine climate can cause them to loosen. A 200' rope is useful on this route and can shorten the climbing time considerably by combining pitches 1 and 2, and pitches 5 and 6.

SPEARHEAD

Spearhead perches above Glacier Gorge, a long glacier-excavated basin flanked by soaring ridges, broken cliffs, and talus slopes, carpeted with wildflower-strewn meadows and dark evergreen forests, and dotted with crystalline alpine lakes. The Spearhead lifts its 12,575-foot point above a burnished 800-foot northeast face. This immaculate granite wall, one of the best in Rocky Mountain National Park, is dwarfed by surrounding peaks, including 13,327-foot McHenry's Peak to the west, 13,326-foot Storm Peak to the east, and the immense bulk of 13,579-foot Chiefs Head Peak to the south. This climber-friendly face is seamed with cracks and dihedrals and studded with incut handholds and flakes. Numerous three-star routes up to 9 pitches long ascend the concave wall, offering brilliant climbing in a pristine, remote setting.

Approach Spearhead by driving west from Estes Park on U.S. Highway 36 into Rocky Mountain National Park. Turn south on Bear Lake Road just past the Beaver Meadows Entrance Station and follow the road to a small parking lot at the 9,240-foot Glacier Gorge Trailhead 1 mile before road's end at Bear Lake. The lot is small. Get there early for a spot or walk the 0.5-mile trail down from the larger Bear Lake parking lot. Hike south on the Glacier Gorge Trail. It's about 6 miles and two hours to the base of Spearhead. The trail intersects the North Longs Peak Trail at 1.4 miles. Keep right and in 0.5 mile turn south toward Mills Lake. The trail climbs steeply 0.6 mile to the lake and continues south along the east shore another 0.4 mile to Jewell Lake. The trail follows the forested floor of Glacier Gorge for another 1.8 miles to Black Lake at 10,620 feet. Hike up steep slopes below a cliff band east of the lake and enter the upper basin below Spearhead. Follow a climber's trail through alpine meadows and across glacier-polished bedrock to the base of the wall.

Spearhead is the ending high point of a ridge that juts north from Chiefshead and the Continental Divide. The northeast face is a sweeping, pyramid-shaped wall broken by several obvious features. A horizontal grassy ledge—Middle Earth—splits the lower wall. The Eye of Mordor is the tilted, shadowy north-facing dihedral just above Middle Earth, while Syke's Sickle is the prominent crescent corner just below the summit block. A huge snowfield skirts the wall's base early in the season.

Descend from Spearhead's summit by dropping down its northwest flank or working south along the ridge to Chiefshead and scrambling down ramps and ledges to the basin below. Watch for cliff bands, steep couloirs, snowpatches, and loose rock.

Spearhead's climbing season generally runs from June through September. The wall receives a fair amount of summer sun, melting any snow on the face and drying the rock. Most of the routes are done as day climbs, but a limited number of bivouac permits are available for overnight stays at the wall base. The free permits are available at the backcountry ranger station at park head-quarters. Objective dangers include quick and heavy afternoon thunderstorms, snow and sleet showers, lightning, loose rock, and lots of parties on the classic lines. To avoid the crowds, try to avoid the weekends.

Every route on Spearhead is worth doing, but the following descriptions are some of the best lines on this great wall. Other worthy climbs include *Axe Age* (III 5.10b), *Three Stoners* (IV 5.11a), *Four Believers* (IV 5.11a), *Barb Gnarly* (III 5.11b), and *The Barb* (III 5.10c), an old classic line that wanders up the face right of Sykes Sickle. Topos and descriptions of these routes are found in Gillet's *Rocky Mountain National Park: The Climber's Guide.*

6. **Stone Monkey** (III 5.12a) This neo-classic route, put up by Chip Chase and Dan Stone in 1985, offers excellent climbing with superb position on the left side of the wall. Jeff Achey calls its fingertip crux crack "one of the hardest and prettiest leads in the high peaks." The route lies on the upper wall. To reach Stone Monkey's 4 pitches, climb the first 3 pitches of UNBE-LIEVERS. **Pitch 1** begins on the far left side of the face. Locate two obvious right-leaning dihedrals. The left one is topped by a roof. Climb the

right dihedral to a 5.9 bulge and belay above on Middle Earth. **Pitch 2** is a full rope-length up the sloping 5.4 dihedral to a belay stance at its top. **Pitch 3** works up a thin, right-facing flake and corner with 5.9 laybacking. Near the top of the corner, make an exciting 5.10b runout traverse along a thin seam to a hanging belay. **Pitch 4** begins STONE MONKEY. Face climb up and right from the belay on thin flakes (5.8). Belay on a wide ledge below a right-leaning corner/crack system. **Pitch 5** is the long, crux lead. Do a 5.9 undercling up and left into the corner. Follow the corner to its end and continue up an extremely thin, fingertip crack (5.12a) to a flake and on to a decent belay platform. **Pitch 6** jams a 5.8 crack up to fractured rock below the summit. Stretch out the rope to the belay stance of your choice. **Pitch 7** works up and right through broken rock to the right side of the summit block. **Rack:** Bring a rack that's generous with small wired nuts, RPs, and TCUs, along with Friends to #3.

7. **Spear Me The Details** (IV 5.11d) This rappel-bolted classic, finished in 1990 by Greg Davis and Neal Beidleman, was first climbed to the top of the 6th pitch by Ed Webster and Joe Frank in 1987. The pair bailed off after rockfall almost killed them. The route is one of the best hard routes on Spearhead for good reason. It's a direct line up the wall with fun and varied climbing including friction, technical edging, and hard jamming. The route combines its 9 pitches above Middle Earth with the first 2 easy leads of OBVIOUSLY FOUR BELIEVERS for an 11-pitch grand tour of the face. **Pitch 1** begins near the south side of the face left of a series of black-streaked overlaps. Follow an easy right-leaning ramp for a long pitch to a belay ledge. **Pitch 2** continues up and right on easy rock to Middle Earth below the Eye of Mordor. **Pitch 3** is the start of SPEAR ME THE DETAILS. Begin on a terrace below and right of the Eye just above Middle Earth. Face climb up and right on 5.7 rock to a series of 5.8 cracks. Belay on a narrow ledge. **Pitch 4** scales easy 5th class rock straight up to belay stance below the left side of a finger. This is a long 175' pitch that requires either a 200' rope or some simul-climbing. **Pitch 5** jams a 5.8 hand crack up the left side of the finger to a ledge on top. **Pitch 6** face climbs up and left past 2 fixed pins and a bolt (5.10b) into a narrow corner. At its top traverse up right to a small belay below a thin roof. **Pitch 7** swings over the roof at its narrowest part via a 5.10d mantle at a bolt. Go up left to a belay stance below a shallow left-facing corner. **Pitch 8** is a long, difficult lead. Climb the corner and the small roof that caps it and face climb (5.11b) past 3 bolts and a piton to a flake. Scale the flake and climb a thin 5.11d face past 4 bolts. Belay below a left-facing corner. **Pitch 9** stems and jams the corner to a 5.11a face above with 2 bolts and a fixed pin. Climb into another thin corner with fixed pro and ascend it (5.11b) to a ledge on the right. **Pitch 10** follows a left-facing dihedral to a good belay atop a pillar. **Pitch 11** traverses left and slightly

ROCKY MTN NAT'L PARK
SPEARHEAD

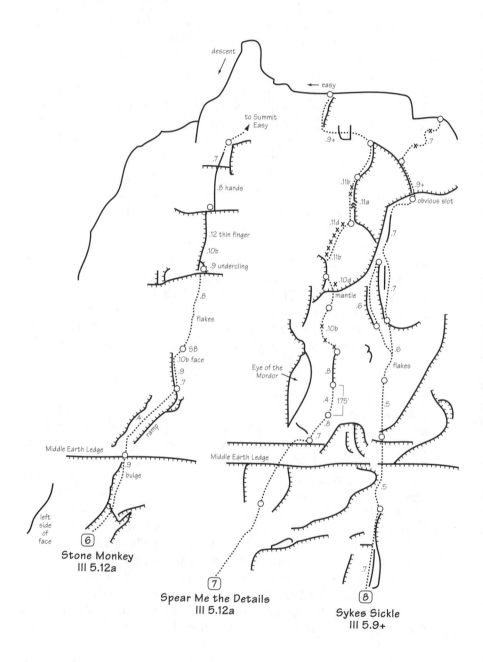

descent

← easy

to Summit
Easy

.9+

.7

.8 hands

.11b

.9+

.11a

obvious slot

.12 thin finger

.11d

.7

.10b

.11b

.9 undercling

.10d

mantle

.8

.7

flakes

.6

.10b

SB
.10b face

.6

.9

Eye of the
Mordor

flakes

.7

.8

.4

175'

.5

.4

.8

ramp

.7

Middle Earth Ledge

Middle Earth Ledge

.9

.7

bulge

.5

left
side
of
face

⑥

Stone Monkey
III 5.12a

⑦

Spear Me the Details
III 5.12a

.7

⑧

Sykes Sickle
III 5.9+

downward (5.9) on thin face climbing into a right-facing corner which leads to the summit ridge. **Rack:** Bring a standard rack and a 200' rope if possible.

8. **Sykes Sickle** (III 5.9+) This route, following the obvious sickle-shaped arch on the upper wall, is Spearhead's all-time classic with mostly moderate climbing, generally adequate protection, and an exciting climax on the last pitch. Established in 1958 and freed by Royal Robbins in 1964, *Sykes Sickle* was the first route on the Northeast Face. The 8-pitch route is quite popular, particularly on summer weekends when parties queue up at the route base. An early start is essential on the route to avoid getting caught by rain on the summit slabs. Begin the line at the wall's base directly below the Sickle and just right of a series of water-streaked overlaps. **Pitch 1** climbs the left of 2 parallel cracks (5.7) 80' to a belay. **Pitch 2** continues up 5.4 slabs to a terraced ledge just above Middle Earth. **Pitch 3** face climbs (5.5) up flakes and occasional cracks to a convenient ledge. **Pitch 4** heads straight up the face above (5.6) to a belay at the base of an obvious left-leaning corner system. **Pitch 5** jams 5.7 cracks up the dihedral to a belay just below the Sickle. Early parties headed out left part-way up Pitch 4 and climbed a series of flakes and cracks (5.6) on the face left of the dihedral to the belay ledge below the Sickle. **Pitch 6** squeezes up a flared 5.7 chimney on the left side of the Sickle and works up right to an exposed ledge directly below a notch in the large roof above. **Pitch 7** is the route's technical crux. Climb up to the notched roof, pull and stem over (5.9+) past some fixed pitons. This section can be wet, especially in early summer. Step left into a crack and follow it up left for another 100' or so to a stance. The hard roof move, somewhat out of character with the rest of the line, is easily aided. **Pitch 8,** the route's psychological crux, has seen its share of epics. Traverse delicately right across a polished slab (5.7) to a fixed pin. Work downward and around a rounded corner to an old bolt and scamper carefully up and right on easier rock to the summit ridge. **Rack:** Bring a standard rack with wired nuts, some medium hexes, and a set of Friends.

9. **North Ridge** (III 5.6) This outstanding line up Spearhead's North Ridge, first ascended by Charles Schobinger and Pete Roberg in 1958, is one of the park's best multi-pitch moderate routes. The route is usually done in 7 pitches plus some scrambling. The generally easy climbing allows plenty of route-finding variations. Use your own judgment for the exact line you want to follow. To begin scramble up and around the Northeast Face to a dark chimney/cleft below the broad ridge. Do a long pitch up through the chimney (5.5) to a belay ledge. Follow grooves up a slab for 3 long pitches (5.5) to a headwall. The next pitch diagonals up and left above the slab to the airy edge of the Northeast Face. Another pitch creeps along the exposed edge to a step below the final difficulties. Scramble south along the

ridge (3rd and 4th class climbing) to a ledge below the spired summit. Squeeze up through a 5.6 slot in a large block to emerge onto the summit. **Rack:** Bring a standard rack.

PETIT GREPON

Loch Vale, a broad U-shaped valley, is one of Rocky Mountain National Park's most scenic spots. The deep valley descends northeast from Taylor Peak and the Continental Divide, dropping past picturesque alpine tarns and dense forests of subalpine fir, spruce, and lodgepole pine. Icy Brook, originating from Taylor Glacier, traverses the valley floor, tumbling over cliffs and boulders and meandering through damp meadows. The upper above-timberline gorge is lined on the north by the Cathedral Spires—a startling collection of splendid summits and abrupt rock faces. The Cathedral Wall, looming west of The Loch, is an 800-foot pillar at the end of a long ridge. Farther up Loch Vale soar the rest of the spires—Sharkstooth, Petit Grepon, The Saber, and The Foil.

The Petit Grepon is the best known and most beautiful of the Cathedral Spires. This amazing semi-detached pinnacle, flanked by bulky Sharkstooth and The Saber, sweeps its 800-foot triangular south face upward like a huge Eiffel Tower to an airy summit platform. This sky summit, a flat rectangle 10 feet wide and 25 feet long, looks like a postage stamp pasted atop a mountainous envelope.

The Petit Grepon's concave South Face hosts two superb routes that wander up ever-steepening cracks, chimneys, slabs, and headwalls to their final 2 pitches up the dramatic and exposed summit blade. *The South Face* route, included in *Fifty Classic Climbs of North America*, is one of Colorado's best known rock climbs. Its inclusion in that book ensured the route's continuing popularity and led occasionally to overcrowded conditions. The climb, however, is well worth waiting in line for. The rock is excellent with numerous incut holds and cracks of all widths, and the climbing is varied and fun with plenty of protection. The tremendous exposure, particularly on the upper pitches and belay stances, gives flashes of vertigo to even jaded rock jocks.

The true first ascensionists of the Petit's *South Face* remain unknown, although Bill Buckingham and Art Davidson made the wall's first ascent in 1961 via a series of moderate pitches up the face's left edge. A pair of Bobs, Culp and Beal, pioneered the first ascent of the *Southwest Corner* route in 1970.

Approach the Petit Grepon by parking at the small Glacier Gorge Junction trailhead on Bear Lake Road 1 mile from road's end at Bear Lake. The small lot fills up early, so no parking spaces may be available. Alternatively, park at the larger Bear Lake lot and hike 0.4 mile down to Glacier Gorge Trailhead. It's 4.6 miles from here to Sky Pond below the Petit Grepon, and another 0.25 mile up to the wall base. Hike south on Glacier Gorge Trail 1.4 miles to its junction with North Longs Peak Trail. Keep right and continue another 0.5 mile to the junction of the Glacier Gorge and Loch Vale trails. Keep right on the Loch Vale Trail. The trail follows the valley for another 2.7 miles to Sky Pond at 10,900 feet, passing The Loch, a large lake. Just before reaching Sky Pond, look for a

PETIT GREPON

climber's trail cutting off toward the talus slopes below The Saber and Petit Grepon. Scramble up loose talus to the face. Allow about two hours to walk in to the spire.

Descent off the Petit Grepon is straight-forward, but a wrong turn can easily turn it into an unexpected adventure. Make one long, double-rope rappel or three shorter single-rope rappels into the steep gully on the northeast side of the tower from fixed anchors. From the base of the rappels, scramble up the gully and locate an easy 5th class chimney. Climb the chimney and scramble up the rest of the gully to the East Col, a notched saddle behind the Petit Grepon and between Sharkstooth and The Saber. Descend north down more gullies and slabs into The Gash, a steep valley that angles northeast. Follow this downward to the Andrews Glacier Trail which leads down to Loch Vale. If you bivouac at the base of the wall, it's best to carry all your gear up the climb. If anything is left at the base the best descent is to scramble up to the notch above The Gash, 3rd class east across the north side of The Saber to another notch, and descend south down a steep but easy gully to Sky Pond. A short rappel over a step from bolts is necessary part way down the gully. Avoid attempting to rappel and downclimb the steep gullies on either side of the Petit Grepon. While they look relatively benign, most parties that do this descent end up with a major epic on their hands because of extremely loose rubble and stuck or cut rappel ropes.

The season on the Petit runs from June through September. Snow generally melts off the south-facing wall early in June. Snowfields may be found on the approach, particularly on the steep trail section below Glass Lake and on the scree slope below the Petit Grepon. Be extremely careful early in the season on the descent into The Gash on the backside. Slippery snow can remain in the steep couloir well into summer. All the routes are done as day climbs. A limited number of bivouac sites are available for overnight stays. The free bivy permit is obtained at the park's backcountry ranger station at park headquarters. Watch for various dangers while climbing that include rockfall from parties above, wet rock sections, loose blocks, afternoon thunderstorms, lightning strikes, and overcrowded conditions. Weekends in July and August are usually the busiest. Try to schedule your climb on a weekday or in September to avoid the rush, or alter your plans and climb one of the excellent routes on Sharkstooth or The Saber. An early start is mandatory to make the approach and do the route before the customary bad weather sets in.

10. **South Face** (III 5.8) Simply an excellent route in a breathtaking mountain setting. The 9-pitch route generally follows an obvious crack/chimney system up the middle of the face to the right ridge, which leads to the summit. If the route is crowded, an easy alternative follows cracks, corners, and slabs just outside of and on the Southeast Ridge to the Pizza Pan Belay 6 pitches up. The South Face route begins left of the main chimney. Scramble up and right onto a ledge 70' above the base. **Pitches 1 and 2** ascend easy, low-angle slabs left of the chimney for 200' to a 30'-wide ledge called First

Terrace. **Pitch 3** climbs the dark chimney to a large chockstone. Climb around it on the left and belay atop the boulder. **Pitch 4** continues up the easy left wall of the chimney to a roof that caps it. Step out of the chimney into an awkward, wide, left-leaning 5.7 crack and follow it to the spacious Second Terrace. **Pitch 5** bridges up the obvious 5.5 chimney above the ledge. Exit left atop the chimney, then work back right on 5.6 face climbing to a belay stance with a fixed piton. **Pitch 6,** the crux lead, begins by working up right on a steep 5.7 slab to a good ledge. Stem, jam, and face climb the thin crack in the right-facing dihedral above (5.8) to a good ledge poised on the right-hand ridge. This long pitch is technical, exposed, and fairly sustained. **Pitch 7** wanders up the steep face 30' to 40' right of the southeast ridge (around the corner from the South Face). This long, sustained 5.7 pitch is scantily protected. Work left up high to the Pizza Pan Belay, a tiny, exposed stance perched on the southeast corner below the jutting summit prow. **Pitch 8** heads up right along a thin crack that leads back onto the spire's east face. Continue up the steep wall to a decent ledge below the top. This 5.7 pitch is long, sustained, under-protected, and requires careful route finding. **Pitch 9** climbs straight up the headwall above to the narrow ridge and on to the summit. It's initially 5.6 but the grade rapidly eases. **Rack:** Bring a standard rack with sets of wired nuts and Friends, and a few hexes.

11. **Southwest Corner** (III 5.9) This 7-pitch route, first climbed by Bob Culp and Bob Beal in 1970, joins the SOUTH FACE line at the Pizza Pan Belay and finishes up its last 2 pitches. The route follows a major crack system left of the regular route up to the Second Terrace, before climbing up and left onto the southwest corner itself. As with the SOUTH FACE, the upper section of this line is sustained and exposed. Begin by picking an easy crack line on the slabs left of the main lower chimney. **Pitch 1** goes up easy cracks and slabs for a full rope-length to the First Terrace. **Pitch 2** follows a large, arching, left-facing 5.5 dihedral to a belay stance above the arch section. **Pitch 3** continues up the dihedral, a spot of 5.6, to the Second Terrace. Go left on the ledge about 50' to start the next lead. **Pitch 4** (5.7) climbs shallow corners, cracks, and steep slabs up and left to a ledge just left of the Southwest Corner itself. **Pitch 5** goes up 5.8 corners and cracks on the sharp ridge for a long, sustained pitch. Belay at the second decent ledge on the exposed ridge. **Pitch 6** continues up the arete to a vertical 5.9 crack. Belay above on a good ledge directly below the narrow prow of the South Face. **Pitch 7** is a short traverse right across the top of the face to the Pizza Pan Belay on the southeast corner. This short lead can be combined with Pitch 6 if there's not too much rope drag. **Pitch 8** is shared with the SOUTH FACE route. Climb a 5.7 crack/flake above the belay and work up right on exposed face climbing to a ledge. **Pitch 9** heads up 5.6 rock to the ridge above. Follow it north to the summit. **Rack:** Bring a standard rack of wired nuts, Friends, and a few hexes.

HALLETT PEAK

The three rocky buttresses of 12,713-foot Hallett Peak loom west of Bear Lake, forming one of the park's most famed mountain vistas. The buttresses, composed of hard metamorphic schist and gneiss and sculpted by Tyndall Glacier, stretch along the mountain's northeast flank. The small First Buttress on the left is somewhat broken by gullies, slabs, and headwalls. The few routes here offer easy introductions to multi-pitch climbs. The 5.7 *Great Dihedral,* following chimneys, cracks, and slabs on the right side of the buttress, is probably the best route on the First Buttress. The dark cleft of Hallett Chimney separates the First and Second buttresses, and offers, when in shape in winter and early spring, a difficult mixed ice and rock climb. The Second Buttress, reaching 900 feet at its high point, yields the best rock routes on Hallett Peak. Most of the rock is clean and studded with edges. Its routes tend to be long and somewhat runout affairs that require common sense and good route-finding skills. The rock on the Third Buttress tends to be looser and not as solid as on the other walls. It offers a couple of trade routes but is complicated by route-finding problems.

Approach Hallett Peak by driving Bear Lake Road from the park entrance all the way to a large parking lot at the road's end by Bear Lake. This lot and the surrounding trails are usually busy with other park visitors. Get there early to grab a parking spot or you might be out of luck. The trail approach to the face base is just over 2 miles (shortest walking approach for the high peaks) and takes about an hour and a half at most. Walk south from the lake a short distance and pick up the Emerald Lake Trail. Follow it west up Tyndall Gorge. The trail passes Nymph Lake (0.5 mile), Dream Lake (1.1 miles), and reaches Emerald Lake at 10,000 feet after 1.8 miles. Pick up a faint path on a terrace above the lake's rocky south shore and follow it up to the talus slopes below the walls. Snowfields are encountered below the wall until late July. Use caution when crossing.

Descent is best accomplished by continuing west from the top of the buttresses up and across the gently tilted summit plateau. A steep scree-filled gully flanks the west edge of the Third Buttress. Drop down the loose gully for a few hundred feet to a fork. Scramble up to a notched saddle and drop down another gully to the wall base. This descent is easy, but has much loose rock. Use caution, especially if others are below. Also watch for steep, slick snow in the gully. An alternative descent route goes south of the First Buttress to a headwall with bolted rappel anchors. Make two single-line raps into a gully. Keep left at the bottom of the gully and follow cliffs north to open slopes below the First Buttress.

Hallett Peak is best climbed in the warm summer months between June and mid-September. The three buttresses all have a northern exposure, and are often cold. The walls are usually shrouded in shadow, with the sun leaving the

**HALLETT PEAK
SECOND BUTTRESS**

cliffs by late morning. The metamorphic rock that composes the cliffs tends to offer a plethora of edges, flakes, and incuts allowing the climber to roam just about anywhere on the wall. The same rock also gives few good crack systems, so the roving climber often runs into a lack of good protection and encounters numerous route-finding difficulties. Eyeball your proposed line from down near Emerald Lake before setting off, and memorize any noticeable landmarks to keep your vertical voyage on course. Get an early start to avoid the area's notorious thunder and lightning storms. Watch for rockfall from parties above, and don't knock anything on those below. Wear a hard-hat for protection from falling objects. Use old fixed pitons with caution; the severe climate can cause them to loosen and fall out when least expected.

12. **Love Route** (III 5.9- or 5.7 A1) This line up the left side of the Second Buttress is one of the better moderate routes on Hallett Peak. The route, first climbed in 1957 by Carl Love, Dean Egget, and William Hurlihee, follows the right side of a broken buttress before weaving up the slabby wall just left of a prominent arching crack system. To begin the route locate the broken, triangular buttress right of Hallett Chimney. **Pitches 1 and 2** follow the large, right-facing dihedral on the right side of the broken buttress for 2 long, easy leads. **Pitch 3** is kept interesting by leaving the dihedral and climbing the blocky face of the buttress (easy 5th class) to its top. Continue above the buttress as high as possible to a good ledge atop a flake. **Pitch 4** face climbs the steep wall above past incipient cracks (5.6) for about 130' to a small stance. Aim for the large dark roof straight overhead near the top of the Second Buttress. **Pitch 5** wanders up the wall with superb 5.7 face climbing for a long pitch to a sloping belay ramp below the obvious overhang. This lead is fairly sustained and somewhat runout. **Pitch 6**, the crux lead, goes up to a left-facing dihedral on the right side of the roof. Edge up the dihedral (5.9-) past numerous fixed pitons. Angle left above the roof up a shallow groove to a belay stance. The hard section of this pitch is easily aided by clipping and pulling through on the fixed pegs. Use caution; not all of them may be secure. **Pitch 7** heads up left to the top of the wall on easy climbing. **Rack:** Bring a standard rack with some additional small wired nuts and some large RPs to protect the face climbing pitches.

13. **Hesse-Ferguson** (III 5.9) This fine 8-pitch route, first climbed by Mark Hesse and Duncan Ferguson in 1974, ascends the flawless shield of rock between the long arching crack system of the Englishman's Route on the left side of the Second Buttress and the nose of the buttress on the right. A right-hand variation on pitches 3 and 4 makes this one of Hallett's best routes and is described as such here. The route offers excellent rock, enjoyable face climbing, plenty of exposure on the upper pitches, and generally adequate but not great protection. The route is also called IN BETWEEN. Begin the route by locating the huge, right-facing dihedral on the broken buttress ascended by the LOVE ROUTE. The HESSE-FERGUSON starts almost 100' right of the big dihedral on a ledge below a left-leaning, right-facing corner. Scramble up to the ledge and belay. **Pitch 1** follows the corner for a long 5.5 pitch to a stance. **Pitch 2** continues up the corner system (5.7) to a

ledge below the obvious white roofs. **Pitch 3** begins the variation pitches. Traverse right from the belay onto a burnished, reddish slab. Continue up right on thin 5.9 face climbing with little pro to a belay stance below a shallow right-facing corner. This pitch is often done by climbing straight up from the belay atop Pitch 2 and over 2 roofs (5.9) to the large ledge reached by Pitch 4. **Pitch 4** ascends the perfect, well-protected 5.9 corner by finger jams and stemming to a good ledge in a large horizontal band of white rock. **Pitch 5** tackles the 5.7, mostly unprotected face just left of the buttress nose to a small stance. **Pitch 6** continues up the devious face (5.7 and runout) to a stance below a narrow left-facing corner. **Pitch 7** heads up the 5.7 corner and traverses up right to a 5.8 crack/groove just left of the nose. The upper part of this pitch and the next one are shared with the CULP-BOSSIER route. **Pitch 8** climbs (5.7) the wall just right of a large right-facing dihedral on small face holds to the cliff top. **Rack:** Bring a standard rack with extra medium stoppers and TCUs for the crack on Pitch 4.

14. **Culp-Bossier** (III 5.8) This is a superb classic line up the prominent nose of the Second Buttress. The route, named for Bob Culp and Tex Bossier after their 1961 first ascent, offers mostly moderate climbing with great position on the upper pitches. The climbing is straight-forward, although a few sections give some problematic route finding to keep one's attention centered. Begin the climb on the same ledge below the same left-leaning, right-facing corner as the HESSE-FERGUSON route. **Pitch 1** climbs about 50' of the corner before striking out right onto the face. Follow a fun 5.7 finger crack up right to a belay stance. **Pitch 2** goes up left into a right-facing dihedral. This is the middle of 3 parallel right-facing dihedrals. Belay atop the corner. **Pitch 3** traverses out right on a 5.8 ramp, reaches over a small roof, follows a right-leaning corner, and face climbs up and left to a large terrace in the obvious band of white rock. This ledge is shared with the HESSE-FERGUSON. **Pitch 4** begins on the right side of the ledge and face climbs up the left edge of the beautiful, sweeping prow above. Belay on a small stance. This long pitch is slightly underprotected, but never goes above 5.6 if the right line is taken. Pay attention to keep on course. **Pitch 5** is a mirror image of Pitch 4. Continue up the prow on exposed, perfect rock. Near the top of the nose, keep left and avoid the ramp that swings up right toward the JACKSON-JOHNSON. Instead work up left to a belay below a groove/crack. **Pitch 6** goes up the 5.8 groove by a series of jams and stems to a ledge. **Pitch 7** scales the wall (5.7) right of a pronounced right-facing dihedral. The angle and difficulty ease higher and the summit is soon reached. **Rack:** Bring a standard rack with wired nuts and RPs for the face climbing pitches and camming gear to 3" for the cracks.

15. **Jackson-Johnson** (III 5.9 or 5.7 A1) This route, put up in 1957 by Dallas Jackson and Dale Johnson, is a long, moderate line up the right side of the

Second Buttress. It follows the left side of an obvious pillar before striking up the steep headwall to the summit plateau. Most of the climbing is low 5th class with occasional harder sections. The 5.9 climbing is enough out of character with the rest of the route that many parties grab carabiners for aid. Begin below the same leaning corner as the CULP-BOSSIER. **Pitch 1** climbs the left-leaning dihedral for about 50' to a small ledge. Traverse out right from the ledge to a short headwall split by a fine 5.7 finger crack. Belay atop a flake. **Pitch 2** follows a steep, awkward crack up and over a 5.5 overhang. Angle up right across slabs to a belay in a right-facing corner. **Pitch 3** traverses up right across an easy 5.0 slab to a belay below a wide chimney. **Pitch 4** ascends the easy chimney before heading up and right again to the left side of a huge pillar. Follow the chimney/crack system (5.6 initially) up the side of the pillar to a convenient belay. **Pitch 5** continues up the easy chimney for a long pitch to a large, excellent ledge atop the pillar. **Pitch 6** angles up and left through a couple of right-facing corners (5.6) to a ledge on the left below a right-leaning, right-facing, slightly overhung dihedral. Watch for rope drag on this long pitch or split it into 2 short leads. **Pitch 7**, the crux lead, stems, jams, and thrutches up the awkward right-facing dihedral past some funky old bolts and fixed pitons (5.9 or A1). Work left around a corner from the top of the dihedral to a final belay stance. The hard climbing on this pitch can be easily aided. **Pitch 8** is a short, easy lead up very loose blocks and boulders to the summit ridge. **Rack:** Bring a standard rack with wired nuts, Friends, and a few hexes.

LUMPY RIDGE

OVERVIEW

Lumpy Ridge, studded with rough, granite crags, stretches across Estes Park's northern skyline in Rocky Mountain National Park. The long ridge, rising from an 8,000-foot base to the windswept summit of 10,068-foot Sundance Buttress, was first named *That-aa-ai-atah* or "Mountain with Little Lumps" by the Arapaho Indians who summered in surrounding valleys. Later settlers and climbers simplified the old name to Lumpy Ridge. The scattered lumps of granite that decorate the ridge's steep slopes offer the rock climber some of Colorado's best vertical challenges. The numerous cliffs, including Crescent Wall, The Twin Owls, Batman Rock, The Book, Bookend, Bookmark, The Pear, and Sundance Buttress, yield excellent crack, face, and slab climbs. Most of the routes are done in a traditional climbing style, requiring the clean placement and removal of gear. A few bolted climbs are found on some crags, but these are the exception.

The ridge's crags, cliffs, pinnacles, and buttresses are made of a hard, crystal-studded granite. The south-facing cliffs repose at a 70-degree angle, allowing routes to use minute features that would be impossible on more vertical surfaces. The crystalline granite surfaces, untouched by valley glaciers that once covered the park's upper reaches, were shaped by water and alternating winter cycles of freeze and thaw that formed exfoliation slabs and flakes, vertical cracks and chimneys along rock weaknesses, and rounded potholes.

Climbing history: The first technical climbs on Lumpy Ridge went up in the 1950s including *Wolf's Tooth* and *West Owl Direct,* but it wasn't until the 1960s that climbing flourished. Numerous now-classic crack and aid lines were established on the main cliffs, including *Osiris, The J Crack,* and *Femp* on *The Book, Kor's Flake* and *Turnkorner* on Sundance, and a host of hard routes on The Twin Owls such as *Tiger's Tooth,* the off-width *Crack of Fear,* and *Twister.* Layton Kor, a Boulder bricklayer, regularly visited the ridge through the decade, putting up many lines with Bob Culp, Paul Mayrose, Bob Bradley, and Larry Dalke. Other active climbers were George Hurley, Jim Logan who did the first free ascent of *Crack of Fear* with Chris Fredericks, and Royal Robbins.

Lumpy Ridge was finally discovered in the 1970s by the greater climbing community. A handful of guides, including Bill Westbay, Douglas Snively, and Dan McClure at Mike Covington's Fantasy Ridge climbing school frequented the crags, seeking out new and difficult lines. Some notable ascents were Westbay and McClure's free ascent of *The J Crack* on The Book, Westbay and George Hurley's runout *X-rated Heavenly Journey* on The Pear, Jim Dunn's desperate off-width *Peaches and Cream* on The Twin Owls, and Snively and John Bacher's all-free ascent of *Silly Putty (West Owl Direct)* on the Owls—Lumpy Ridge's first 5.12 route. The 1980s were a time of continued discovery and standard-

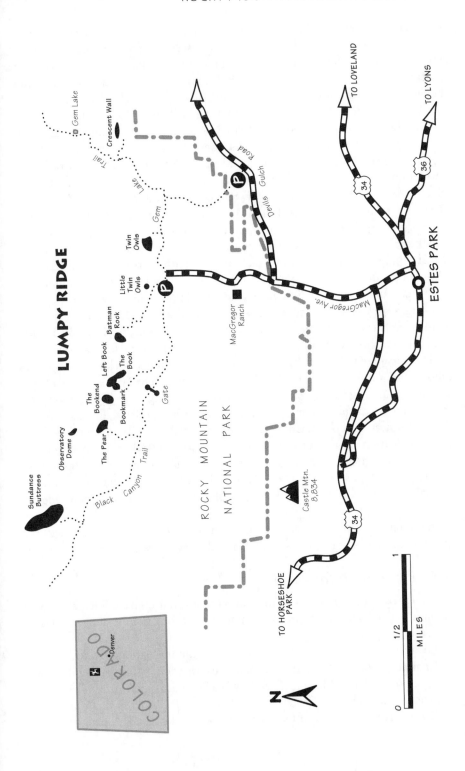

pushing. New routes and variations were established between the classics, while new crags were found and climbed. Active ascensionists were Scott Kimball, Hidetaka Suzuki, Bernard Gillet, and, of course, local guru Doug Snively. First ascents are still being found in the 1990s, with the most notable new route being Alan Lester's brilliant free climb of *Anaconda* on The Twin Owls. This 5.13b overhanging thin crack/seam follows a beaten-out Kor A4 horror pitch.

Almost 500 routes ascend more than 30 named crags on Lumpy Ridge. The vast majority of these lines are cracks done in traditional style, while a few newer ones are bolt-protected faces and slabs. Fixed protection is a rarity on most Lumpy climbs, except for the newer routes. Use caution when clipping fixed pitons and bolts here, especially the old 1/4" studs found on older routes. The newer lines are equipped with 3/8" bolts and good rappel or lowering anchors. Rappels on many routes are from trees, old fixed gear, or tied-off blocks or flakes. Carry an extra sling to reinforce the existing webbing. **Rack:** Most climbs here require a full rack and a 165-foot rope. A standard rack should include sets of RPs, wired stoppers, and Friends or other camming devices, as well as a few medium hexentrics and TCUs, and at least three or four runners. Carry some free carabiners and quick draws. Many routes also have off-size sections that can be protected with large Camalots, Big Bros, Big Dudes, and tube chocks. Scope the route before you set out and rack up accordingly.

Dangers here include ticks in spring and early summer, rockfall from parties above, and loose boulders and blocks on ledges. Watch for heavy summer thunderstorms and lightning. Bring appropriate clothes to stay dry and keep off high points to avoid becoming a lightning rod. Some cliffs might be seasonally closed for nesting raptors. Check the bulletin board at the Twin Owls Trailhead for information on this or other problems. Use trails whenever possible and don't cut switchbacks. Lumpy Ridge is a traditional climbing area. Respect the boldness of first ascensionists on runout routes by not placing needless bolts. Don't chip holds on routes or boulder problems. It's a small and inconsiderate lout who lowers routes to their own lowly standards by chipping instead of lifting themselves to a higher level. Don't drink stream or lake water without purifying it. Drinking water is available at the Twin Owls Trailhead.

Trip Planning Information

General description: One of Colorado's finest traditional climbing areas with numerous crack and face routes ascending south-facing granite domes and cliffs on a long ridge.

Location: North of Estes Park in Rocky Mountain National Park.

Camping: Rocky Mountain National Park operates 4 campgrounds on the east side of the park. Moraine Park Campground (250 sites) is 3 miles west of the Headquarters Visitor Center off Bear Lake Road. Glacier Basin Campground (152 sites) is 9 miles west of Estes Park off Bear Lake Road. Aspenglen Campground is 5 miles northwest of Estes Park near the park's Fall River entrance off U.S. Highway 34. Longs Peak Campground (30 tents-only sites) is 11 miles south of Estes Park and 1 mile west of Colorado Highway 7. Stays at Longs Peak CG are limited to only 3 days from June through September. Camping in the park is limited to 7 days from June through September. Aspenglen and Longs Peak campgrounds operate on a first-come, first-served basis. Moraine Park and Glacier Basin operate on an advance reservation system in summer. Contact the park for more info. Several commercial campgrounds are found in the Estes Park area. Longer term and cheaper public camping is found in Roosevelt National Forest south of Estes Park along CO 7, including Olive Ridge Campground near Allenspark.

Climbing season: Year-round. The best weather is from April through October. April and May can be windy with unpredictable weather that includes snow, sleet, and rain. Summers offer excellent conditions for rock climbing with warm days and temperatures ranging from 60 to 85 degrees. The south-facing cliffs are sometimes too hot for comfort. Severe thunderstorms regularly occur on summer afternoons. Pay attention to the weather and get off high points and cliffs during lightning storms. September and October are great climbing months with comfortable daytime highs and chilly nights. Winters are fickle, with periods of intense cold and snow mixed with warm, sunny days. The south-facing cliffs are often climbable in winter.

Ian Spencer-Green jams a thin finger crack on *Pressure Drop* on Crescent Wall at Lumpy Ridge. *Photo by Stewart M. Green.*

Restrictions and access issues: National Park regulations pertaining to rock climbing include: the use of motorized drills is prohibited; bolts can be placed by hand; it is illegal to remove vegetation from cracks; don't bother wildlife; no littering; dogs are not allowed in the backcountry and must be leashed in the parking areas and campgrounds; bivouac permits are required for overnight bivouacs in the backcountry (call the Backcountry Station at (970) 586-1242 for info and permits).

Guidebooks: *Rocky Mountain National Park: The Climber's Guide* by Bernard Gillet, Earthbound Sports, 1993. An excellent overall guide to Lumpy Ridge with complete topos and descriptions of the major crags and most of the satellite cliffs.

Nearby mountain shops, guide services, and gyms: Wilderness Sports, Komito Boots, Colorado Mountain School (Estes Park); Neptune Mountaineering, Boulder Mountaineer, Basecamp Mountain Sports, Boulder Rock Club (Boulder); Desert Ice Mountain Guides (Fort Collins).

Services: Full services—lodging, dining, gas, groceries, beer, fast food, campgrounds, and showers—in Estes Park.

Emergency services: For rescues and emergency situations call 911 or (970) 586-2371. Estes Park Medical Center, 555 Prospect, Estes Park, CO 80517, (970) 586-2317. McKee Medical Center, 2000 Boise Ave., Loveland, CO 80538, (970) 669-4640.

Nearby climbing areas: The Diamond, Mount Meeker, Spearhead, Chiefs Head, Notchtop, Hallett Peak, Petit Grepon, Sharkstooth, The Saber, Estes Valley crags, Combat Rock, Big Thompson Canyon, South St. Vrain Canyon, Carter Lake boulders, Button Rock Reservoir crags, Boulder Canyon, The Flatirons, Eldorado Canyon State Park.

Nearby attractions: Trail Ridge Road, Longs Peak, Enos Mills Cabin, Big Thompson Canyon, Indian Peaks Wilderness Area, Peak to Peak Highway.

Finding the crags: Estes Park is 30 miles west of Loveland and 34 miles west of Interstate 25 via US 34. The park can be reached from Boulder and Denver by heading north from Boulder on US 36 to Lyons and driving 19 miles west on US 36 to Estes Park. Lumpy Ridge is accessed by driving 2 miles north on MacGregor Avenue from the east side of Estes Park. Turn left into MacGregor Ranch and Rocky Mountain National Park where the road makes a sharp right turn and becomes Devils Gulch Road. Follow this narrow road up to a parking area at the Twin Owls Trailhead. The lot is usually full on summer weekends. Get there early for a spot. The Gem Lake Trail runs east from here to Twin Owls and Crescent Wall. The Black Canyon Trail heads west along the edge of the valley and provides access to The Book, Bookend, Bookmark, Citadel, Pear, and Sundance Buttress. For more park info contact: Rocky Mountain National Park, Estes Park, CO 80517, (970) 586-2371.

CRESCENT WALL

The Crescent Wall, an immense slab high atop the east end of Lumpy Ridge, is easily identified by the huge crescent-shaped arch in its center. The wall offers an assortment of excellent thin crack routes along with good edging and friction climbing on steep slabs. The difficulty of most routes here limits its popularity. It's rare to find another party here. The wall can be very hot on sunny days. For several short, moderate crack routes, go to Fin City immediately north and above the Crescent Wall's summit. Approach the wall by hiking northeast on Gem Lake Trail from the Twin Owls parking area. Follow the trail uphill for about 1.5 miles to a point where the trail bends north above a shallow, boulder-choked ravine. Crescent Wall is visible directly east. Drop down a crude trail into the ravine and scramble over boulders to the base of the south-facing wall. The routes are listed from east to west, or right to left. **Descent** off the wall is by walking west down ramps and ledges toward Gem Lake Trail.

1. **Poultry in Motion** (5.11d) A very good 125' face route that wanders up the steep wall right of the obvious arch past 7 bolts. **Descent:** Rappel with 2 ropes from anchors atop the arch.

2. **Crescent Arch** (5.11c) This off-width classic grunts up the arching, left-facing dihedral 120' to a belay ledge and anchors just up right of the arch. **Descent:** Rappel with 2 ropes to the ground. **Rack:** Bring pro to 6".

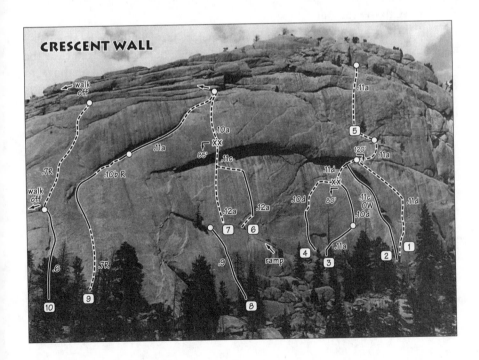

CRESCENT WALL

3. **Finger Lickin' Good** (5.11a) This route, commonly done in 2 short pitches to avoid rope drag, offers one of Lumpy's finest finger cracks. Follow a thin crack that diagonals up and right. The first 20' are hardest with dicey 5.11 face climbing. Belay on a small stance below a beautiful finger crack. Jam the crack for 50' or so to a belay atop a flake and rappel. **Rack:** Bring small gear.

4. **Pressure Drop** (5.11a) Another great crack line. Begin left of a small, inset arch. Jam a good hand and finger crack for 40'. Work right on scary face climbing onto the edge of a thin, arching flake. Jam and face climbing up and right to FINGER LICKIN' GOOD'S belay. Rappel 80'.

5. **Strategic Arms** (5.11d R) Climb either FINGER LICKIN' GOOD or PRESSURE DROP to the upper belay ledge. 3 short face pitches go up right from here to the wall's summit. **Pitch 1** climbs up right (5.11d) past 2 bolts to the CRESCENT ARCH belay ledge. **Pitch 2** traverses up right on thin face climbing to a shallow groove and ends on a ledge by a belay tree. **Pitch 3** goes up a steep, mostly unprotected wall and over a couple of overlaps to the summit.

6. **Lycra Bikers From Hell** (5.12a) Scramble up a ramp below the left side of the arch to a large leaning block. Follow a thin seam up right past 2 old pins to a finger crack. Jam the tips crack up and left past 3 bolts. Climb delicately up left to a bolt below the arch-roof. Pull over (5.11c) and belay at anchors. Rappel 80' back to the ledge or do a 5.10a face pitch (1bolt) above to the summit.

7. **Flight For Life** (5.12a) A good but desperate face climb up the steep slab under the arch's left side. Begin on the left side of a ramp/ledge below the arch. Follow a line of 5 bolts up the face, 5.12a initially but easier above, to a bolt under the roof. Pull over (5.11c) and finish at the same stance as LYCRA BIKERS FROM HELL. Rappel 80' or continue up 5.10a face climbing (at a bolt) to the summit slabs.

8. **Heaven Can Wait** (5.9) Jam cracks up a left-facing corner to a tree on a large ledge. Walk off to the right. A 2nd pitch goes up unprotected 5.5 rock to the left end of the arch and then reverses the moves.

9. **Cleft Palate** (5.11a) This nice 2-pitch line follows a right-angling arch on the left side of the wall. Start almost directly below the left side of the right-angling arch. Climb a moderate unprotected slab up to a thin, curving crack. Follow the crack up and right and traverse under the arch to a belay stance. **Pitch 2** continues hand-traversing and face climbing up the arch (a spot of 5.11a) to easier rock and a belay above.

10. **Milk Run** (5.7 R) Begin on the far left side of the wall. **Pitch 1** climbs a shallow right-facing corner (5.6) to a belay ledge with a small tree. **Pitch 2** frictions up and right on an unprotected slab.

THE TWIN OWLS

The Twin Owls, a pair of steep gray buttresses, roost atop the ridge north-east of the parking area. The Owls' 300' overhanging south walls host some of Lumpy Ridge's best and hardest crack climbs, including a number of fierce off-width testpieces, as well as some hard aid routes. The south face is split by the deep Central Chimney, which separates the two owls. A gently angled ramp, called the Roosting Ramp, sweeps up left and gives access to routes on the west owl. A lower, more broken buttress sits below The Twin Owls, while a small blocky formation, the Hen and Chickens, lies below the crag's southeast corner.

The approach to the Owls is short and steep. Walk east from the parking area on the Gem Lake Trail and follow its switchbacks up the slope below the Owls. The marked climber's access trail begins about 0.25 mile up the main trail. Turn north and follow it to the base of the Roosting Ramp. Don't shortcut and cause erosion; use the access path. **Descent:** The best descent from the summit of The Twin Owls is from the saddle between the two owls. Drop north down a polished groove to a crack threaded with rappel slings. Make a 75' single-rope rappel to the ground. An alternative is to downclimb the Bowels of the Owls route. Go left near the bottom of the groove to a tunnel/chimney. Squeeze down the passage (5.0) to the base. Descend around the southeast corner of the formation to reach the south side.

11. **Tighter Squeeze** (5.8) Locate an obvious chimney just west of the southeast ridge. Chimney up to a wide off-width crack (5.8) and struggle up to a good ledge on the ridge above. Continue up the ridge for either 1 long or 2 pitches to the east summit. **Rack:** Bring a few pieces of large pro to protect the off-width.

12. **Twister** (5.10b) This 3-pitch line follows a long chimney system in a large left-facing dihedral. The difficulties start immediately on **Pitch 1** with a pinched 5.10b chimney just off the ground. Thrash upward to a tight squeeze chimney, struggle through this 5.10b crux, and belay above on a ledge on the left. **Pitch 2** continues up the chimney, muscles over a chockstone (5.9), and heads up easier rock to a good ledge. **Pitch 3** heads up left on easy rock to an obvious horizontal break topped by a roof with a crack. Climb this awkward 5.9 fist crack (BARRACUDA) to the summit slabs.

13. **Peaches and Cream** (5.11c) This fierce, off-width affair, first ascended by Jim Dunn in 1977, is for the rock masochist. It jams the insecure, leaning, left side of a 75' flake just left of TWISTER. Rack up at the base with lots of big pro and tape the hands. Start up the first few feet of RIP CURL and swing left across flakes to the flared crack. Struggle, claw, and curse your way up the 5.11c off-size crack using hand-stacks and arm bars. Higher up the crack pinches to hand-size and then the leader steps out of the crack

and laybacks strenuously up the flake to a good ledge. **Descent:** Rappel 75' to the ground.

14. **Rip Curl** and **Epitaph** (5.12a) This route combo avoids the 5.11 X unprotected 1st pitch of EPITAPH. RIP CURL begins just left of the PEACHES AND CREAM crack. Jam the crack on the right side of a large boulder leaning against the wall. Continue up a finger-tips seam (5.12a) past a couple

of fixed pins and face climb up left past a bolt to a small stance in the EPITAPH crack system. **Pitches 2** (5.10b) and **3** (5.9) continue up the crack to the summit.

15. **Crack of Fear** (5.10d) This fearsome off-size crack, Colorado's most famous off-width, remains 5" or wider for 250' up the East Owl. Chris Fredericks, a Yosemite crack specialist, and Jim Logan free climbed the line in 1966 using bongs for protection. Layton Kor free climbed the actual route crux on its first ascent in 1963. The route is strenuous, continuous, and unrelenting in difficulty. It was once somewhat unprotected, but can be safely climbed now with a rack of modern off-width pro that includes Big Bros, tube chocks, and lots of big Friends and Camalots to #4. It is climbed in either 3 or 4 pitches, although many parties rap from anchors at 75' just before the route crux after doing the initial 5.9 section. Locate the splitter crack system right of the CENTRAL CHIMNEY at the base of the Roosting Ramp. **Pitch 1** fist jams the 5.9 left side of the Rat's Tooth, a stubby pillar below the crack, and climbs the 5.9 off-width crack (right-side in) to a belay ledge on the left. **Pitch 2** struggles up the 5.10d 10" crack to a dogleg, and then underclings up and left (5.10c) to a comfortable belay. **Pitch 3** continues up the off-width past some 5.10 and 5.9 sections. It's not as difficult as the lower pitches, but still strenuous and sustained. **Pitch 4** goes up and left from the horizontal break to the summit on easier rock.

16. **Central Chimney** (5.8) Walk left from CRACK OF FEAR past a couple of aid routes to the cavernous chimney. **Pitch 1** climbs the right side of a pedestal above blocks, then heads up left onto a flake belay. **Pitch 2** continues up a slick squeeze chimney (5.7+) past some fixed pitons to a large chockstone. Turn it on the left and belay above in an alcove. **Pitch 3** heads up the chimney to a funky roof (5.7) or face climbs (5.7) up the left wall of the chimney. **Pitch 4,** the short, last lead, wanders up the wall above to the saddle.

17. **Anaconda** (5.13b/c) This dramatic and difficult route, one of Colorado's hardest cracks, follows an overhanging thin crack above the Roosting Ramp. Alan Lester managed the first free ascent in 1994 of this long-standing problem using preplaced gear. **Pitch 1** The crux, jams the obvious crack to a bolted belay. Rap here or if you have the energy **Pitch 2** continues up the 5.10c offset crack to a belay under a big roof. **Pitch 3** swings over the roof (5.11a) and climbs easy rock to the summit of the West Owl.

18. **Silly Putty (AKA West Owl Direct)** (5.12a R) A very serious and hard free climb up a large dihedral on the West Owl. The route, a landmark ascent at Lumpy Ridge, was first climbed by John Bacher and Doug Snively in 1978 and renamed SILLY PUTTY. Approach by walking west up the Roosting Ramp and belay below the dihedral. **Pitch 1** climbs the left side of a large

flake at the base of the dihedral via excellent laybacks and jams (5.9) to a belay stance. Most rap from here. The right side of the flake is a 5.11d toprope. **Pitch 2** stems the dihedral using jams in the thin crack (5.12a and difficult to place pro) to a stance below the roof cap. **Pitch 3** traverses left and follows easier cracks to the top. **Rack:** Bring lots of small gear.

19. **Coyote** (5.12b) A great sport route up the outside arete of the SILLY PUTTY dihedral. **Pitch 1** climbs excellent rock right of the arete past 5 bolts (5.12b up high) to bolted anchors. Lower or rap 85' from here. **Pitch 2** is also good. Go left from the belay onto the arete and a thin crack above. Work left higher into the TIGER'S TOOTH crack.

20. **Tiger's Tooth** (5.9+) This classic Kor route scales the right side of a semi-detached pillar on the southwest corner of The Twin Owls. Begin atop the Roosting Ramp below the obvious off-width crack. Wide fist jams and awkward off-width moves (5.9+) grunt up the strenuous crack 60' to a runout but easier 5.8 squeeze chimney. Belay on the pillar. **Pitch 2** steps off the tooth onto the main face and follows a flared groove (5.7) and then easier rock to the top. Or work right into a thin 5.9 crack. WOLF'S TOOTH, the crack opposite TIGER'S TOOTH on the other side of the pillar, is a superb 5.8 classic off-width and chimney route to the ledge atop the pillar.

21. **Tilted Mitten** (5.8) This route lies on the Lower Owls below the southwest corner of The Twin Owls. Begin at the lowest point of the south face. **Pitch 1** follows either of two low-angle chimneys that head up right to a good ledge. **Pitch 2** climbs an arching crack to the bottom of The Mitten formation. Jam the mitten's right side (5.8) to a hole that leads to a ledge. **Pitch 3** works right up a chimney and cracks to the Roosting Ramp.

22. **Prow** (5.10c) A fun route up the prow of the Lower Owls. Start by climbing the first 2 pitches of TILTED MITTEN. Belay on the left side of the ledge. Work left to the prow and follow a crack up and over a roof (5.10c), and continue on easier rock to the Roosting Ramp.

THE BOOK

The Book is perhaps the best of Lumpy Ridge's many crags. This large, south-facing cliff, reaching heights of 500', offers numerous routes up its clean faces and long crack systems. The granite itself is made for rock climbing and flaw-lessly perfect, with incuts, edges, knobs, and crystals that allow for superb face climbing and excellent friction. The cracks readily take protection, permitting even marginal leaders to sew up their chosen line. And the belay ledge views are great—the pastoral valley, edged by pine forest, spreads out below while the park's high, snowcapped peaks along the Continental Divide tower over lower ridges.

A huge, left-facing dihedral splits The Book in half, with the right side further divided into two sections: the Pages Wall on the left creased by numerous vertical cracks that form the book pages, and the smooth J Crack Slab on the right. This guide documents the excellent classic lines on the right half of The Book.

Approach The Book by hiking west along the Black Canyon Trail from The Twin Owls parking lot. The Book access trail heads northwest after a mile and steeply climbs the mountainside to the crag's base below J-Crack Slab. **Descend** from the rock summit by hiking southeast down slabs and gullies around the crag's forested east flank.

23. **The Cavity** (5.10a) This 1-pitch Doug Snively route is a good 1st pitch to FEMP and J CRACK. Scramble into a large crystal-filled cavity or solution pocket with a lone ponderosa pine tree above the wall's base. Lieback up the obvious left-facing corner above to a large ledge below J CRACK Slab.

24. **Femp** (5.9) This superb and beautiful route jams up a striking hand crack on the right side of J CRACK Slab. The name came from the combined last names of first ascensionists Ren Fenton and Charles Femp in 1962. **Pitch 1** climbs THE CAVITY or goes up 4th class corners and ledges to the right for about 75' to the highest ledge. **Pitch 2** jams the crack 155' to a sloping stance. This is continuous 5.7 with two 5.9 sections. The first crux is where the first crack ends and it's necessary to jog left into another crack. The second is in a thin corner just below the belay. **Pitch 3** is done in various ways. The standard finish follows a left-leaning dihedral capped by a 5.7 roof, and then angles up right through a 5.7 break in the obvious band of roofs and onto easier rock. The short, overhanging corner directly above the belay is HEMP 5.10b. Climb above it to a belay under a 5.9 roof slot. A good 5.9+ thin crack (Pitch 3 of ENDLESS CRACK) follows the left edge of KITE SLAB to the belay stance under the roof slot. Or climb KITE SLAB (5.11d).

25. **Kite Slab** (5.11d) This line, the 3rd pitch of PIZZA FACE, is a good second lead to FEMP. Work left from FEMP'S first belay to the base of the slab. Edge up right past 3 bolts to a belay. Traverse off on easy rock to the right.

26. **J Crack** (5.11c or 5.10a) Lumpy Ridge's most famed classic route follows the backwards J on the left side of the slab. **Pitch 1** begins by climbing THE CAVITY or a groove to a crack and chimney pitch (5.7 up high) to the left of the pocket to the long ledge below FEMP. Set up a belay on the far left side of the ledge. **Pitch 2** is long. Traverse delicately up left (5.10-) into the J Crack. Jam the slightly flared finger and thin hand crack (sustained 5.9) for 140' to a sloping alcove below the headwall. **Pitch 3** offers several alternatives. The hardest line continues up the crack, now a virtual seam, on the headwall (5.11c) to a wide ledge atop the crack. **Rack:** Bring RPs. The

THE BOOK

popular line jams up to the headwall and traverses right on 5.10a unprotected face climbing to an easy slanting groove/crack. Place some pro high
in the crack to add security to the traverse. **Pitch 4** also offers alternatives.
The best finishing pitch angles up right over a 5.7 roof, up a slab, and
through a 5.7 break in the roof band above. Or climb easy grooves up left

and then right to The Cave. **Rack:** Bring a good selection of wired stoppers, TCUs, and small Friends, along with RPs for the headwall.

27. **Loose Ends** (5.9) This excellent route up the left side of J CRACK slab is usually done in 5 pitches. Start below a pillar/flake directly below J CRACK. **Pitch 1** jams a finger crack or liebacks up a left-facing 5.9 corner on the flake. Undercling left onto a ramp and climb (5.8) up left to a belay niche. **Pitch 2** goes left to the second of 2 parallel cracks. It's 5.9 initially, then continuous 5.8 jamming to a belay stance above a flake. The right crack is VISUAL AIDS 5.10b. **Pitch 3** climbs a short face into the large, left-leaning, left-facing dihedral above. Layback up (5.9) to a spacious ledge. **Pitch 4** works right over an easy slab and up a groove to The Cave. Continue up easy rock to The Book's right skyline.

28. **Pear Buttress** (5.8) Another superb Book classic crack. Begin left of the LOOSE ENDS flake on a face right of a right-facing flake/corner. **Pitch 1** face climbs up left (unprotected 5.7) to a stance 20' up. Step right into the flake's crack and follow to its top. Make a hard move into twin cracks (5.8+) and jam to LOOSE ENDS' belay niche on a sloping ramp. **Pitch 2** follows the ramp up left to the buttress corner and climbs up right to a good ledge. **Pitch 3** jams the beautiful crack above the ledge; fingers (5.8) at first then widening to excellent hands (5.7). Undercling right (5.7) under a roof up high to a wide ledge shared with LOOSE ENDS. **Pitch 4** heads up easy slabs and cracks to The Cave and continues up right.

29. **Stretch Marks** (5.11a) Go left from the start of PEAR BUTTRESS and scramble up a slab to a ledge. Face climb up a 5.11a seam and work into a higher crack and a chimney slot. Finish at a stance on the edge of the buttress. Rappel from anchors 65' to the ledge.

30. **Thinstone** (5.9) Begin around the arete from STRETCH MARKS. Climb an excellent thin crack in the open book and then go right to a chimney slot. Rap from STRETCH MARKS anchors.

31. **Fat City** (5.10c) This brilliant classic crack route, lying on the east side of the Pages Wall, was first ascended by Ray Jardine, the inventor of Friends, and Bill Forrest with some aid in 1970. Scramble up to a large ledge with trees just left of the huge dihedral. **Pitch 1** jams an excellent crack (some 5.8) up the center of the slab to a small stance with anchors. **Pitch 2**, the route crux, fingerlocks up the narrowing crack (5.10a), hand-traverses left into a flared slot (5.8), and jams insecurely over the roof above (5.10c). Belay on ledge. **Pitch 3** follows a long right-angling crack and flakes system (5.9) to The Cave. Continue up and right on easier rock to the skyline ridge.

32. **The 44** (5.10c) This is a companion route to FAT CITY and shares its upper pitches. Begin 25' left of FAT CITY. **Pitch 1** follows a waterworn chimney and steps left into an excellent 5.7 hand crack. Belay in the crack at a bolt. **Pitch 2** liebacks or hand jams (5.8) up and right and joins FAT CITY at the flared slot under the roof. Continue upward via FAT CITY.

33. **High Plains Drifter** (5.10b) This technical slab pitch makes a fun third lead to FAT CITY or THE 44. Climb either route to the second belay over the roof. Step left from the ledge into an thin arching corner. Climb the corner (5.10b) and work up left onto the exquisite slab. Continue up past 4 bolts and belay on a ledge. Continue up GEORGE'S TREE to The Book's summit.

34. **Frisky Puppies** (5.12b) Begin just left of the Tombstone block below FAT CITY for this hard face climbing pitch. Follow 10 bolts up a white vertical dike up to and over a small roof to a belay from a large horn. **Descent:** Rappel 165' from slings on the horn. **Rack:** Bring some TCUs for the roof.

35. **George's Tree** (5.9) This 5-pitch line, first climbed by George Hurley and Steve Pomerance with aid in 1967, follows cracks up the right side of The Book pages. Find a crack left of FRISKY PUPPIES with a small pine tree (George's) in it. **Pitch 1** jams the flared, awkward finger crack (5.9 and harder than it appears) for a long pitch and works left onto a good ledge. **Pitch 2** ascends flakes and cracks up left for about 50' before striking back right into a crack system or climbs a wide crack over a bulge (5.10b) above the first belay. Either way work up to a convenient stance where the cracks meet. **Pitch 3** follows the right-hand crack (5.8) for a long pitch over a headwall to Fang Ledge, a large ledge that splits the upper face. Move left a few feet to an inset topped by an arch by a juniper tree. **Pitch 4** jams a crack up the right side (5.9) and continues up various cracks to a ledge below the final wall. **Pitch 5** scales the large 5.7 dihedral 50' to the summit.

36. **Osiris** (5.7) This 3-star Lumpy classic crack route, named for the Egyptian god of the dead, wanders up the maze of cracks on the Pages Wall. Find an obvious chimney in a large left-facing dihedral just left of GEORGE'S TREE. **Pitch 1** follows the chimney (5.6) 140' to a good ledge on the right that is shared with GEORGE'S TREE. **Pitch 2** climbs left on moderate flakes and cracks up a series of steps (5.5) to a spacious ledge with a tree. **Pitch 3** ascends the obvious right-facing corner or good cracks just right to double cracks up a headwall (5.7). Belay at The Fang, a small pillar, on Fang Ledge. **Pitch 4** jams The Fang and then follows the left crack up and over a bulging roof (5.7) and belays at a tree. **Pitch 5** works up and left on easier rock to the summit slabs.

THE PEAR

The Pear is a 400' slabby granite shield perched just above the valley floor. The pear-shaped buttress offers an excellent assortment of friction and thin face routes, most of which end on lower angle slabs two-thirds of the way up. Approach The Pear by walking west on the Black Canyon Trail from The Twin Owls parking lot for just over 1 mile. After passing through a gate in a barbed wire fence, look for a trail heading northwest toward the crag's base. **Descent** is accomplished on many routes by walking east on a ledge system and easy slabs and down onto the rock's east flank. From the summit, make a 1-rope, 65' foot rappel north from anchors into a narrow gully. **Descend** east down the gully and around The Pear's east shoulder.

37. **Gina's Surprise** (5.4 R) This is a fine beginner's route, although somewhat runout for the leader. The 1-pitch line ascends a prominent vertical dike on the far east side of The Pear. Climb up unprotected slabs to the dike and waltz upward on either side to a ledge with a tree. Right of the dike is slightly easier than the left side. Continue on to the summit on 5.0 rock or walk-off east.

38. **East Slabs** (5.6) Climb moderate slabs and water grooves just left of GINA'S SURPRISE for 1 pitch to the ledge with a tree.

39. **Northern Lights** (5.10d) Face climb up the steep slab right on the outside corner of RIGHT DIHEDRAL past 3 bolts to a stance on a horizontal crack/ledge. Crux is at the third bolt.

40. **Right Dihedral** (5.9) **Pitch 1** jams and stems up the large left-facing dihedral (5.9) to a belay stance where the system swings left as a roof. **Pitch 2** continues up the corner (some 5.7) to whatever belay is convenient to the walk-off.

41. **Heavenly Journey** (5.10b X) This runout Bill Westbay classic has seen few pure ascents and a number of serious tumbles. **Pitch 1** works up a crescent-shaped finger crack (5.10b) to a bolted belay stance 65' up. Rap from the 1/4" bolts or continue up and left on the smooth, unprotected 5.10a slab to a belay stance. A fall from the upper 5.9 crux section would result in a groundfall and possible death. Most climbers now clip 1 or 2 of the bolts on neighboring WEIGHT LOSS CLINIC to mitigate the disaster.

42. **Fat-Bottomed Groove** (5.10d) One of The Pear's best routes. Find a deep water groove on the right side of the long roof band. **Pitch 1** chimneys up the wide 5.8 groove to the roof, or takes a strenuous 5.10c hand crack to the roof. Either way hand traverse left along a horizontal flake/roof and swing over by a knee-bar rest to a belay stance above. **Pitch 2** climbs a 5.9 dike to a ledge up left.

43. **The Whole Thing** (5.10a) Begin left of the groove and scramble onto a ledge by a tree. **Pitch 1** climbs a short crack to a face with a bolt and crosses the roof at a notch (5.10a). Belay in the crack above. **Pitch 2** face climbs up left on a thin 5.8 slab to a thin 5.9 seam. Continue up in the left-facing corner above (5.9) to a good belay. **Rack:** Bring some RPs for the second pitch seam.

44. **Slippage** (5.9+) Begin at a tree just right of a deep groove. **Pitch 1** face climbs right of the groove (5.8) past a bolt to a thin corner in a break in the roof band. Work right up it (5.9+) and then left to a belay stance. **Pitch 2** heads up a thin 5.9 seam for a long pitch to a belay on the slabs above. **Rack:** Bring RPs and small wires.

45. **Trippage** (5.10b) Begin left of the obvious deep water groove. **Pitch 1** frictions up a runout 5.6 slab to the roof band. Pull over on good holds (5.8) and edge into a shallow left-leaning corner with 2 bolts. Step left above (5.10b) and belay at the base of a crack. **Pitch 2** follows the moderate crack for a long pitch.

46. **Root of All Evil** and **Sibling Rivalry** (5.9-) This 2-route link-up yields a neo-classic line. Begin just right of a huge left-facing dihedral. **Pitch 1** is ROOT OF ALL EVIL. Climb a slab to a 5.8 crack and continue up to and through the roof (5.9 at a bolt). Belay in a groove above. **Pitch 2**, the superb

THE PEAR

and airy SIBLING RIVALRY, follows the outside arete of the dihedral past 4 bolts to a 2-bolt belay. Rappel 165' to the ground with 2 ropes.

47. **Magical Chrome Plated Semi-Automatic Enema Syringe** (5.6) One of The Pear's popular old classics. Scramble onto a small buttress below the big dihedral. **Pitch 1** angles up and left in hand crack to a 5.6 traverse. Belay below a pretty, right-facing corner. **Pitch 2** liebacks up the corner (5.6) to a good ledge. Walk off west here or continue to the summit. **Pitch 3** angles up left on ramps and cracks for a long lead. **Pitch 4** goes up a 5.5 crack to a good ledge below the final headwall. **Pitch 5** goes right to a flake/crack (5.7) and up the headwall to the top. Rap off the back from bolts.

48. **L'Chaim** (5.7) A fun 2-pitch line up the slabs left of MAGICAL. Locate the superb finger crack in the slab above the roof band. Climb an easy but runout dike up a slab past a tree (tie it off) to a stance below the crack. Jam the 5.7 finger crack to the walk-off ledge. **Rack:** Bring some RPs and wires.

SUNDANCE BUTTRESS

Sundance Buttress, almost 1,000' high, is the tallest and most remote crag at Lumpy Ridge. Its immense granite wall is broken by dihedrals, creased with cracks and chimneys, and fractured into steep slabs and faces. Sundance offers everything a climber could wish for—superb views, excellent rock, and numerous classic routes. The wall is divided into four main sections by distinct rock features: North Slabs, Turnkorner Buttress, Guillotine Wall, and Eumenides Slab. All the lines on Sundance are multi-pitch affairs that generally require a whole day to approach, climb, and descend. **Rack:** Carry a standard rack and 165' rope. It might be wise to toss an off-size piece on the rack for the occasional off-width crack.

Approach the cliff by hiking east on the Black Canyon Trail from the Twin Owls parking area for just over 2 miles. A climber's trail, marked by either a sign or a cairn, heads northwest up the steep, wooded slopes below the Turnkorner Buttress. Allow about an hour for the walk in to the base. **Descent** is somewhat complex, time-consuming, and involves 4th class downclimbing and/or rappels. A direct descent scrambles north from the top of the Turnkorner Buttress to a wide saddle. Drop over a series of short walls to a gully that swings east and southeast around the North Slabs. Follow the gully down and around to the base. It may be wise, depending on conditions, to rig rappels from trees on parts of this descent. Use your judgment, especially in winter.

49. **The Nose** (III 5.10b) An excellent 6-pitch line up the exposed nose of Turnkorner Buttress. The route starts directly below The Nose left of a large, left-facing dihedral and just left of the buttress low point. **Pitch 1** (150') follows a right-angle ramp for 50'. Work left into a right-facing di-

hedral on a pillar. Jam and lieback (5.9) to the top of the pillar. **Pitch 2** climbs right up a flake and face climbs left (no pro) into a wide crack (5.8). Belay from 2 bolts on a small ledge. **Pitch 3** follows a crack and corner to the right edge of the prominent roof band. Step left from the corner, climb left to the edge of the roof. Continue straight up on exposed 5.9+ face climbing to a small stance. **Pitch 4** works up right along a shallow right-facing corner to a thin seam that angles left over a crux bulge. Climb the seam (5.10b) and then head up right on runout 5.8 face climbing to a groove belay. Hard climbing is found just before the groove. **Pitch 5** climbs the groove to the right side of a roof. Exit right (5.8) and follow easy rock to a convenient belay. **Pitches 6 and 7** ascend low 5th class slabs to the summit of the buttress. **Descend** to the saddle behind the buttress for the descent route.

50. **Idiot Wind** (III 5.10a/b) A good 7-pitch route, put up in 1986 by Ed Webster and Peter Athens, that combines parts of THE NOSE and FIREBIRD. Begin below a left-arching corner about 40' left of THE NOSE and below a thin, vertical crack. **Pitch 1** jams the 40' finger crack (5.9) and face climbs right into a left-facing corner. Follow the crack in the corner (5.9) to a belay ledge on the right. A long pitch. **Pitch 2** face climbs up and left from a flake (5.7 and no pro) and parallel to THE NOSE to an easy groove/corner. Continue up a short crack to a stance with 2 bolts (shared with THE NOSE). **Pitch 3** (70') follows the first part of THE NOSE'S 3rd pitch. Jam a crack to the right edge of the huge roof. Step left from the corner (5.9+) and

SUNDANCE BUTTRESS

continue traversing horizontally above the roof on exposed 5.10a face climbing past 2 bolts. End at a small stance with 2 bolts on a slab. **Pitch 4** heads diagonally up left on airy 5.9 face climbing above the roof past several bolts. Reach a short 5.9 finger crack and belay above at a very exposed hanging belay from a bolt and pin below the left end of the second band of roofs. **Pitch 5**, with superb position, laybacks and jams around the left side of the roof (5.9) to a 5.9 finger crack. Belay after 150' on a small ledge. **Pitch 6** scales easy 4th and 5th class rock to a large terrace. **Pitch 7** climbs a flake to the right (5.6) and follows easy rock to the summit.

51. **Turnkorner** (III 5.10b) This all-time crack classic, freed by Royal Robbins in 1964, is still an intimidating Lumpy testpiece. The line was originally climbed by Layton Kor and Jack Turner in 1962 and named the Kor-Turner. Robbins, using an imaginative play on the first ascensionist's names, redubbed the route TURNKORNER. The sustained 6-pitch route follows a long crack system up the middle of Turnkorner Buttress to the left side of the large roof band. Begin at a right-facing dihedral just left of a large flakelike boulder. **Pitch 1** stems and jams up the dihedral (5.9) to a good stance on the left. **Pitch 2** jams a rounded hand crack (5.9) to a good belay on a large, boulder-strewn ledge. **Pitch 3** follows a shallow dihedral up left and then face climbs (5.9) to a left-angling ramp with an old bolt. Thrash up the crux, overhanging, off-width crack/slot (5.10b) above the left end of the ramp, and continue up the 5.9 off-width past a couple of old bolts to a semi-hanging belay below the roof band. **Pitch 4** continues up the strenuous crack system, off-widthing over the large roof (5.10a) and following the flared crack above with hand and fist jams to a stance. **Pitch 5** works right into a flared 5.6 crack. Belay on a wide terrace. **Pitch 6** angles left up another 5.6 crack to the low-angle summit slabs. **Rack:** Bring a standard rack up to a #4 Friend, along with doubles of Friends #3 to #4. A #4 Camalot is useful too.

52. **Mr. President** (III 5.10d) Another strenuous crack classic. This line goes up a crack directly to the saddle on the left side of Turnkorner Buttress. Begin below a flared wide crack in a right-facing dihedral. **Pitch 1** climbs the flared crack (5.9) by stemming and jamming a hand crack inside the flare. **Pitch 2** continues up the crack as it eases right and thins (5.10d). Step left and follow some 5.9 cracks to a belay ledge. **Pitch 3** jams the left of two parallel cracks up the wall above; some 5.9 up high. **Pitches 4** and **5** climb the groove cracks above to the saddle behind Turnkorner Buttress.

53. **Bonzo** and **Chain of Command** (II 5.11a) This link-up of two routes makes a superb but difficult day's outing. Begin just left of MR. PRESIDENT below a thin, right-facing dihedral. **Pitch 1** is Bonzo. Thin face climbing (5.9) heads right into the hanging right-facing corner. Strenuous jamming (5.10a initially and 5.10b at the top) up the corner ends at a double-bolt

belay stance. Rappel 110' to the ground or continue. **Pitch 2** works up left past 6 bolts along the edge of the buttress on excellent 5.10 face climbing (5.10c above third bolt) and then goes left to a small 2-bolt belay. **Pitch 3** is short. Climb the steep headwall above past 2 bolts on thin 5.11a face climbing. Belay on a ledge with 2 bolts. Pitches 2 and 3 can be combined as 1, but use runners wisely to avoid rope drag. Make two double-rope rappels to the ground: first is 130' to BONZO'S anchors; second is 110' to ground. Or continue on to the saddle behind Turnkorner Buttress with 2 moderate pitches.

BOULDERAREA

THE RIVER WALL

OVERVIEW

The North St. Vrain River, named for nineteenth-century fur trapper and trader Ceran St. Vrain, begins from snowmelt high atop the Continental Divide in Rocky Mountain National Park's Wild Basin. The river threads down wide glacial valleys before twisting through a rugged canyon northwest of Boulder. Several small but excellent granite outcrops line the canyon walls west of Lyons, below Button Rock and Longmont reservoirs. The River Wall, a compact cliff towering above a river pool below Longmont Reservoir's spillway, is the best of the lot, yielding a surprising number of superb routes. Local climbers rave about the River Wall, calling it "the best little crag in Colorado." Paul Piana writes, "For the rock climber interested in something beautiful, unique, and a little less pedestrian, the granite imperatives of the Button Rock area are gems to be savored."

The wall rises out of the North St. Vrain River, offering fractured overhanging walls and steep lichen-colored slabs. The climbing itself is equally diverse with difficult finger cracks, sharp incut edges and sidepulls, and arm-pumping jug hauls. The cliff measures 80 feet at its highest and stretches almost 200 feet along the river. Many of the routes are bolt-protected, while others require careful and competent natural protection. Old Yellar Dome, a southeast-facing crag on the hill north of the reservoir, offers several excellent routes, including *Bambi* (5.12d), an eight cold-shut route up the wall's left side, and *Old Yellar* (5.13a), a superb Steve Hong route with nine bolts up the center of the steep wall.

Approach the crag by walking up the road from the steel gate and parking area. The River Wall lies a scant 100 yards up-river. A short trail leads to the river's southwest bank. Climbs can be approached by rock-hopping across the river. Watch in spring and early summer for swift, cold currents. During high-water times, climb a short, 5th class gully east of the wall and follow a rough path along the cliff top. Fixed rappel anchors west of *New Horizon* allow access to the canyon floor. Routes are listed from left to right looking at the cliff.

DENVER/ BOULDER

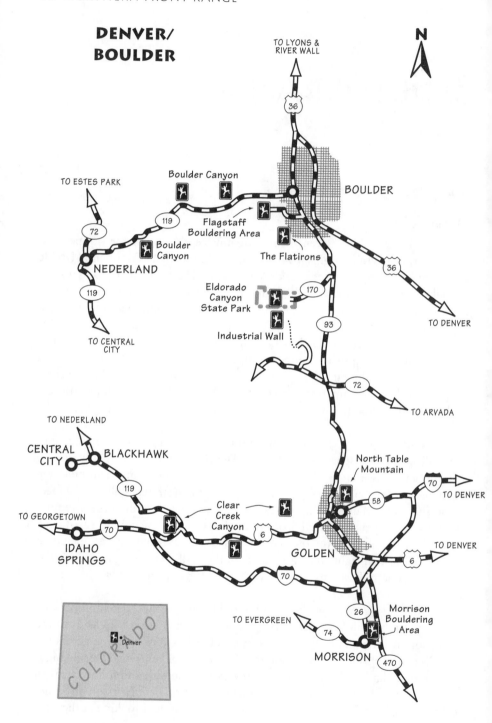

N

TO LYONS & RIVER WALL

36

TO ESTES PARK

Boulder Canyon

72

119

BOULDER

Flagstaff Bouldering Area

The Flatirons

36

Boulder Canyon

NEDERLAND

119

TO DENVER

Eldorado Canyon State Park

170

93

Industrial Wall

TO CENTRAL CITY

72

TO ARVADA

TO NEDERLAND

CENTRAL CITY

BLACKHAWK

North Table Mountain

70

TO DENVER

58

119

Clear Creek Canyon

TO GEORGETOWN

70

6

TO DENVER

IDAHO SPRINGS

GOLDEN

6

70

Morrison Bouldering Area

26

TO EVERGREEN

74

470

MORRISON

COLORADO

Denver

Ian Spencer-Green moves up *Red Neck Hero*, a great sport line on The River Wall.
Photo by Stewart M. Green.

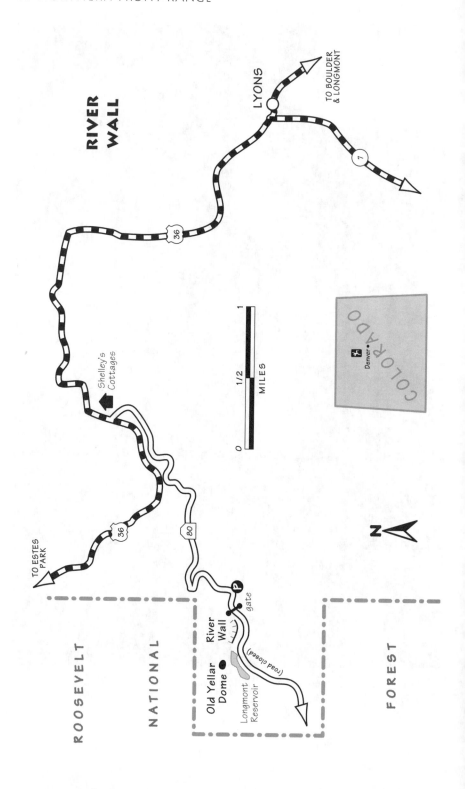

Trip Planning Information

General description: A spectacular selection of short, high-quality routes on a compact granite cliff.

Location: Northwest of Boulder (west of Lyons on U.S. Highway 36) along the North St. Vrain River.

Camping: No camping in the immediate vicinity or along the river. The nearest public campgrounds are in Roosevelt National Forest and Rocky Mountain National Park. Private campgrounds are found in Estes Park just up the highway from the River Wall.

Climbing season: Year-round. The west-facing cliff offers shade on hot summer mornings. Late summer and autumn are good times to visit. Spring days can be windy, and the river runs very high. Winter afternoons are often warm enough for climbing.

Restrictions and access issues: The River Wall and adjacent cliffs are on land administered by the City of Longmont for its water supply. Bathing, swimming, and inner-tubing are not allowed in the river. Pick up your trash and respect other users, including anglers and hikers.

Guidebooks: The River Wall and other North St. Vrain canyon cliffs are well-covered in the *1995 Boulder Sport Climber's Guide* by Mark Rolofson. Also *Front Range Crags* by Peter Hubbel, Chockstone Press, 1994 and *Boulder Climbs North* by Richard Rossiter, Chockstone Press, 1988.

Nearby mountain shops, guide services, and gyms: Basecamp Mountain Sports, Boulder Mountaineer, Mountain Sports, Neptune Mountaineering, Boulder Mountaineering Climbing School, Boulder Rock Club (Boulder); International Alpine School (Eldorado Springs).

Services: All services, including groceries, dining, lodging, and espresso, in Boulder and Lyons.

Emergency services: Call 911. Boulder Community Hospital, N. Broadway and Balsam, Boulder, CO 80301, (303) 440-2273. Memorial Hospital Boulder, 311 Mapleton Ave., Boulder, CO 80302, (303) 443-0230.

Nearby climbing areas: Flagstaff Mountain, the Flatirons and Green Mountain, Eldorado Canyon State Park, Clear Creek Canyon, Golden Gate Canyon State Park, North Table Mountain, Rocky Mountain National Park, Lumpy Ridge, South St. Vrain Canyon, Combat Rock.

Nearby attractions: Rocky Mountain National Park, Longs Peak, Trail Ridge Road, Indian Peaks Wilderness Area, Rollins Pass, Golden Gate Canyon State Park, Central City-Blackhawk National Historic District, Golden, Coors Brewery, Eldorado Canyon State Park, Boulder Mountain Park, Mount Evans Wilderness Area, Mount Evans Highway.

Finding the crag: From Boulder drive north 17 miles to Lyons via US 36. Turn northwest in Lyons on US 36 toward Estes Park and drive 3.7 miles. Turn south or left onto a dirt road, County Road 80, at Shelly's Cottages. Follow the road west along the North St. Vrain River, over a rise, and back along the river 2.3 miles to a steel gate. Park well off the road and walk 100 yards up the road. The River Wall rises from the river's north bank below the road.

1. **New Horizon (5.12d)** A perfect overhanging arete protected by 5 bolts on the far west side of the wall. Difficult layaways and sidepulls lead up and left. Step right from the 2nd bolt then move back left onto the arete at the 3rd bolt.

2. **Lost Horizon (5.14a)** Rob Candelaria gave this thin 40' crack its severe rating after finally leading it. It's the hardest crack pitch in Colorado and maybe in the United States. Follow the obvious overhanging crack right of NEW HORIZON and bring lots of small wired nuts and tape.

3. **Brother From Another Planet (5.13a/b)** Follow the line of 4 bolts up incipient cracks.

4. **Big, Big Gunky Man (5.12a R)** Begin on a river-side ledge and climb the blocky roof above. 2 bolts above the lip protect hard face moves. Run it out to the top.

5. **Pocket Hercules (5.12a)** An excellent finger crack over a series of small roofs with thin hand jams and fingerlocks. Occasional incut face holds offer relief. **Rack:** Bring an assortment of small to medium Friends including at least 3 #1.5s.

RIVER WALL

6. **Big, Big Monkey Man** (5.12b) Climb POCKET HERCULES to its crux and swing up and right on buckets over steep overlaps and flakes past 5 bolts. **Rack:** Bring pro to #1.5 Friend, including several #1.5 Friends, to protect the POCKET HERCULES crack.

7. **Red Neck Hero** (5.12a) Cross the river and belay on a small pedestal. Traverse left above the waterline to a shallow cave. Follow 6 bolts up and out on the overhanging wall. A very powerful and fun route. The anchors are set well back on top. Better to belay on the ledge there, have your second clean it, and rappel from the anchors of ESCAPE FROM ALCATRAZ immediately east.

8. **Escape from Alcatraz** (5.11b) A brilliant line up a steep slab using sidepulls and underclings. 5 bolts to 2-bolt anchor.

9. **Introducing Meteor Dad** (5.10d) A steep slab festooned with incut holds. The crux is an awkward mantle half-way up. 7 bolts to 2-bolt lowering anchor.

10. **Diamonds are Forever** (5.13b) A thin, continuous, bolt-protected face just right of The Box, a deep chimney. 8 bolts to anchors.

11. **Neurosurgeon** (5.12a R) One of the best finger cracks around and comparable to the 1st pitch of THE NAKED EDGE. Jam the thin crack over small roof, continue jamming and then face-climb where the crack peters out. Traverse up and right onto the prow of the buttress and finish with poorly protected moves (5.9) on the right side of the arete. A direct finish continues straight up the headwall and goes at 5.11c/d X. **Rack:** Bring a rack of wired stoppers and Friends up to #2.5.

BOULDER CANYON

OVERVIEW

Boulder Canyon twists for 14 miles through fir- and spruce-cloaked mountains between Boulder on the edge of the Front Range and Nederland below the snow-capped Continental Divide. Numerous granite crags, buttresses, and domes stud the abrupt canyon slopes and give a spectacular assortment of impressive and classic lines that range from one to four pitches in length. More than 25 named crags, laced with literally hundreds of routes that scale both crack and face, perch above the winding highway.

Climbing history: Only minutes from downtown Boulder, the canyon has a rich climbing history. Local hardmen climbed many of the canyon classics in the 1950s, including *Empor,* a 5.7+ crack testpiece on Cob Rock. Layton Kor and Pat Ament dominated the canyon scene in the 1960s. Kor did a plethora of first ascents on the crags, while Ament specialized in hard free climbs. His remarkable achievements include the first free ascent of 5.11b/c *Country Club Crack* in 1967 and the first ascent of 5.11a *Athlete's Feat* in 1964 with Royal Robbins, which was probably the hardest free climb in the United States at that time. Exploration of Boulder Canyon's more remote crags boomed during the 1970s and '80s, with excellent lines put up on Blob Rock, Happy Hour Crag, and Bell Buttress. The early 1990s brought new exploration to the canyon's classic crags as well as difficult bolted routes to new cliffs like Centopah Crag and Coney Island from climbers the likes of Mark Rolofson and Dan Hare. Ben Moon, one of Britain's top climbers, established the canyon's current hardest route, *The Borg* (5.13c), in a spring snowstorm in 1994. Other superb canyon testpieces include Christian Griffith's *Verve* (5.13b), a thin face route up a flat arete on Bell Buttress, and *Give the Dog a Bone* (5.13a) on Coney Island Crag.

Boulder Canyon's numerous crags are easily reached from Colorado Highway 119. Roadside pullouts are found near all the major crags. Be careful crossing the highway.

Trip Planning Information

General description: Numerous granite crags, laced with hundreds of routes that ascend cracks, steep faces, and slabs, line a 16-mile canyon.

Location: Immediately west of Boulder on Colorado 119.

Camping: No camping is allowed in the canyon. The nearest Roosevelt National Forest campgrounds are 46-site Kelly Dahl Campground south of Nederland on CO 119 and 55-site Pawnee Campground at Brainard Lake north of Nederland off CO 72. Golden Gate Canyon State Park, southwest of Nederland, offers several excellent high-elevation campgrounds off CO 119.

Climbing season: Year-round. Boulder Canyon's sunny, north-slope crags afford excellent and dry winter climbing opportunities. Boulder Falls, mid-way

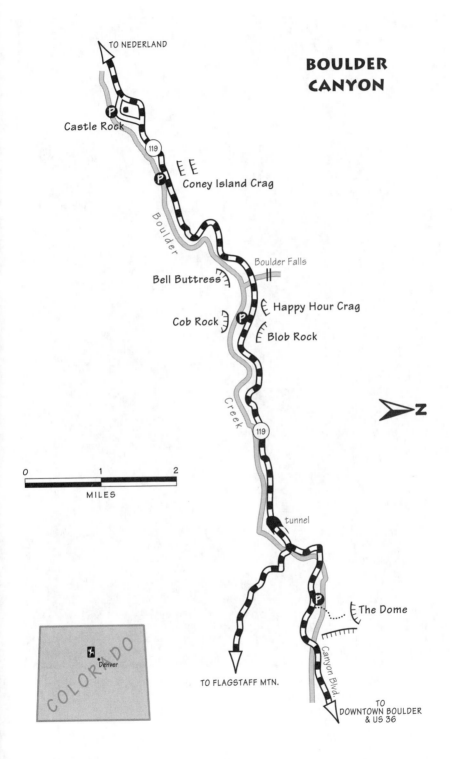

TO NEDERLAND

BOULDER CANYON

Castle Rock

119

Coney Island Crag

Boulder

Boulder Falls

Bell Buttress

Happy Hour Crag

Cob Rock

Blob Rock

Creek

119

N

0   1   2

MILES

tunnel

The Dome

COLORADO

Denver

TO FLAGSTAFF MTN.

Canyon Blvd.

TO
DOWNTOWN BOULDER
& US 36

Ian Spencer-Green on *Der Letzer Zug*, a technical line up Coney Island in Boulder Canyon. *Photo by Stewart M. Green.*

up the canyon, forms into a good moderate ice climb during cold periods. Spring and fall offer pleasant weather, although high winds often sweep down the canyon on spring afternoons. Summer days are often hot on the south-facing cliffs. Relief, however, is across the canyon on shady crags including Cob Rock.

Restrictions and access issues: Boulder Canyon is a mixture of Roosevelt National Forest and private land. Almost all the crags sit on public lands and access is not an issue. Avoid climbing near the highway, park at wide pull-outs, and use existing trails to the cliff bases. Boulder Creek becomes dangerously swollen with snowmelt in late spring and early summer. Avoid any creek crossing during this period.

Guidebooks: *Boulder Climbs North* by Richard Rossiter is an excellent and comprehensive guide to almost all the crags and routes in Boulder Canyon. It includes maps and detailed topos. *Best of Boulder Climbs,* also by Rossiter, looks closely at the canyon's main crags. *1995 Boulder Sport Climbs* by Mark Rolofson, 1995, includes up-to-date topos of the canyon's sport crags including Coney Island, Bitty Buttress, Centopah Crag, Fisky Cliff, and Surprising Crag.

Nearby mountain shops, guide services, and gyms: Basecamp Mountain Sports, Boulder Mountaineer, Mountain Sports, Neptune Mountaineering, Boulder Mountaineering Climbing School, Boulder Rock Club (Boulder); High Peaks Mountain Shop (Nederland); International Alpine School (Eldorado Springs).

Services: All services, including groceries, dining, lodging, and espresso, in Boulder. Limited services in Nederland.

Emergency services: Call 911. Boulder Community Hospital, N. Broadway and Balsam, Boulder, CO 80301, (303) 440-2273. Memorial Hospital Boulder, 311 Mapleton Ave., Boulder, CO 80302, (303) 443-0230.

Nearby climbing areas: Flagstaff Mountain, the Flatirons and Green Mountain, Eldorado Canyon State Park, Clear Creek Canyon, Golden Gate Canyon State Park, North Table Mountain, Morrison, Rocky Mountain National Park, Lumpy Ridge, St. Vrain Canyon, Button Rock Reservoir, Combat Rock.

Nearby attractions: Rocky Mountain National Park, Longs Peak, Trail Ridge Road, Indian Peaks Wilderness Area, Rollins Pass, Golden Gate Canyon State Park, Central City-Blackhawk National Historic District, Golden, Coors Brewery, Eldorado Canyon State Park, Boulder Mountain Park, Mount Evans Wilderness Area, Mount Evans Highway.

Finding the crags: Boulder Canyon begins on Boulder's west side and ends at Barker Dam just below Nederland. The canyon is easily accessed from downtown Boulder via Pearl Street, Canyon Boulevard, or Arapahoe Avenue. Canyon Boulevard becomes Colorado 119 as it leaves town and is the best approach. All mileages begin from the bridge at the junction of Canyon and Arapahoe immediately west of the Boulder city limits at the canyon's mouth.

THE DOME

The Dome perches north of Colorado 119 high above Boulder Creek's frothy torrent just 0.5 mile up the canyon from Boulder. The crag yields several excellent, classic routes that edge up steep slabs and jam a variety of superb cracks. The dry, south-facing cliff offers great climbing on winter afternoons when snow and shadow blanket everything else in the canyon. Most pitches are short, allowing climbers to communicate over the roar of the creek below. To approach The Dome, park at a large, obvious pull-out on the north side of the highway immediately past a large roadcut. A wide path swings around a blocky buttress and crosses the creek on a large steel bridge. Turn right on the bridge's north side and follow a trail east along the creek bank. After a short walk, the marked Dome Trail heads north up bouldery slopes to the crag base. **Descend** from the summit by dropping down rocky gullies on either the east or west side.

1. **East Slab** (5.5) This pleasant 1-pitch route, one of the best beginner pitches in the Boulder area, ascends The Dome's prominent east slab. Begin about half-way up the talus slope on the crag's east flank. Scale a corner and waltz up the open slab above to the summit. **Rack:** Bring medium wires and a few Friends for pro.

2. **Cozyhang** (5.7) This Boulder classic, first ascended in 1953, attains the summit via a somewhat circuitous but fun line in 3 short pitches. Begin just east of the crag's low point. **Pitch 1** surmounts 3 small overhangs, the high-

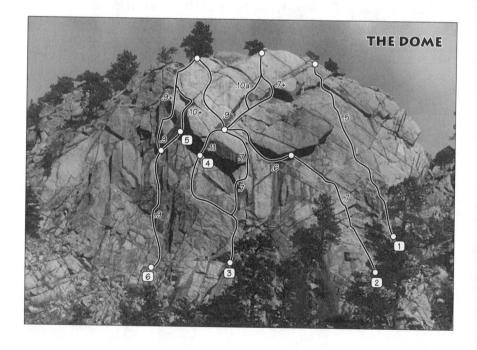

est with a 5.7 move at the lip, to a belay stance below the right side of the prominent roof. **Pitch 2** traverses under the roof and up to a ledge. **Pitch 3** climbs up right and over a V-shaped roof (5.7). A great variation heads directly up a leaning 5.10a hand crack to the summit slab.

3. **The Owl** (5.7) A superb 2-pitch route up cracks, corners, and slabs. **Pitch 1** begins by the rock's low point and scrambles up easy rock to a belay stance below a sloping ramp. **Pitch 2** climbs into a short, left-facing corner below a bulging roof via an awkward 5.7 move. Reach right and mantle past a couple large chicken heads and follow a perfect hand crack (5.7) to the large ledge at the end of the COZYHANG'S 2nd pitch.

4. **The Umph Slot** (5.11- to 5.11+) The name says it all—you abandon the classic three points of contact and thrutch, scratch, and umph your way up a narrow slot to THE OWL'S spacious ledge. Difficulty varies on this 1960s Chuck Pratt testpiece depending on body type. Thin anorexic types easily squeeze up the slot, while beefier ones use desperate off-size techniques on the overhanging outside edge.

5. **Super Squeeze** (5.10d) Masochists love this delightful stem and squeeze problem up the prominent A-shaped roof on The Dome's west side.

6. **Prelude to King Kong** and **Gorilla's Delight** (5.9+) Combine these two 1-pitch routes for a 3-star line. Scramble up to a belay stance on a gentle ramp on The Dome's west side just left of a black water streak. PRELUDE TO KING KONG ascends a shallow finger crack (5.9) up a left-facing corner to a ledge. GORILLA'S DELIGHT follows the obvious overhanging dihedral above via a 5.9 hand crack. After the crack falters, step right into another crack. After a couple of jams, a committing, dicey 5.9+ smear exits the crack onto the summit slabs.

COB ROCK

Cob Rock, a dark slabby buttress, rises south of the highway and Boulder Creek 6.8 miles up the canyon. Several high-quality, moderate lines scale the numerous delightful cracks that cleave the smooth cliff. Park at the large pulloff on the south side of the highway directly across from Cob Rock. Cross the creek and scramble to the rock base. The creek crossing can be the crux of any ascent. Use extreme caution at high water in late spring and early summer. Cob Rock, on the canyon's shady south slope, is an excellent summer and autumn crag. **Descent:** The best descent scrambles down the rock's broken south side and steep forested slopes below the west buttress.

7. **Northwest Corner** (5.7+) This quality route generally follows, as it's name implies, the northwest corner of Cob Rock. A long pitch climbs from huge boulders at its base up cracks and shallow corners (5.6) to an airy belay

stance. The short final lead pulls over an exciting 5.7 bulge to the summit slab.

8. **Empor** (5.7+) This superb line, first ascended in 1954 by Dallas Jackson and George Lamb, climbs the obvious dihedral that bisects Cob Rock's

north face. Begin atop the same boulders as the NORTHWEST CORNER route. **Pitch 1** diagonals up and left on a steep face via some 5.7+ moves and climbs into the prominent right-facing corner. Belay atop the corner in a V-shaped trough. **Pitch 2** climbs the steep finger and hand crack (5.7+) to the summit.

9. **North Face Center** (5.7) This 1959 Layton Kor and George Hurley route begins at the bottom of the north face. **Pitch 1** follows a 5.6 crack for 50', steps right into a right-trending system, and climbs to a ledge. **Pitch 2** continues up the obvious off-width and chimney crack (5.7) to EMPOR'S second belay.

10. **North Face Left** (5.8) This superb 1959 Kor route begins with the same start as the NORTH FACE CENTER line. Continue up and left on a steep finger and hand crack (5.8) to a bouldery ledge. A final pitch scales an easy corner to the top.

11. **East Crack** (5.10b) An elegant route up the north face's east edge. Begin just east of NORTH FACE LEFT and ascend an easy 5th-class corner to a large belay ledge. The route's difficulties are immediately obvious. Scale a thin, poorly protected corner (5.9) to a small roof. Above stretches a fingertip crack (5.10a) that leads to a blocky belay ledge on the rock's east corner.

12. **Huston Crack** (5.8) This 60' 1950s classic testpiece, first climbed by Cary Huston, makes a good direct start to EAST CRACK. Follow the obvious fist and off-size crack on the bulging buttress below the crag's east edge. Bring some large Camalots for protection. The thin crack immediately to the west, a former practice aid climb, goes free at 5.10d.

CONEY ISLAND

Coney Island, a large crag broken into an upper and lower cliff, sits on the north side of the canyon 9 miles up Colorado 119 on a sharp highway turn. The crag is somewhat hard to spot from the road. Park on a pullout on the south side of the highway and approach the Lower Wall via a short trail. The trail continues east around the Lower Wall and climbs gravel slopes to the Upper Wall. The Lower Wall is short and steep. The Upper Wall is broken by dihedrals and crack systems, with a large shield on its left side. Many excellent bolted sport routes as well as a few good traditional lines grace Coney Island. **Descent** from all routes is via rappel or lowering from fixed anchors.

13. **Twist and Shout** (5.13b) 6 bolts up the left side of a steep arete on the west end of the Lower Wall lead to a 2-bolt anchor.

14. **Flytrap** (5.11c) A very good and pumpy 5-bolt route up jugs right of the arete to anchors.

15. **Flies in the Soup** (5.11c) 3 bolts up the steep wall to anchors.

16. **Fly Swatter** (5.10c) A good 3-bolt line up a steep slab right of the overhanging face.

17. **Dampened Enthusiasm** (5.12a) 3 bolts to hook anchors on a leaning boulder-problem face on the Lower Wall's right side.

18. **Red Badger** (5.11d) Another 3-bolt boulder-problem route on the Lower Wall's right side. Ends at DAMPENED ENTHUSIASM'S hook anchors.

19. **Joyride** (5.12b) A good line up the far left side of the Upper Wall. Edge up past 7 bolts to anchors on a ledge.

20. **Der Letzer Zug** (5.12c) Climb a slab to a roof and up the obvious water streak on the upper shield on thin edges. Excellent climbing, but hard and sequential. 6 bolts to a 2-bolt anchor on a ledge.

21. **Der Reeperbahn** (5.13b) This excellent route scales the right edge of the shield on small holds. Climb past 3 bolts up a slab and over a roof onto the edge. Continue up on thin climbing past 5 more bolts to 2 bolts on a ledge.

22. **Loading Zone** (5.10d) Climb the obvious right-facing dihedral. **Rack:** Bring nuts and Friends.

23. **Quintet** (5.10b/c) A good crack/corner route in a right-facing zig-zag dihedral that swings over 5 roofs. Belay on a ledge. **Pitch 2** climbs a 5.10d fist crack over a roof. **Rack:** Bring an assortment of gear from wired stoppers to medium Friends.

24. **Give the Dog a Bone** (5.13a) Climb an arching 5.10 corner past a couple of bolts. When the corner bends right, turn the roof to the left and continue on steep rock to a ledge with a 2-bolt anchor.

25. **Coney Island Baby** (5.12a R) Same start as GIVE THE DOG A BONE, but continue up the right-facing dihedral to a vertical crack system. **Rack:** Bring RPs, wired stoppers, and Friends to 2.5. Bring some extra #1 to 2 Friends.

26. **Project** (5.14) This extreme thin face route/project edges up the steep wall below CONEY ISLAND BABY'S arch. Turn the arch and continue up the headwall above to the ledge with anchors. 9 bolts to 2-bolt anchor.

CASTLE ROCK

Castle Rock, one of the Boulder area's most famous crags, yields almost 50 routes and variations of all levels of difficulty from 5.0 to 5.13. The rock, jutting castle-like above the highway and Boulder Creek, is 11.9 miles up the canyon. A gravel road turns south off the highway and swings around Castle Rock's south face. Numerous parking areas are found below the impressive south face of this popular cliff. The longest approach is 30 seconds. **Descent** is accomplished down ledges, corners, and ramps on the north slope with the final descent down the rock's west side. Use caution, particularly in winter when snow coats everything. Rappels off trees or from anchors atop some routes might be advisable in snowy conditions.

27. **The Final Exam** (5.11a) This classic short problem, put up by Robbins and Ament in 1964, struggles up a 20' bulge via fingertip laybacking left of a large roof on the rock's west side. Once atop the bulge continue up slabs to the 5.11a PASS/FAIL OPTION roof, traverse right into the COFFIN CRACK system, or downclimb slabs to the left. Pat Ament says the route was named "when, as the leader struggled to a point short of falling, a tourist in her late eighties yelled from a car window, 'That must be the final exam!'" A couple of good crack climbs—5.9 CURVING CRACK and 5.10b/c COMEBACK CRACK—ascend the buttress northwest of Final Exam.

28. **Coffin Crack** (5.10b) Climb the strenuous off-width, 5" crack just right of FINAL EXAM to a belay above the slot. Continue up the crack, over a roof, and on to the top of Castle Rock.

29. **The By Gully** (5.9+) Immediately right of COFFIN CRACK. This route, called "a masterpiece of insecurity" by Pat Ament, scales an overhanging off-size crack and tight squeeze chimney. A 2nd pitch climbs a 5.7 roof and continues upward.

30. **Cussin' Crack** (5.7) This 1950s route right of the obvious roof climbs a prominent diagonal cleft for 50' before balancing left to a couple small

CASTLE ROCK
SOUTHEAST FACE

ledges and a belay stance at the base of the Cussin' Crack. Climb the flared 5.7 crack above and continue to the summit in a long pitch.

31. **Jackson's Wall** (5.6) This popular route, the easiest on the south face, was first climbed in 1953 by Dallas Jackson and Chuck Merley. It's somewhat funky. Climb the same diagonal trough as CUSSIN' CRACK, only continue higher to a ledge. Above the trough the route surmounts the crux headwall with a loose block and scrambles on to the summit.

32. **Tongo** (5.11a) This good route begins around the corner from JACKSON'S WALL. Follow a thin right-leaning ramp to a belay ledge with rappel anchors. This 5.10a pitch is poorly protected with small wires. The crux, a short fingery crack, (5.11a) climbs above to another good ledge.

33. **Gill Crack** (5.12a) This 25' crack, once a popular practice nail-up, sits a few paces east of TONGO near a smoke-blackened streak. The problem, first freed by John Gill in 1968, consists of painful finger jams in smooth piton scars. Downclimb the crack to the left or continue on up 5.11b/c THE STING to TONGO'S lower belay stance.

34. **The South Face** (5.9) A fine moderate route that scales 3 pitches to JACKSON'S WALL. **Pitch 1** climbs a short, obvious right-facing dihedral (5.8) and hand-traverses left onto a ledge. **Pitches 2** and **3** continue up hand and finger cracks to the last lead of JACKSON'S WALL.

35. **Athlete's Feat** (5.11a) This superb line breaks naturally into 5 short pitches up the southeast side of Castle Rock. First free-climbed in 1964 by Royal Robbins and Pat Ament, ATHLETE'S FEAT offers a 5.11 pitch, 3 (5.10) pitches, and a 5.9 pitch. Begin atop a pointed boulder near the southeast corner and crank the crux 5.11a mantle onto a sloping slab. Follow the right-facing corner system above for 4 difficult crack pitches to the summit. **Rack:** The first lead is protected by a couple of bolts, otherwise bring stoppers, TCUs, and Friends to 4".

36. **Country Club Crack** (5.11b/c) This must-do climb follows a series of sustained vertical and overhanging cracks up the crag's smooth southeast corner. Royal Robbins freed almost all of the route in 1964, resorting only to a couple of aid pitons near the top. Pat Ament, his belayer, returned in 1966 to free-climb the entire route. **Pitch 1** starts just right of ATHLETE'S FEAT and edges delicately up polished holds using bolts for protection. This boulder problem start is the route's 5.11 crux. A 5.8 hand crack above leads to The Bar, an airy ledge 65' off the ground. **Pitch 2** jams 70' up an excellent hand crack to a roof. Pull the roof and climb the steep 5.11b finger crack to a broad ledge. Find a knee-lock at the roof to rest before the final difficulties and be careful not to overprotect the 90' pitch to avoid rope drag. **Rack:** Bring gear to 3".

FLAGSTAFF MOUNTAIN BOULDERING AREA

OVERVIEW

Flagstaff Mountain, with its easy access from Boulder and a plethora of both difficult and moderate problems, is Colorado's historic and most popular bouldering area. Numerous boulders scatter across the upper flanks of 6,872-foot Flagstaff Mountain, forming a climbing playground for both the beginner and the way-honed alike. The boulders, composed of a ruddy conglomerate sandstone, offer a wide variety of moves and problems with pebble-pinches, shallow sloped dishes, sharp flakes, finger pockets, and gritty edges. The granular rock quickly shreds finger-tips, especially after multiple attempts. After a few days of bouldering here, however, the tips begin to adapt and problems become less painful.

Use care when bouldering on Flagstaff. While most of the problems have good landings, some do not. Use a spotter to avoid twisted or broken ankles. A crash-pad is useful. Use chalk sparingly and brush the holds before you leave. Also, do not hog problems or boulders. If others are waiting, let them have a go while you rest.

Trip Planning Information

General description: A wide variety of problems on numerous sandstone boulders and outcrops scattered across piney ridges.

Location: On the western edge of Boulder.

Camping: No camping on Flagstaff Mountain or in the immediate Boulder area. The nearest Roosevelt National Forest campgrounds lie west of the mountain near Nederland.

Climbing season: Year-round. The bouldering area is accessible throughout the winter, although snow may pile up below the north-facing boulders. Summer days can be very hot. Evenings are more comfortable.

Restrictions and access issues: Flagstaff Mountain is within Boulder Mountain Park, a large enclave of public land that preserves Boulder's mountain skyline. Residents can use the park for free. Out-of-towners must purchase a daily park pass at a kiosk at Panorama Point 0.5 mile up the road and display the pass in a rear window. Boulder Mountain Parks have a no-bolting restriction.

Guidebooks: *Front Range Bouldering* by Bob Horan, Chockstone Press, 1989, details almost all of the bouldering with maps, topos, and descriptions on Flagstaff Mountain.

Nearby mountain shops, guide services, and gyms: Basecamp Mountain Sports, Boulder Mountaineer, Mountain Sports, Neptune Mountaineering, Boulder Mountaineering Climbing School, Boulder Rock Club (Boulder); International Alpine School (Eldorado Springs).

Services: All services, including groceries, dining, lodging, and espresso, in Boulder.

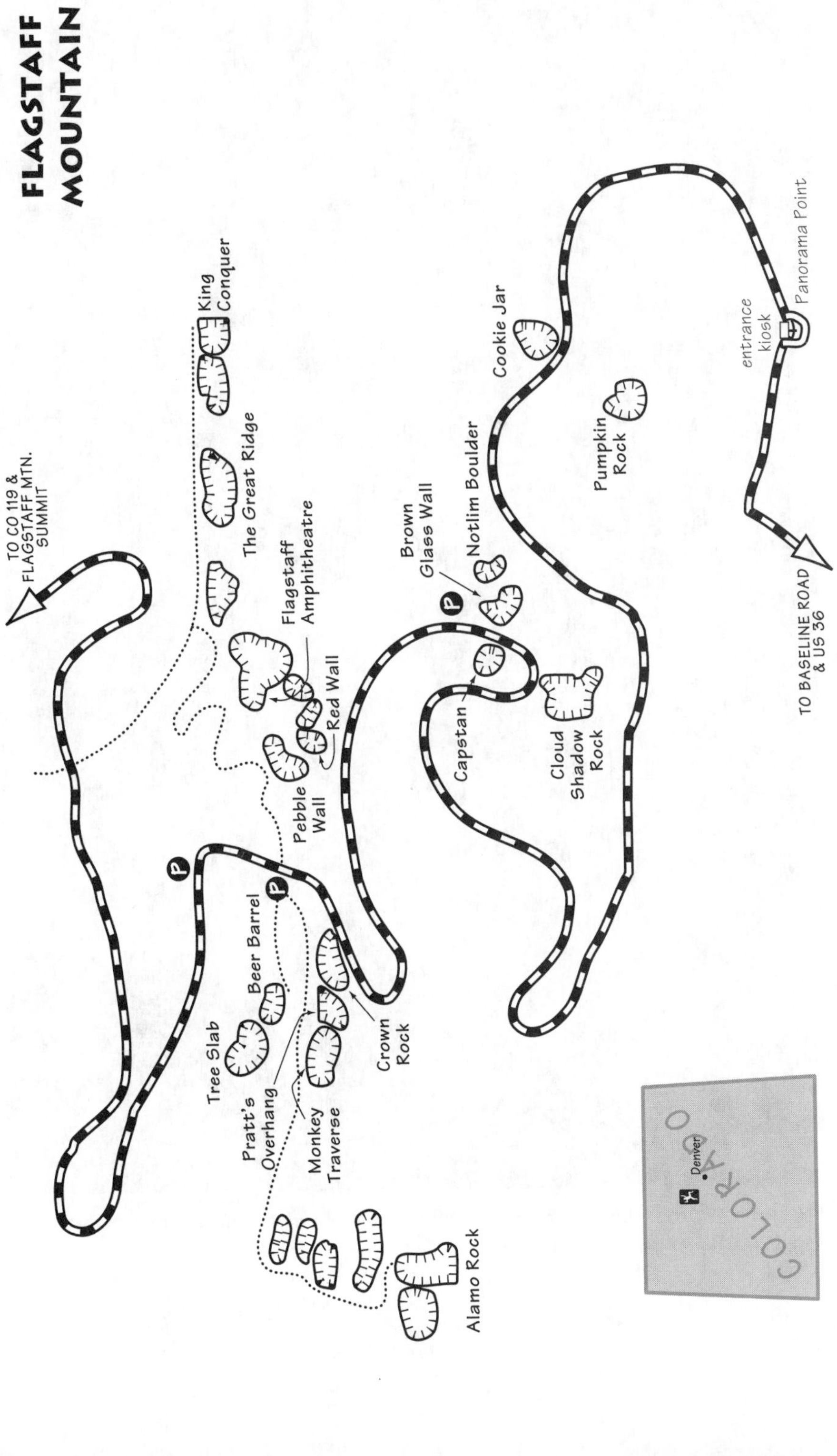

FLAGSTAFF MOUNTAIN

TO CO 119 &
FLAGSTAFF MTN.
SUMMIT

King Conquer

The Great Ridge

Flagstaff Amphitheatre

Red Wall

Pebble Wall

Tree Slab

Beer Barrel

Pratt's Overhang

Monkey Traverse

Crown Rock

Alamo Rock

Brown Glass Wall

Notlim Boulder

Capstan

Cloud Shadow Rock

Cookie Jar

Pumpkin Rock

entrance kiosk

Panorama Point

TO BASELINE ROAD
& US 36

P

COLORADO

Denver

Boulderers test their skill on Capstan Rock's classic B1 *South Overhang* problem, Flagstaff Mountain. *Photo by Stewart M. Green.*

Emergency services: Call 911. Boulder Community Hospital, N. Broadway and Balsam, Boulder, CO 80301, (303) 440-2273. Memorial Hospital Boulder, 311 Mapleton Ave., Boulder, CO 80302, (303) 443-0230.

Nearby climbing areas: The Flatirons and Green Mountain, Eldorado Canyon State Park, Clear Creek Canyon, Golden Gate Canyon State Park, North Table Mountain, Morrison, Rocky Mountain National Park, Lumpy Ridge, St. Vrain Canyon, Button Rock Reservoir, Combat Rock.

Nearby attractions: Rocky Mountain National Park, Longs Peak, Trail Ridge Road, Indian Peaks Wilderness Area, Rollins Pass, Golden Gate Canyon State Park, Central City-Blackhawk National Historic District, Golden, Coors Brewery, Eldorado Canyon State Park, Boulder Mountain Park, Mount Evans Wilderness Area, Mount Evans Highway.

Finding the boulders: The area is easily reached from Boulder via Baseline Road. Exit U.S. Highway 36 from Denver at Baseline Road, or follow Broadway to Baseline Road at the south edge of the University of Colorado. Either way, head straight west on Baseline through a residential area to the foot of Flagstaff Mountain. Most of the best boulders lie near the mountain crest. All mileages used here are taken from Armstrong Bridge, the small bridge at the mountain base. Baseline Road turns into Flagstaff Road here. Park well off the road at designated pulloffs and watch for bicyclists on the road.

COOKIE JAR AREA

Cookie Jar Rock sits 0.8 mile from Armstrong Bridge on the west side of the road. This large block hosts numerous classic problems. Eyebolts on top offer toprope anchors. **Cookie Jar Crack,** on the boulder's south face, is an excellent 5.7 and one of the Boulder area's most climbed problems. Immediately right of *Cookie Jar Crack* is **The Shield** (B1-) on a bulging face and **Northcutt's Roll** (B1), an overhanging wall on the southeast corner above the road. **Russian's Nose** (B5.10) ascends the overhang left of *Cookie Jar Crack*. A couple of good problems lie on the north face. **Commitment** (B1-) climbs a bulge on the right side of the face, while **Jackson's Pitch** (B1-) reaches over a bulge from an undercling left of *Commitment.*

CLOUD SHADOW AREA

Capstan Rock, Brown Glass Wall, and Cloud Shadow sit off a sharp, hairpin turn 1.5 miles up the road. Park in a small pulloff just west of the Brown Glass Wall. Capstan Rock is a large, obvious pillar sitting alongside the road. The south and west faces offer the longest and best problems. **South Crack** (B1-) jams piton scars up the obvious crack that slices across Capstan's south face. **Sarabande** (B5.10+) edges up the steep face where the crack bends east. **South

Overhang (B1) climbs the slight bulge just right of *South Crack* on slopers and pebbles. **Just Right** (B1+), a desperate Jim Holloway problem, tackles the overhanging face just right of *South Overhang* with sloping holds, laybacks, and delicate friction moves. The excellent **West Face** (B5.10) climbs shallow huecos and pockets on the boulder's west side. It's scary up high; don't fall.

Brown Glass Wall lies north of Capstan on the opposite side of the road. The best problems face north into the forest. The problems are long with bad landings. A toprope is advisable for safety. Four good problems climb the boulder's concave north face. **Brigg's Bridges** (B1) scales the arete on the right side of the face. **V Crack** (B5.9) is a superb problem up the obvious flake system. **Crack Slot** (B5.10) jams an off-width crack on the left side of the wall, while **Back Extension** (B5.10+) climbs the overhanging wall left of the crack. Notlim Boulder in the forest just below Brown Glass Wall hosts **Hollow's Way**, an overhanging B2 lieback problem.

Cloud Shadow, a large pile of boulders, sits immediately east of the hairpin turn at 1.5 miles. Park just west of Brown Glass Wall, walk east on the road, and cut down on a short trail to the south side of Cloud Shadow and its best problems. The excellent classic problem **Hagan's Wall** (B1) climbs a steep bulge on the left side of the long wall. Crank off a painful flake and shallow two-finger pocket up and right to easier rock. Just left is **Dandy Line** (B1), a hard pebble-pulling route. An upper and lower traverse swing across a band of pockets and sloping ramps on the south face. The lower B2 traverse is much harder than the upper traverse. The steep southeast corner of the rock offers several great problems. **Contemplation** (B1-) follows a left-leaning seam to a scary headwall. **Consideration** (B1-), one of Flagstaff's best problems, climbs up and right from an obvious hole to the angled ridge. Just right of *Consideration* is **A.H.R.** (Another Holloway Route), an almost unimaginable B2 line up minute edges and pebbles done by Jim Holloway in 1975. It has a very specific set of holds and is as yet unrepeated, although Ben Moon climbed the basic line. To the right is **The Bulge** (B1). Climb the bulge from an undercling to the ridgeline above. **East Inside Corner** (B5.9) climbs a small dihedral just right of the southeast corner. A few superb problems climb The Alcove, a cul-de-sac west around the corner from Hagan's Wall. **East Overhang** (B5.10+) mantles over the prominent roof. The excellent **Sailor's Delight** (B5.10) swings up and over the bulging roof above The Alcove with cut-loose jugs at the lip.

PRATT'S OVERHANG AREA

Some of Flagstaff Mountain's best classic problems lie north and south of the road at 1.6 miles. Park in a small parking area on the south side of the road. A lot of problems lie south of the lot in a maze of tilted sandstone hogbacks stretching down the mountainside. Crown Rock sits southeast of the lot alongside the road. This low-angle flatiron offers many good beginner topropes on its east, south, and west faces.

Follow a trail about 150' south of the parking area to *Pratt's Overhang*, a well-traveled, west-facing overhang on the path. Some great problems edge up this boulder. **Pratt's Mantle** (B5.9) is an obvious awkward mantle on the left-side bulge. **Pratt's Overhang** (B5.10), first ascended by Bob Culp in 1960, climbs the right-leaning shallow crack/slot. The classic **Smith Overhang** (B1+) pulls up the overhanging wall right of the slot using a left-hand layback flake. Excellent **Crystal Corner** (5.10+) climbs the steep, blunt arete on the right via the large crystal.

Just down the trail from Pratt's Overhang is the **Monkey Traverse,** probably Flagstaff's most frequented problem. This popular pump follows the obvious chalked holds back and forth across the wall and offers many variations and eliminates. A few other lunge and roof problems bisect the traverse. Farther south downslope are more boulders, traverses, and topropes including *William's Mantle,* The Rib Boulder, and Alamo Rock, a large flatiron with some very good 5.10s on its steep west face.

Another selection of boulders sits west and downhill from *Pratt's Overhang.* Beer Barrel Rock, the first large block encountered, yields a dozen problems. The East Slab is the standard descent route and a good beginner's problem. The rock's south face hosts some excellent problems: **Poling Pebble Route** (B1-) pinches pebbles up the southeast corner; **South Face** (B5.9) climbs to an overhanging crack; **Southwest Corner** (B5.9) is a fun layback up good holds. **West Traverse** (B1-) reaches across the boulder's steep west flank. **Double Clutch** (B1+), on the northwest corner, is a great dyno problem.

THE FLAGSTAFF AMPHITHEATER AREA

North of the parking area at 1.6 miles lies a splendid assortment of boulders and problems that are of particular interest to the bouldering aficionado. The first grouping of boulders sits about 100 yards up the Flagstaff Trail from the road. The Pebble Wall, shaded by pine trees, is the first encountered. This excellent boulder offers some of Flagstaff's classic hard problems on its bulging and pebble-covered south face. Problems are listed east to west. **The Original Route** (B5.7), the easiest one, scales the southeast corner. Pat Ament's **Crystal Mantle** (B5.10) mantles the large crystal. **Direct South Face** (B1) starts off a tree root and pinches pebbles and crystals to the rounded summit. **High Step** (B5.10+) climbs the pebbled wall left of the Direct. **Southwest Face** (B1-) is thin, high, and committing. **Southwest Corner** (B5.9) is a superb but airy layback problem up a rounded arete. **West Overhang** (B1-) and **North Overhang** (B1-) lie around the corner on the northwest side of the boulder.

Northeast of The Pebble Wall and North Rock, a pair of boulders, is Red Wall. This boulder's vertical south face yields six extreme problems and several variations. The popular **Left Side** (B5.10) uses the obvious fingertip pocket.

Standard Route (B1) reaches up to a hole. **Right Side** (B1) climbs the smooth wall just left of the pine tree using a soap dish handhold.

Flagstaff Amphitheater, a south-facing cul-de-sac of boulders, lies immediately north of The Pebble Wall. Many fine problems ascend these boulders. **South Corner** (B5.10) is a good, overhanging corner on the east wall of the amphitheater. To its left are **South Bulge** (B5.10), **Direct Route** (B1-), **Gill Direct** (B1), and **Overhanging Hand Traverse** (B5.9). The north wall of the amphitheater offers four B1 problems: **Crystal Swing, Direct South Face, Briggs Route,** and **South Face Left. High Overhang** (B5.9) is an overhang with a scary finishing mantle in the northwest corner. Around the corner and up the hill from the amphitheater is **Overhang Wall** with some good steep problems. Continue up the trail from here to the Great Ridge and many more excellent problems.

THE FLATIRONS

OVERVIEW

The slabby east faces of the First and Third Flatirons, pasted on the northeast flank of 8,144-foot Green Mountain, form Boulder's distinctive skyline. From town the rocks appear monolithic, with their abrupt, conspicuous faces looming above the city noise and bustle. Up close, however, the Flatirons assume a more friendly aspect—broken by gullies, seamed with cracks, liberally studded with flakes, and tilted back to a reasonable 50-degree angle. Green Mountain and its Flatirons lie within Boulder Mountain Park, a spectacular 5,500-acre preserve, part of Colorado's largest urban park system and administered by the City of Boulder's Parks and Recreation Department. Boulder, long aware of its unique scenic assets, has protected its mountain backdrop from commercial development and ringed the city with numerous enclaves of open space. Green Mountain and its southerly neighbor Dinosaur Mountain attract Boulder's outdoor recreationists to a lengthy network of trails, diverse wildlife and flora, and superb rock climbing opportunities. The numerous crags offer a myriad of challenges ranging from 4th class scrambles for beginners to sharply overhanging 5.13 routes that test every hardman's mettle. Gerry Roach in his *Flatiron Classics* book describes more than 20 miles of routes under 5.8 that lace the cliffs in Boulder Mountain Park.

Green Mountain is a rough, bulky peak, coated with thick evergreen forests and littered by numerous crags including the renowned First and Third Flatirons. Their sandstone and conglomerate rock layers were deposited almost 300 million years ago during the Pennsylvanian Period. The rock began as coarse alluvial run-off from Colorado's Ancestral Rockies. It was then dragged, heaved, tilted, and uplifted during the rebirth of the Rocky Mountains some 30 million years ago. Erosion quickly attacked the rising layers, excavating sharp canyons and slowly chiseling the immense rock faces.

Climbing history: The Flatirons, always drawing the eye from Boulder, are Colorado's first technical rock climbing area. The first recorded ascent of the Third Flatiron came in 1906 by Floyd and Earl Millard, who scaled the 1,300-foot east face. Afterwards, the local Rocky Mountain Climber's Club regularly scaled the Flatirons. One member, Rudolph Johnson, wrote in 1923: "These are the most dangerous climbs I have ever attempted, but the thrill and pleasure have tempted me to perform the feat a number of times, as it has tempted other thrill seekers in Boulder.... I am not recommending the Flatiron climb for any except the most foolhardy rock climbers, but to mountaineers who want real thrills no better climb can be found." The Third Flatiron remains the most popular route in the Boulder area. The East Face route has been scaled in roller skates, soloed in less than ten minutes, streaked by Gary Nepture in the early 1970s, and it sees thousands of ascents annually. Yvon Chouinard called it the "finest beginner's climb in the country."

THE FLATIRONS

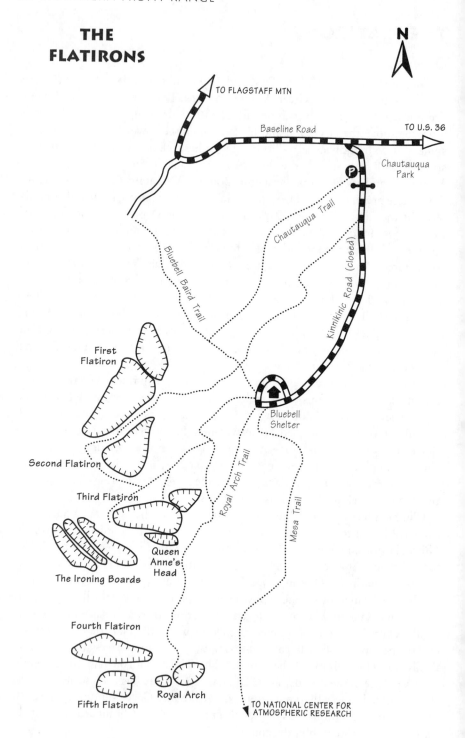

N

TO FLAGSTAFF MTN

Baseline Road

TO U.S. 36

Chautauqua Park

Chautauqua Trail

Bluebell Baird Trail

Kinnikinic Road (closed)

First Flatiron

Second Flatiron

Third Flatiron

The Ironing Boards

Queen Anne's Head

Royal Arch Trail

Bluebell Shelter

Mesa Trail

Fourth Flatiron

Fifth Flatiron

Royal Arch

TO NATIONAL CENTER FOR ATMOSPHERIC RESEARCH

Still, despite its relative ease and bucolic atmosphere, the Third Flatiron along with the First Flatiron remains a serious rock climb that has claimed its share of victims. Both are well over 1,000 feet long and offer nebulous route finding and sparse protection. Retreat is difficult. The crux of the Third Flatiron, particularly for beginners and on busy days, is the three-rappel descent down the vertical backside. Climbers are well-advised not to take a Flatiron outing too lightly. Carry sufficient clothing for the weather, including a raincoat on summer afternoons. Watch the weather. Thunderstorms brew quickly and can move in unseen from the west. Lightning regularly strikes the mountain high-points, including the Flatiron summits. Route finding on the Flatirons can be problematic. The low angle and numerous holds allow climbing almost anywhere on their slabs. It's best to pick the line that looks easiest and proceed with caution.

Trip Planning Information

General description: Slabby sandstone faces pitched at 50 degrees offer excellent moderate and easy routes.

Location: Immediately west of Boulder.

Camping: No public camping is in the immediate vicinity of Boulder. The nearest campgrounds lie in Golden Gate Canyon State Park and Roosevelt National Forest about an hour's drive away.

Climbing season: Year-round. The best time to climb on the Flatirons is between March and November. Spring brings windy days and unsettled weather. Summers are hot. Start early and carry lots of water. Watch for heavy afternoon thunderstorms and lightning while climbing and on top. Autumn offers excellent climbing weather, with warm days and low precipitation. Winters can be cold, but warm, sunny days are not unusual. The descent trails usually remain snow-covered in winter.

Restrictions and access issues: The Flatirons are in Boulder Mountain Park and users are subject to park rules. A bolting moratorium is in effect in Boulder Mountain Park. The Third Flatiron and surrounding crags may be closed from February through July for nesting raptors. Obey all area closures. Signs are usually posted on the perimeter of the closed area. Call the Boulder Open Space office at (303) 441-4142 for more information on cliff closure dates.

Guidebooks: *Boulder Climbs North* by Richard Rossiter, Chockstone Press, 1988, is a very complete, user-friendly guide to all the Flatiron crags on Green Mountain. *Best of Boulder Climbs* by Rossiter, Chockstone Press, 1992, also details the area. *Flatiron Classics* by Gerry Roach, Fulcrum Inc., 1987, is an excellent guide and compendium of all the moderate Flatiron routes and hiking trails.

Nearby mountain shops, guide services, and gyms: Basecamp Mountain Sports, Boulder Mountaineer, Mountain Sports, Neptune Mountaineering, Boulder Mountaineering Climbing School, Boulder Rock Club, (Boulder); International Alpine School (Eldorado Springs).

Services: All services, including groceries, dining, lodging, and a private campground, in Boulder.

Emergency services: Call 911. Boulder Community Hospital, N. Broadway and Balsam, Boulder, CO 80301, (303) 440-2273. Memorial Hospital Boulder, 311 Mapleton Ave., Boulder, CO 80302, (303) 443-0230.

Nearby climbing areas: Flagstaff Mountain, Eldorado Canyon State Park, Clear Creek Canyon, Golden Gate Canyon State Park, North Table Mountain, Morrison, Rocky Mountain National Park, Lumpy Ridge, St. Vrain Canyon, Button Rock Reservoir, Combat Rock.

Nearby attractions: Rocky Mountain National Park, Longs Peak, Trail Ridge Road, Indian Peaks Wilderness Area, Rollins Pass, Golden Gate Canyon State Park, Central City-Blackhawk National Historic District, Golden, Coors Brewery, Eldorado Canyon State Park, Boulder Mountain Park, Mount Evans Wilderness Area, Mount Evans Highway.

Finding the crags: From downtown Boulder head west on Baseline Road or south on 9th Street. A half-block west of their intersection, at the mountain base, is Chatauqua Park. Park in designated lots here. Hike south 0.75 mile on closed Kinnikinic Road from the parking area to Bluebell Shelter and the road's end. To reach the First Flatiron, walk northwest on Bluebell Baird Trail a short distance to the marked First Flatiron Trail. Follow it west up a steepening ridge before cutting north to the base of the Flatiron's east face on a rough path. The trail continues west to the saddle between the First and Second Flatirons and is used for the descent.

The Third Flatiron Trail begins southwest of Bluebell Shelter. Follow the marked trail as it climbs steeply through forests and across boulder fields. Aim for the East Bench on the Flatiron's northeast flank, not the face's low point. Allow up to an hour to reach the Third Flatiron's base.

FIRST FLATIRON

The immense slab of the First Flatiron, the northernmost Flatiron face, perches on Green Mountain's northeast flank high over Boulder. This huge rock yields some of the Boulder area's longest routes—up to 1,000' and 10 pitches in length.

Descent: From the First Flatiron's summit rappel 100' (2 ropes are needed) to the west off a fixed eyebolt; rappel 25' west to a large ledge, scramble south 30' to another eyebolt; and rappel another 60' south to the ground. Or downclimb the *South Ridge* route, a tricky 5.0 route down ramps and ledges.

1. **North Arete** (5.4) This spectacular, easy line up the serrated north arete of the Flatiron is one of Boulder's "must-do" routes. It offers superb climbing with great views of the Continental Divide peaks to the northwest and of Boulder spread out below. This classic route, usually climbed in 6 pitches,

FIRST FLATIRON

traditionally starts on the ridge proper after scrambling around the rock's north flank. Climb onto the arete from the west and belay on a good stance. Continue up the ridgeline, surmounting several abrupt steps along the way. The second step yields the route's hardest move—a 5.5 pull onto the slab above. **Rack:** Carry a small rack of wires and Friends.

2. **Direct East Face** (5.6 R) One of Boulder's finest routes, this line scales the First Flatiron's 1,000' east face from its low point 10 pitches to the summit. Like most Flatiron routes, innumerable variations can draw the climber off-route. Pay attention and follow the obvious line. The first pitch is the hardest. The upper pitches follow the NORTH ARETE route from its second step crux. Begin at the Flatiron's lowest point. **Pitch 1** climbs up and right to a shallow corner past a bolt. Continue up on thin climbing to a belay at a flake. Scant protection is found on this sustained 5.6 friction pitch. **Pitch 2** angles up left to a belay ledge at a tree. **Pitch 3** climbs a 5.5 slab to an angling crack to a 2-bolt belay. **Pitches 4** and 5 ascend straight up the steepening headwall above on excellent holds. From the large ledge atop the headwall, **Pitch 6** angles up and left to a belay stance below an obvious chimney slot. **Pitch 7** stems the 5.5 slot and continues up a gully to the skyline ridge. Here the route joins the NORTH ARETE. **Rack:** Carry a small selection of wired nuts and Friends.

3. **Baker's Way** (5.4) This easy tour of the First Flatiron's east face begins about halfway up the face's southern margin below 2 small pine trees perched 40' above the ground. Climb the route's crux, the steep 5.4 wall to the trees, and follow a large right-angling ramp system for several pitches up and north to the NORTH ARETE route.

4. **South Ridge** (5.0) This short easy route to the crag's summit is often used as the descent route. Begin north of the col between the First and Second Flatirons and follow ramps and ledges north to the summit in 1 long pitch. It can be done in 2 pitches by belaying from the rappel eyebolt at 90'.

THIRD FLATIRON

The Third Flatiron, perched high over Boulder, is the area's most visible and most traveled crag. Its 1,300' east face, now only faintly scarred with giant CU letters, offers one of the nation's best easy rock climbs as well as more serious slab routes. The abrupt south and west faces, dropping sharply away from the summit, host excellent steep face climbs. The *East Face* route, the most popular climb in the Boulder area, is not a route to be taken casually. It's very committing, under-protected, treacherous when wet or snowy, difficult to retreat from, and generally busy. The descent, involving 3 rappels, is complicated and dangerous, particularly for beginners. Use caution and common sense, and carry proper clothing, water, and snacks.

The East Face is usually approached from Bluebell Shelter. The Third Flat-iron Trail begins southwest of the shelter. Follow the trail up a shallow draw, across a talus field, and up to the East Bench on the northeast corner of the Flatiron's East Face. The trail continues steeply up the crag's north face to the West Bench below the West Face and is used for the descent back to the parking lot.

Descent from the Third Flatiron's summit is by rappel only. 3 rappels with a single rope or 2 rappels with double ropes from fixed eyebolts lead to the ground. Large eyebolts with attached rappel directions offer safe anchors. **Rappel 1:** 40' over an overhang to the South Bowl. **Rappel 2:** 50' from the south edge of the bowl to Friday's Folly Ledge, a narrow, exposed ledge on a vertical face. Be sure to knot the end of your rope to ensure you do not rappel off its end. Traverse west from an eyebolt along the ledge to another eyebolt and the third rappel. **Rappel 3:** 70' west to the West Bench. Do not rappel from the first eyebolt on the ledge without double ropes—it's a 140' semi-free rappel to the ground from there.

5. **Extra Point** (5.7 R) Begin on the East Bench, a large ledge below the north-east ridge and some 300' above the East Face's low point. This 6-pitch route generally follows the right or north side of a large gully system and crosses the U of the painted CU logo. Begin by climbing up past a small tree and angling left to the gully edge. Continue up easy climbing along the gully's right side to a ledge system. Ascend up the middle of the painted U on runout 5.6 or 5.7 climbing, depending on the exact route taken. An-other pitch leads to the summit. **Rack:** Carry a small rack of stoppers and Friends.

6. **East Face** (5.4 R) This superb classic route wanders up the 50-degree face for 7 or 8 pitches. The route follows 6 large belay eyebolts that were placed in 1931 for guided parties. The first and last pitches are the hardest. Begin at the same place as EXTRA POINT. **Pitch 1** traverses up and left past a bolt, crosses the smooth water trough, and climbs a rib south of the gully to an eyebolt belay. **Pitch 2** continues straight up to a small belay stance at a flake. **Pitch 3** scales easy rock to an eyebolt and ledge; climbing left is 4th class, while right along the gully edge is 5.2. **Pitch 4** is easy 5.0 climbing to a 5th eyebolt below the C on the painted CU. **Pitch 5** moves up and across the C on easy rock to the last eyebolt just left of base of the Gash, a large chimney that splits the upper face. The standard finish (**Pitch 6**) climbs left of the Gash up steep, easy rock 100' to a belay. **Pitch 7** ascends another 100' to a belay atop a huge chockstone at the head of the Gash. Finally, **Pitch 8** crosses the Gash and climbs Desolation Flats, a friction face with runout easy rock, to the summit. The direct finish goes right of the Gash for 2 long pitches to the summit. The last belay is hard to find on this varia-tion. **Rack:** Carry a small rack with wired stoppers and small to medium Friends.

THIRD FLATIRON

3 rappels off back

.6R

.7R

8&9

7

6

5

descent trail

approach trail

7. **East Face Left** (5.5 R) This excellent route, the longest in the Boulder area and a good alternative when the EAST FACE route is busy, ascends the left edge of the East Face. Approach by hiking up the Royal Arch Trail from Bluebell Shelter 0.3 mile to Bluebell Canyon, then take a rough path up the canyon to the face's foot. The 10-pitch route begins at the bottom of the buttress. Climb up and right along a rib for a pitch. Above angle to ramps on the left side of the large overhang or climb directly over it via a 5.7 crack. Continue up another 5 pitches to the top of the Gash and finish up the regular EAST FACE route. Protection, as on most Flatiron slabs, is sparse and somewhat marginal. **Rack:** A small rack of wired stoppers and a few Friends should suffice.

8. **Friday's Folly** (5.8) A superb route on the backside of the Third Flatiron, this line climbs the crag's west face in 2 steep pitches. This sensational, exposed route, first climbed in 1950, ascends the vertical wall on almost perfect holds. Start on a ledge at the bottom of the third rappel near the rock's southwest corner. **Pitch 1** climbs up, steps onto the airy south face, and follows a crack. Swing over a roof on good holds, and continue on flakes to Friday's Folly Ledge. Rappel here or do a good 5.7 pitch up to the South Bowl.

9. **Saturday's Folly** (5.8+) A steep 1-pitch route that begins just left of FRIDAY'S FOLLY. Follow a pin-scarred crack up and right to a right-facing dihedral. Belay on the west end of FRIDAY'S FOLLY Ledge.

ELDORADO CANYON STATE PARK

OVERVIEW

Eldorado Canyon is an awesome gash sliced into Colorado's Front Range by South Boulder Creek as it races from its snowy Continental Divide origins to the high plains south of Boulder. The spectacular canyon, one of the few west of Denver without a highway, is flanked by soaring, angular sandstone cliffs that range in hue from gold and rust to ebony and gray. The tall cliffs are broken by ramps and ledges, seamed by cracks, beetled with overhangs, and laced with vertical climber's trails. Eldorado Canyon, preserved as a Colorado State Park, is a rock climber's paradise with hundreds of routes edging up its famed crags, including the Redgarden Wall, The Bastille, Wind Tower, Rincon Wall, and the West Ridge.

The canyon's vertical landscape is eroded out of the Fountain Formation, a thick 300-million-year-old rock layer of sandstone, siltstone, and conglomerate deposited along the eastern edge of the Ancestral Rocky Mountains. Some 65 million years ago, as today's Rockies lifted, the formation was dragged and tilted upward along the fringe of the rising uplift. Water erosion quickly attacked the sandstone, stripping away softer layers and excavating the impressive canyon and today's stunning rock topography.

This rock landscape attracts climbers. Eldorado, one of Colorado's oldest technical climbing areas, is, along with Yosemite National Park in California and the Shawangunks in New York, one of the top three areas in the United States. Climbers flock here every year from all over the globe to test their skill and nerve on almost 600 climbing routes. Almost 75 percent of the state park's annual visitors are climbers.

Climbing history: Eldorado Canyon's cliffs tell the story of modern Colorado rock climbing. This small area, explored by a strong Boulder climbing community, has long pushed standards and styles as well as provided testpieces for each generation to prove themselves on. The canyon's first landmark ascents were the first ascent of *Redguard* on the Redgarden Wall in 1956 and the first free ascent of *Bastille Crack* on The Bastille in 1957. The year 1957 also saw the emergence of Layton Kor, a tall, gangly Boulder bricklayer who became the dominant figure not only in Eldorado but in Colorado climbing in the next decade. Kor, in only his second year of climbing, made the first ascent of *The Bulge*, a devious 5.7 face route on the east side of Redgarden Wall. Afterwards Kor embarked on an inexhaustible search for first ascents in Eldo, putting up almost all of the canyon classics over the ensuing years including *T2*, *Anthill Direct*, *Grand Giraffe*, *The Naked Edge*, *Psycho*, *Rosy Crucifixion*, *Ruper*, *The Yellow Spur*, *Outer Space*, and *The Northwest Corner* and *West Buttress of The Bastille*.

Other climbers also participated in this orgy of new routes. Ray Northcutt

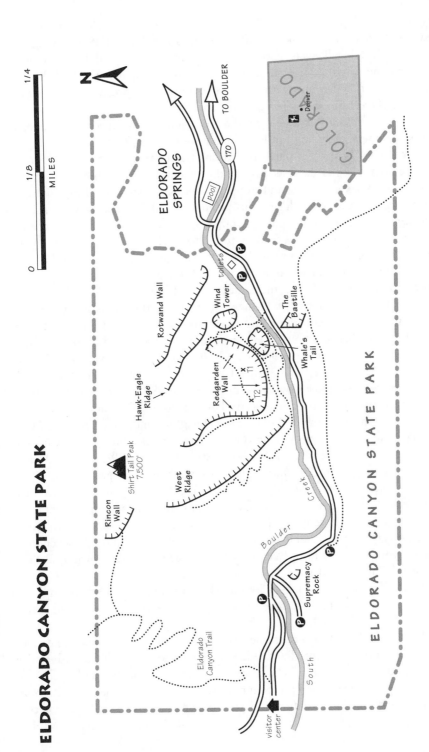

ELDORADO CANYON STATE PARK

N

MILES

0   1/8   1/4

TO BOULDER

170

ELDORADO SPRINGS

Pool

COLORADO

Denver

toilets

Rotwand Wall

Wind Tower

The Bastille

Whale's Tail

Hawk-Eagle Ridge

Redgarden Wall

×T1

×T2

Shirt Tail Peak 7,500'

West Ridge

Rincon Wall

ELDORADO CANYON STATE PARK

Boulder Creek

Supremacy Rock

South

Eldorado Canyon Trail

visitor center

established the canyon's first 5.10 with his ascent of the *Northcutt Start* to the Bastille Crack. Larry Dalke and Pat Ament, apprentices to Kor, put up their own testpieces. Dalke was renowned for his dicey aid lines, while Ament began pushing the canyon's free standards. In 1966 Ament firmly established the canyon's first 5.11 routes with free ascents of overhanging *Supremacy Crack, The Northwest Corner of The Bastille,* and *Vertigo.*

As the 1960s closed, a new band of rock junkies swarmed onto the scene. These climbers, including Jim Erickson, Steve Wunsch, Duncan Ferguson, and Roger Briggs, brought a pure ground-up style of free climbing to Eldorado. They eschewed bolts and fixed protection whenever possible, relying instead on new-fangled hexentric nuts and stoppers to protect their severe free routes. Jim Erickson, the trailblazer during this prolific period, brought new intensity to the scene by free-climbing old aid routes up the canyon's overhanging walls. *Tagger* on Wind Tower was the first to fall to Erickson in 1968. The following year he freed *Grandmother's Challenge,* with its strenuous layback, and *Rincon.* In 1971 Erickson and Duncan Ferguson made the pivotal first free ascent of the spectacular *Naked Edge* up the center prow of Redgarden Wall. This superb route with three 5.11 pitches brought the realm of the impossible to the possible and opened a new era of hard free climbs in Eldorado Canyon. Through the 1970s climbers continued to convert numerous scary aid routes into modern free climbs, including *Guenese, Kloeberdanz, Jules Verne, The Wisdom, Psycho* (Eldorado's first 5.12), *Cinch Crack,* and Jim Collins' ascent of Genesis.

The torch passed to a new bunch by the early 1980s, a group that continued freeing the canyon's old aid lines as well as establishing dramatic new and difficult routes on both new and old crags. This group included Jeff Achey, Chip Chace, Bob Horan, Skip Guerin, Charlie Fowler, Alec Sharp, and Christian Griffith. Notable ascents were Achey's 1980, 5.12 leads of *Wendego* and *Salvation;* Horan's ascent of *Rainbow Wall,* the canyon's first 5.13 pitch; and Griffith's 5.13 testpieces *Desdichado* and *Lakme.* In the 1990s few new routes remain for the next generation. Eldorado Canyon has reached a saturation point and is considered almost totally developed. The few new routes going up are mostly variations to already established lines, and, of course, a bolting restriction on the canyon cliffs has forced climbers to look at other areas such as Rifle to pursue the upper grades.

Descent from some routes is by rappel. Most rappels can be accomplished with a single rope, but it's sometimes convenient to make a long double-rope rappel. Plan accordingly.

Rack: Eldo's vertical sandstone walls offer a unique climbing experience. The steep cliffs are featured with edges and incut holds that allow for technical and devious face climbing. The crack systems tend to be thin and discontinuous, but yield lots of good protection possibilities. Most of the canyon's routes were first climbed in a traditional style. Some newer routes are bolt-protected.

Many of the older classic routes still sport ancient bolts and pitons for protection and belay/rappel anchors. Most of these are being replaced with modern gear. Use any old bolts or fixed pro with caution and back them up whenever possible. Most Eldorado classic climbs require a standard rack that includes sets of RPs, wired stoppers, and Friends to 3 inches, as well as a few medium hexes or Tri-cams, six to ten quick draws, a few long runners, and a few free carabiners. Use a 165-foot rope.

As a state parkland, Eldorado Canyon is subject to a number of regulations to control the crowds and protect the environment. These regulations include: stay on trails to reduce erosion; keep your pets on a leash and under control at all times; no camping or leaving a vehicle overnight; fires only in designated areas; mountain biking is restricted to specific trails only; motor vehicles must remain on roads; do not gather or collect wood or rocks; do not carry or discharge firearms; and no bolting without permission. The state park uses a permit system administered by the Fixed Hardware Review Committee to approve or deny new routes and the replacement of old bolts. Besides the bolting restriction, the regulation that most applies to climbers is to stay on trails. The greatest impact climbers have on the canyon is caused by walking to and from their chosen route. Vegetation is damaged and trampled along the way, and trail-cutting leads to erosion.

Numerous objective dangers exist in the park. The sheer number of climbers that use the park ensure that accidents will happen. Pay attention to yourself, your party, and others to avoid problems and mitigate hazards. Rockfall from parties above is one of the greatest causes of accidents. Try to avoid climbing beneath another party. While much of the canyon's rock is sound, loose boulders can be dislodged. Even a small pebble can be fatal. Wear a hard-hat whenever possible to protect yourself. It's not always cool-looking, but it might save your life. Place enough good protection to stop you in case of a fall and don't rely totally on old fixed pitons or bolts. Back them up whenever possible. Remember that you're not off the route until you're back on the ground. Use care when rappelling and on the cliff descents. Several fatalities have occurred on the Redgarden Wall's descent slabs. Watch the descent when it's wet or dark out. Watch for severe summer thunderstorms and lightning strikes. Keep an eye on the weather and retreat during storms. Keep off high points to avoid lightning. Ticks are found in the springtime. Rattlesnakes live on the talus slopes and are active in summer and fall. Use caution on approaches and descents, and watch where you put your hands and feet.

Besides climbing, other activities at Eldorado Canyon State Park include hiking, fishing, and nature study. The park's visitor center dispenses information and sells books and maps. Eldorado Springs Resort, just east of the park boundary, offers swimming in its large pool during the hot summer months. A couple of climbing shops and guide services are located in Eldorado Springs.

Pete Williams stems across the airy first pitch of *Rosy Crucifixion* on Redgarden Wall in Eldorado Canyon. *Photo by Peter Gallagher.*

Besides the routes described here, popular and hard sport lines include *The Web* (5.13b) and *Supremacy Crack* (5.11b) on Supremacy Rock; *Captain Crunch* (5.13b), *White Lies* (5.13a), *Wasabe* (5.12b/c), and *Paris Girl* (5.13a R) on Redgarden Wall; *The Monument* (5.12d/.13a) on Whales Tail; and *Lips Like Sugar* (5.12b/c) on Hawk-Eagle Ridge. Other good canyon crags not included here are lofty and peaceful Rincon Wall with its mega-classic routes like *Wendego* (5.12a/b), *Rincon* (5.11a/b), and *Climb of the Century* (5.11b/c), and The Upper and Lower Peanuts Walls on the canyon's south side. Route descriptions, topos, and directions to these and other cliffs are found in the comprehensive *Boulder Climbs South* guidebook.

Trip Planning Information

General description: One of Colorado's oldest, finest, and most developed climbing areas offers numerous excellent routes of all grades and lengths on colorful sandstone crags.

Location: 7 miles southwest of Boulder.

Camping: No camping is allowed in the canyon or state park. There is no public camping available in the immediate Boulder area. Several private campgrounds are in Boulder. The nearest Roosevelt National Forest campgrounds are 46-site Kelly Dahl Campground south of Nederland on Colorado Highway 119 and 55-site Pawnee Campground at Brainard Lake north of Nederland off Colorado 72. Golden Gate Canyon State Park, southwest of Nederland, offers several excellent high-elevation campgrounds off CO 119.

Climbing season: Year-round. Winters can be cold, especially on the cliffs on the south side of the canyon, but long mild spells offer superb climbing weather. High winds occur in the canyon in winter and spring. Summer days are often very hot, with highs reaching the upper 90s. Heavy thunderstorms regularly occur on summer afternoons. Autumn offers some of the best weather with clear, warm days and cool nights.

Restrictions and access issues: A bolting restriction is in effect. A $3 daily fee is charged to enter and use the park. Annual passes are available. (See the Overview section for other regulations.)

Guidebooks: *Boulder Climbs South* by Richard Rossiter, Chockstone Press, 1989, is a comprehensive and excellent guide to Eldorado Canyon and its environs. *Best of Boulder Climbs* by Richard Rossiter, Chockstone Press, 1992, details most of the canyon's best routes with topos and brief descriptions.

Nearby mountain shops, guide services, and gyms: Basecamp Mountain Sports, Boulder Mountaineer, Mountain Sports, Neptune Mountaineering, Boulder Rock Club (Boulder); Naked Edge Mountaineering, Bob Culp Climbing School, International Alpine School (Eldorado Springs).

Services: All services, including groceries, dining, and lodging, in Boulder.

Emergency services: Call 911. Boulder Community Hospital, N. Broadway and Balsam, Boulder, CO 80301, (303) 440-2273. Memorial Hospital Boulder, 311 Mapleton Ave., Boulder, CO 80302, (303) 443-0230.

Nearby climbing areas: Flagstaff Mountain, the Flatirons and Green Mountain, Boulder Canyon, Mickey Mouse Wall, Clear Creek Canyon, Golden Gate Canyon State Park, North Table Mountain, Morrison, Rocky Mountain National Park, Lumpy Ridge, St. Vrain Canyon, Button Rock Reservoir, Combat Rock.

Nearby attractions: Rocky Mountain National Park, Longs Peak, Trail Ridge Road, Indian Peaks Wilderness Area, Rollins Pass, Golden Gate Canyon State Park, Central City-Blackhawk National Historic District, Golden, Coors Brewery, Eldorado Canyon State Park, Boulder Mountain Park, Mount Evans Wilderness Area, Mount Evans Highway.

Finding the canyon: Drive south from Boulder or north from Golden on Colorado 93 (Broadway Avenue, in Boulder) to Colorado 170. Drive 3 miles west on CO 170 to the town of Eldorado Springs. The canyon entrance lies on the west side of town. A park entrance station sits at the entrance. Pay your daily fee here. Parking is found in several lots just up the road from the station. The parking lots can be full on summer and autumn days, especially on weekends. Arrive early to ensure you're allowed to enter the park. Continue up the road to the far west end of the canyon to the park's visitor center and the Eldorado Canyon Trailhead. A network of climber access trails wind around the inner canyon, making approaches relatively easy. Stay on the trails to reduce erosion.

WIND TOWER

Wind Tower, a 300' pyramid-shaped crag sitting directly north of the canyon's lower parking area, offers an excellent selection of multi-pitch routes up its vertical south and slabby west faces. The popular moderate routes on the west face—*Calypso, Recon,* and *West Ridge*—are the most well-traveled lines in the entire canyon. Indeed, *West Ridge* is often said to be the most climbed route in all Colorado. It's a rare day that sees no traffic on these trade routes. Queues often form at the route starts. The west face routes are generally well-protected slabs, while the south face offers hard, vertical, poorly protected routes. Beware of climbing beneath another party, especially on the west face. Much loose rock is found on the upper reaches of the tower and is often dislodged by careless climbers.

Approach Wind Tower by crossing the plank footbridge across South Boulder Creek just west of the parking area. A path runs east along the base of the south face. Another path branches up and right from the bridge and accesses the west face. **Descent** from the top of Wind Tower is best accomplished by scrambling northeast from the summit over broken ledges and slabs to a sharp notch. A short single-rope rappel from double bolt anchors leads to a talus slope. This section can also be down-climbed (5.4). The descent trail from Redgarden Wall is followed from the base of the rappel down the gully on the west side of Wind Tower.

1. **The Yellow Traverse** and **Metamorphosis** (5.9+ R) The 1-pitch YELLOW TRAVERSE (5.9-) coupled with METAMORPHOSIS yields a superb line up the south face. Follow the path along the base of the south face to a left-angling ramp that begins near the southeast corner. Scramble up the ramp (3rd class) about 100' to a belay stance atop a V-shaped pedestal. Rope up here. For THE YELLOW TRAVERSE work down and left from the belay to a small ledge. Traverse up left from here (5.9-) below a black groove on poorly protected rock to a belay ledge at a small tree. **Pitch 2** (METAMOR-PHOSIS) heads up vertical rock right from the belay. Work into a left-facing corner (5.9+), then up left past an old 2-bolt belay. Continue up right past another bolt and past a 5.9+ flake. A 5.9 bulge above leads to a left-leaning ramp to a ledge belay with a bolt atop the face.

2. **Rainbow Wall** (5.13a) A difficult face pitch that saw many attempts before Bob Horan's 1984 success. The route scales a beautiful rainbow-tinted, vertical wall left of a steep, right-leaning ramp on the lower south face. The route begins by scrambling up the ramp and working up left (5.9) to the 1st bolt. Continue up and left on increasingly harder climbing to a devious crux past the 4th bolt. Easier climbing leads to the southwest ridge and a belay stance. **Rack:** Bring some nuts and a #1 Friend for pro to the first bolt.

3. **Recon** (5.4) This line, one of the earliest routes up Wind Tower, follows an obvious crack system up the right side of the west face. Begin below an obvious crack/groove. Climb a shallow left-facing corner to a crack (5.4) and belay on a wide ledge after 140'. Many possibilities exist for **Pitch 2.** The best for beginners is to move a few feet left to the base of a chimney. Climb the chimney (5.4) and belay on a ledge. **Pitch 3** works onto the loose south ridge (5.4) and up to the summit.

4. **Calypso** (5.6) A superb and popular route for moderate leaders. Begin just left of a huge block at the base of the west face. Chimney up behind the boulder (5.6), or better yet, traverse in from the left (5.5) into the large, right-facing dihedral above. Fun climbing up the corner leads to a roof, lieback up and right (5.6) to a ledge. Step down a few feet to a double-bolt belay. **Pitch 2** goes up left via a thin 20' crack (5.6). Climb easier rock above to a belay ledge. **Pitch 3** goes right into a corner (5.5) and then up left to the summit.

5. **Reggae** (5.8) A great but harder 2nd pitch for CALYPSO. Climb the 1st pitch of CALYPSO to the bolted belay. Go right a few feet to the base of a

prominent right-facing dihedral. Climb the dihedral to a 5.8 finger crack on the left side of a large flake near its top and work right to a belay ledge above the large roof that caps the dihedral. Continue to the summit on easy rock.

6. **Salvation** (5.12a R) A serious route first freed by Jeff Achey in 1980. Begin left of the huge block below a slab and roof. Edge up the 5.10 runout slab to the underneath right side of ceiling. Use RPs in opposition to protect 5.11d moves left to a bolt on the roof. Get an undercling in the roof, lunge out to the lip holds, and mantle over. Belay and rappel 75' from bolt anchors above.

7. **Tagger** (5.10b/c R) An Eldorado classic with a scary 1st pitch that is difficult to protect since all of the old fixed pitons have disappeared. Begin uphill from the block below the left side of the SALVATION roof. **Pitch 1** follows the obvious chalked lieback crack up and left around the edge of the roof (a couple 5.9 spots) to an easy crack. Belay at the tree above. **Pitch 2** (short and easy) goes up left to a stance below a large right-facing dihedral. **Pitch 3** climbs the dihedral (5.6) to the obvious roof that caps it. Work out left on the edge of the roof (5.10b/c) to the lip, swing over, and continue up a shallow corner to a good ledge. Follow the ledge left to traverse off or do a short easy pitch to the summit. **Rack:** Bring wired nuts for the 1st pitch.

8. **Wind Ridge** (5.6 or 5.8-) The canyon's mega-classic moderate route was, of course, first climbed by Layton Kor in 1959. The line roughly follows the left skyline ridge of the west face. Scramble up to a ledge with a tree directly below the ridge. **Pitch 1** offers a couple of options. The easy way goes left up a ramp (5.6) before traversing back right onto the ridge. The better way is to surmount a large flake above the ledge (some 5.8- moves) and head straight up the ridge itself. Continue up the ridge on moderate rock to a good ledge. **Pitch 2** steps right on a narrow ledge to a fun crack (5.5). Follow the crack, some 5.6 hand-jamming up high, to another ledge. It's possible to traverse left here on the ledge to get off. **Pitch 3** swings over a roof on a flake (5.6), climbs easy rock past a large tree, and belays on a ledge left of the summit. Scramble northeast to the descent rappel.

REDGARDEN WALL

The Redgarden Wall, reaching heights of 700', dominates Eldorado Canyon. The complex crag is broken by angling ramps; featured with sharp aretes, steep slabs, bands of roofs, and vertical walls; and topped by several distinctive sharp summits. The wall, with many routes that range from 1 to 8 pitches long, offers superlative climbing with good protection and lots of exposure. Pat Ament writes in his guidebook *High Over Boulder*, "The Redgarden Wall is a graceful rock with some of Colorado's most imaginative routes."

Approach the Redgarden Wall by crossing the footbridge over the creek and turning left or west on Streamside Trail below The Whale's Tail. At the concrete slab on the far side of The Whale's Tail, turn right or north and scramble up a boulder field to the base of the wall below *C'est La Vie*. A good climber's trail follows the base of the wall west from here, providing access to the roof routes, the routes above the Lower Ramp, and the west flank of the crag. The west face is also reached by walking upstream or west on Streamside Trail past The Whale's Tail. An access trail begins just past a low buttress below the Lower Ramp and winds uphill to the face. Keep on the trails and don't cut switchbacks. Severe erosion occurred before the trails were constructed in the early 1990s.

Descent: The descent routes can be difficult to find. The East Slabs Descent is the easiest and most common route down from the summits of Redgarden Wall. Work east and southeast down steep gullies below the notches between the summits and onto the east-sloping slabs. Carefully drop eastward down the slabs via grooves and cracks into a narrow wooded gully. Downclimbing is necessary in places, particularly if you lose the easier route. Eventually drop into a broad, boulder-choked gully that swings southeast between Hawk-Eagle Ridge and the Redgarden Wall's east slabs. Follow a trail down the gully past Wind Tower to the creek. This descent is very dangerous in the dark or when wet. Use extreme caution and rope up if necessary. Fatalities have occurred on the descent. A common descent from the Upper Ramp makes 2 rappels from bolted anchors below *The Naked Edge*. Descend the ramp to its eastern base and traverse east around a corner to a bolted belay/rappel ledge below *The Naked Edge*. Rappel 75' from here to another bolted rappel anchor. Rappel 150' from here to the ground, or make 2, 75' rappels using the anchors at the end of T2's 1st pitch.

9. **C'est La Vie** (5.11a/b) A brilliant 2-pitch route up the lower right side of the south face. Many parties only climb the great 1st pitch and rap off. Some like to set up a toprope for a large party and hog the route for hours. Begin below an immense right-angling dihedral almost directly north of the concrete slab by The Whale's Tail. **Pitch 1** begins on a broken ledge above the wall base. Climb up a shallow corner to a flake. Step right (5.9) and lieback up an obvious left-facing flake to a V-shaped notch. Swing over the notch (5.8) and work up left across a 5.9- slab to a double-bolt belay. **Pitch 2** edges up thin holds in the large dihedral to a 2-move crux (5.11b) and past a couple of fixed pins. Exit right to a small belay stance. **Descent:** Rappel with double ropes from anchors 150' to the ground.

10. **Desdichado** (5.13b/c) An extreme bolt-protected Christian Griffith route. Climb C'EST LA VIE'S 1st pitch. Continue up through the .11c crux and then head out across the severely overhanging headwall past 4 bolts. Swing over the roof lip (5.12a) and belay above from 3 bolts. **Descent:** Rappel 165' or back clean down to the belay.

11. **Pansee Savage** (5.11b R) A good face climbing pitch for the confident leader, but somewhat runout. Begin left of C'EST LA VIE partway up a left-angling ramp. Climb straight up the face past 3 bolts and 3 cruxes to the C'EST LA VIE belay. **Descent:** Rappel 80'.

12. **Genesis (5.12d)** This excellent route, one of Eldorado's best hard climbs, was an old A4 horror show before Jim Collins freed it in 1979 after many attempts. Begin atop some boulders on a leaning ramp left of C'EST LA VIE. **Pitch 1** follows a thin, left-facing corner (5.8) to an A-shaped roof; exit left with awkward 5.10d moves. Edge up a steep slab (5.11a) past some bolts to a left-facing expando flake (5.9). A belay, rappel, or lower-off

can be set up off 2 bolts above the flake. Otherwise continue up the red headwall on small holds (5.12d) past 1 bolt to the big roof; traverse right to a double-bolt belay. Most parties rap 110' here. A 2nd pitch heads up corners to the right (5.9) to a ledge.

13. **Anthill Direct** (5.9 R) THE ANTHILL DIRECT, first ascended by Layton Kor and Rick Tidrick in 1961, is one of Eldorado's enduring classic climbs. The route, generally done in 5 pitches, offers varied and interesting climbing, some intricate route finding, and is somewhat runout in spots. The 1st pitch is the least interesting lead. A better start is TOUCH AND GO around the corner to the west. Begin left of GENESIS below a left-angling black ramp. **Pitch 1** follows the narrow, black ramp up left to a loose roof; traverse left and work up to a bulging 5.8 corner. Continue up the easy ramp to a bolted belay ledge; a long lead. **Pitch 2** climbs up right onto a pretty slab (5.4), heads up to a crack (5.6), and pulls over an obvious, exposed overhang (5.8) to a good belay on a ledge. **Pitch 3** is fairly short. Head diagonally left up a runout black 5.6 slab to a ledge belay. **Pitch 4** climbs up right on 5.5 rock to a thin, right-facing corner. Climb a fun, vertical 5.5 crack and angle left to a belay stance below a bulge. **Pitch 5** heads up right under the bulge to a dihedral. Lieback up a steep crack (5.9) in the dihedral to easier rock and a belay platform atop the South Buttress. Head northwest across easy slabs above the wall to the East Slabs Descent.

14. **Redguard** (5.8 R) This 5-pitch classic, the first to ascend the wall, gives some good, exposed climbing but is somewhat loose in places and slightly runout. It's not quite as good as ANTHILL DIRECT, but still worth doing. The route begins by boulders behind some trees and left of ANTHILL DIRECT. **Pitch 1**, the technical crux, climbs up left on sloping rock (5.8+) and back right up a crack in a corner (5.8-). Traverse left 20' at the top to a spacious platform with 2 bolts. This 85' pitch is dicey in spots with marginal pro, especially if the fixed pins are gone. Several serious falls have occurred here—proceed with caution. **Pitch 2** heads right up an easy crack to a left-angling groove/ramp. Head up the ramp to a double bolt belay (first belay on ANTHILL DIRECT). **Pitch 3** liebacks up right into a huge black dihedral. Stem and layback up the dihedral using its left wall to a narrow stance on the left. **Pitch 4** goes left up a thin ramp (5.4) for a long lead to a belay niche. **Pitch 5** continues up the ramp system (5.4) for another long pitch to a cave belay. **Pitch 6** is intimidating. Work right up a vertical wall (5.7) to a ledge. Climb back left into a groove, go out the left edge of a massive chockstone, and belay above. **Descend** by scrambling northeast onto the East Slabs and working down and left into a gully.

15. **Touch and Go** (5.9) A superb and popular 1-pitch line that makes a great start to REDGUARD and ANTHILL DIRECT. It's climbed so much the holds are getting polished. Begin around a corner and uphill from

REDGUARD below a thin, slanted roof. Climb under the roof and out left up flakes (5.9) into a short, left-facing corner. Work above into an upside-down V-slot and up a good 5.7 finger crack to a sloping ramp and an alternate belay/rap station with 2 bolts. Traverse left to an excellent right-facing corner. Jam, lieback, and stem up the corner (5.8) to a ledge with 2 bolts. Rappel 125' with double ropes to the ground from here or continue up to REDGUARD, ANTHILL DIRECT, or THE NAKED EDGE.

16. **Bolting For Glory** (5.10a) A great variation to TOUCH AND GO. At the sloping, incut ramp halfway up TOUCH AND GO, edge directly up a steep slab on pebbles and edges (5.10a) past 3 bolts. Work left past the 3rd bolt to another bolt and the double-bolt belay ledge. **Descent:** Rap with 2 ropes to the ground.

17. **The Naked Edge** (5.11b) This famous route offers everything a great rock climb should have: lots of exposure, superb position, hard climbing, and a direct line. The Edge was first climbed by Layton Kor and Bob Culp in 1962, and finally freed by Jim Erickson and Duncan Ferguson in 1971. It's been free-soloed by Derek Hersey and Jim Collins, and climbed naked. To reach the start, climb TOUCH AND GO to its belay ledge and then work left up a sloping ramp to a bolted, sloping belay ledge directly below the Edge. **Pitch 1** jams and stems up a thin finger crack just right of the edge (5.11a) 75' to a stance with 2 bolts. **Pitch 2** is both spectacular and unnerving. Face climb the left side of a slab above the belay (some fixed pro) to a leaning roof. Traverse left around the edge (5.9) and jam a thin crack (5.10b) to an exposed stance. **Pitch 3** follows the edge (5.6) to a niche, steps right to an awkward 5.8 mantle, and works up and right to a sloping ledge beneath an overhung chimney. **Pitch 4** heads up strenuous cracks and corners (5.11a) to the top of the chimney slot. Exit over the roof capping the slot (5.10c) to a small broken ledge. **Pitch 5** continues up a shallow, continuous corner (5.11a) to the right side of the hanging prow. Jam or lieback a strenuous, overhanging hand and fist crack (5.10d) to a small stance on the right. **Pitch 6** climbs up and left around the arete and up easy slabs to the summit. **Descent:** Scramble northeast to the descent route. **Rack:** Bring a rack with lots of finger-sized pro including RPs and wired stoppers, and Friends to #4.

18. **T2** (5.10d) Another true Eldorado classic free route. The starting hard bouldery moves are out of character with the rest of T2. Start uphill from TOUCH AND GO beneath a long roof with a drilled piton above it. **Pitch 1** pulls over the roof on strenuous flakes (5.10d) to a fixed piton. Leaders should be confident; otherwise use a shoulder stand or stick-clip the pin. Climb up right on steep but moderate rock (a spot of 5.8) to a bolted belay on a left-angling ramp. **Pitch 2** starts a few feet west up the ramp and follows a shallow, grungy chimney (5.8) to a stance in a slot cave. **Pitch 3**

works diagonally left onto the right side of the Upper Ramp. This short pitch can be combined with Pitch 2 for a long lead. **Pitch 4** begins about 75' west up the ramp below a shallow black gully. Climb up the grooved gully (5.8) to a narrow shelf 60' up. A scary 5.8 traverse goes left to an excellent 5.9 finger crack that arcs up and left. Belay on a small stance in the crack. **Pitch 5** angles left up the widening crack to a huge right-facing dihedral. Climb the ramp/slab on the right side of the dihedral (5.7) to an airy belay below a large roof. **Pitch 6** climbs left out the overhanging side of the dihedral (5.9 R) along a rotten red band with bad fall potential. Belay up left on a groove/ramp above. **Pitches 7** and **8** follow the left-ascending groove/ramp to a large tree in the saddle west of Tower 2. **Descend** northeast onto the East Slabs.

19. **Kloeberdanz** (5.11a R) A swinging route usually done as 1 pitch. Begin uphill from T2 below a double roof. Climb straight up a broken red corner (5.8 and protected by 1 upward-driven peg). Go right past a good bolt and swing over the roof on jugs (5.11a but harder for short folks), and continue right to a hanging belay. Rappel 75' to the ground or continue up a 2nd pitch on 5.10 R climbing.

20. **Guenese** (5.11a) One of the easier roof routes. Begin uphill from KLOEBERDANZ below some down-hanging flakes. Traverse up and right along the flakes using liebacks and underclings to a small roof. Climb straight up (5.11a) to a sucker rest under the roof. Many parties lower here. Best to continue by pulling over the roof on a jug (5.11a) and following a shallow corner up right to a bolted stance. Rappel 80' to the ground or do **Pitch 2** up left on runout 5.8 climbing to the Upper Ramp. Mark Rolofson's super classic 1-pitch DOWNPRESSOR MAN (5.12a/b) begins partway up the lower traverse. Work straight up past 2 bolts to FIRE AND ICE'S belay.

21. **Fire and Ice** (5.12a) An old Pat Ament aid route that's now a thin, technical face climb. Start just uphill from GUENESE. Devious face climbing diagonals right past 3 bolts to a belay under the roof. Lower or rappel to the ground. The roof above goes at 5.11d with runout 5.10 climbing above to a Friend placement.

22. **Psycho** (5.12d) A scary Kor aid route that's now a classic free line with 4 short pitches to alleviate rope drag. Begin uphill from FIRE AND ICE beneath the right end of a low roof band. **Pitch 1** climbs up and right through shallow corners (5.11a up high) to a belay under the roof. **Pitch 2** offers desperate free climbing (5.12d) or an A1 bolt ladder across the wide roof to a hanging belay in a crescent corner directly above. Rap 100' with double ropes from here or do the last 2 excellent pitches. Continue Pitch 2 by traversing left above the lip of the roof (5.8+) to a bolted stance; move up right on runout 5.8 face climbing, then work up left into a shallow corner

and a belay. **Pitch 3** traverses right on 5.7 rock to a diagonaling groove. Belay at the top of the groove up left beneath a large overhang. **Pitch 4** crosses the famed Psycho Slab. Traverse up right to a bolt and onto the smooth slab. Some dicey 5.9 climbing heads up and right to easier rock and the Upper Ramp.

23. **Temporary Like Achilles** (5.10c A1) **Pitch 1** begins west of PSYCHO below the left side of the lower roof band. Boulder up a flake (5.10c) to a rotten rock band, traverse up left below the roof, and climb straight up good rock (5.9) past 3 bolts to a 2-bolt anchor. Another start, 5.11a/b, begins left of the flake. Follow a left-angling RP crack to roof. Climb the route by heading up a crack and face to rotten band. Rap 75' to ground. **Pitch 2** aids over the large roof on bolts to a 2-bolt belay. **Pitch 3** ascends Hands in the Clouds (5.12a). Climb steep rock past 2 bolts to a thin roof with a bolt. Pull over and work up and right past another bolt to the belay stance next to Psycho Slab. Finish with the last pitch of PSYCHO.

24. **Rosy Crucifixion** (5.10a) A must-do Kor classic with great climbing and airy situations. The circuitous route is done in 4 short pitches. A fair amount of old fixed pro is found on the route. Begin by scrambling up the Lower Ramp, the wide low-angle 3rd-class ramp west of the roof routes. From the top of the ramp, chimney behind a large block to a short corner to a narrow angling ramp and a belay shelf. **Pitch 1** traverses straight right (5.10a) above a large roof past 4 bolts/pins to an airy belay in a corner. **Pitch 2** follows a crack system (5.9+) 45' to a bolted belay. Pitches 1 and 2 can be combined. **Pitch 3** goes straight up 40' and then does a tricky downward traverse (5.9) to the right and ends on a good ledge with a tree. **Pitch 4** climbs straight up easy rock to the Upper Ramp. **Descent:** Do 2 rappels from the base of THE NAKED EDGE to the ground.

25. **Ruper** (5.8) A brilliant route that climbs the wall in 6 interesting pitches. Many parties only climb the first 3 leads and rap off. Scramble up the Lower Ramp and set up a belay on a ledge above a large boulder at the top of the ramp. **Pitch 1** climbs cracks and corners (5.8) above the ramp to a good ledge. **Pitch 2** traverses right about 20' to the base of the infamous Ruper Crack. Struggle up the off-size 5" crack (5.8) for 75' and then step up right to a good ledge. Bring some large Camalots or Friends for pro. **Pitch 3**, the exposed Ruper Traverse, is a classic Eldo pitch. Traverse right from the ledge across a series of shallow corners (5.7) to a moderate left-facing corner that leads to the Upper Ramp. Belay from a tree. Make 2 rappels from the ledge below THE NAKED EDGE or continue up the last 3 leads. **Pitch 4** is reached by hiking down the ramp to the right side of a large scooped cave. Belay by a large boulder. The pitch goes up a left-facing corner (5.6) and works left up a vertical wall (5.8) 25', then diagonals right into the corner again. Continue up the steep 5.6 corner to a scanty belay

ledge atop a flake. This long pitch is somewhat unprotected. **Pitch 5** heads straight up the corner above (5.6) for almost 100'. Belay on a stance beneath a large red roof. **Pitch 6** traverses up left (5.8) past old fixed pitons and hand traverses under the roof to its left side. Diagonal up left on easier rock to a large tree in a saddle. **Descend** northeast to the slabs.

26. **Grand Giraffe** (5.10a) Another superb Eldo classic put up by Layton Kor and George Hurley in 1960. Hurley later wrote, "The name we gave our new route, The Grand Giraffe, was a take-off on the Grand Jorasses and a way of debunking ourselves and our efforts in a canyon in the foothills of the gentle Rockies." Begin atop the Lower Ramp at the start of RUPER. **Pitch 1** follows the same first lead of RUPER up easy corners to a belay alcove below an overhanging flake. **Pitch 2** moves diagonally up left on a steep wall to a leaning crack. Climb the crack (5.8+) to a good belay ledge. **Pitch 3** ascends an easy groove straight up to a shallow right-facing corner. Belay in a niche below the obvious off-width crack over the left side of a long roof. **Pitch 4** thrutches up the off-width (left side in) to a strenuous bulge (5.10a) and belays above on the Upper Ramp. Bring some large pro for this pitch. **Pitch 5** begins on the north side of the ramp on the left edge of a large, arcing cave. Climb straight up vertical 5.6 rock 80', traverse a line of holds right, and then move up to a belay stance with a bolt. **Pitch 6** diagonals up left on 5.6 rock 20', then angles right on jugs for another 100' to the saddle above. **Descend** northeast to the East Slabs.

27. **Super Slab** (5.10dR) A spectacular and intimidating classic route up the colorful slab left of GRAND GIRAFFE'S off-width pitch. To find the start go west on an angling ledge from the top of the Lower Ramp past a tree. Look for a line of old fixed pitons on the steep wall above. **Pitch 1** climbs the vertical face past the fixed pins and over a 5.10c undercling flake. Above work left into a shallow corner, climb for almost 50', and make a long traverse down and up (5.9 and fixed pro) to a narrow belay ledge. **Pitch 2** follows a left-facing corner (5.6) to a ledge on the right. **Pitch 3** heads up 15' to a fixed pin, works left around a blind edge (5.8) onto the bottom of the Super Slab, and climbs directly up to an airy belay shelf. **Pitch 4** offers high drama on the steep, colorful slab. Climb up past a bolt and fixed pin to a narrow corner (5.9) and work right up thin face holds (5.10d). A few feet higher head back left below a thin roof and then straight up easier rock to the top of the Upper Ramp. **Descend** by scrambling down the ramp to the 2 rappels below THE NAKED EDGE or walk north along the top of the ramp and locate slings around a large block atop Pigeon Crack. Make a 2-rope 165' rappel west to the base of the west wall. Or find a ledge just below the ramp's west edge. Rap 150' from a tree to a walk-off ledge or do 2 75' rappels from the tree and anchors with 1 rope. Bring RPs and Loweballs.

28. **Mellow Yellow** (5.12a) A superb and difficult line up the south face of Tower One. To start, climb one of the lower routes—TOUCH AND GO, RUPER, or GRAND GIRAFFE—to the Upper Ramp. Begin at the far northwest corner of the ramp just left of a tree. **Pitch 1** pulls over a roof, then

works left and then right into a right-facing corner (5.9). Belay beneath the upside-down V-shaped roof. **Pitch 2** climbs up and over the intimidating roof (5.11d) and reaches a belay just above. **Pitch 3** goes up a shallow corner to the next roof (5.11c) and belays above a left-facing corner. **Pitch 4** follows an incipient seam (once A4, now 5.12a) up a steep headwall with 2 bolts and 1 peg to an immense slanting roof. Diagonal up and left below the roof (5.6) to a ledge just right of the YELLOW SPUR arete. **Pitch 5** steps left onto the sharp arete and waltzes up it (5.6) to the summit of Tower One. **Descend** by scrambling northeast to the East Slabs.

29. **The Yellow Spur** (5.10a) This time-tested classic, put up by Layton Kor and Dave Dornan in 1959 and free-climbed by Royal Robbins and Pat Ament in 1964 (although they avoided the crux bolt ladder), is one of Eldorado's most sought after routes. It's a long, beautiful free climb with excellent rock and airy position. Robbins wrote after his ascent, "One moves delicately upward on small holds, with the rock falling away steeply below. One here can experience some of the finest beauties rock climbing offers." The 7-pitch route is approached via the Streamside Trail. Walk west on the trail to a climber's path that zigzags up the wide ravine below the west face of Redgarden Wall. Hike up below the face and scramble up slabs to a large ledge that runs along the bottom of the wall. The route begins in trees below some large roofs. **Pitch 1** begins directly below the largest roof. Climb a right-facing corner (5.7) to the base of the roof and traverse left to the left edge of the roof. A direct, poorly protected 5.10 R start goes up to the left edge of the roof from the ledge. Turn the awkward left side of the roof (5.8) and angle up right on easier rock to a tree belay right of a roof. Put some gear in to protect your second on this pitch's traversing sections. **Pitch 2** diagonals up left to a right-facing dihedral (5.8). Above, climb left on a rotten horizontal band to another tree belay. **Pitch 3** works up a 5.7 corner to a ledge, pulls over a small roof (5.7), and stems up a tight dihedral (5.8) to a spacious ledge. **Pitch 4** traverses right on the ledge and climbs a huge easy dihedral to a belay stance below an immense roof. **Pitch 5** hand traverses right under the roof, exits around a blunt arete (5.8), and climbs an insecure left-facing corner (5.8) to an exposed belay stance on the ridge. **Pitch 6** jams a thin crack to an airy step right onto a vertical yellow wall. Face climb up right on continuous 5.9 past several fixed pitons to a narrow shelf atop a flake. Rest and then continue up right on sustained 5.9 face climbing (a spot of 5.10b) to a thin corner. Easier climbing leads to a belay nest on the arete. If you chicken out at the final crux, take the Robbins Traverse left from the flake stance. Traverse up and left to a 5.8 headwall. Continue to the belay stance on the ridge. **Pitch 7** offers beautiful but runout climbing up the exposed arete. Follow the spectacular ridge 100' (5.6) to the summit of Tower One. **Descend** northeast to the East Slabs descent route.

THE BASTILLE

The Bastille, jutting out from the south side of Eldorado Canyon, towers over the creek and canyon floor. The 300' buttress rises sharply from the road. The cliff offers numerous excellent routes with hard face and crack climbing coupled with airy situations. The crag is easily approached by walking up the road from the parking area. The west face routes are accessed via a steep, loose gully on the slopes west of the rock. **Descent:** To descend from the summit, work south along the ridgetop and on ledges to the old railroad cut behind The Bastille. The safest way from here is to walk west almost a mile on the Fowler Trail to its intersection with the canyon road. Otherwise, descend down the steep talus slopes on the west side of the crag. This descent is very loose with lots of precarious boulders. Take care not to dislodge any rocks on your partners or other climbers below. Numerous accidents have occurred on this descent. Use extreme caution!

30. **Werk Supp** (5.9+) A decent 2-pitch crack line up the far east side of The Bastille's north face. Begin from the road just right of a broken right-facing corner system. **Pitch 1,** a long 150' lead, climbs thin cracks and flakes to a large sloping ledge. **Pitch 2** struggles up a right-leaning crack that ranges from a tight squeeze chimney at its base to a hand crack up high (5.9+). **Descent:** Scramble east down ramps and shelves to the road.

31. **The Bastille Crack** (5.7) This mega-classic crack route, first climbed by a pair of GIs in 1954 and free-climbed by Stan Shepard and Allen Bergen in 1957, is undoubtedly the most popular route not only in Eldorado Canyon but in all of Colorado. The route is usually done in 5 pitches to ease rope drag, but this can easily be condensed to 3 with good rope handling. A queue of climbers at the base is the norm for summer afternoons. On weekends a steady stream of rock warriors fight their way upwards. Watch out for loose rock dislodged by careless climbers above. Don't set up a toprope at the first anchors and hog the route. Begin the route on some broken blocks directly below the obvious crack system. **Pitch 1** (65') works up a thin flake and stems left into the crack. Lieback and jam up the hand-sized crack (5.7) to a small stance with double bolts. Put protection in the flake and crack before stepping into it. Numerous groundfalls have occurred at this spot. A historic variation to the 1st pitch, *The Northcutt Start*, climbs an open book left of the regular pitch. It's 5.10d crux is a delicate rightward traverse at the top of the corner. **Pitch 2** jams and liebacks up the flake/crack (5.6 and 5.7) 90' to a good ledge. The first 2 pitches can easily be combined into 1 long lead. **Pitch 3,** with the technical crux, scales twin cracks (5.7) up the steep headwall for 45' to a sloping ramp belay. **Pitch 4** begins with a descending traverse into a broken corner system. Climb moderate rock upward to another sloping stance. **Pitch 5** continues up ledges

and short walls to a chimney and the summit. **Rack:** Bring a rack with a few large stoppers and Friends to #4.

32. **Outer Space** (5.10c R) An airy route up the steep upper north face. To start ascend the first 2 pitches of THE BASTILLE CRACK to a ledge. **Pitch 1** diagonals right 35' up a ramp to a left-facing red dihedral system. Climb the steep dihedral (5.9+ and 5.10a cruxes) to another sloping ramp. Belay up and right below an arching corner. **Pitch 2** climbs steep rock up left below the corner to a wild undercling (5.10c). Continue up a left-facing corner (5.9) to a left-leaning crack. Face climb on easier rock above to the summit. Use enough runners to avoid rope drag on this pitch.

33. **X-M** (5.10c R) A sustained and brilliant face climb up the dark face right of THE BASTILLE CRACK. Larry Dalke first led it all free in 1967 and rated it 5.9 (the upper end of the ratings at that time). The best finishing pitch is the upper lead of OUTER SPACE. Begin just right of THE BASTILLE CRACK atop broken ledges. **Pitch 1** climbs straight up through some runout 5.7 flake corners to a right-trending crack. Jam the hand and finger crack and make a delicate step right (5.10b) into a narrow chimney on the left side of a pillar. Belay atop the pillar. Another start climbs the off-size/chimney crack (5.9+) 70' to the belay. **Pitch 2** is serious and committing. Traverse left from the pillar (5.10c) to a thin seam that diagonals up left. Try to work some thin wires into the seam (originally A4 rurps) before leaving the safety of the pillar. The leader will slam into the pillar with a fall here. Continue traversing up left on easier rock along the seam to a shallow vertical corner. Belay from bolts on a blocky shelf above the corner. **Pitch 3** liebacks up left (5.10c) past some fixed pitons to an awkward, committing mantle onto a narrow shelf. Continue up to a ledge. **Pitch 4** works up right along the strata (a runout 5.9 section under a slanted roof) to a large open book. Stem and jam 25' up the dihedral (5.8) to OUTER SPACE'S ramp belay. **Pitch 5** is done in 2 ways. The original path followed the ramp up right and around the corner to the west face and finished up an easy crack. The better way is to climb the last airy pitch (5.10c) of OUTER SPACE for a sustained 5-pitch tour of the north wall. **Rack:** Bring a rack that's heavy on thin crack and seam pro and Friends to #3.

34. **The Northwest Corner** (5.11a) This exposed classic up the nose of The Bastille used to be an aspiring hardman's testpiece. It was one of Eldo's first 5.11s after Pat Ament's 1966 free ascent. Begin just right of the pillar below the nose. **Pitch 1** climbs left up an angling corner (5.7) and works straight up (5.9) to the chimney on the right side of the pillar. Work up the chimney to a bolted belay stance in the chimney. **Pitch 2**, the crux lead, jams a difficult crack in a thin, left-facing corner 15' to a roof. Jam over it (5.9+), step left onto a rounded edge left of a crack, and work upward on thin face holds (5.11a). Work right after about 15' on 5.9 rock to a thin corner.

THE BASTILLE

Belay above from bolts on a small, exposed stance on the prow. The original free way went up the thin crack above the roof for a few moves and leaned right to a hairy 5.10c mantle hold that has dropped many leaders. Climb up right from the mantle to the belay. **Pitch 3** follows a 5.8 crack up a narrow, slightly flared dihedral to a ledge. **Pitch 4** works up left past a fixed piton, over a 5.9 bulge, and finishes up a steep slab to a good stance on the ramp right of OUTER SPACE. **Pitch 5** is done any number of ways. Traverse left and finish with OUTER SPACE'S final 5.10c pitch; climb OUTER FACE, a 5.10c line directly above the belay ledge; or step right around the corner and climb an easy chimney to the summit.

35. **Rain** (5.10d R) A superb face route right of THE NORTHWEST CORNER on the West Buttress that is usually done as 1 pitch to rappel anchors. Begin just south of the nose. Work up a slab to some small roofs, undercling left and pull over (5.10d), and work up difficult rock to a 2-bolt anchor. Descent: Rappel with double ropes 145' to the ground.

36. **The West Buttress** (5.9) Another time-tested classic. Scramble up a bouldery talus slope to a belay atop some broken blocks and below a room-sized boulder. **Pitch 1** climbs up and hand traverses left 10' (5.7) to a thin, vertical finger crack. Jam up it a few moves (5.9) and work left to easier rock. Climb straight up (5.6 R) and rejoin the crack where the angle eases. Or jam up the excellent and sustained crack (5.10b) to the belay. Either way, climb fun rock above the crack to a stance beneath a looming off-width crack on the left side of a huge flake. **Pitch 2** climbs the crack by off-width technique or laybacking past a bolt (5.9), then chimneys up the flake to a large ledge with 2 bolts. **Pitch 3** works up left along a broken ledge and climbs a chimney (5.7) over an overhang to a spacious ledge. **Pitch 4** cruises to the summit via an easy chimney or a 5.4 slab to the right.

37. **Hair City** (5.9 R) This great face route climbs the outside of the flake right of THE WEST BUTTRESS. **Pitch 1** climbs left into a shallow corner and then works straight up past a couple of bolts to the flake's overhanging wall. Pull over on jugs (5.8+) and finish on the ledge atop the flake. This pitch is a full rope length. **Pitch 2** goes up left on broken rock and climbs a 5.9 crack right of THE WEST BUTTRESS chimney to a ledge. Continue up easy rock to the top.

38. **Out to Lunge** (5.9) 2 pitches up the upper west wall. Approach by carefully scrambling up along the base of THE WEST BUTTRESS past the recess of the West Chimney. Walk left onto a ledge to belay. **Pitch 1** climbs up right and mantles (5.9) onto a ledge. Fun climbing goes up the vertical wall above to a roof and angles left (5.8) into an easy left-facing dihedral. Belay on the walk-off ledge above. **Pitch 2** edges up a slab to a big roof. Lieback a crack to the lip and pull over on a jug (5.9).

39. **Your Mother** (5.12d) A neo-classic sport route, established by Colin Lantz in 1988, up the leaning west wall of the summit tower. Access by trudging up the base of the west face to the railroad cut behind The Bastille or driving up the road and hiking almost a level mile along the old railroad grade to the cut. Walk north up the huge ledge to an obvious belay point. Climb straight up the strenuous overhanging wall past 7 bolts to a 2-bolt anchor. Lower off.

INDUSTRIAL WALL &
MICKEY MOUSE WALL

OVERVIEW

The Mickey Mouse Wall and the Industrial Wall perch high over Boulder and the rolling high plains, forming a remote climbing refuge on the edge of the urban sprawl. The walls are sharply tilted sandstone beds with slabby east faces and sheer south- and west-facing exposures. The colorful crags, composed of the same sandstone conglomerate formation found in nearby Eldorado Canyon and the Flatirons, are studded with myriad handholds, sharp incuts, and steep crack systems. The Mickey Mouse Wall is naturally divided into three buttresses by the North Tower, Central Tower, and South Tower. The wall is named for its fanciful resemblance to the two "ears" of a Mouseketeer beanie when the cliff is viewed from Boulder. The Industrial Wall, a lower, eastern continuation of the South Tower, lifts an overhanging red wall above the Denver and Rio Grande Railroad tracks.

Numerous routes thread up the sunny rock faces. The Mickey Mouse Wall yields some of the Boulder area's classic multi-pitch, traditional routes including *Red Dihedral* and *Perversion,* while the Industrial Wall sports a host of excellent and difficult bolted routes.

Climbing history: Although a route was pushed up the Central Tower in the mid-1950s, Layton Kor, the legendary Boulder climber, was the first to seriously explore the Mickey Mouse Wall's climbing potential. In 1963, in the company of Paul Mayrose, Charles Kemp, and Bob Bradley, Kor ascended the now-classic *Perversion.* The following year he established *The Red Dihedral,* an impressive, airy 5-pitch aid route up the South Tower. The Mickey Mouse is also home to *Perilous Journey,* a serious, no-pro 5.11b face climb ascended by Dave Breashears in 1974 on a steep slab on the South Tower. Breashears later said, "It was the most emotional climb I've every done.... First of all, it was not a good climb to fall off of at the crux—you'd certainly hit the ground. You probably wouldn't die—but you might." Needless to say, *Perilous Journey* and *Krystal Klyr,* Breashear's other unprotected line to the left, still see few ascents. *The Red Dihedral,* a spectacular, overhanging dihedral high on the South Tower, was a Mickey Mouse testpiece as an aid climb until Christian Griffith and Eric Doub free-climbed it at 5.12d in 1985.

The Industrial Wall, looming above the path to the Mickey Mouse Wall, remained unclimbed except for Larry and Roger Dalke's *Rene,* a horrific A5 aid route, until early 1991. That winter a number of Boulder climbers, including Colin Lantz, discovered its steep wall, mild winter weather, and relatively easy access. The first routes put up were *Terminal, Tunnel Vision,* and *Soul Train.* A grid of bolted lines ascend the Industrial Wall, including some 5.14 projects.

The Mickey Mouse and Industrial walls are accessed via the railroad tracks

Steve Landin warms up on *Soul Train*, a popular 5.12b on lower Industrial Wall. *Photo by Stewart M. Green.*

from Plainview to the south or from Eldorado Canyon. The parking situation and hiking along the tracks both come with some objective hazards. Park on the east side of the tracks well off the road (see "Finding the crags" below) and don't block any gates to adjoining ranch land or the train yard. Be sensitive when parking here; overcrowded parking could lead to restrictions and problems. Mark Rolofson, author of *Boulder Sport Climbs*, warns climbers to "watch for gun-toting locals from Plainview." Locals here haven't taken a liking to having folks parking here and walking on the train tracks. This approach is currently closed. Trespassers are being ticketed. The best approach is from the town of Eldorado Springs. The railroad right-of-way is private property.

Rack: Bring a standard rack with RPs, stoppers, TCUs, and Friends for the traditional lines on the Mickey Mouse Wall. A dozen quick draws and a 165-foot rope are necessary for the sport routes on the Industrial Wall.

Trip Planning Information

General description: A variety of excellent traditional and sport routes on steep sandstone cliffs high above Boulder and the high plains.

Location: Northern Front Range just south of Boulder.

Camping: No camping in the immediate area. The nearest Roosevelt National Forest campgrounds are 46-site Kelly Dahl Campground south of Nederland on Colorado 119 and 55-site Pawnee Campground at Brainard Lake north of Nederland off Colorado 72. Golden Gate Canyon State Park, southwest of Nederland, offers several excellent high-elevation campgrounds off CO 119.

Climbing season: Year-round. Summer days are hot on the sunny south-facing cliffs, especially the Industrial Wall. Winter days are often warm, although the sun sinks behind the ridge at an early hour.

Restrictions and access issues: The crags lie on Boulder County Open Space land and are subject to all park rules, including no power drills or bolting, no dogs, and no camping. The South Tower as well as the other towers and the Industrial Walls are often closed to rock climbing from February through July because of nesting raptors. Signs are posted along the cliff base detailing the closures. Call at Boulder Open Space office at (303) 441-4142 for more info on cliff closure dates.

Guidebooks: *Boulder Climbs South* by Richard Rossiter, Chockstone Press, 1989, is an excellent and comprehensive guide to the Mickey Mouse area. The Industrial Wall is not included. *Best of Boulder Climbs*, also by Rossiter and published by Chockstone Press, 1992, highlights selected climbs on Mickey Mouse Wall. *1995 Boulder Sport Climber's Guide*, by Mark Rolofson, topos of sport routes on both cliffs as well as surrounding crags.

Nearby mountain shops, guide services, and gyms: Basecamp Mountain Sports, Boulder Mountaineer, Mountain Sports, Neptune Mountaineering, Boul-

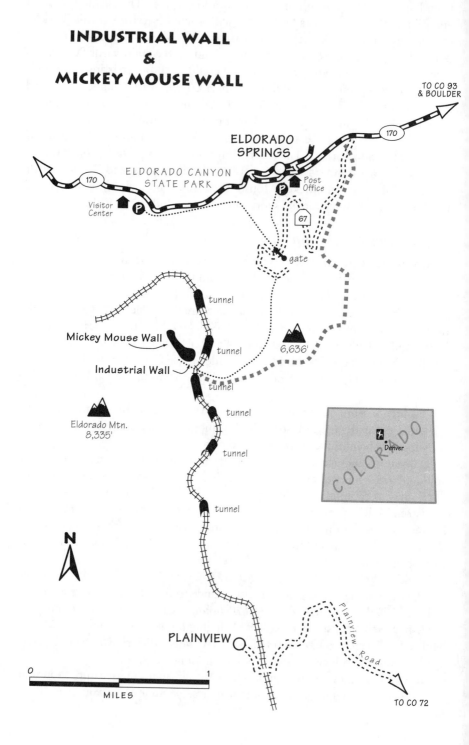

INDUSTRIAL WALL
&
MICKEY MOUSE WALL

TO CO 93
& BOULDER

170

ELDORADO
SPRINGS

170

ELDORADO CANYON
STATE PARK

Post
Office

P

Visitor
Center

P

67

gate

tunnel

Mickey Mouse Wall

tunnel

6,636'

Industrial Wall

tunnel

tunnel

Eldorado Mtn.
8,335'

tunnel

COLORADO

Denver

tunnel

N

tunnel

Plainview Road

PLAINVIEW

0   1

MILES

TO CO 72

der Mountaineering Climbing School, Boulder Rock Club, (Boulder); International Alpine School (Eldorado Springs).

Services: All services, including groceries, dining, and lodging in Boulder and Golden.

Emergency services: Call 911. Boulder Community Hospital, N. Broadway and Balsam, Boulder, CO 80301, (303) 440-2273. Memorial Hospital Boulder, 311 Mapleton Ave., Boulder, CO 80302, (303) 443-0230.

Nearby climbing areas: Flagstaff Mountain, the Flatirons and Green Mountain, Eldorado Canyon State Park, Clear Creek Canyon, Golden Gate Canyon State Park, North Table Mountain, Morrison, Rocky Mountain National Park, Lumpy Ridge, St. Vrain Canyon, Button Rock Reservoir, Combat Rock.

Nearby attractions: Rocky Mountain National Park, Longs Peak, Trail Ridge Road, Indian Peaks Wilderness Area, Rollins Pass, Golden Gate Canyon State Park, Central City-Blackhawk National Historic District, Golden, Coors Brewery, Eldorado Canyon State Park, Boulder Mountain Park, Mount Evans Wilderness Area, Mount Evans Highway.

Finding the crags: The easiest and traditional approach is via the railroad tracks that run beneath the wall. These are accessed from Plainview north of CO 72. This approach is currently closed by the railroad. Trespassers are being ticketed! The best approach now is from the town of Eldorado Springs. Park at the town post office. Head south past some old stone pillars and follow a trail up to an aqueduct. Follow this south to a dirt road. Head up the dirt road a short distance and pick up another trail near its end. Follow this trail through meadows and pine forests in a shallow valley to a broad saddle. Continue west into a canyon and follow the dim trail up steepening slopes to the railroad tracks and the Industrial Wall. Continue up the trail alongside the cliffs to the Mickey Mouse Wall. Trail distance is about 2 miles. Allow up to an hour for the approach.

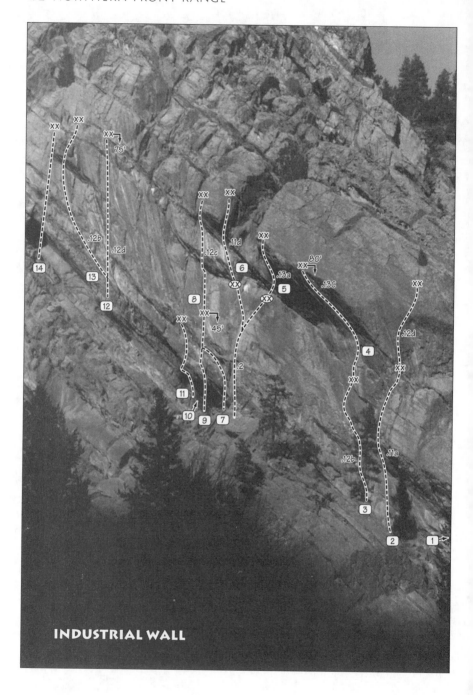

INDUSTRIAL WALL

INDUSTRIAL WALL

The Industrial Wall is the overhanging red cliff that forms the lower south face of the Mickey Mouse Wall. The wall towers above the railroad tracks beyond the fourth railroad tunnel. Access the cliff by walking the railroad tracks to a short trail that clambers up to the lower cave on the wall's east side. Continue up slabs above the lower cave to the Catwalk, an easy traverse into the upper cave. **Descent** from all routes is from rappel/lowering anchors. Routes are listed from east to west.

1. **Tunnel Vision** (5.13a) A short, hard route up an overhanging wall with long reaches and underclings. 6 bolts to a 2-bolt anchor.

2. **Trackton** (5.12d) This good route climbs 2 pitches. **Pitch 1** (5.11a) is commonly climbed as a warm-up. Climb a wide slot/corner system 40', past 3 bolts and 4 fixed pitons to anchors on a large ledge. Belay or lower from here. **Pitch 2** climbs the left side of a steep headwall past 7 bolts to a 2-bolt station.

3. **Soul Train** (5.12b) An excellent and popular 50' route with powerful laybacks and pulls out of the lower cave. A good kneebar is found half-way up. 6 bolts to 2-bolt lowering anchors.

4. **TGV** (5.13c) A superb 5-bolt line up the severely overhanging wall above SOUL TRAIN. Climb SOUL TRAIN, rest, and then work on TGV, or climb an easy corner with an aid sling right of TUNNEL VISION and begin on the ledge above. The route's hardest moves are at the top—hard bouldery pulls lead to a dyno and the finishing jug at the anchors above the lip. Clean the pitch from a fixed carabiner at the last bolt rather than the anchors. 5 bolts to 2-bolt anchors.

5. **Auntie Dez** (5.13a) Climb a short 5.2 pitch from the ledge just right of the Upper Cave to anchors. This route ascends the left side of the big roof past 5 bolts to a 2-bolt anchor.

6. **Spike** (5.11d) Scale the 5.2 pitch to a belay below a crack/gully. Climb up and over a roof to the right side of an arete. 6 bolts to a 2-bolt anchor.

7. **Railing** (5.12b) This 45' pitch is a popular warm-up. Begin in the Upper Cave and climb past 5 bolts to cold-shut lowering anchors. A good kneebar rest is found near the 3rd bolt.

8. **Railslide** (5.12b/c) A good 2nd pitch to RAILING that climbs past 6 bolts and a fixed piton to a 2-bolt anchor on the steep upper wall.

9. **Terminal** (5.12d) Powerful underclings and sidepulls lead past 6 bolts to RAILING'S anchors.

10. **Rene** (A5) A fixed copperhead marks the start of Larry and Roger Dalke's hairy nail-up. The 1st pitch is usually done now. Rap from RAILING'S

anchors.

11. **Jumping Someone Else's Train** (5.13a) This excellent pitch, usually called JUMP, powers up the overhanging wall at the left end of the cave. Stick-clip the 1st bolt, and jump for the starting holds from the slab. Pumpy climbing past 5 bolts to anchors.

12. **Driver Eight** (5.12d) Belay near the top of the slab. Straight up past 11 bolts to anchors.

13. **Coltrane** (5.12b) Begin at same belay as DRIVER EIGHT, only climb up and left past 12 bolts to a 2-bolt anchor.

14. **The Auctioneer** (5.11d) Begin on a ledge at the top of the slab. Stick-clip the 1st bolt and climb the wall above past 6 bolts to anchors.

MICKEY MOUSE WALL

Approach the wall by continuing up a rough and eroded cliff-base trail or a talus-field trail just south of the crag. **Descent:** There are no good walk-off descents. The best descent is between the North and Central towers. Make 4 half-rope (80') rappels from anchors to a large ledge below *Perversion*. Walk north off the ledge. Some of the newer sport routes have rappel anchors. The South Tower is closed to climbing half the year from February 1 through July 31 for nesting raptors.

15. **Perilous Journey** (5.11b X) The classic no-pro route up the obvious smooth slab below THE RED DIHEDRAL. Climb pebbles, small edges, and pockets for 125' to a large ledge. The initial 40' are most difficult. Bring a rope and large huevos. Rappel from anchors on the west end of the ledge.

16. **Krystal Klyr** (5.11b R) Another Breashears runout classic, but more reasonable than PERILOUS JOURNEY. Begin just left of a blunt arete around the corner from PERILOUS JOURNEY. Climb up and right around the arete (5.11a) and over a small roof (second 5.11 crux). Continue up to the large ledge. **Descent:** Rap from anchors. **Rack:** Bring a small rack that includes Friends to #2.5.

17. **The Red Dihedral** (5.12d R) This serious and spectacular 4-pitch line up the South Tower offers hard, dicey climbing and lots of exposure. Begin in the obvious broken corner left of KRYSTAL KLYR. **Pitch 1** follows the corner (5.6) to a belay/rappel stance on the west end of a large ledge. **Pitch 2** begins on the east end of the ledge and climbs a shallow left-facing corner (5.8) to a small roof. Turn the roof and follow the strata to a belay below the red dihedral. **Pitch 3** is exhilarating. Climb the obvious dihedral (5.12d) for 80' to a bolted hanging belay. Some fixed pro including a 1/4" bolt and possibly fixed wires and pins may be found in the crack. **Pitch 4** continues

MICKEY MOUSE WALL
SOUTH TOWER

up the severely overhanging dihedral with little pro and much excitement. Some fixed pins may be in place. Some 5.8 climbing leads above the dihedral to a belay. Do an easy **Pitch 5** up and left along the strata to the notch west of South Tower. Most parties only climb the first dihedral pitch and rap from the anchors. **Rack:** Bring a rack from RPs to medium Friends.

18. **Stigmata** (5.13b) A superb George Squibb 1-pitch route up a spectacular arete right of THE RED DIHEDRAL. Climb 2 pitches to the base of the dihedral and belay. Climb the first 40' of the dihedral—the 5.12d crux section—and then head up and right onto the steep arete. Pass 8 bolts and a couple 5.12 segments to a 5.13b crux above the last bolt. The 120' pitch ends at double bolts. **Descent:** Rappel with double ropes back to the base of the dihedral and make 2 more rappels to the ground (200').

19. **Green Dihedral** (5.7) A good moderate line. Climb the first 5.6 pitch of THE RED DIHEDRAL. Follow the obvious arching left-facing corner for a long pitch to rappel slings. Make a 165' rappel off left.

20. **Green Space** (5.12a) Begin at a huge flake below RED DIHEDRAL'S 1st pitch. Difficult and thin face climbing leads up and left past 7 bolts to a 2-bolt belay. The next pitch climbs up and left past 3 bolts along a flake system, finishing at GREEN DIHEDRAL'S belay. **Rack:** Bring a rack of draws if you only do the 1st pitch. The 2nd pitch requires some TCUs.

21. **Simian's Way** (5.11b) You'll go ape over this classic 4-pitch line. **Pitch 1** climbs a superb finger crack (5.9+) to a ledge belay. It's possible to rap from here. Head left up the ledge to **Pitch 2.** Climb a broken, right-facing corner (5.6) to a good belay. **Pitch 3**—the crux—jams the obvious 4" off-width crack (5.11a) above. **Pitch 4** continues up a large right-facing dihedral to a 5.8 roof. Belay above it and scramble up and left on easy rock. **Rack:** Bring a rack to 4" and a single off-width piece.

22. **Mighty Mouse** (5.12a/b) Simply one of the best sport routes on Mickey Mouse. Thin 5.12b face climbing and 7 bolts lead up and left on the smooth wall left of the 1st pitch crack of SIMIAN'S WAY to a 2-bolt belay/rappel anchor.

23. **Three Mouseketeers** (5.11c) Another superb line, but easier than MIGHTY MOUSE. Start just left of a tree and follow 6 bolts and 2 fixed pins up a steep slab to a 2-bolt belay/rap station left of a pine tree on a ledge. Watch the long, loose flake just below the top.

24. **Culp's Fault** (5.8) A classic 2-pitch line to the saddle between the Central and North towers. **Pitch 1** begins on a ledge 20' up. Jam and stem a left-facing corner, 5.8 initially, but easier up high. Belay on a ledge. **Pitch 2** continues up the corner to a roof. Turn the roof at 5.7 on the right or 5.9 on the left. Head up moderate rock to the saddle.

25. **Captain Beyond** (5.10c) An excellent 5-pitch crack line to the summit of the Central Tower. **Pitch 1** climbs a narrow, left-facing corner to a 5.10a

MICKEY MOUSE WALL
CENTRAL TOWER

roof. Belay above or rap from slings. **Pitch 2** traverses left 15' to another crack system; jam a 5.9 finger crack to a spacious belay. Walk a few feet left for **Pitch 3**—a short, under-protected 5.8 slab. Belay on a ledge below a leaning off-width crack. **Pitch 4** jams the crux 12" crack (5.10c) and heads up and left on easier rock to a stance below the huge open-book. **Pitch 5** goes up and left on broken rock to a right-facing dihedral. Climb the corner, some 5.10a at the second roof, and belay at a tree just below the top. **Rack:** Bring a rack of stoppers, a couple of hexes or Tri-cams, a few tri-cams, and a set of Friends to #4.

26. **Beginner's Mind** (5.12a R) A superb 1-pitch route, first done by Jeff Achey and Mark Sonnenfeld, up the sustained, thin crack in a narrow, right-facing corner just right of a tree. After the difficulties ease, traverse right 15' to CAPTAIN BEYOND'S first belay and rappel 80'. **Rack:** Should include RPs, small stoppers, and a large Crack 'n' Up.

27. **Better Red Than Dead** (5.12c) A hard route that is seldom done, but often failed on. Follow a line of bolts that wander up a vertical slab to a double-bolt anchor.

28. **Rodent Lust** (5.12c) A difficult face route with 12 bolts that ends at a belay anchor on a ledge just left of a small tree.

29. **Perversion** (5.9) A 3-pitch Mickey Mouse classic first ascended by Layton Kor in 1963. Scramble up broken rock to the foot of a right-facing dihedral. **Pitch 1** (80') jams a finger/hand crack in the corner, some 5.9 low and high, to a large ledge. **Pitch 2** begins just right on the ledge. Climb a 150' corner (5.7) to a belay ledge below the immense dihedral. Layback up the 5.8 dihedral, traverse right under the huge roof, and finish atop the Central Tower.

30. **Parallel Journey** (5.9) A good 2-pitch route up the right-hand of two crack systems on the east side of The Shield, a steep wall below and right of the overhanging North Tower summit. The Shield routes are best approached via a large left-facing, 1-pitch dihedral (5.5) to the big ledge. This route begins on the right side of the ledge atop a large block. Climb the right-hand crack system in a long pitch to a niche belay. Continue up the corner above to the saddle between the North and Central towers. The standard rappel route starts here.

31. **Fake Right Go Left** (5.10b R) Begin on the large ledge just left of the obvious crack system. Do a dicey, no-pro traverse (5.9) up and right into the crack, or climb up the crack off the ledge at 5.10c. Continue up in a long pitch to a ledge. Do a short traverse right to the niche belay of PARALLEL JOURNEY.

32. **Beagle's Ear** (5.11a) 2 pitches. **Pitch 1** (150') starts on a small ledge just above the main ledge. Climb a left-facing 5.9 corner and head up the crack above, passing the crux 4" off-width half-way up. Belay on a ledge directly

MICKEY MOUSE WALL
NORTH TOWER

.9+

rappel
route

XX
65'

.8

XX
145'

.10b

75'

.11a

.10b

XX
80'

.9

.12b

.10a

.8

.11c

XX
75'

.11a

34

.9

.9R

33

32

31

.10c

30

.10d

.5

80'

34

← walk off

below the Beagle's Ear block. **Pitch 2** works up a left-facing corner (5.9+) to the notch above.

33. **Zen Effects** (5.12a) A spectacular and exposed face climbing route on the left edge of The Shield. Begin on the left side of the same small ledge that BEAGLE'S EAR begins on. Edge up a difficult seam past 3 bolts (bring some RPs also), and work up and left above on thin face climbing (5.12b) to a rounded arete. A double anchor with rappel slings are on a ledge here. Watch that the loose block sitting on the ledge doesn't trundle off. Rap 80' to the big ledge or continue up LIFESTREAM for 70' more to 2-bolt anchors and rap with 2 ropes 145' back down.

34. **Lifestream** (5.11a) Another superb and beautiful route, one of the best on the wall. **Pitch 1** starts directly below the arete. Climb a corner to a large roof. Pass the roof at a bolt (5.10d) and edge up the slab above to the large ledge. **Pitch 2** begins below the arete that marks the left side of The Shield. The crux 5.11a face climbing is getting past the first 2 bolts. Continue up and right on easier climbing to a small stance with 2 bolts and a loose block. Difficult face climbing leads up and left back onto the arete and waltzes past 3 bolts to an airy belay. Make a long double-rope rappel back to the big ledge.

DENVER AREA

CLEAR CREEK CANYON

OVERVIEW

Clear Creek begins high above timberline near Loveland Pass on the Continental Divide. Its snow-fed waters plunge downward through a broad glaciated valley, gathering tributaries and strength as it descends. Just west of Idaho Springs the creek leaves its glacier-carved, U-shaped valley and drops into Clear Creek Canyon, a tight, twisted gorge sliced into the lower Front Range mountains. Here also the creek crosses the Colorado Mineral Belt, a wide swath of mountains veined with rich ores including gold and silver that spawned Colorado's first gold rush in 1859 to Gregory Gulch near Central City, an area dubbed by early miners as "The richest square mile on Earth." Gold seekers still sift the creek's sands in search of precious nuggets, while numerous crags, buttresses, and cliffs stud the dry canyon walls and attract rock climbers with their angular handholds, steep faces, and sharp overhangs. The rocks, composed of 1.7-billion-year-old gneiss and schist, are ancient layers twisted, heaved, wrenched, heated, and metamorphosed by repeated epochs of mountain uplift and erosion.

Climbing history: The canyon saw little climbing action until 1989 when new bolting regulations went into effect at Boulder Mountain Parks to the north. Boulder rock climbers, needing a new place to run their Boschs, turned their attention south to Clear Creek Canyon. Kurt Smith called it in a 1990 issue of *Climbing* magazine "the most traveled and most overlooked canyon on the Front Range." That quickly changed when climbers, including Smith, Alan Nelson, Pete Zoeller, and Mike Pont, discovered that the canyon's rock was amazingly solid and surprisingly steep.

The canyon's almost 200 routes on over 30 crags range in difficulty from 5.4 to 5.13. Most are bolt-protected sport routes, although a number of routes requiring gear also ascend the cliffs. Holds range from fingertip crimps on micro-flakes to huge, incut jugs on overhanging walls. Several routes in Nomad Cave near the west end of the canyon are almost totally manufactured with

Ian Spencer-Green on *Pizza Dick* on the right side of Nomad Cave in Clear Creek Canyon. *Photo by Stewart M. Green.*

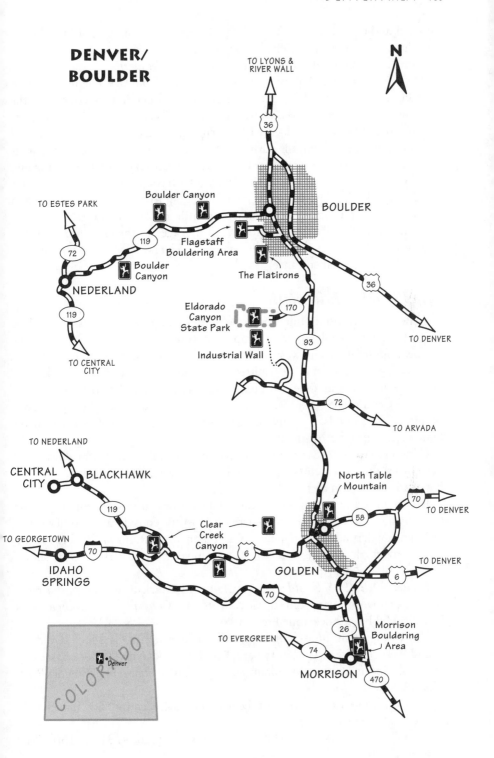

DENVER/ BOULDER

N

TO LYONS & RIVER WALL

36

TO ESTES PARK

Boulder Canyon

BOULDER

119

Flagstaff Bouldering Area

72

Boulder Canyon

NEDERLAND

The Flatirons

36

119

Eldorado Canyon State Park

170

TO DENVER

93

Industrial Wall

TO CENTRAL CITY

72

TO ARVADA

TO NEDERLAND

North Table Mountain

CENTRAL CITY   BLACKHAWK

70

TO DENVER

119

58

Clear Creek Canyon

TO GEORGETOWN

70

6

TO DENVER

IDAHO SPRINGS

GOLDEN

6

70

Morrison Bouldering Area

26

TO EVERGREEN

74

COLORADO

Denver

MORRISON

470

chiseled and drilled holds. These chipped routes are omitted from this guide. The three routes in Pete's Wicked Cave (Sex Cave), however, are natural, except for some drilled pockets at the start of *Stone Cold Modern*.

Clear Creek Canyon's crags are easily accessible from U.S. Highway 6, with the longest approach only minutes from the car—depending, of course, on the creek level. Some approaches, such as for Nomad Cave and Primo Wall, require a creek crossing. Clear Creek is swift and cold; use extreme caution when crossing and don't even attempt it during high water in May and June. Climbing is possible year-round, making Clear Creek Canyon a brilliant off-season cragging area. Sunny cliffs are easily found on dry winter days, while shaded walls offer good summer climbing. Use caution when hiking to the cliff bases and when crossing scree and rock slopes. Numerous rattlesnakes live in the canyon and are active between May and October. All mileages to the cliffs are from the intersection of US 6 and Colorado highways 58 and 93 on the west side of Golden at the canyon entrance.

Trip Planning Information

General description: Numerous small crags composed of gneiss and schist line steep canyon walls, offering almost 200 routes.

Location: Immediately west of Denver and Golden, along US 6.

Camping: No camping is permitted along the highway in Clear Creek Canyon. The nearest Arapahoe National Forest campgrounds lie north of the canyon and Central City along Colorado 119 and include Columbine and Cold Springs campgrounds. A couple of campgrounds are in Golden Gate Canyon State Park a little farther north.

Climbing season: Year-round. Winters can be cold, but warm days often occur on south-facing cliffs. Spring and fall are best. Summers can be very hot but shaded cliffs can be found.

Restrictions and access issues: Clear Creek Canyon is a mixture of public and private land. No restrictions currently exist. Be considerate of other users, including anglers and gold panners. Note that many sections of Clear Creek are under private placer mining claims. Clean up your trash. Park on wide shoulders well off the busy highway.

Guidebooks: *1995 Boulder Sport Climbs* by Mark Rolofson, is the most complete and up-to-date guide to the canyon. Also *Colorado Front Range Crags* by Peter Hubbel, Chockstone Press, 1994.

Nearby mountain shops, guide services, and gyms: Bent Gate Inc., (Golden); Grand West Outfitters, The North Face, Paradise Rock Gym (Denver); Basecamp Mountain Sports, Boulder Mountaineer, Neptune Mountaineering, Boulder Rock Club (Boulder).

Services: All services in Golden, Denver, Boulder, Central City, Blackhawk, and Idaho Springs.

Emergency services: Dial 911. St. Anthony Hospital, 4231 W. 16th Ave., Denver, CO 80204, (303) 629-3511.

CLEAR CREEK CANYON

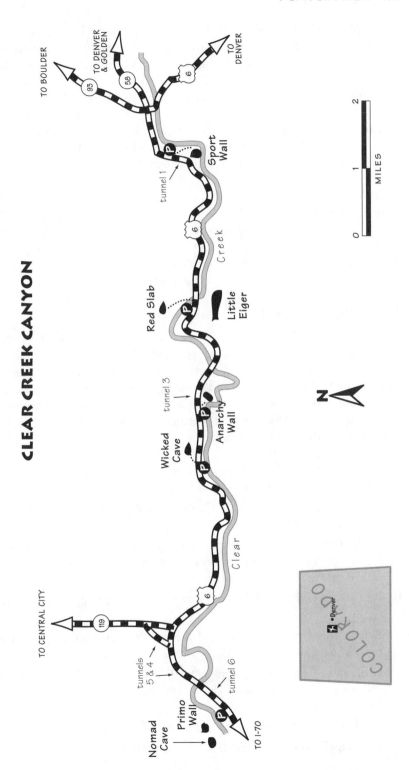

TO BOULDER

TO DENVER & GOLDEN

93

58

TO DENVER

6

P

tunnel 1

Sport Wall

6

Creek

Red Slab

P

Little Eiger

tunnel 3

Wicked Cave

P

Anarchy Wall

P

P

Clear

6

TO CENTRAL CITY

119

tunnels 5 & 4

Primo Wall

Nomad Cave

P

tunnel 6

TO I-70

N

COLORADO

• Denver

0   1   2

MILES

Nearby climbing areas: South Platte domes, Mount Evans, Lover's Leap, Golden Gate State Park, North Table Mountain, Morrison bouldering, Eldorado Canyon State Park, Flatirons, Boulder Canyon, Buttonrock Reservoir, Flagstaff Mountain, Industrial Wall.

Nearby attractions: Central City-Blackhawk National Historic District, Mount Evans Wilderness Area, Mount Evans Highway, Mount Goliath Natural Area, Georgetown, Guanella Pass Scenic Byway, Golden Gate Canyon State Park, Eldorado Canyon State Park, Lookout Mountain, Buffalo Bill's Grave, Mother Cabrini Shrine, White Ranch County Park.

Finding the crags: The canyon is traversed by US 6 and is easily accessed from Denver via West 6th Avenue (US 6), Colfax Avenue, Interstate 70, or Colorado 58. Colorado 93 connects Golden with Boulder. Follow any of those roads to the junction of US 6 and CO 58 and 93 on the west side of Golden at the canyon's entrance. Turn west up US 6 into Clear Creek Canyon. The crags scatter along the 15-mile highway stretch between Golden and I-70.

THE SPORT WALL

The Sport Wall lies 1.1 miles up the canyon above and south of the first tunnel. Park in a roadside lot just east or before Tunnel 1. Follow an old road-bed/trail south around a hairpin canyon turn to the west side of the tunnel and scramble up to the cliff base. This west-facing crag, broken by steep cracks and blocky roofs, gets late afternoon sun and offers great winter climbing. Some routes require gear. **Descend** by lowering or rappelling off fixed anchors or walking off from the traditional routes.

1. **Rufus' Roof** (5.12b) A toprope roof problem. Use anchors on OLAF'S ROOF. Right side of roof goes at 5.10c.

2. **Olaf's Roof** (5.11b R) Turns the blocky left side of roof at 5.11b. Small gear and cold shuts.

3. **Coffin Crack** (5.9) A traditional route up a hand-and-finger crack. **Rack** of wires and Friends. End at belay station on OLAF'S ROOF or PET SEMETARY.

4. **Pet Semetary** (5.11b) A bolted corner system capped by a roof. 5 bolts to chains.

5. **Balkan Dirt Diving** (5.11d/12a) Up a steep slabby wall and over a 5.11a roof. Thin crux on lower slab. 7 bolts to chains.

6. **Generation Gap** (5.10a) Begin as for BALKAN DIRT DIVING, but keep left in the shallow dihedral. Three 5.10 crux sections. 7 bolts and 1 fixed pin to chains.

7. **The Crack** (5.9-) Climb prominent crack to summit.

8. **The Happiness of Pursuit** (5.10b) A short bolted route to anchors.

THE SPORT WALL

RED SLAB

The prominent 80' Red Slab, lying north and above the creek, yields numerous excellent routes for the 5.10 climber. Weekends are often crowded here. Park at the 4.1-mile mark on the north side of the highway just past the bridge. Cross the bridge and traverse a short, rough trail to the crag base. On the shaded south side of the highway towers Little Eiger. Its lower face offers 8 bolted routes for hot days. Rainy Day Rock, with a 5.12a, is 100 yards downstream from the bridge on the canyon's south side.

9. **Snakes for Snacks** (5.10a) A good bolted slab on the crag's right side. 4 bolts to 2 bolt anchors.

10. **Slip and Slide** (5.10d) Long, steep slab to anchors. 7 bolts to chains.

11. **Pink Slip** (5.12b) Thin face moves just past the third bolt. 8 bolts to chains.

12. **Diamondback** (5.10c) Begin on right side of long roof, with tricky high-step crux. 6 bolts to double anchors.

13. **Spring Fever** (5.10c) Over roof and up through broken rock. 6 bolts to anchors.

14. **Wicked Game** (5.10d) Crux is pulling roof lip. 6 bolts to chains.

15. **Trundelero** (5.10b) Thin moves below and over roof. Ends at WICKED GAME anchors. 7 bolts to chains.

16. **Vapor Trail** (5.9) Climbs slab to left edge of roof and up left to anchors. 6 bolts to chains.

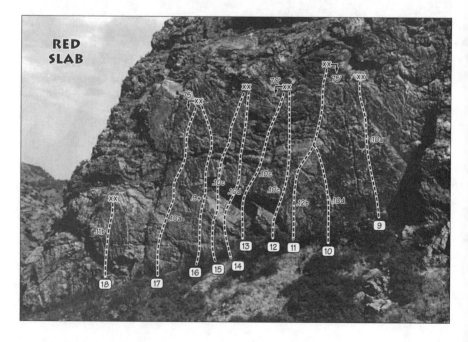

17. **Bumblies for Breakfast** (5.10a) Easy climbing to high, sloping crux moves. 5 bolts to chains.

18. **Slip It In** (5.11b) Short, thin slab with 3 bolts. 3 bolts to anchors.

ANARCHY WALL

West-facing Anarchy Wall is one of Clear Creek Canyon's best crags, with numerous 5.12s scaling its steep, smooth face using off-balance crimpers and slopers for a maximum pump. The 35' to 65' cliff hosts numerous sport routes and variations with bolts and chained anchors. Park at 6.4 miles on the south side of the highway just past Tunnel 2 and scramble up to the rock base.

19. **Question Authority** (5.12a) 3 bolts to chains.

20. **Chaos** (5.12d/13a) Hard, bouldery route with a crux by the first bolt. 3 bolts to chains.

21. **Anarchitect** (5.12d) A masterful route that scales the 110-degree overhanging wall on greasy slopers. 7 bolts to open cold shuts.

22. **Maestro** (5.12d) Climb up and right past 6 bolts to open cold shut anchors.

23. **Presto** (5.12c) An excellent route that shares the same start as MAESTRO. Move up and left after the fourth bolt and continue up left past 4 more bolts to hook anchors.

24. **Matriarch** (5.12d) A direct start to PRESTO up the left side of the smooth wall to 2-bolt anchor. 7 bolts to open cold shuts.

25. **Monkey Wrench** (5.11c) Short, steep, and sweet with sloper holds. The cliff's easiest route. 4 bolts to open cold shuts.

26. **Anarchy Rules** (5.12b) Another short route, ends at MONKEY WRENCH anchors. 5 bolts to open cold shuts.

27. **Anarchy in the UK** (5.12b) Climbs to anchors above the steep section. 3 bolts to open cold shuts.

28. **Hazardous Waste** (5.11d) Up the blocky edge on the wall's left side to a small roof. 4 bolts to chains.

29. **Anatomic** (5.12c) This good traversing route begins at the first bolt of MONKEY WRENCH and works up left past 9 bolts to the chain anchors of HAZARDOUS WASTE.

PETE'S WICKED CAVE (SEX CAVE)

This small cave, tucked into the base of a broken south-facing buttress, offers 3 pumpy routes. The cave sits above the highway at 7.1 miles. Park just west around the corner at 7.2 miles in a pullout on the south side of the highway. Cross the highway with caution and walk down the highway to a short trail that scrambles north to the cave. The 3 routes are listed left to right. No topos.

30. **Rubble** (5.13a/b) Begin on the left side of the cave. Crank up and right past 7 bolts to a 2-bolt anchor.

31. **Stone Cold Modern** (5.13a) A decent route but 2 manufactured/drilled holds at the start make it an ethical debacle. Climbs the middle of the cave past 7 bolts to chains.

32. **Head Like a Hole** (5.13d) Start on the right side of the cave by a boulder. Swing right and back left under the roof and up an overhanging headwall (5.12d) above to chains.

NOMAD CAVE AND PRIMO WALL

These crags sit on the north bank of the creek. Park in a pulloff at 12 miles just past Tunnel 6. Wade the creek (may be impossible in high water). Nomad Cave is on the left (routes right to left), while Primo Wall is on the right (routes left to right). No topos.

33. **Pizza Dick** (5.12b) Great 5-bolt line up Nomad Cave's right side.

34. **Project** (5.13?) 5 bolts.

35. **Pro-Choice** (5.12c) Begin in back of cave. Go up left then back right to anchors. 7 bolts.

36. **Mirthmobile** (5.10a) Popular 3 bolt to anchors on far left side of Primo Wall.

37. **Sucking My Will To Live** (5.12d) 6 bolts.

NORTH TABLE MOUNTAIN

Overview

North Table Mountain, forming Golden's northern skyline, offers numerous bolted routes and crack climbs on its lofty basalt escarpment. The dark south- and west-facing cliff rims the mountain's summit plateau like a medieval battlement, towering above suburban subdivisions and the Coors Brewery in the broad valley below. Both North Table Mountain and its twin South Table Mountain on the opposite side of Clear Creek are composed of basalt, an igneous rock deposited as lava. These thick lava flows, originating from a volcanic vent to the northwest, spread across underlying sandstone and shale formations during the Tertiary Period during the uplift of the Rocky Mountains.

North Table Mountain's hard basalt cliffs, ranging from 20 to 80 feet high, yield tough face climbs with thin cruxes on small edges and sidepulls. Crack systems separate aesthetic aretes and vertical slabs. While most of the cracks have been jammed, the majority are rather chossy affairs characterized by loose blocks and broken steps. The bolted face routes, however, offer good, clean climbing fun on well-protected rock. Most of the lines are sequential, technical affairs, rather than overhanging pumpfests. The climbing here also offers a distinctly urban experience. The climber, looking down on neat homes that line suburban streets, hears the sound of barking dogs and the roar of highway traffic below. Across the valley scatters the gray concrete Coors Brewery complex. It's a constant buzz of activity punctuated by factory whistles, rolling keg-laden trains, and the heavy scent of brewing hops. The brewery offers an interesting tour of its facilities that ends with a free sample—the perfect end to a perfect afternoon of cragging.

North Table Mountain, with its generally mild weather, is one of the most popular Front Range climbing areas. It not only boasts numerous sport routes rated 5.10 and lower, but is a marvelous winter climbing area with its sunny afternoon exposures. The cliff basks in lots of sunshine through the winter and snow quickly melts off the routes and the cliff-bottom trail, which allows for an afternoon of cranking even on chilly winter days. Summer days, however, are a different story. The sunny walls are generally too hot for enjoyable climbing, except on overcast afternoons or when the western cliffs lie in the morning shade.

Climbing history: The area has a short climbing history. Although locals began ascending the obvious crack lines in the 1950s, it wasn't until 1991 that activity reached a feverish pitch. Early that year Denver climbers, including Ken Trout, Guy Lords, Dave Field, Ernie Moskiovics, and Rick Lightner, discovered this "climbing banana-belt" and began bolting sport routes on the vertical cliffs.

Because North Table Mountain lies on the edge of a housing development, climbers need to be aware of local homeowner's cares and concerns. Observe

Ian Spencer-Green pulls over a roof on *Mr. Squirrel Places a Nut* at The Overhang Area on North Table Mountain. *Photo by Stewart M. Green.*

local speed limits, keep dogs on leashes, and keep noise and music to a minimum at the parking area and while walking to and from the crag. Park only in the climber parking area, not on the neighborhood streets. Also pick up your trash at the parking area and the crag base. The owner of the crags is donating the property to The Access Fund. A new access road and parking area will be constructed on the southeast flank of the mountain. Facilities, including better trails, toilets, and signs, will be installed in the near future.

A handful of objective hazards are found at the crag. Be aware of rattlesnakes. The place teems with them in summer and fall, particularly on bouldery slopes above and below the cliffs. Keep an eye out for the snakes cooling themselves in bushes above ground or coiled in the shade under boulders. Raptors occasionally nest in the cliffs. Be aware of their nests, respect their right to be there, and don't climb near their nests. Some of the routes are bolted with unwelded cold-shuts. Do not implicitly trust these. They can and do open under loading. The anchors atop many routes are open 1/2-inch cold shuts for easy lowering off. Avoid toproping off these anchors; the rope can slip out of their open hooks. If you do toprope, keep the last quick draw clipped to the rope and don't climb above the cold-shuts. Loose blocks abound on the cliff face, particularly on unclimbed areas and atop the cliffs. Be extremely careful to avoid knocking rocks onto your partner or others below.

North Table Mountain's long cliff wall is divided into eleven different sectors—Pinnacle Area, Risk Area, Winterfest Wall, Hot Spot Area, Cold Shut Area, Fence Area, Twelve-Pack Wall, Industrial Buttress, Overhang Area, Brown Cloud Crags, and Child Free Zone. This guide offers a selection of routes at the four best areas. Information on routes in the other areas is available in other guidebooks or from climbers at the cliff.

Rack: All the sport routes can be climbed with a single rope (a shorter rope works fine) and a dozen quick draws. The crack climbs require an assortment of gear including a set of wired stoppers and a set of Friends. The climbing grades at Table Mountain are notoriously soft. If you want to lead your first 5.11, this is probably the place to do it.

Trip Planning Information

General description: A semi-urban crag with numerous bolted sport routes as well as a handful of good cracks.

Location: West of Denver; immediately north of the Coors Brewery at Golden.

Camping: No camping is permitted at or near North Table Mountain. The nearest Arapahoe National Forest campgrounds lie northwest of Golden along Colorado Highway 119 near Central City and include Columbine and Cold Springs campgrounds. A couple of campgrounds are in Golden Gate Canyon State Park a little farther north.

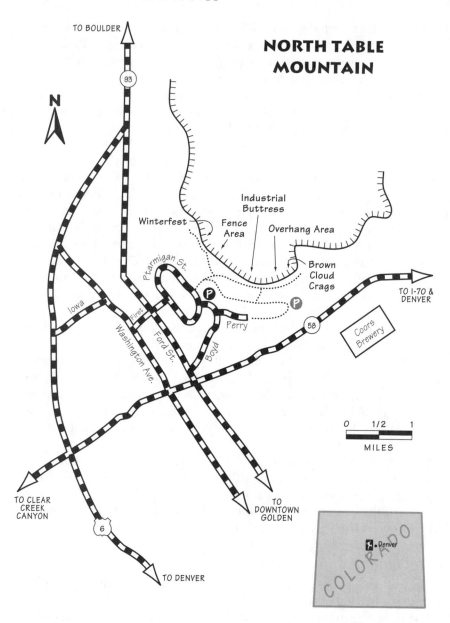

Climbing season: Year-round. Summers can be very hot. Spring and fall offer great climbing weather but can be hot in the afternoons. Table Mountain is one of Colorado's best winter crags. The temperature on sunny days quickly warms to a comfortable level. Winter afternoons are often pleasant. Snow quickly melts on these south-facing slopes.

Restrictions and access issues: The crags are on land deeded to the Access Fund. A parking area, a portable toilet, and a trail to the cliff were installed in 1995. The Friends of Golden Cliffs oversees management of the property. Climbers should respect area homeowners by not parking on residential streets, keeping a low profile, keeping noise and music to a minimum, and staying under the local speed limits.

Guidebooks: *1995 Boulder Sport Climber's Guide* by Mark Rolofson, 1995, is a complete and up-to-date crag guide. *Colorado Front Range Crags* by Peter Hubbel, Chockstone Press, 1994.

Nearby mountain shops, guide services, and gyms: Bent Gate, Inc. (Golden); Grand West Outfitters, The North Face, Paradise Rock Gym (Denver); Basecamp Mountain Sports, Boulder Mountaineer, Neptune Mountaineering, Boulder Rock Club (Boulder).

Services: All services in Golden, Denver, and Boulder.

Emergency services: Call 911. St. Anthony Hospital, 4231 W. 16th Ave., Denver, CO 80204, (303) 629-3511.

Nearby climbing areas: Clear Creek Canyon, South Platte domes, Mount Evans, Lover's Leap, Golden Gate State Park, Morrison bouldering, Eldorado Canyon State Park, Flatirons, Boulder Canyon, Buttonrock Reservoir, Flagstaff Mountain, Industrial Wall.

Nearby attractions: Coors Brewery, Central City-Blackhawk National Historic District, Mount Evans Wilderness Area, Mount Evans Highway, Mount Goliath Natural Area, Georgetown, Guanella Pass Scenic Byway, Golden Gate Canyon State Park, Eldorado Canyon State Park, Denver area attractions, Lookout Mountain, Buffalo Bill's Grave, Mother Cabrini Shrine, Roosevelt National Forest, Arapaho National Forest, White Ranch County Park.

Finding the crag: From Interstate 70 at Denver drive west on Colorado Highway 58, which joins U.S. Highway 6 and continues west from Golden up Clear Creek Canyon. Exit on Washington Avenue in Golden. Drive north, or right, a few blocks to 1st Street. Turn right here and follow to Ptarmigan. Take another right and drive up to the obvious dirt parking area. From Boulder head south on Colorado 93 and exit left or south on either Ford or Washington streets. Drive a few blocks southeast and turn left or east on 1st Street. Follow to Ptarmigan and the parking lot. A steep fence-line trail leads up to the Winterfest Wall. An alternate trail follows an old road southeast along the slope base to another steep trail that climbs up to the Industrial Buttress. Both trails are thankfully short. The parking area and trail will be rerouted in the future.

WINTERFEST WALL

The Winterfest Wall, named for a popular Coors Christmas beer, sits above the western access trail's end. This west-facing wall, beginning on the north at obvious Sunset Arete and ending on the south where the cliff becomes broken, offers an assortment of Table Mountain's best bolted routes.

1. **Sunset Arete** (5.11a) 6 bolts lead to a 2-bolt anchor atop a clean, sharp arete. A hard, off-balance clip in the arete's midsection is the crux.

2. **Rebel Yell** (5.11b) A superb 5-cold-shut line up the left side of a bulging arete to anchors.

3. **Driving Over Stella** (5.11b) Another good one up a steep slab right of REBEL YELL'S arete. Climb past 5 bolts to a double anchor. The crux is a long reach over a thin bulge.

4. **Interstellar Overdrive** (5.11a) 6 bolts lead up a spectacular stemming corner to anchors.

5. **Pseudo Bullet** (5.12a) Step right onto a dicey arete to a steep 5.9 face to the upper crux arete. 7 bolts and a 2-bolt anchor.

6. **Bush Loves Detroit** (5.8) A good crack climb. Broken at the bottom but a smooth hand crack in the dihedral at the top. Friends to #3.

7. **Crawling up Rosanne's Belly** (5.11a) Climbs the pillar's face right of BUSH LOVES DETROIT past 6 bolts to anchors. (Not on topo.)

WINTERFEST WALL

8. **Bimbo in Limbo** (5.10a) 6 bolts and a 2-bolt anchor on a good face route.

9. **Killian's Red** (5.11d) A hard, technical crux below the 3rd bolt leads to loose face-climbing above. 6 bolts and 2 open cold-shut anchors.

10. **Tanning Butter** (5.11d) 6 bolts and a stiff start to a steep face to anchors.

11. **Silver Bullet** (5.10c) A good and popular face route with 6 bolts and anchors.

12. **An Artichoke** (5.10d) A 7-bolt line right of an arete with the crux getting to the double anchors.

13. **Under the Wire** (5.10a) 5 bolts and 2 anchors up a steep face.

14. **Leaning Pillar** (5.10a) 4 bolts up a leaning pillar to cold-shut hooks on a ledge.

15. **The Dissolution** (5.11d) 7 bolts up a steep slab to THE RESOLUTION'S anchors.

16. **The Resolution** (5.11c) An excellent route with fingertip sidepulls up a steep slab. 5 bolts to double chains.

17. **Whole Lotta Drunk** (5.10d) A bouldery start leads to face climbing on the right wall of the right-facing corner. 6 bolts to cold-shut anchors.

INDUSTRIAL BUTTRESS

To reach the Industrial Buttress, follow the cliff-bottom trail southeast for 0.25 mile or so past the Hot Spot Area, Cold Shut Area, Fence Area, and Twelve-Pack Wall. The popular Fence Area offers some good 5.10 routes, including *Winter Warmer*, the cliff's longest climb. The Industrial Buttress is easily identified by the large white "67" painted on the rock. A walk-off descent gully splits the Industrial Buttress in 2 distinct halves.

18. **Heidi Hi** (5.8) A pretty good crack. Bring some nuts and Friends.

19. **Politicians, Priests, and Body Bags** (5.10a) Scale a short crack and face climb above up clean rock past 4 bolts to a double anchor.

20. **Fast Boat to China** (5.8) A crack in a corner system. Bring nuts and Friends for pro.

21. **Salad Bar** (5.10a) This fun route climbs a steep face with 4 bolts to anchors. Bring some wires for additional protection.

22. **Flight 67** (5.11a) A superb line up the left side of a smooth face. 4 bolts to a 2-bolt anchor. Some wired stoppers offer extra security on runouts.

23. **Industrial Disease** (5.11c) This route, one of Table Mountain's best, climbs a tips-crack to a horizontal break. Above is the crux bulge. 5 bolts and 2 anchors. Bring a couple of wired stoppers for the lower crack.

24. **Feeding Frenzy** (5.11c/d) A spectacular line up a steep slab and large left-facing corner. The crux in the corner is a stem problem. 6 bolts and anchors.

25. **Major Bolt Achievement** (5.11a) 6 bolts lead up the outside of a large pillar with the crux a reach over the big roof near the top. Lower off cold-shuts.

26. **Brain Cloud** (5.9+) A great line up a sharp arete with 4 bolts and anchors on a ledge.

27. **Shadow of a Hangdog** (5.10a) A nice layback and thin crack line right of the arete. Bring pro including stoppers and small Friends. It's easily toproped from BRAIN CLOUD'S anchors.

28. **Table Manners** (5.11c) A south-facing wall with 6 bolts and double anchors on top.

THE OVERHANG AREA

This somewhat broken cliff section nonetheless offers some very good routes. The Overhang Area lies east of a prominent descent gully on the east side of the Industrial Buttress. The first good route, *Table Top*, a 5.10a with 2 bolts, sits about 100' east of the end of the buttress. The better routes are even farther east.

29. **Lying on the Ground** (5.11d) A short, steep boulder-problem route with 3 bolts and anchors on the outside of a pillar.

30. **The Ground Doesn't Lie** (5.10c) This short line sits back in a shallow alcove. Crank up steep rock on decent holds past 3 bolts to an open hook and an unwelded cold-shut.

31. **Beer Barrel Buttress** (5.10c) Scramble onto a pedestal and ascend the clean buttress above past 5 bolts to cold-shut anchors. Don't blow the first few clips or you'll hit the pedestal below.

32. **Mr. Squirrel Places a Nut** (5.11c) Thin face climbing leads to a roof and an upper headwall. 5 bolts and open cold-shut hooks.

33. **Tora, Tora, Tora** (5.11b/c) Jam a 5.8 crack to a roof. The headwall above is protected by 3 bolts. Bring some medium pro for the crack.

34. **Mrs. Hen Places a Peck** (5.11d) An excellent, pumpy route up a steep wall. 5 bolts and open cold-shut hooks.

35. **This Ain't Naturita, Pilgrim** (5.9) Wander past 5 bolts on the outside edge of a pillar on this classic climb. Cold-shut lowering anchors.

36. **The Fabulous Flying Carr's Route** (5.11a) A 5-bolt route to lowering anchors. Keep left out of the corner on the lower section to keep it harder.

37. **Sloping Forehead** (5.7+) A short 4-bolt line up the left side of an arete to a ledge with anchors.

38. **Ivory Tower** (5.7) A 4-bolt companion to SLOPING FOREHEAD to same ledge.

BROWN CLOUD CRAGS

A section of broken cliff without any quality routes lies between The Overhang Area and Brown Cloud Crags. The Brown Cloud Crags run east to a wide descent gully. Numerous good routes ascend this cliff section. Also good views east of downtown Denver.

39. **Deck Chairs on the Titanic** (5.9) A good 5-bolt line up a vertical face. The crux is a dyno past the first bolt. It can be avoided by jamming the 5.8 crack to the left.

40. **Killian's Dead** (5.6) A fun moderate hand crack. Bring pro to 3".

41. **Bullet the Brown Cloud** (5.11a) A classic line with the difficult climbing on the lower arete. 3 bolts and lowering chains. A little runout, but the hard climbing is protected.

42. **Tenacious** (5.9+) 4 bolts to cold-shut anchors.

43. **Interface** (5.8) A good short face route with 2 bolts and open hooks.

44. **Lemons, Limes, and Tangerines** (5.8) This route lies east of a broken section with a descent chimney. Climb the steep buttress past 4 bolts. Belay on top and descend via the chimney to the west.

45. **New River Gorge Homesick Blues** (5.11b/c) 3 bolts and anchors.

46. **Kid's Climb** (5.9+) An east-facing warm-up route with 3 bolts and lowering anchors.

47. **Thelma** (5.7) A pretty good but short line on a blunt arete facing the gully. 3 bolts to lowering anchors.

48. **Louise** (5.8) Climb the open face right of THELMA. It's 5.10a if you don't use the right-hand edge. 3 bolts to anchors.

BROWN CLOUD CRAGS

Brett Spencer-Green on Project X's pebble-studded wall in Castlewood Canyon State Park. *Photo by Stewart M. Green.*

CASTLEWOOD CANYON STATE PARK

OVERVIEW

Cherry Creek, springing from rolling ranch country on the Palmer Divide between Colorado Springs and Denver, meanders north until it slices into Castlewood Canyon. This sharp, shallow canyon is administered as an 873-acre Colorado State Park to protect the scenic gorge as well as a unique high plains environment. The canyon is 30 miles east of the Front Range and receives 19 inches of annual rainfall, 4 more than Denver. This precipitation allows a number of plant communities, more representative of the Rocky Mountains than the Great Plains, to flourish on the canyon slopes and bottomlands, including forests of ponderosa pine and Douglas-fir, quaking aspen tucked into damp draws, dense thickets of Gambel oak, and open grassy meadows dotted with summer wildflowers.

Castlewood Canyon State Park is one of those little-known and seldom-visited places reserved for those in the know. The park offers quiet recreational opportunities—hiking its excellent trail system, picnicking under the pines, and climbing the steep walls of the canyon's rimrock. A spate of recent publicity has just made Denver and Colorado Springs climbers aware of Castlewood Canyon's unique and interesting rock and routes. The 10-mile canyon, Colorado's easternmost developed climbing area, offers a superb collection of cracks, topropes, and bolted routes on its short, steep cliffs.

The canyon's 25-million-year-old rock, called Castlerock Conglomerate, stretches along the canyon's east and west rims. It's a strange rock to get used to climbing on. It's hard as concrete, but coarsely studded with pebbles, cobbles, and boulders that jut out at odd angles. Numerous pockets, generally formed when a pebble falls out, range from shallow dishes to sinker in-cuts and allow positive upward movement. Learning to trust and pull on the embedded cobblestones is an intricate part of the Castlewood climbing experience. It feels odd at first, but they're mostly solid.

The rock allows for a diversity of routes, including cracks, corners, slabs, vertical faces, and overhanging aretes, ranging in height from 20 to 50 feet. Climbers divide the canyon into three main areas: East Rim, West Rim, and Inner Canyon. The East Rim, with the greatest profusion of difficult bolted lines, is probably the best area for the sport climber. The West Rim, site of the canyon's oldest routes, yields numerous good crack and toprope lines. It's an ideal site for beginners and moderate leaders. The Inner Canyon, north of the park's visitor center, offers some fine sport walls as well as some of the canyon's best bouldering. A number of good ice climbs also form in the Inner Canyon during winter.

Essential equipment includes a rope (a shortened one works fine), a dozen quick draws, and a few long slings for rimrock belays or anchors set back from the edge. A rack of wired stoppers, a set of Friends, a few TCUs, and a couple Tri-cams for pockets is adequate for the trad routes. Topropes require tying off trees or setting anchors. Pad the rope or anchor slings where they run over edges. The rock's coarse and abrasive character can quickly trash a rope. Descent from routes is from lowering anchors set below the cliff-top or scrambling descent routes.

Castlewood Canyon State Park has a number of important rules and regulations climbers should be aware of. The park is a fee area. The $3 entry permit, paid at the Visitor Center or the north entrance station, goes on your front windshield. Tickets are issued to those who skip payment. The entrance station is usually staffed during the busy summer months, but is self-service the rest of the year. The installation of bolts and fixed protection is currently prohibited. Most of the bolted routes were put up in the late 1980s before a bolting moratorium. New route permits may eventually be allowed. Use existing and designated access trails to reach the various cliff sectors. When hiking stay on designated trails. Mountain bikes are allowed only on roads and designated bike paths. Some other rules include keeping pets on a leash no longer than six feet, no camping, and no ground fires. Park only in designated parking areas, not along the road. Be advised that the road through the upper canyon is not maintained in winter. Travel at your own risk. It becomes very icy and towing fees can be very expensive. When visiting in winter, it's better to park at the Homestead Trail lot or at the Visitor Center and walk to the crags.

A number of objective dangers are found at Castlewood Canyon. Loose rock is generally not a problem; but use caution on the rims or on descent walk-offs. Bee hives and wasp nests are found in cavities and cracks on the walls and on existing routes. Mosquitoes can be a problem in summer. Bring bug juice to ward off the hungry hordes. Poison ivy occurs in the canyon. Watch for its shiny three leaves. The biggest danger is rattlesnakes. The canyon's boulders, dense underbrush, warm climate, and plentiful prey, offers ideal habitat for the prairie rattlesnake. If you do much walking here between May and October, you will probably encounter a snake. Be particularly careful along the access paths. They blend in quite well with the grass and oak leaves. Watch your hands on descent or scrambling routes. Rattlesnakes like to sun on open ledges or under bushes. If you do meet a snake, don't kill it. Remember this is their home, and you're the intruder.

Trip Planning Information

General description: A selection of topropes, cracks, and bolted routes on a thin band of conglomerate in a shallow canyon.

Location: On the high plains southeast of Denver and northeast of Colorado Springs, along upper Cherry Creek.

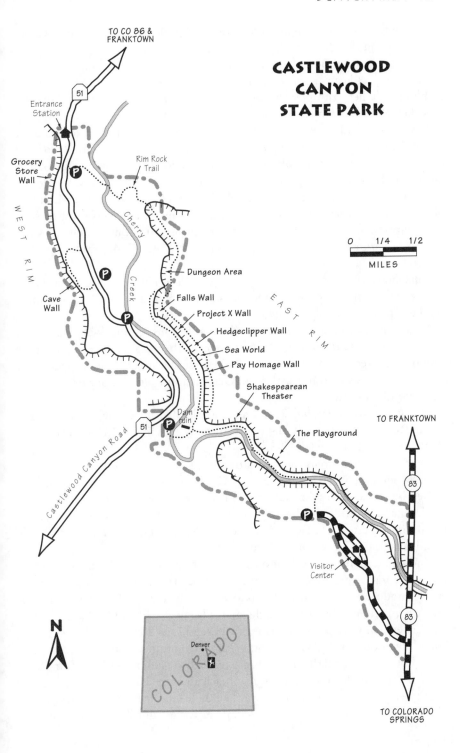

CASTLEWOOD
CANYON
STATE PARK

TO CO 86 &
FRANKTOWN

51

Entrance
Station

Grocery
Store
Wall

Rim Rock
Trail

W
E
S
T

R
I
M

Cherry

Creek

P

P

P

Dungeon Area

Cave
Wall

Falls Wall

Project X Wall

Hedgeclipper Wall

Sea World

Pay Homage Wall

E
A
S
T

R
I
M

Shakespearean
Theater

TO FRANKTOWN

Castlewood Canyon Road

51

P

Dam
ruin

The Playground

83

P

Visitor
Center

83

N

0   1/4   1/2

MILES

Denver

COLORADO

TO COLORADO
SPRINGS

Camping: No camping is allowed in the state park. The nearest public campgrounds are in Pike National Forest 40 miles to the west.

Climbing season: Year-round. Summers can be very hot and rattlesnakes abound. Expect heavy afternoon thunderstorms. Fall and spring offer the best climbing weather, with pleasant temperatures. Winter days on the south- and west-facing cliffs can be excellent.

Restrictions and access issues: A daily pass or annual permit is required for use of the park. Stay on designated trails and use only designated trails for cliff access. The installation of bolts and fixed protection is prohibited. Do not garden routes by removing vegetation or trees from cracks and pockets; and do not remove bird nests, especially those of cliff swallows, from the cliffs. Mountain bikes are allowed only on roads and designated bike trails. Pets must be on a leash. Ground fires are prohibited. For more information on Castlewood Canyon State Park call (303) 688-5242 or write: P.O. Box 504, Franktown, CO 80116.

Guidebooks: *Colorado Front Range Crags* by Peter Hubbel, Chockstone Press, 1994. Some of the topos and names are inaccurate in this book. A good sport climber's guide is found in *Rock & Ice* #60.

Nearby mountain shops, guide services, and gyms: Grand West Outfitters, The North Face, Paradise Rock Gym (Denver); 8th Street Climbing Club, Sport Climbing Center, Mountain Chalet, Grand West Outfitters (Colorado Springs).

Services: All services in Castlerock, Denver, and Colorado Springs. Limited services in Franktown.

Emergency services: Dial 911. Castle Rock Medical Clinic, 515 Jerry St., Castle Rock, CO, (303) 688-0660. St. Anthony Hospital, 4231 W. 16th Ave., Denver, CO 80204, (303) 629-3511.

Nearby climbing areas: South Platte domes, Jackson Creek Dome, North Table Mountain, Morrison bouldering, Garden of the Gods, Scorpio Dome.

Nearby attractions: Pike National Forest, Devils Head National Recreation Trail, Cherry Creek State Recreation Area, Chatfield State Recreation Area, Roxborough State Park, Denver Museum of Natural History, Air Force Academy, Pikes Peak, Garden of the Gods.

Finding the canyon: The easiest access is via Interstate 25. From either Denver or Colorado Springs, exit I-25 at Castle Rock (Exit 182). Head east 6 miles on Colorado Highway 86 to Franktown. About 0.25 mile before reaching Franktown and just before the highway bridge over Cherry Creek, turn south on Castlewood Canyon Road. This gravel road runs 2 miles southwest to the boundary of Castlewood Canyon State Park. An entrance station sits just south of the boundary. The East Rim cliffs are reached via Homestead and Rim Rock trails or Dam and Rim Rock trails. Approach all of the East Rim sectors via the rim rather than from below to protect the fragile hillside habitats from erosion. The West Rim cliffs are accessed via Climber's Cave Trail. The park road can be treacherous in winter and is not maintained. Travel at your own risk. It's wiser in winter to park at the Homestead Trail lot just south of the entrance station and access the cliffs via Rim Rock Trail. This is far cheaper than being towed out of a ditch farther south.

THE INNER CANYON

The Inner Canyon area (and park visitor center) is accessed by driving south on Colorado 83 from Franktown 5 miles to the park's east entrance. To reach the area's excellent walls, hike north on Inner Canyon Trail from the large picnic area north of the visitor center. The best sector is The Juggernaut Area. Walk down the trail through the canyon to the power lines that span the gorge. The area lies on the north side of the canyon under the power lines. *Seem to Seam* (5.12a) climbs the obvious bulging arete past 5 bolts. Stick-clip the first bolt for the first-move dyno. Around the corner is *Bat Face* (5.10a), an excellent 4-bolt line up the left side of a steep slab. A couple more 5.10s lie northwest from the power lines. Many excellent boulders with a diversity of hard problems scatter throughout the Inner Canyon. Some excellent ice routes form up on the shady south side of the canyon.

THE WEST RIM

The West Rim offers numerous toprope and crack climbs on seven different sectors—Five & Dime Wall, Grocery Store Wall, Neanderthal Wall, Cave Wall, Morning Sun Wall, Porky's Wall, and Alien Tuna Area. The West Rim is probably the best place for the beginner and moderate-grade climber at Castlewood. Many lower-grade routes are found on these cliffs. The area is also cooler in summer than the East Rim cliffs.

The Grocery Store Wall, reached from the road via Climber's Cave Trail, has many traditional climbs and topropes ranging from 5.6 to 5.12. There are many moderate cracks and faces, some with toprope anchors. Good routes in this sector include *Pretzel Logic* (5.11b), *Hamburger Helper* (5.10b), and *Tuna Helper* (5.10a). The Morning Sun Wall, the only bolted sector on the West Rim, is reached by hiking up Cave Trail from the parking area just north of the Falls parking lot to Cave Wall. Walk south along the cliff base about 150 yards to the Morning Sun Wall. Four bolted routes ascend the wall. From north to south they are *Pointillist* (5.11a; 6 bolts and anchors), *Renaissance* (5.11a; 5 bolts and anchors), *Marijuana* (5.10d; 5 bolts and anchors), and *Magician's Apprentice* (5.10d; 4 bolts and anchors).

EAST RIM

The East Rim is Castlewood Canyon's most developed sport climbing area, with numerous bolted routes ascending the short rimrock cliffs. The rim is divided into seven sectors—The Dungeon Area, Falls Wall, The Zoids, Project X Wall, Hedgeclipper Area, Sea World, and Pay Homage Wall.

The area is accessed by driving just south from the park's north entrance booth to the parking area at the old homestead. Park here and walk east and south on Homestead/Rim Rock Trail onto the East Rim. Walk south along the rim for a short distance to the top of Falls Wall at the farthest west rim point. A scramble descent lies just north of the wall. Continue south along the rim for the other walls.

An alternate approach is to drive south on the canyon road and park at the dam ruins. Follow the Dam Trail east across the creek and pick up the Rim Rock Trail. Follow it north to the top of Pay Homage Wall and Sea World. A short, steep, and eroded approach is east of the Falls parking area in the central canyon. This rough path crosses the creek and climbs the hillside above to the base of Falls Wall.

Several large boulders, including one with a tree growing from its summit and The Buoux Block (a huge boulder with a bolted line (5.12c) on its west face), lie below Falls Wall. A rough, sometimes hard-to-find climber's trail follows the cliff base north to The Dungeon Area and south to the other sectors. Watch for snakes on this path. The best access is via the wide Rim Rock Trail, accessible via several easy scrambles, along the East Rim. All the cliffs are easily found below the trail.

FALLS WALL

Falls Wall offers some excellent bolted routes as well as some of the canyon's best cracks and topropes. Routes are listed from north to south. Walk north from The Buoux Block to find the first route, which lies just east of a large west-leaning block. A couple of B1 boulder problems ascend the block's overhanging wall.

1. **Swinging Sirloin** (5.11c) This tricky route, on a steep face just left of a ramp, is more difficult than it looks. Climb up and left past 4 bolts with homemade hangers to double anchors.

2. **Out of Arms Reach** (5.10d) Climbs the right wall of an obvious dihedral behind a large fir tree. Dicey 5.9 climbing leads to the first bolt 20' up. 2 more bolts lead to the top. Rap from slings in the tree. No anchors.

3. **Arborist Arms** (5.12a or 5.10c) Climb past a bolt to a big hole. Going left of bolts is 5.12a, while going right is 5.10c. 3 bolts and 2 cold-shut anchors.

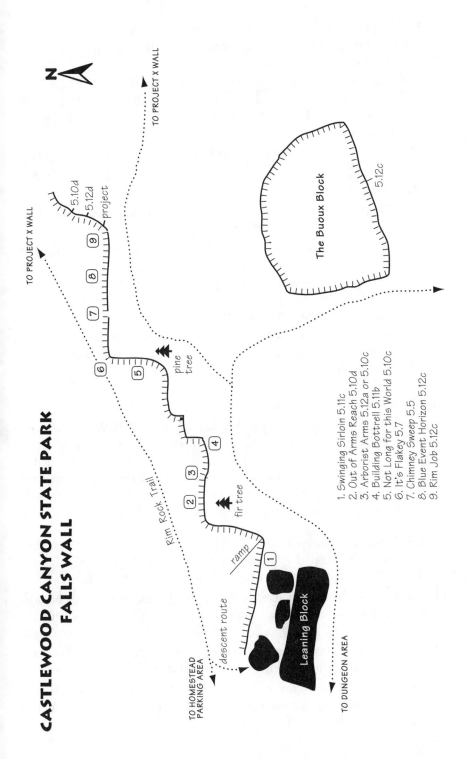

CASTLEWOOD CANYON STATE PARK
FALLS WALL

N

TO PROJECT X WALL

TO PROJECT X WALL

TO PROJECT X WALL

5.10d
5.12d
project

9
8
7
6
5

pine tree

Rim Rock Trail

2 3
4

fir tree

ramp

1

descent route

TO HOMESTEAD PARKING AREA

Leaning Block

TO DUNGEON AREA

The Buoux Block

5.12c

1. Swinging Sirloin 5.11c
2. Out of Arms Reach 5.10d
3. Arborist Arms 5.12a or 5.10c
4. Building Bottrell 5.11b
5. Not Long for this World 5.10c
6. It's Flakey 5.7
7. Chimney Sweep 5.5
8. Blue Event Horizon 5.12c
9. Rim Job 5.12c

4. **Building Bottrell** (5.11b) This good route follows the leaning edge on the south end of the face right of the large fir. The third clip is hard. 4 cold-shuts to double cold-shut anchors.

5. **Not Long For This World** (5.10c) Walk south from the above routes past a pine tree to a huge open dihedral. This route, usually toproped, lies on the north wall of the dihedral. Climb up and into the shallow right-facing corner. Bring wired stoppers and small cams.

6. **It's Flakey** (5.7) Follow the thin cracks in the dihedral. Bring small pro.

7. **Chimney Sweep** (5.5) The deep chimney on the right wall of the dihedral. Don't wear shorts.

8. **Blue Event Horizon** (5.12c) Toprope the good-looking face right of the chimney off a tree anchor on the rim.

9. **Rim Job** (5.12c) This spectacular route, one of the best at Castlewood, climbs the sharply overhanging arete. Start behind a fir tree right of the big dihedral and crank up and right past 6 bolts to a double cold-shut anchor. The route, originally rated 5.13a, has mostly good holds. It's tricky getting to the anchors without dynoing to the ridge.

An open project with 4 black bolts is just around the corner from *Rim Job*. A few yards farther east is *Blackout* (5.12d), the 1" to 3" crack splitting a big roof. The roof crack/corner right of *Blackout* is *Lactic Tactics* (5.10d).

PROJECT X WALL

This excellent sector lies a few hundred yards south of Falls Wall. Find a trail below RIM JOB at the south end of Falls Wall and walk south through dense oak thickets to the Project X Wall. It's better to scramble onto the East Rim from the north end of Falls Wall and follow the good trail on top south to Project X. This wall is partly hidden by a huge clump of boulders. Routes are listed from north to south. The first two routes are not on the Project X Wall.

10. **Skunk Buttress** (5.10a) This short, fun route begins among tall pine trees along the cliff base path just north of the large boulders and the Project X Wall. Climb up the blunt arete past 2 bolts to 2 cold-shut anchors.

11. **Lothar** (5.9+) This short line climbs the shady side of the huge boulder north of the Project X Wall. Climb the pebbled wall past 3 cold-shuts to cold-shut anchors. Just opposite LOTHAR is a 5.5 ascent/descent route.

12. **Rest in Pieces** (5.9+) A steep, pumpy route on the left side of the Project X Wall. Begin by the big boulder blocking the lower gully.

13. **Nuclear Blue** (5.11a) Traverse right from REST IN PIECES for the .11a start. Direct start up past the first bolt is a bouldery .11c. A cool undercling move over the upper roof is the route crux.

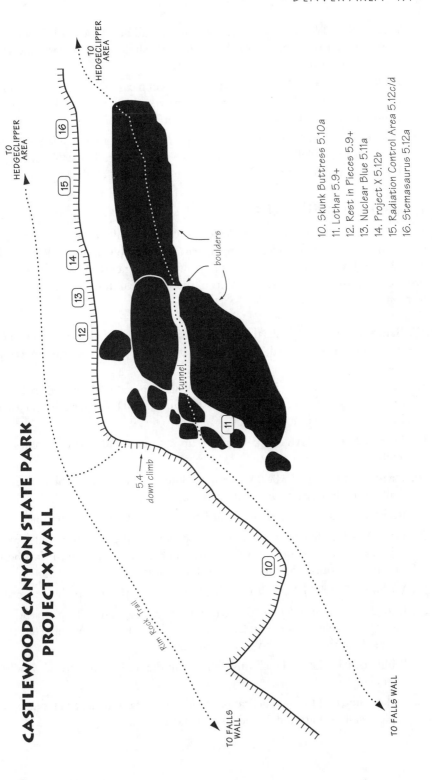

CASTLEWOOD CANYON STATE PARK
PROJECT X WALL

TO HEDGECLIPPER AREA

TO HEDGECLIPPER AREA

boulders

tunnel

5.4 → down climb

Rim Rock Trail

TO FALLS WALL

TO FALLS WALL

10. Skunk Buttress 5.10a
11. Lothar 5.9+
12. Rest in Pieces 5.9+
13. Nuclear Blue 5.11a
14. Project X 5.12b
15. Radiation Control Area 5.12c/d
16. Stemasaurus 5.12a

14. **Project X** (5.12b) A good, hard line up the middle of the wall. 5 bolts to single anchor over the top of the wall. Use a sling on the anchor and last bolt to lower off.

15. **Radiation Control Area** (5.12c/d) A thin, technical, height-dependent line on the right side of the wall. The crux moves above the roof involve sick pebble-pinching. 4 bolts to cold-shut lowering anchors.

16. **Stemasaurus** (5.12a) Climb .11c rock past 2 bolts to the huge ledge. Stem up the leaning right-facing corner above past 2 more bolts. No anchors. Use the last bolt and a #2.5 or 3 Friend to lower and clean.

HEDGECLIPPER AREA

Follow the trail south from the Project X Wall around a buttress and over a jumble of boulders to the Hedgeclipper Area, or scramble up to the Rim Rock Trail and follow the rim south to this northwest-facing cliff. A large fallen tree propped against the rim marks the start of the sector. Routes are listed from left to right.

17. **Beta Slave** (5.10c) Climbs the vertical wall right of the fallen tree. It's somewhat devious, sequential, with a couple of long reaches. 5 bolts to lowering anchors.

18. **Patrick Hedgeclipper** (5.11b) A superb route up water-blackened rock left of a leaning arete. 5 bolts to 2 cold-shut anchors. The upper crux is easier by deadpointing to a cobble jug.

19. **Entry Level** (5.8) A good 5-bolt line up a seam studded with pebbles to anchors.

20. **Heavy Duty Judy** (5.10c) A popular route up the yellow lichen-covered wall with 4 bolts and cold-shut anchors.

21. **Radiation Fear** (5.11a) A short, hard crank past 3 bolts to double anchors.

22. **First Dibs** (5.10a) Begin right of a steep ramp and climb up pebbles and cobbles to the crux roof above a horizontal break. Go right at the last bolt for an easier finish. 5 bolts to double cold-shuts.

23. **Wishbone Crack** (5.10a) A thin, right-leaning crack that is usually toproped.

24. **Bolted by Committee** (5.12a) Excellent but tweaky mono-doights lead to easier rock. The upper bouldery section is best climbed by going up the right side of the arete. 5 bolts to 2 cold-shuts.

25. **Pebble Beach** (5.11d) Pinch tiny pebbles up the dark water streak. 5 bolts to anchors.

26. **Peckerwood** (5.11a) Thin delicate climbing up the far right side of the steeply angled wall. 4 bolts and 2 cold-shut anchors.

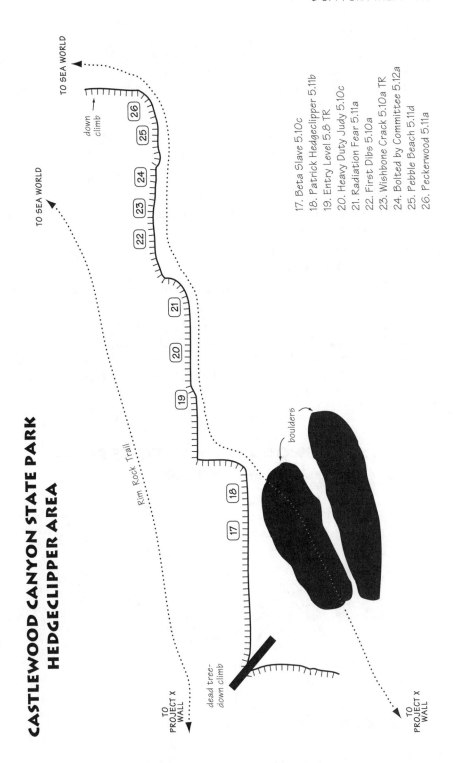

CASTLEWOOD CANYON STATE PARK
HEDGECLIPPER AREA

TO PROJECT X WALL

Rim Rock Trail

dead tree-down climb

TO SEA WORLD

TO SEA WORLD

down climb

17 18 19 20 21 22 23 24 25 26

boulders

TO PROJECT X WALL

17. Beta Slave 5.10c
18. Patrick Hedgeclipper 5.11b
19. Entry Level 5.8 TR
20. Heavy Duty Judy 5.10c
21. Radiation Fear 5.11a
22. First Dibs 5.10a
23. Wishbone Crack 5.10a TR
24. Bolted by Committee 5.12a
25. Pebble Beach 5.11d
26. Peckerwood 5.11a

SEA WORLD

This sector, also called Hanson's Wall, sits about 100 yards south of the Hedgeclipper Area. Follow the trail along the cliff base from the far right side of Hedgeclipper to this steep wall blackened by two wide water streaks. Routes are from left to right.

27. **Trade Winds** (5.11a) Climb over a roof and follow the left edge of the left water streak to double anchors over the top. 5 bolts.

28. **Horse Latitudes** (5.11b) Steep pebble climbing up the right side of the water streak past 5 bolts to cold-shut anchors over the top.

29. **Doldrums** (5.12a) Crank over the big roof and follow the left side of the right water streak to 2 cold-shuts. 4 bolts.

30. **It's a Nor'easter Outta Thar Southwest** (5.12a/b) 4 bolts to double anchors on the right side of the black streak.

31. **Sea Breeze** (5.11d) Hard climbing up the yellow wall just around the corner. 5 bolts to 2 cold-shut anchors.

The Pay Homage Wall, a.k.a. the Vulture Wall, sits farther south from Sea World. Follow the trail along the cliff base to it. 4 good bolted walls scale it including 70' *Scandinavian Dream*, a 7-bolt 5.11a, and *Pay Homage*, an excellent 7-bolt 5.12a up the center of the wall.

CASTLEWOOD CANYON STATE PARK
SEA WORLD

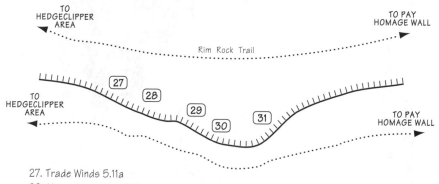

27. Trade Winds 5.11a
28. Horse Latitudes 5.11b
29. Doldrums 5.12a
30. It's a Nor'easter Outta Thar Southwest 5.12a/b
31. Sea Breeze 5.11d

Southern Front Range

REGION

SOUTH PLATTE

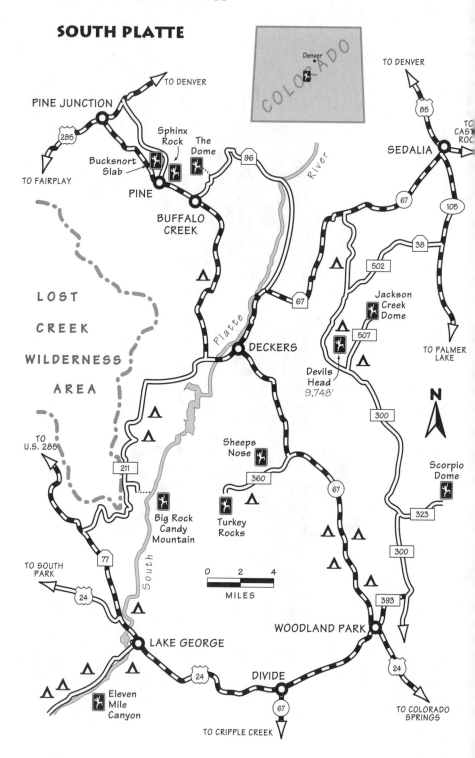

SOUTH PLATTE AREA

BUCKSNORT SLAB & SPHINX ROCK

OVERVIEW

Bucksnort Slab and Sphinx Rock, lying along the Elk Creek Road in the northern South Platte region, offer some of the area's best roadside cragging opportunities. Both are composed of fine, flawless granite, darkened by occasional water streaks and broken by occasional crack systems. Bucksnort and Sphinx, facing southeast, allow good cold weather cragging when nearby higher cliffs remain encased in snow and shadow.

Sphinx Rock, towering east of the town of Pine, is one of Colorado's most famed crags. Its testpiece is the obvious *Sphinx Crack,* an abrupt splitter that slices through the rock's right-hand summit block. A series of unnatural and natural events formed the crack. During the 1940s some yahoos drilled several deep holes into the rock's solid summit and fired at least one dynamite charge in the holes before Pine's townsfolk decided that the big granite block wouldn't look too good in their front yard. Unknown natural events, possibly frost-wedging, then went to work on the weakened rock and eventually split the block in half. An almost perfect crack formed on the summit block's southwest face, throwing up a challenge to rock climbers with its thin, overhanging finger jams.

Several climbers began working on the project in the late 1970s with renowned crackmaster Steve Hong finally succeeding in April, 1981, some two years after first trying the route. Californian Tony Yaniro repeated the route in four days that autumn with a yo-yo ascent. Although Peter Croft came close to on-sighting the 5.13b/c crack in 1993, Japan's Yuji Hirayama placed gear and on-sighted the route in 1995. The crack, despite the hard grades put up by sport climbers, has yielded few ascents and none without preplaced protection until Hirayama's ascent. The crack was first aid-climbed by Boulder climbers Paul Sibley and Bill Roos in the late 1960s. Besides *Sphinx Crack,* Sphinx Rock also offers some good crack, slab, and aid routes.

Bucksnort Slab, a granite dome eroding out of a pine-clad hillside just up the canyon from Sphinx Rock, is a smooth, almost featureless expanse of rock

Bob D'Antonio moves up *Nuclear Burn/China Syndrome* on Bucksnort Slab.
Photo by Stewart M. Green.

broken only by occasional discontinuous cracks, dihedrals, and roofs. Some brilliant bolt-protected face routes lace the slab's steep lower face, while one of the South Platte's best 5.7 cracks ascends an open book up the crag's midriff. *The Classic Dihedral,* first climbed by Ron Cox, Paul Sibley, and Carl Arndt in 1967, was Bucksnort Slab's first route. Most of the others were put up in the 1980s.

Trip Planning Information

General description: Two roadside crags offer several excellent crack routes and numerous bolted slabs.

Location: Southwest of Denver near the town of Pine.

Camping: There is no camping in the immediate area. The nearest public campgrounds are to the south in Pike National Forest, including Kelsey on Colorado Highway 126 and Top of the World just off Colorado 126. Several other campgrounds lie up Buffalo Creek along Forest Road 543.

Climbing season: Year-round. Spring and fall offer the best weather. Summers can be hot, with afternoon storms. Winters are often snowy, but short-sleeve days regularly occur.

Restrictions and access issues: The slab lies on private land. Treat climbing here as a privilege, not a right. Keep a low profile; don't build fires or leave

BUCKSNORT SLAB
&
SPHINX ROCK

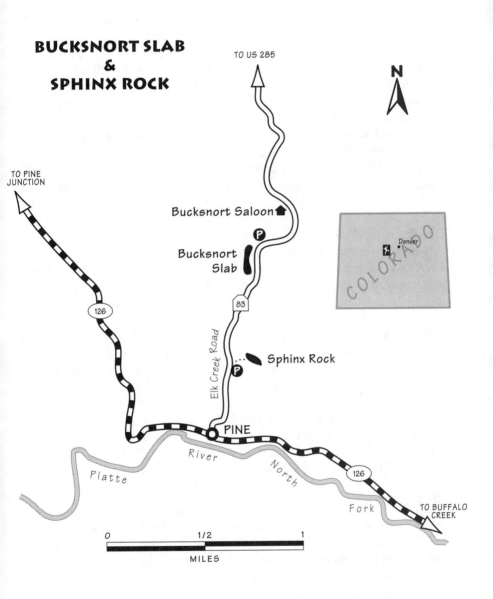

TO US 285

N

TO PINE
JUNCTION

Bucksnort Saloon

Bucksnort
Slab

126

83

Elk Creek Road

Sphinx Rock

PINE

River

Platte

North

Fork

126

TO BUFFALO
CREEK

COLORADO

Denver

0   1/2   1

MILES

trash. Keep off adjoining private property with summer cabins. Park well off the road.

Guidebooks: *South Platte Rock Climbing and the Garden of the Gods* by Peter Hubbel and Mark Rolofson, Chockstone Press, 1988. *Rock and Ice #25* published a very good South Platte guide by Ken Trout.

Nearby mountain shops, guide services, and gyms: Denver area stores and gyms are closest. Grand West Outfitters, The North Face, Paradise Rock Gym.

Services: Limited services in Pine, Buffalo Creek, and Pine Junction. The Bucksnort Saloon offers sustenance 0.5 mile up the road from the slab. Complete services in the Denver area.

Emergency services: Call 911. St. Anthony Hospital, 4231 W. 16th Ave, Denver, CO 80204, (303) 629-3511.

Nearby climbing areas: Squat Rock, The Dome, The Bishop, Cynical Pinnacle, Etive Slabs, Poe Buttress, Chair Rocks, The Castle, Little Scraggy Dome, Helen's Dome, Acid Rock, Sheep Rock, Sunshine Dome, Wigwam Domes, Couch Potatoes, Turkey Rock, Turkey Tail, Sheeps Nose, Clear Creek Canyon, North Table Mountain, Morrison bouldering.

Nearby attractions: Pine-North Fork National Historic District, South Platte River, Pike National Forest, Devil's Head National Recreation Trail, Lost Creek Wilderness Area, Cheesman Lake, Rampart Range Road, Mount Evans Wilderness Area, Guanella Pass Scenic Byway, Denver attractions.

Finding the crags: Bucksnort Slab and Sphinx Rock sit along Jefferson County Road 83 (Elk Creek Road) northeast of Pine. Pine, a National Historic District, lies 6 miles south of U.S. Highway 285 and Pine Junction on Colorado 126. Turn north in Pine at the Pine Grocery Store onto gravel Elk Creek Road. Drive 0.4 mile to reach Sphinx Rock. Park in the obvious pulloff and hike 0.25 mile south to the rock. To reach Bucksnort Slab continue up the road and narrowing canyon for 2.1 miles from Pine. The crag lies northwest above the road. Park just past the slab at a couple of small pulloffs. Parking is limited. The famed Bucksnort Saloon sits another 0.6 mile farther upcanyon.

SPHINX ROCK

Sphinx Rock is visible from Pine. From the pulloff follow a rough trail south into the valley, across the creek, and up the gravel slopes to the rock's base. Approach time is less than 10 minutes. *Sphinx Crack* is reached by walking up to a ledge on the rock's east flank. **Descend** from the top by rappelling 50' off the backside of the west summit.

1. **Talus Food Crack** (5.9+) This route follows a right-leaning crack system on the far left side of the wall. Begin below the obvious crack on the rock's southwest face. Climb a slightly rotten slab past 2 bolts (5.9+) and follow the hands-to-fist crack up and right.

SPHINX ROCK

2. **Cave Route** (5.6) Scramble right up a northwest-facing, fourth-class slab to the base of the left summit block and the start of this good, short lieback pitch. **Descend** by scrambling north.

3. **Plinth** (5.8 R) A good friction route up the prominent right-leaning slab that splits the face. Climb easy rock to a belay stance and follow bolts upward in either 1 or 2 pitches. **Rack:** Bring quick draws, TCUs, wires, and other small pro.

4. **Lickety Split** (5.7 R) Another bolted, friction route up the right edge of the slab.

5. **Dihedral Route** (5.10-) 2 pitches up a prominent right-facing dihedral. Begin below the dihedral above some blocks. **Pitch 1** climbs a chimney to a large ledge. **Pitch 2** liebacks the large corner (5.8) above to a 5.10- finger crack. Bring extra pro to 3".

6. **Cheops** (5.10c) This good bolted route begins at the end of the ledge midway up the DIHEDRAL ROUTE. Reach the route base by traversing across a huge broken ledge below SPHINX CRACK to the base of the prominent dihedral. Follow 8 bolts up the blunt arete to a ledge. It's a little flakey up high. Belay from 2 bolts on a ledge. **Descent:** Rappel or lower 80' to the ground.

7. **Thinner** (5.9 A4) A steep aid route up the seam left of SPHINX CRACK. **Rack:** Bring rurps, knifeblades, and copperheads.

8. **Sphinx Crack** (5.13b/c) This is it—Colorado's most famous crack climb. Reach its start by scrambling around the east flank of the rock to a large, broken ledge that leads to the crack base. The difficulties above are readily obvious. Climb the 5.11a crack/corner to the roof. Swing over and jam a painfully thin and insecure finger crack up the overhanging face above. Higher the crack widens to secure thin hands. **Rack:** Tape your hands and fingers well and bring extra Friends from #1 to #3. The crack is also an excellent clean A1 aid route. Several runout friction routes climb the slabs below the crack.

BUCKSNORT SLAB

Bucksnort Slab sits above the Elk Creek Road 2.1 miles from Pine and Colorado 126. Park past the slab at a couple pulloffs. Parking is limited and traffic is heavy on the road. Avoid parking on the roadway itself. Most routes need only quick draws and a rope, while the few worthwhile cracks require a rack of stoppers and Friends. Many bolts found here are old 1/4" bolts; user beware. **Descend** from the top of the dome by walking south along the summit crest and dropping into the shallow canyon to the south. Many routes end at rappel stations on the face; some require 2 ropes to reach the base.

1. **Left Out** (5.10a) Begin atop a flake/block on the south side of the slab and wind upward and left past several 1/4" bolts to a bolted belay under an arch near the top. Rappel with 2 ropes from slings 120' to the ground or clamber up and walk off. A good 5.10 6-bolt face route lies immediately left and ends on a ramp 90' up left. **Descent:** Downclimb south on easy slabs. **Rack:** Bring some medium Friends and large stoppers to set up a belay.

2. **Buck Fever** (5.9+) Duck through a tunnel under several large boulders to the base of a large right-facing dihedral. **Pitch 1** climbs a hand and finger crack (5.9-) up the corner. A hard exit move (5.9) leaves the crack at a crescent roof and leads up left to a 3-bolt belay stance with a chain rap anchor (85' down). **Pitch 2** frictions up the bolted slab above (5.9 and 3 bolts) to the same slinged belay as LEFT OUT. Rap 125' with 2 ropes. Bring pro to 3" for the crack. A good, direct start to this route begins atop the boulders just right of LEFT OUT. Edge up and right past 5, 3/8" bolts (5.10) to the chain anchor.

3. **Buouxsnort** (5.11b/c) A superb and continuous line up the steep, blank wall 20' right of BUCK FEVER. Begin right of the obvious dihedral. Weave up the dark water streak for about 125' past 11 bolts to a 2-bolt, chained rappel stance below a shallow corner on the lower-angle upper slab. It's kinda scary getting to the first bolt 15' up. Also watch the run-out to the second bolt—you'll crater if you blow the clip. **Rack:** Bring some RPs and small wires for some extra creative pro.

4. **Shake n' Bake** (5.10c) A superb 3-pitch line up Bucksnort's mid-section. **Pitch 1** begins on the left side of the large flake/boulder leaning against the main face. Ascend its left edge past a few 5.9 moves on rotten, flakey rock to an easy runout slab. Belay from bolts atop the flake. **Pitch 2** scales the waterstreak above (5.10c) past several bolts to a belay/rappel stance below a small roof. Rap 165' with 2 ropes to the ground or finish up with **Pitch 3**—a short 5.7 hand crack that waltzes to the summit. **Rack:** Bring pro to 3" for the crack.

5. **Grand Slam** (5.11) A strange pitch that face climbs up behind the huge flake below SHAKE N' BAKE. Begin in the shadow under the flake and follow 4 bolts up and left. Finish with weird chimneying up the bombay flake to the top. **Rack:** There may be some fixed pro at the contact of the flake and face, otherwise bring some small and medium stuff.

6. **Hurricane Gloria** (5.12a/b) This good route up the dark streak on the steep central slab offers desperate bolt-protected face climbing. It can be done in 2 pitches, with a bolted sling belay, or 1 long rope-length to the summit slabs. Many parties rap from chains at the first belay stance. Begin right of the huge flake and follow 7, 1/4" bolts upward to 5.12 moves on the steep headwall. From the 2-bolt stance, work up and left (5.11a) to a crack (5.8+) that finishes the route. Bring pro to 3". The hanging belay stance sits right in the middle of a crux section and, if used, is considered a rest point.

BUCKSNORT SLAB

7. **The Good, Bad, and the Ugly** (5.12b) **Pitch 1** climbs a 5.9 crack in a shallow, left-leaning corner for 20' and exits left onto a steep slab. Difficult 5.12 moves lead up right past 4 1/4" bolts to 3 belay bolts. **Pitch 2** heads up a friction face (5.10c) and a runout 5.9 slab.

8. **Classic Dihedral** (5.7+) This classic route, one of the South Platte's best 5.7s, climbs a sustained crack line in the central dihedral—fingers-to-hands to an off-width or layback at the top. It's a full rope length to the belay ledge atop the slab. Rappel 160' with 2 ropes to the ground or continue to the summit on easy rock.

9. **Slippery When Wet** (5.11b) Ascend CLASSIC DIHEDRAL'S initial easy corner and angle right onto the blank slab. Bolts (1/4") and 5.9 climbing lead left and above a roof; traverse up left on a 5.11a headwall past 5 bolts to a bolted belay ledge. A variation, SLIPPERY WHEN DRY (5.11d), climbs thin flakes directly up the headwall. Use caution with the route's many 1/4" bolts. Rap 135' with 2 ropes from the ledge or climb up right (5.10) to the summit.

10. **Nuclear Burn/China Syndrome** (5.12a) Continuous and excellent thin face climbing leads up a steep, ultra-thin slab to a 2-bolt chained lowering station. 5 bolts. A good 5.8 crack is immediately to the right.

11. **Core Dump** (5.11c/d) Hard bolt-protected slab climbing (4 bolts) off the ground leads to a 5.7 crack and a belay stance. Continue up cracks to the summit.

12. **Gumby Groove** (5.10a/b) An excellent 1-pitch, 80' route up a steep slab and groove on the right side of the wall. Work up to a black water groove and edge up and right (5.10a) to a spacious ledge below some big bulging roofs. 4 bolts. The last one is somewhat funky. Rappel from a 2-bolt rap station on the ledge. THE BOYS ARE BACK, an awkward 5.11 off-width, thrashes up the leaning corner above and right of the ledge.

13. **Over and Out** (5.8) Climb up the slab past a bolt, then angle left past another bolt to the GUMBY GROOVE belay and rap anchors.

THE DOME

OVERVIEW

The Dome perches on a lofty ridge high above the North Fork of the South Platte River. Its immense southeast-facing slab, broken by occasional roofs and creased by polished water streaks, reaches 400 feet above a boulder-littered base. The smooth slab, reached by an hour-long forced march up the steep slopes below, yields a marvelous selection of sustained, generally well-protected friction routes including the popular *Topographic Oceans* and the classic *Bishop's Jaggers*. The routes, ranging from 2 to 4 pitches in length, ascend cracks and smooth bolted slabs. Expect occasional runouts on easier climbing, some quite serious. **Descent** is accomplished by rappelling the routes with double ropes, although *Bishop's Jaggers* goes to The Dome's summit. Descend from it by downclimbing north and skirting the formation's east flank.

Climbing history: The Dome and The Bishop, a crag immediately southwest of The Dome on the same ridge, boast some of the South Platte's earliest technical climbs. Albert Ellingwood, a Colorado College professor who learned rope work and rock technique in England as a Rhodes scholar, scaled the 5.7 *Ellingwood Chimney* on The Bishop with Agnes Vaille and Stephen Hart in 1924. The route ascends a classic deep chimney splitting the monolith. While today's climbers make a quick 150-foot rappel alongside the chimney, Ellingwood, going last, downclimbed the fissure.

Ian Spencer-Green on *Bolts to Somewhere* on The Dome. *Photo by Stewart M. Green.*

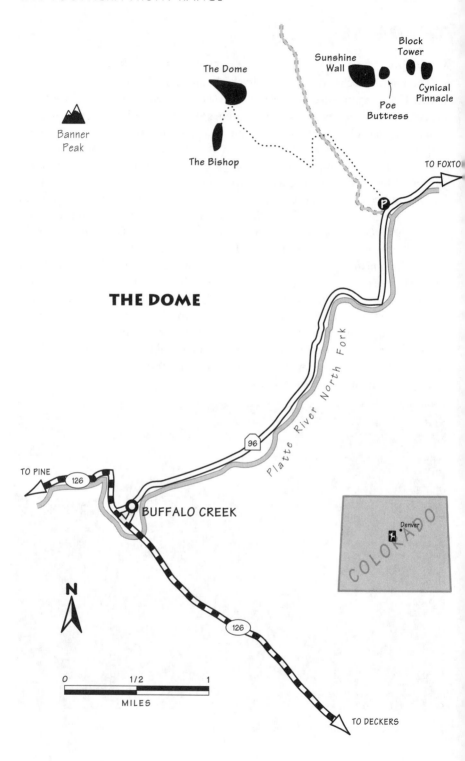

The Dome

Sunshine Wall

Block Tower

Cynical Pinnacle

Poe Buttress

Banner Peak

The Bishop

TO FOXTO[N]

THE DOME

Platte River North Fork

96

TO PINE

126

BUFFALO CREEK

COLORADO

Denver

N

0   1/2   1

MILES

126

TO DECKERS

Bishop's Jaggers, The Dome's first route, was ascended by Duncan Ferguson and Jim Walsh in long underwear or "jaggers" on a cold January day in 1971. Ferguson returned a couple of years later and scaled *Dire Straits.* In 1975 Chris Reveley and Art Higbee put up the *Reveley-Higbee Route,* a very serious climb that still harbors an X rating for the possible crater fall from the hard-to-protect, off-width first pitch. Other routes went up during the 1980s, including *Topographic Oceans* by Peter Hubbel and Mike Smith; *Sea of Holes* by Ken Trout, Paul Frank, and Brian Hansen; and the sustained *PTL Club* by Pete Gallagher and Bob Robertson.

The Dome's other routes, including a selection of cracks and a few more slab climbs, lie on its shorter south face. Many other superb lines grace the numerous formations near The Dome. The Bishop, besides the *Ellingwood Chimney,* offers the excellent *Bishop Finger Crack,* a long thin 5.12c crack first freed by Christian Griffith and Alan Lester. The Cathedral Spires clump atop the lofty ridge east of The Dome. This group of crags, including Poe Buttress, Cynical Pinnacle, and Sunshine Wall, offer perhaps Colorado's best assortment of three-star crack climbs. Cynical Pinnacle is the best. Must-do routes on this soaring thumb are the *Center Route,* perhaps Colorado's best 5.9 crack line, 5.11b *Route 66,* and the sustained and brilliant 5.11a *Wunsch's Dihedral* up the central corner system. Cynical Pinnacle is not included in this guide, however, because of sensitive environmental considerations. The crag is closed for much of the year, including the prime climbing season, by active raptor nesting.

Trip Planning Information

General description: A 400-foot slab perched atop a high ridge offers some of Colorado's finest slab climbs.

Location: Above the North Fork of the South Platte River south of Denver.

Camping: No camping is allowed along the river east of Buffalo Creek. Four Pike National Forest campgrounds—Baldy, Tramway, Buffalo, and Green Mountain—lie along Buffalo Creek on Forest Road 543 southwest of the town of Buffalo Creek. Top of the World and Kelsey campgrounds are south of town along County Road 126.

Climbing season: Year-round. May through October offers the best weather, although summer afternoons on the south-facing slab are usually too hot. Watch for afternoon thunderstorms and lightning in summer. September and October are the best times for climbing with warm days. Spring days are often windy, with unpredictable weather. Winter days, although short, can be pleasantly warm. Snow quickly melts off the slab, except during periods of prolonged cold weather.

Restrictions and access issues: The Dome is on Pike National Forest land. No climbing restrictions currently exist although The Dome and The Bishop may be closed to climbing from February 1 to July 31 because of raptor nesting. Call the Division of Wildlife office in Colorado Springs at (719) 473-2945 for closure info. The South Platte River corridor, so close to the Denver metro area, is heavily used and abused. Pike National Forest heavily manages the area to protect the natural resources and provide a positive recreational experience. The 15-mile road section from Buffalo Creek to Nighthawk is a restricted day-use-only area. Park only in designated areas, or your car will be ticketed. Camping is allowed only in designated campgrounds.

Guidebooks: *South Platte Rock Climbing* by Peter Hubbel, Chockstone Press, 1988, offers complete topos to The Dome's south and southeast faces, as well as the surrounding crags including Cynical Pinnacle and The Bishop.

Nearby mountain shops, guide services, and gyms: Denver area stores and gyms are closest.

Services: Limited services in Pine, Buffalo Creek, and Pine Junction. The historic Green Store in Buffalo Creek offers cold sodas, groceries, and gas. Complete services in the Denver area.

Emergency services: Call 911. St. Anthony Hospital, 4231 W. 16th Ave, Denver, CO 80204, (303) 629-3511.

Nearby climbing areas: Squat Rock, Sphinx Rock, Bucksnort Slab, The Bishop, Cynical Pinnacle, Etive Slabs, Poe Buttress, Chair Rocks, The Castle, Little Scraggy Dome, Helen's Dome, Acid Rock, Sheep Rock, Sunshine Dome, Wigwam Domes, Couch Potatoes, Jackson Creek Dome, Turkey Rock, Turkey Tail, Sheeps Nose, Clear Creek Canyon, North Table Mountain, Morrison bouldering.

Nearby attractions: Pine-North Fork National Historic District, South Platte River, Pike National Forest, Devils Head National Recreation Trail, Lost Creek Wilderness Area, Cheesman Lake, Rampart Range Road, Mount Evans Wilderness Area, Guanella Pass Scenic Byway.

Finding the crag: The Dome is best approached via County Road 126. From Pine Junction and U.S. Highway 285, drive south 10 miles on County 126 to Buffalo Creek. (Or, from Woodland Park, drive north on Colorado Highway 67 to Deckers and turn west on County 126 to Buffalo Creek.) Head east 2 miles on gravel County 96 and park in a large designated area on the road's north side. Because of over-use and parking problems, you must park only in designated parking lots along this section of the South Platte River corridor. Hike northwest up a trail in a dry gulch until The Dome is in sight and then scramble up a gully trail and across a boulder field to its southeast face.

THE DOME

1. **Day at the Beach** (5.9+) A 2-pitch line up the southeast face's far west margin. **Pitch 1** begins by a large boulder and climbs a wide crack (5.8) to a belay stance below a small roof. **Pitch 2** continues up some 5.9 moves and heads up a 5.7 slab when the crack thins out. **Rack:** Bring pro to #4 Camalot.

2. **Burke-Box-Ball** (5.10a R) Start atop a large boulder and climb up and right past 3 bolts—some scary and runout 5.9 here—to a belay with 2 bolts

above a roof. **Pitch 2** goes up a water streak (5.10) above to a tree. **Descent:** Rappel from here or continue up a 5.5 crack to the top. **Rack:** Bring some Friends to 3".

3. **Stars of Mars** (5.10a R) Begin just right of BURKE-BOX-BALL and head up the runout slab past 5 bolts to a 2-bolt anchor. Be careful on the 5.10 between the second and third bolts; a fall could be serious. Continue up the last pitch of the REVELEY-HIGBEE ROUTE to the top or rap from the station.

4. **Reveley-Higbee Route** (5.10 X) A very serious route up the slab's left side. Climb a wide, off-width crack (5.10) with slight protection to a 1-bolt stance. **Pitch 2** heads up the thinning crack, steps left past a bolt, and climbs up to the 2-bolt station on STARS OF MARS. The last long pitch (5.9) goes up and right past 2 bolts. There may or may not be an anchor at the upper belay. The first ascent party used butt friction as an anchor. **Rack:** Carry pro to 6" including large Camalots, Big Dudes, Big Bros, and/or tube chocks.

5. **Dos Equis** (5.10c A2) Climb a 4-bolt slab (5.8) just right of a pillar below a left-leaning crack system. Clip 3 bolts at a hanging belay or traverse 10' to a spacious ledge atop a flake. Do 2 more bolt-protected pitches (5.9- and 5.10) to the left side of the obvious arching roof halfway up the wall. Surmount the roof on aid, traverse right, and finish up BISHOP'S JAGGERS or rappel from a tree above the arch. **Descent:** Most parties rap after the 2nd pitch. **Rack:** Bring pro to #3 Friend.

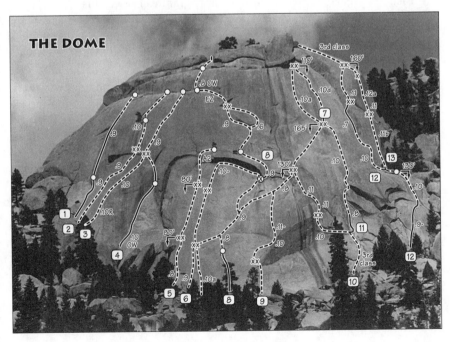

THE DOME

6. **Dire Straits** (5.10b R) A good route that climbs to the arch in 3 pitches. Begin right of DOS EQUIS and ascend the 1st pitch of TOPOGRAPHIC OCEANS. Head left from the belay stance up bolted 5.8 and 5.9 friction to a 3-bolt belay. Continue smearing above, a couple of thin 5.10 spots, to the arch and traverse right and down to BISHOP'S JAGGERS on the far right side of the arch. Continue up BISHOP'S JAGGERS to the top. **Rack:** Bring Friends to #4 for the arch traverse.

7. **Topographic Oceans** (5.10c) This excellent 4-pitch line, wandering up the face, is a good test of one's friction ability and calf strength. **Pitch 1** climbs a slab (spot of 5.9) past 3 bolts, somewhat runout up high, to a bolted belay stance. An alternative pitch climbs the slab immediately right (5.10a) with several bolts. **Pitch 2** frictions up and right past 6 bolts (5.9 and 5.7) to a 3-bolt rappel/belay station right of the prominent arch. **Pitch 3** moves up right (5.7) past more bolts to another 3-bolt stance. **Pitch 4** the best lead, stretches up the long line of bolts above. Smear straight up on sustained but well-protected 5.9 and 5.10 friction to a 3-bolt belay station below some blocky roofs. **Descent:** Make 3 rappels down the route with double ropes. **Variation:** BOLTS TO SOMEWHERE (5.10a), with superb friction climbing, climbs the left-land line of bolts (7) to the top belay stance. Do it after rapping from the top anchors or as an alternative last pitch. **Rack:** Bring at least 15 quick draws. A few medium Friends and stoppers might be useful for the timid.

8. **Bishop's Jaggers** (5.9) An all-time Platte granite classic. This 5-pitch route wanders up the central face. **Pitch 1** begins in an easy crack just east of the face's low point. Belay atop the crack. **Pitch 2** smears up and joins TOPOGRAPHIC OCEANS' 2nd pitch at its first bolt, follow past the third bolt (5.9) before striking up to a belay (1 bolt) on the right side of the large arch. **Pitch 3** turns the arch's right side with a few 5.9 moves and follows a ramp/crack system up and left to a belay above the arch. **Pitch 4** frictions up the runout slab (5.7) above toward an obvious small roof, keep right of the roof for 5.6 climbing or go left at 5.9. Either way reach a 2-bolt belay on the ramp above. **Pitch 5** continues up the ramp to a 5.8 off-width pitch on a steep headwall. Finish on the sloping summit slabs. **Descent:** Downclimb east along the dome's flank. **Rack:** Friends, TCUs, and stoppers.

9. **Sea of Holes** (5.11a) A good alternate start to TOPOGRAPHIC OCEANS. **Pitch 1** climbs a slab below and left of a prominent slice. Bring RPs to protect a 5.8 traverse left from the slice to a bolted belay stance. **Pitch 2** edges up the steep slab above on 5.10 and 5.11 climbing past 7 bolts and joins TOPOGRAPHIC OCEANS' 2nd pitch. **Descent:** Make a double rope rappel from the end of TOPO'S 2nd pitch or continue upward.

10. **Pecker Wrecker** (5.11a R) Another direct 2-pitch start to TOPOGRAPHIC OCEANS. Begin just left of a clump of trees and jam an easy 4th class crack to a belay stance right of a long roof. **Pitch 2** traverses left below the roof and turn its left side (5.10b) to a 2-bolt belay stance. Continue up a thin left-leaning crack/corner (5.11) to a 3-bolt slab above. End at TOPO'S second belay. **Rack:** Bring Friends to 3" to protect the traverse and RPs for the thin crack.

11. **Connections** (5.10a) This good, long pitch joins TOPOGRAPHIC OCEANS at its third belay station. Belay at the stance for PECKER WRECKER'S traverse or set the belay as high as possible in the crack system above. Climb a hand-crack and face climb, smear, and jam past the left side of 2 obvious overlapping roofs (5.8). Head up the slab above on 5.10 climbing past 4 bolts to TOPOGRAPHIC OCEANS. Rap to its second stance with two ropes. A 200' rope is handy for this long pitch. **Rack:** Bring pro to 4".

12. **Pornographic Motions** (5.11) A 3-pitch line up the steep east margin of the face. **Pitch 1** goes 130' up a finger crack (5.9) to a 1-bolt 5.10 slab and ends on a ledge by a tree. **Pitch 2** begins on the left side of the ledge and wanders up and left through cracks and over slabs to a 2-bolt anchor. **Pitch 3** scales a steep slabby edge (5.11) past 6, 1/4" bolts to a runout section (5.9) and old rap anchors. **Descent:** Make 2 rappels—160' to the tree and then 130' to the ground or downclimb east from the summit. **Rack:** Stoppers and Friends to #3.5.

13. **PTL Club** (5.12a) A sustained and difficult line which may not have a second ascent. Do the 1st pitch of PORNOGRAPHIC MOTIONS to the large ledge with a tree. **Pitch 1** edges up the steep slab above the tree (5.10c and 5.11b) past 5, 1/4" bolts to a belay stance at a break. **Pitch 2** yields only after sustained 5.11 and 5.12 climbing up the abrupt headwall above (6, 1/4" bolts). Belay from anchors. **Descent:** Rap with 2 ropes or downclimb east from the top of the rock.

SHEEPS NOSE

OVERVIEW

Sheeps Nose rears its slabby granite flanks above low rolling ridges and shallow valleys blanketed with ponderosa pine and Douglas-fir in the southern South Platte River region of central Colorado. The abrupt 8,894-foot-high dome yields many excellent climbing routes that ascend discontinuous crack systems and steep slabs studded with sharp crystals and chicken heads. The south-facing exposure offers great winter climbing when other Front Range mountain areas are snowed in.

Numerous routes lace Sheeps Nose, with great climbing on 3- and 4-pitch routes that range from 5.7 to 5.11. Good routes can be pieced together from established lines. The best is probably the first 3 pitches of *Lost in Space*, 5.9, with an airy finish up 5.10b *Ozone Direct*. Another good route ascends the 5.6 first pitch of *When Sheep Are Nervous*, stems wildly up 5.10d *Golden Fleece*, and finishes with the exposed 5.11b *Assassination Slab* to the summit. Other great routes include Ten Years After, an excellent 5.9 layback up the prominent open-book on the dome's west flank; thin friction climbing on 5.11a *Seamis*; and the *Southeast Face*, a meandering four-pitch 5.8 route on the buttress just right of *Lost in Space*. **Descend** by downclimbing north along a broken ridge. Watch for loose rock. Snow often covers the descent in winter. Make a rappel

Ian Spencer-Green at the crux of *Room with a View* on Sheep's Nose.
Photo by Stewart M. Green.

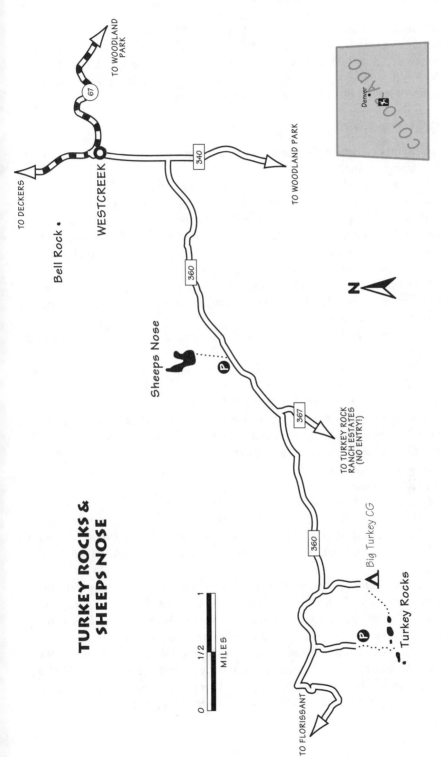

TURKEY ROCKS &
SHEEPS NOSE

off blocks or trees to avoid slippery spots. Behind the dome, scramble down through woods along the crag's north and east flanks. **Rack:** A rack for Sheeps Nose should include a set of RPs, stoppers, Rocks, a few TCUs, and a set of Friends through #4. Don't rely exclusively on existing bolts here for your safety. Most are 1/4" bolts placed in the 1970s and 1980s.

Trip Planning Information

General description: Numerous excellent crack and face routes ascend a 500-foot granite dome.

Location: Northwest of Woodland Park near the South Platte River.

Camping: Primitive, off-road camping is permitted on Pike National Forest land below Sheeps Nose. Keep off adjoining private property. Nearby forest campgrounds include Big Turkey on Forest Road 360 and Trail Creek on Teller County 3. Several forest campgrounds lie south along Colorado Highway 67 near Manitou Lake and Woodland Park.

Climbing season: Year-round. South-facing cliffs offer excellent winter climbing on warm days. Watch for lightning strikes on this high, isolated dome during summer thunderstorms.

Restrictions and access issues: Within Pike National Forest. No climbing restrictions.

Guidebooks: *For Turkeys Only* by Steve Cheyney and Bob Couchman, 1984. *South Platte Rock Climbing and the Garden of the Gods* by Peter Hubbel and Mark Rolofson, Chockstone Press, 1988, contains a topo of Sheeps Nose.

Nearby mountain shops, guide services, and gyms: 8th Street Climbing Club, Sport Climbing Center of Colorado Springs, Mountain Chalet, Grand West Outfitters, Pikes Peak Mountain Sports, (Colorado Springs).

Services: All services in Woodland Park. Limited services in Deckers, Buffalo Creek, and Pine.

Emergency services: Call 911. Memorial Hospital, 1400 E. Boulder, Colorado Springs, CO 80909, (719) 475-5000. Penrose-St. Francis Healthcare System, 2215 N. Cascade, Colorado Springs, CO 80907, (719) 630-5000. Langstaff-Brown Medical Center, Hwy. 67 at Hwy. 24, Woodland Park, CO, (719) 687-6022.

Nearby climbing areas: South Platte domes and crags, Bucksnort Slab, Sphinx Rock, The Dome, Bishop Rock, Cynical Pinnacle, The Big Rock Candy Mountain, Turkey Rocks, Jackson Creek Dome, Scorpio Dome, Eleven Mile Canyon, Pericle, Bigger Bagger, The Crags, Mueller State Park domes.

Nearby Attractions: Devils Head National Recreation Trail, Rampart Range Road, Mount Evans Wilderness Area, Guanella Pass, Mount Evans Highway, Lost Creek Wilderness Area, South Platte River, Florissant Fossil Beds National Monument, Pikes Peak, Eleven Mile State Recreation Area.

Finding the crag: From Woodland Park drive north 14 miles on Colorado Highway 67. Or from Colorado 126 at Pine Junction, drive south on Colorado 67 to Deckers and continue 9 miles to Westcreek. From either direction, turn west on Douglas County Road 68 at Westcreek. Drop down the gravel road from the highway to Westcreek and go 0.8 mile south. Road 68 (Stump Road) turns west above a small reservoir and after a 1.5 miles reaches Sheeps Nose, a prominent dome north of the road. Access is via a rough forest road just east of the rock at 1.5 miles, or park at a wide pulloff south of the crag at 1.8 miles. Hike north up boulder-strewn slopes to the cliff base. Approach time from the road to the crag is about 15 minutes.

1. **Room with a View** (5.11b) An excellent 70' bolted route up the overhanging west-facing wall in the obvious gully on Sheeps Nose's eastern flank. Scramble up the gully over boulders and through numerous sticker bushes to a chimney. Climb the easy chimney and exit right onto a sloping ramp system and belay. The route climbs the beautiful yellow wall above past 5, 3/8" bolts to lowering anchors.

2. **Southeast Face** (5.8+) A good 3- to 4-pitch route that climbs the blunt prow on the rock's southeast flank. Begin near the toe of the buttress and follow crack systems to the summit slabs. Many variations are possible en route. **Rack:** Bring a standard rack with full sets of stoppers and Friends.

3. **Lost in Space** (5.9) and the **Ozone Direct** (5.10b) This excellent 4-pitch route scales the left side of the prominent southeast buttress of Sheeps Nose. LOST IN SPACE, first climbed in 1974, begins at the lowest point of the dome on its southeast corner among tall ponderosa pine trees. Locate a small pine tree growing in a right-leaning corner 70' off the ground. **Pitch 1** begins below this. Climb hand cracks up and right (5.7) past the tree into a large left-facing dihedral and belay on a spacious ledge above. **Pitch 2** (150') moves above the belay and traverses right 15' around a dull arete. Watch for the loose flake directly above the belay stance. Scale shallow finger cracks near the arete, step left with an airy move, and climb thin, discontinuous cracks (5.7) to a large ledge. The last 5.9 stemming moves onto the ledge are the most difficult. **Pitch 3** climbs an easy corner (5.4) 70' to another ledge. **Pitch 4** jams a moderate 5.7 corner system to the summit slabs above the belay ledge. The best finish, however, is the 5.10b OZONE DIRECT on the intimidating slab to the left. Step left past a bolt and jam a finger crack for 40' with a couple of hard fingertip laybacks (5.10b) to the prominent arch above. Hand-traverse left on good holds under the arch and make an awkward exit (5.8) into a moderate left-facing corner (5.7) that ends below the summit. **Descend** via the loose northwest ridge to a saddle on the dome's backside. A couple of rappels might be necessary in winter.

4. **When Sheep are Nervous** (5.9) Climb the first pitch of LOST IN SPACE to the large belay ledge (The Hinterland). Walk left to an obvious crack system. This is WHEN SHEEP ARE NERVOUS. **Pitch 1** climbs a 5.6 hand and finger crack to a ledge. **Pitch 2** scales a right-facing 5.9 corner to a couple of overlaps and finishes on a small ledge below OZONE DIRECT. Continue to the summit via route #3.

5. **Golden Fleece** (5.10d) and **Assassination Slab** (5.11b) This excellent 2-pitch route combines with the first lead of LOST IN SPACE and the 1st pitch of WHEN SHEEP ARE NERVOUS to form a long 4-pitch climb. Begin on the ledge atop the 1st pitch of WHEN SHEEP ARE NERVOUS. **Pitch 1**, GOLDEN FLEECE, works left into a crack that leads to a right-facing 5.10d corner. Thin stemming leads to a belay stance. **Pitch 2**, ASSASSINA-TION SLAB, edges left from the stance onto a runout (5.11b) protected by 4, 1/4" bolts. Easier climbing above leads to the summit slabs.

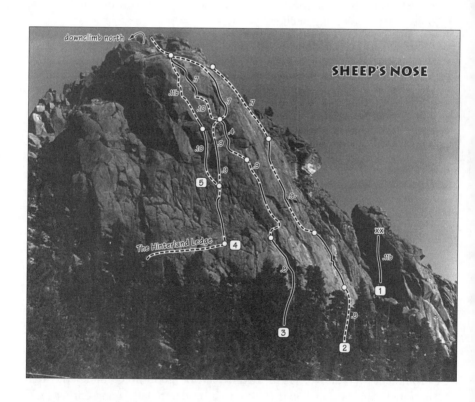

TURKEY ROCK, TURKEY PERCH, & TURKEY TAIL

OVERVIEW

Low mountains clad with thick pine forests and studded by rounded granite domes characterize the central Front Range between the Mount Evans and Pikes Peak massifs. The South Platte River, originating on the Continental Divide near Hoosier Pass, creases these mountains with deep canyons. The Turkey Rocks, a collection of five crags—Turkey Rock, Turkey Tail, Turkey Perch, The Leftovers, and The Rightovers—sit atop a lofty peak overlooking the South Platte drainage. The 8,000-foot-high rocks are composed of a compact, erosion-resistant granite studded with crystals, edges, and chicken heads, and are seamed by slicing vertical cracks that range from thin finger seams to wide chimneys. The bold, jutting formations yield some of Colorado's best crack climbs as well as a few good bolted face routes. More than 200 routes and variations scale the Turkey Rocks.

Climbing history: Turkey Rock has long been a bastion of traditional climbing. The cracks here are readily protected by stoppers, hexentrics, and Friends. The first routes went up in the mid-1960s, including *Gobbler's Grunt* and the mega-classic *Turkey Shoot*. In those early days, residents of adjoining Turkey Rock Estates considered the rocks part of their backyard, although the formations lie on national forest land. A couple of locals, taking offense at the "trespassers" climbing their rocks, took a few potshots at the party doing the first ascent of what is now *Turkey Shoot*.

The 1970s brought a clean, free-climbing ethic to Turkey Rock and Turkey Tail, with numerous classic and difficult routes established on the steep crack systems. Jim Dunn, with a host of partners, set the new standard with hard routes up Turkey Tail including *Piece of Cake, Whimsical Dreams, For Turkey's Only, Turkey Turn, Roofus,* and *Wudamudafuka*. Other active ascensionists were Douglas Snively, Steve Cheyney, Earl Wiggins, Bryan Becker, Kurt Rasmussen, Ed Webster, Steve Hong, Dennis Jackson, and Leonard Coyne. The 1980s brought controversy to the crags when a couple of problems, *The Infraction* and *I Turkey*, were rappel-bolted and subsequently chopped. Both were later rebolted on the lead as *Learning to Fly* and *The Resurrection*. In 1983 Harrison Dekker led *Jello Party*, a technical 5.12c face climb and one of the Tail's hardest face routes. Today, few new lines are being established on the Turkey Rocks. Most of the choice routes were done long ago, with only a few variations remaining to be ascended.

Five rocks compose Turkey Rocks. The Leftovers sit on the far western or left edge of the peak. Turkey Rock, offering mostly moderate routes to 350 feet, dominates the outcrop with its bold buttresses. Turkey Perch, with a marvelous assortment of 1-pitch beginner and moderate routes, hides east of the saddle

Henry Barber belays Dennis Jackson up the final moves of the first pitch of *Messner's Delight* on Turkey Rock. *Photo by Stewart M. Green.*

between Turkey Rock and Turkey Tail. Turkey Tail, the other major formation, lifts a 250-foot craggy south face adorned with roofs, dihedrals, and vertical fissures. The Rightovers, a brushy, somewhat broken wall, sits below Turkey Tail's east flank. The Leftovers and Rightovers, not covered in this guide, yield some very fine routes. *Captain Fist* (5.8) and *Too Much Crack* (5.10a) are the recommended lines on The Leftovers, while *Back to the Zodiac* (5.11d) and *Learning to Fly* (5.12b) are two of the best on The Rightovers. Many excellent routes also climb the shaded north faces of Turkey Rock and Turkey Tail, and offer respite from the summer sun.

Trip Planning Information

General description: A marvelous crack climbing preserve with almost 200 routes scaling excellent granite buttresses, faces, and cracks.

Location: In the central Front Range south of Denver and north of Woodland Park.

Camping: Big Turkey Campground sits along Turkey Creek among tall pines and firs just east of the rocks. Water, restrooms, and grills are available. A fee is charged. Free camping is available along the dead-end road north of Turkey Rock.

Climbing season: Year-round. April through October offers the best climbing weather. Summer days can be hot, but the north side of the crags is shaded. Watch for afternoon thunderstorms and accompanying lightning in summer. Warm winter days with highs of 40 degrees or more on the south-facing walls yield pleasant climbing weather.

Restrictions and access issues: The cliffs are in Pike National Forest. No restrictions are in effect. Climbers should not trespass or drive on private property at Turkey Rock Estates immediately south of the cliffs. Landowners will call the sheriff and have shot at trespassers.

Guidebooks: *For Turkeys Only* by Steve Cheyney and Bob Couchman, revised edition 1989. A comprehensive guide with cliff photos. *South Platte Rock Climbing* and *The Garden of the Gods* by Peter Hubbel and Mark Rolofson, Chockstone Press, 1988.

Nearby mountain shops, guide services, and gyms: 8th Street Climbing Club, Sport Climbing Center of Colorado Springs, Mountain Chalet, Grand West Outfitters, Pikes Peak Mountain Sports (Colorado Springs).

Services: All services in Woodland Park. Limited services in Deckers, Buffalo Creek, and Pine.

Emergency services: Call 911. Memorial Hospital, 1400 E. Boulder, Colorado Springs, CO 80909, (719) 475-5000. Penrose-St. Francis Healthcare System, 2215 N. Cascade, Colorado Springs, CO 80907, (719) 630-5000. Langstaff-Brown Medical Center, Hwy. 67 at Hwy. 24, Woodland Park, CO, (719) 687-6022.

Nearby climbing areas: Big Rock Candy Mountain, Sheeps Nose, Eleven Mile Canyon, Pikes Peak crags, Scorpio Dome, Jackson Creek Dome, South Platte crags and domes.

Nearby Attractions: Devils Head National Recreation Trail, Rampart Range Road, Mount Evans Wilderness Area, Guanella Pass, Mount Evans Highway, Lost Creek Wilderness Area, South Platte River, Florissant Fossil Beds National Monument, Pikes Peak, Eleven Mile State Recreation Area.

Finding the area: From Woodland Park drive 14 miles north on Colorado Highway 67 to Westcreek. Or, from Pine Junction and U.S. Highway 285 in the north, drive south to Deckers and continue 9 miles to Westcreek. Turn west on gravel County Road 68 at Westcreek and drive 0.4 mile to Westcreek itself and head 0.8 mile south. Turn west on County 68, the Stump Road, and follow it 2.5 miles to Forest Road 360. Follow the bumpy road down 1.7 miles to Big Turkey Campground. The campground makes a good base camp. Walk south and west 15 minutes to the rocks. Or continue up FR 360 for 0.8 mile to an unmarked turnoff north of Turkey Rock. Follow the track south a few hundred yards to a turn-around. A short trail heads south and switchbacks up to the saddle between Turkey Rock and Turkey Tail. The forest road is very rough and full of holes. Drive slowly. The road may be impassable in winter and early spring.

TURKEY ROCK

Turkey Rock's south face is approached from the saddle above the parking area by walking west on a short trail to the cliff's base. The routes are listed from left to right or west to east. Many good routes also ascend the rock's north face, including *Rastafarian, Finger Lickin' Good, Shear Shark Attack,* and *Mobius Trip.*

1. **Direct Hit** (5.9 R) A superb 2-pitch face climb. Begins near the top of the gully on the west side of the face. **Pitch 1** climbs vertical rock up right out of gully (5.9 R and scant pro) to small belay stance. **Pitch 2** follows a 5.6 crack to summit slabs. **Descend** west. **Rack:** Pro includes RPs, wired stoppers, and TCUs.

2. **Southern Comfort** (5.10-) A face and crack route commonly done in 3 pitches. Begin just left of wide crack. **Pitch 1** jams thin 5.9 finger crack to a stance in wide crack. **Pitch 2** heads up right into right-leaning, shallow corner system (5.8) to a traverse right on knobs into a niche in wide GOBBLER'S GRUNT crack system. Belay up crack at a shelf. **Pitch 3** climbs unprotected but lower-angle rock (5.7) to summit. **Rack:** Wires and TCUs are helpful.

3. **Messner's Delight** (5.9+ X) A seldom climbed but excellent route with serious groundfall potential on the 1st pitch. **Pitch 1** climbs an overhanging, off-width crack (5.9) 40' to ledge right of large tree. Ledge can be reached by scrambling up from left. **Pitch 2** ascends a thin 5.9 crack. Traverse left and up where crack peters out on unprotected face climbing (5.8-5.9) for 70' to good belay ledge. **Pitch 3** is a 5.7 crack and face on GOBBLER'S GRUNT. **Rack:** Bring some big pro.

4. **Gobbler's Grunt** (5.9) 3 pitches of cracks and chimneys up an obvious crack system on the left side of the central buttress. **Pitch 1** is a 5.7 chimney. **Pitch 2** jams good double finger cracks (5.9) to a flake roof. Work up left on face (5.6) to a good stance. **Pitch 3** follows the large crack above (5.7) and then a no-pro face to summit. **Rack:** Bring pro to 3".

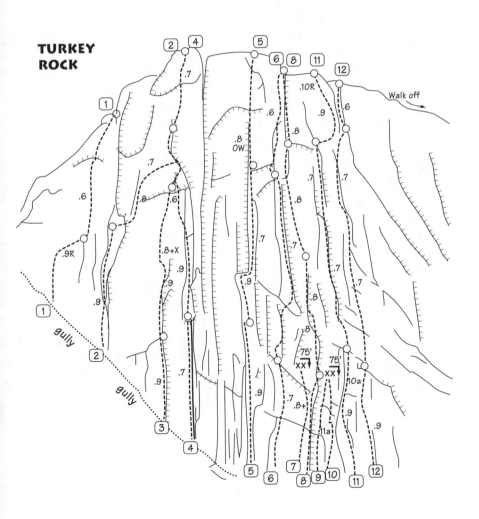

TURKEY ROCK

5. **Turkey Shoot** (5.9) A superb and classic line up cracks on the right side of the central buttress. Begin just left of some large trees at face base. **Pitch 1** works up a wide crack to a stance. Continue up crack and exit (5.9-) from flare into a hand crack. Belay in crack above. **Pitch 2** offers excellent hand jamming up a right-facing corner. Jam crack (5.9), traverse right under obvious roof, and jam a great hand crack (5.8) to a spacious belay. **Pitch 3** works up an awkward 5.8 off-width. **Rack:** Bring pro to 3.5".

6. **Nighttime Madness** (5.7) This grand moderate tour of Turkey Rock yields 3 pitches of cracks from hand-sized to chimney. Begin behind large tree. **Pitch 1** hand jams a 5.7 crack to top of a flake. Move up another crack (5.7) to a large ledge. **Pitch 2** works up a flared crack to a ledge on right. Step up right on ledge to good hand crack (5.7) Belay above on a ledge. **Pitch 3** goes up right in a left-facing corner (5.6) to a chimney and the summit; or move left on ledge and jam TURKEY SHOOT'S 5.8 off-width crack. **Rack:** Bring pro to 3.5".

7. **Vanishing Point** (5.10d) This excellent 1-pitch route, first led by Earl Wiggens, climbs 2 slashing finger-cracks to a spacious ledge. Begin right of tree. **Descent:** Rappel 75' from anchors to the ground. **Rack:** Protection requires wires and small to medium Friends.

8. **Stewart's Crack** (5.8+) **Pitch 1** climbs the flared but fun off-width right of VANISHING POINT. Continue up good chimneys above (5.8) for 3 pitches to summit.

9. **In Style Out of Fashion** (5.11c) A not-so-great blunt arete left of GREAT WHITE CRIME with 4 bolts.

10. **Great White Crime** (5.11a) Another fine 1-pitch (75') finger crack to a belay/rappel station. **Rack:** Bring small pro.

11. **Satyr's Asshole** (5.10a) A 3-pitch line up hand and off-width cracks and chimneys. **Pitch 1** jams and face climbs a couple of thin cracks (5.9 up high) to off-width crack over a bulge and a good ledge. **Pitch 2** works up a long 5.7 crack system to a stance. **Pitch 3** finger jams a thin crack (5.9) in a shallow corner to a runout 5.10 R face with loose flakes. **Rack:** Bring pro to 3.5 Friend.

12. **Straw Turkey** (5.10a) A great 1st pitch. **Pitch 1** jams a series of cracks (5.9 and 5.10-) to belay stance on a diagonaling crack. **Pitch 2** goes left and up into a long crack with some off-width (5.7 and 5.8). Belay high on a good sloping ledge. **Pitch 3** steps right and finishes up a 5.6 crack. **Rack:** Bring wires and medium Friends.

TURKEY PERCH

This great little crag, perched below the saddle between Turkey Rock and Turkey Tail, yields a marvelous collection of 1-pitch, moderate crack routes. All routes end atop the crag, with belays from tied-off boulders or trees. Routes are listed left to right.

13. **Liquid Acrobat** (5.12a R) A short, fierce testpiece on the rock's far left side. Climb thin crack above fallen log, fill with small pro, and step right on a committing face move (5.12-) to shallow, flared crack. **Rack** should include RPs and small wires.

14. **Ragger Bagger** (5.8) Crack in left-facing corner. **Rack:** Bring pro to 3".

15. **Gobble Up** (5.9) An excellent, sustained off-width and fist crack up steep face. **Rack:** Bring lots of big pro; #4 Camalots work good. Keep rope out of the crack when belaying—it tends to gobble it up.

16. **Stiff Little Fingers** (5.11c) Ascend bolted face right of GOBBLE UP on small edges and crystals.

17. **Steppenwolf** (5.9) A good route up somewhat discontinuous cracks. **Rack:** Pro to 3".

18. **Honky Jam Ass Crack** (5.7) Fun hand jams up nut-eating crack. Belay from boulders on large ledge to right.

19. **Left Handed Jew** (5.7) Climb excellent, shallow corner to an awkward step left into another crack system.

TURKEY TAIL

Turkey Tail's impressive south-facing wall, beetled with roofs and seamed by vertical corners, is the place to hone one's crack climbing skills. This 250' face offers a succession of three-star routes ranging from finger cracks to hideous overhanging off-widths. **Descent** is accomplished by scrambling down steep gullies and chimneys on either end of the rock. Use your discretion and judgment as to the best descent. Routes are listed from west to east.

20. **Quiver and Quill** (5.10c) A great route up a leaning hand crack on the far west end of Turkey Tail facing Turkey Perch. **Descent:** Rappel 75' from bolts on west edge of belay ledge. **Rack:** Bring Friends to 3.5".

21. **Johnny Lat** (5.12c) Ascend bolted arete left of QUIVER AND QUILL to 2-bolt anchors. Sustained and excellent.

22. **Unknown** (5.12a) This route ascends west side of large block on Turkey Tail's upper west side around corner from QUIVER AND QUILL. Climb technical face past 2 bolts and jam hand crack to a belay.

23. **Captain Hook** (5.12a) Right side of small west face above ramp. Good face climbing past 5 bolts to anchor over top.

24. **Piece of Cake** (5.11c) A short, strenuous hand crack over prominent south-facing roof. **Rack:** Pro to #2.5 Friend.

25. **Turkey's Delight** (5.7) Locate a large right-facing dihedral on left side of sunny south wall. **Pitch 1** jams bushy double hand cracks (5.7) up corner to a ledge. **Pitch 2** steps right and stems up into thin, left-facing corner. Jam (5.7) to top.

26. **Rasmussen's Crack** (5.10b) A superb hand and finger crack up a steep slab right of TURKEY'S DELIGHT. **Descend** by traversing west on a 3rd-class ledge system from belay ledge or finishing up PIECE OF CAKE. **Rack** with wires and Friends to #2.5.

27. **Hummingbird Way** (5.9) **Pitch 1** jams 5.8 off-width in large left-facing dihedral right of TURKEY'S DELIGHT to good ledge with 2 bolts on right. Rap 80' here or do **Pitch 2** above ledge. Jam hand to fist cracks (5.8) up and over bulge left of a large roof to a ledge. **Pitch 3** continues up the awkward crack (some 5.9) in a left-facing corner to summit. **Rack:** Pro to 4".

28. **The Resurrection** (5.12a) A bolted arete left of WHIMSICAL DREAMS. Belay or lower from 2-bolt anchors (85') from the ledge above.

29. **Whimsical Dreams** (5.11b) This excellent route, one of the Tail's best, scales a thin, continuous finger crack over a series of roofs (5.11b) to a belay ledge with rappel/belay anchors (85') **Pitch 2** continues up wider cracks from right side of ledge (5.10d over the roof) to summit. **Rack:** Bring a rack with an emphasis on RPs, small wires, TCUs, as well as Friends to 3".

TURKEY TAIL

30. **Wudamudafuka** (5.11a) A difficult 3-pitch crack route; the 1st pitch is best. Rappel from anchors above the roof (80') after the 1st pitch. **Pitch 1** jams sustained finger crack (5.11a) 40' to a sloping right-facing dihedral. Climb corner and surmount roof above (5.10c) or climb bolted 5.11 arete on left to a 2-bolt belay/rappel station. **Pitch 2** off-widths through roofs above (5.10b) in same crack system. **Pitch 3** works up a 5.6 chimney to summit. **Rack:** Bring thin pro, TCUs, and Friends to #2, and off-width gear.

31. **For Turkeys Only** (5.11d) A very difficult and strenuous off-width route up the rock's central buttress. Begin in next system right of WHIMSICAL DREAMS. **Pitch 1** jams a finger crack to a large roof. Turn the roof via off-width (5.11d) on right and continue up wide crack (5.11a) past another roof to belay stance with a bolt. **Pitch 2** off-widths out third roof (5.10c) and works up left into 5.6 chimney. **Rack:** Bring Big Bros or Big Dudes for peace of mind.

32. **Drumstick Direct** (5.10d) A classic hand and fist crack. Start right of FOR TURKEYS ONLY. **Pitch 1** climbs a 5.8 flake and moves up left into the left corner of a huge slot. Strenuous fist jamming up overhanging crack (5.10d) leads to a stance up and right from top of the slot. Rap from here with double ropes. **Pitch 2** works up right into a 5.8 corner. **Rack:** Pro includes medium wires and a generous selection of Friends to 4".

33. **Turkey Turd** (5.11c) Begin in a crack right of DRUMSTICK DIRECT'S start. **Pitch 1** jams 5.8 crack and works up left side of a pillar—The Turkey Turd—to a belay atop. **Pitch 2** works up a thin finger and hand crack and over a small roof. Continue up sustained crack (5.11c) to a good belay. **Pitch 3** moves up right into a finger crack (5.9) to a bulging face (5.9+) with a bolt. **Rack:** Pro is RPs and wires to a #4 Friend.

34. **Spider Lady** (5.9) A good, fairly moderate route. **Pitch 1** begins in a right-facing corner right of TURKEY TURD. Jam corner (5.7) to a ledge. **Pitch 2** goes off the right side of ledge. Traverse right into long, left-facing corner and jam crack (some 5.9) to a ledge. **Pitch 3** continues up easy crack above to a notch. **Descend** by scrambling west along top of the rock. **Rack:** Bring a generous rack of Friends.

35. **Brushed Turkey** (5.12a) A 1-pitch route with thin face climbing up a 3-bolt arete. **Rack:** Bring some RPs and wires to medium Friends for first crack.

36. **Jello Party** (5.12c) Brilliant and difficult crack climbing. Begin right of SPIDER LADY. Jam finger crack to thin face climbing and a belay/rappel ledge 75' up. **Rack:** Bring RPs, wired stoppers, TCUs, and small Friends.

37. **Future Chic** (5.12d) Hard and scary climbing. Incipient fingertip cracks lead to leaning arete with a few bolts.

38. **Journey to Ixtlan** (5.12a) A sustained 4-pitch route up steep slabs on the Tail's right side. **Pitch 1** begins with a wild undercling and layback (5.12a) under roofs. Use careful protection; a few leaders have grounded. Belay at a bolt. **Pitch 2** offers thin 5.10+ face climbing along a seam to sling belay at bolts under a large roof. **Pitch 3** goes out right up a 5.11d crack out and over big roof. A second roof is turned on left (5.10d). **Pitch 4** works left along a horizontal crack to an easy slabby crack. **Rack** from RPs to #3 Friend.

39. **Roofus** (5.11d) Start below a crack on the slab right of JOURNEY TO IXTLAN. **Pitch 1** jams a 5.9 hand crack to prominent roof. Traverse left and up to sling belay on JOURNEY TO IXTLAN. Continue over 5.11d roof and upward. **Rack** from RPs to #4 Friend. BEAUTY AND THE BEAST (5.12c) scales the roof above the 5.9 crack and heads up a left-facing corner.

BIG ROCK CANDY MOUNTAIN

OVERVIEW

The Big Rock Candy Mountain, an immense granite crag perched above the South Platte River, offers Colorado's longest slab routes on its 1,500-foot central buttress. The huge cliff, named for the candy-cane stripes coloring its upper slab, hides its face from the casual viewer. The crag, simply called the Big Rock by climbers, sits near the bottom of the South Platte's canyon east of the Tarryall Range's lofty escarpment. The rock is seen only from the Matukat Road, a dirt track that twists along a high bench west of the canyon. At first glimpse the Big Rock looks unclimbable, its bulky mass broken into three distinct buttresses by a few crack systems. Otherwise it's a blank slab, creased only by water streaks.

Climbing history: This formidable appearance deterred would-be ascensionists for years, until Colorado Springs climbers Don Doucette and Earl Wiggens attacked the central crack system between the north and central buttresses in the mid-1970s. The duo, finding easy climbing, jammed cracks to the hanging forest and finished up low-angle slabs to the broad summit in a few hours. A pair of Petes—Pete Williams and Pete Gallagher—attempted the Big Rock's best line, the central buttress, in 1979. In a series of attempts spread over five days in three months, the two were stymied by broken drill bits and high winds. Despite the setbacks they pushed the 11-pitch route to the summit and returned the next week to garner the all-free ascent. They named the route *Fields of Dreams Growing Wild* after a line in a Tom Waits song. The following year Williams and Gallagher climbed *Sweet Catastrophe*, a 7-pitch line up the south buttress to Gumdrop Spire. *Childhood's End,* the last great line put up on the Big Rock, fell after a ten-day, ground-up effort by Ken Trout, Brian Hansen, and Eric Winkelman. This 12-pitch route, with it's well-protected 5.12- crux lead and superb climbing, became an instant classic and remains the Big Rock's most popular line. The Big Rock's newest major route is Kevin McLaughlin and Glenn Schuler's *Shock Treatment* (5.12b/c) on the crag's abrupt north wall. The pair required eight days in 1992 to complete the 6-pitch line, one of the South Platte area's most sustained routes. The climb, following a large corner system on the north face's left side, includes a 5.12 finger crack, a 5.11+ off-width, and a 165-foot thin face pitch to finish. The route recieved its name after a bolt of lightning zipped down the crack system, zapping the climbers while they attempted the line's first continuous ascent.

The Big Rock, while one of the most remote South Platte domes, is fairly easy to reach (see "Finding the crag" below). All the Big Rock routes are long outings. Plan on a full day to approach, do the climb, descend, and hike back to the car. Many of the bolts found on the routes are old 1/4" bolts. Larger 3/8" bolts back up many of the belays and have replaced older protection bolts now on *Childhood's End.* Many pitches on the upper slabs are runout with few to

Pete Williams frictions up slabs during the first ascent of *Fields of Dreams* on the Big Rock. *Photo by Peter Gallagher.*

no bolts for protection. Climb carefully, but don't retrobolt and demean the character of the routes by adding unnecessary bolts. These are serious routes for competent climbers. A rack with wired stoppers and a set of Friends to #4 should be carried for most routes along with a dozen quick draws, some free carabiners, and a few long slings. A full 165-foot lead rope is needed, especially on *Sweet Catastrophe*. Descend from Big Rock's summit by rappelling 150 feet (two ropes) off bolts on the southeast corner. Scramble down scree slopes below the south flank to reach the base of the cliff's west face.

Trip Planning Information

General description: Colorado's longest slab routes—up to 14 pitches—on towering twin granite buttresses.

Location: Northwest of Colorado Springs along the South Platte River.

Camping: Lots of good free campsites lie along the access roads. Bring water and use existing sites whenever possible. Nearby Pike National Forest campgrounds include Happy Meadows and Spruce Grove off Park County 77 to the southwest; Goose Creek and Molly Gulch northwest along the Matukat Road; and Big Turkey to the northeast off Forest Road 360.

Climbing season: Year-round. Spring and autumn months offer the best weather. Expect windy days in March and April. Summer days on the slabs can be hot—not particularly conducive to climbing hard friction. Thunderstorms occur regularly on summer afternoons. Watch for lightning. Winter ascents are possible during dry, warm spells. The west buttresses receive only afternoon light in winter, so expect cold temperatures during the morning.

Restrictions and access issues: None; on the Pike National Forest.

Guidebooks: *South Platte Rock Climbing and the Garden of the Gods* by Peter Hubbel and Mark Rolofson, Chockstone Press, 1988.

Nearby mountain shops, guide services, and gyms: 8th Street Climbing Club, Sport Climbing Center of Colorado Springs, Mountain Chalet, Grand West Outfitters, Pikes Peak Mountain Sports (Colorado Springs).

Services: All services in Woodland Park. Limited services in Deckers, Florissant, and Lake George.

Emergency services: Call 911. Memorial Hospital, 1400 E. Boulder, Colorado Springs, CO 80909, (719) 475-5000. Penrose-St. Francis Healthcare System, 2215 N. Cascade, Colorado Springs, CO 80907, (719) 630-5000. Langstaff-Brown Medical Center, Hwy. 67 at Hwy. 24, Woodland Park, CO, (719) 687-6022.

Nearby climbing areas: Sunshine Dome, Helen's Dome, Wigwam Dome, Lost Creek Wilderness Area crags, Turkey Rocks, Sheeps Nose, Elevenmile Canyon, Pikes Peak crags, The Crags, Mueller State Park, Scorpio Dome.

Nearby Attractions: Lost Creek Wilderness Area, South Platte River, Florissant Fossil Beds National Monument, Pikes Peak, Eleven Mile State Recreation Area, Mueller State Park, Cripple Creek-Victor National Historic District, South Park.

BIG ROCK
CANDY
MOUNTAIN

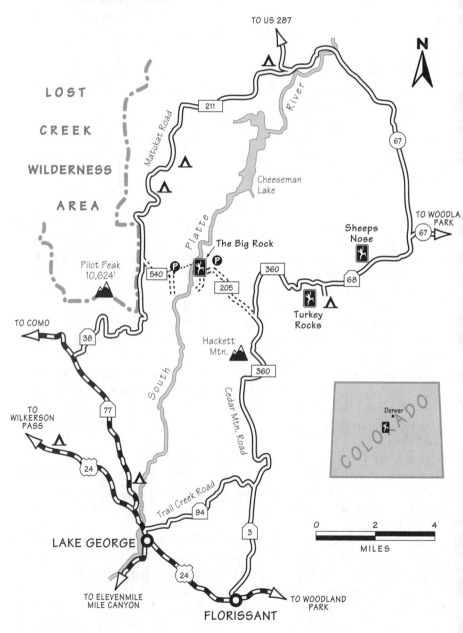

TO US 287

N

LOST

CREEK

WILDERNESS

AREA

211

Matukat Road

River

Cheeseman
Lake

67

Platte

TO WOODLA
PARK

67

Sheeps
Nose

The Big Rock

Pilot Peak
10,624'

P   P

540

205

360

68

Turkey
Rocks

TO COMO

38

Hackett
Mtn.

360

Cedar Mtn. Road

TO
WILKERSON
PASS

77

South

COLORADO

Denver

24

MILES

Trail Creek Road

94

3

0   2   4

MILES

LAKE GEORGE

24

TO ELEVENMILE
MILE CANYON

FLORISSANT

TO WOODLAND
PARK

Finding the crag: The best and easiest route into Big Rock, particularly with a two-wheel-drive vehicle, is from the west. From the north, turn southwest on Matukat Road (FR 211), off Colorado Highway 126 just east of Wigwam Campground. Drive southwest on the dirt road for a few miles to Goose Creek Campground, continue south almost 4 miles to FR 540. This road is marked Corral Creek. From the south, drive north from Lake George and U.S. 24 on Park County Road 77 for 7 miles to Matukat Road. Turn north and follow it almost 10 miles to FR 540. Head down FR 540 a couple of miles and park where it begins to get rough. Continue down the broad, open ridge to a saddle. Big Rock is readily visible directly east. This area was burned in a forest fire and is sparsely vegetated. The jeep trail drops south from the saddle. Hike north down open slopes into a shallow canyon. Continue east down the canyon on a rough trail to the South Platte River. The river is easily forded during late summer and fall but can be high and dangerous during spring runoff. Otherwise, look for a crossing at a boulder pile. The approach takes up to an hour, depending on how far you drive.

The eastern approach to Big Rock requires a four-wheel-drive vehicle or a longer walk. Turn north at Florissant on US 24 onto Teller County 3. After a few miles, turn west on FR 360 and follow to FR 205, marked Mayberry Gulch. Follow this jeep road via a four-wheel-drive vehicle, mountain bike, or foot for about 4 miles to the backside of the Big Rock. Drop down the dome's south flank and scramble around to the west side of the rock. This approach is probably the best way in during high water in late spring and early summer. Total approach time varies from 1 to 2 hours.

1. **Rotten Teeth** (III 5.10 R) This long route, put up by Pete Williams and Pete Gallagher in 1979, climbs the Big Rock's northern buttress in 14 pitches. The route begins just left of the lowermost toe of the rock. The first 3 pitches were mostly erased in 1994 by a large rockfall. Pete Gallagher is reestablishing them from a gully left of the original start. **Pitch 1** climbs an unprotected 5.9 slab to a tree belay. **Pitches 2** and **3** continue up a series of cracks and slabs. **Pitch 4** climbs left via a fingertip crack on a steep headwall and edges up a thin 2-bolt slab above to a groove. **Pitches 5** and **6** angle left in cracks and corners (5.9 and 5.8+) to another angling groove. **Pitch 7** climbs the groove (5.8) to the base of an excellent left-facing corner. **Pitch 8** jams the corner (5.9) to a ledge. **Pitch 9** climbs up a slab and into a crack system (5.9). **Pitches 10** and **11** friction up unprotected 5.8 R slabs to a pedestal/ledge system. **Pitch 12** downclimbs a chimney behind the pedestal to its base, then traverses left into a gully/crack system. **Pitch 13** climbs the gully to the top of a small pedestal. **Pitch 14** is an easy but unprotected 300' pitch or 2, 150' pitches—belay where it's convenient. The first ascent party simul-climbed this pitch. **Rack:** Bring a standard rack, with some extra pro for a 5" off-width crack.

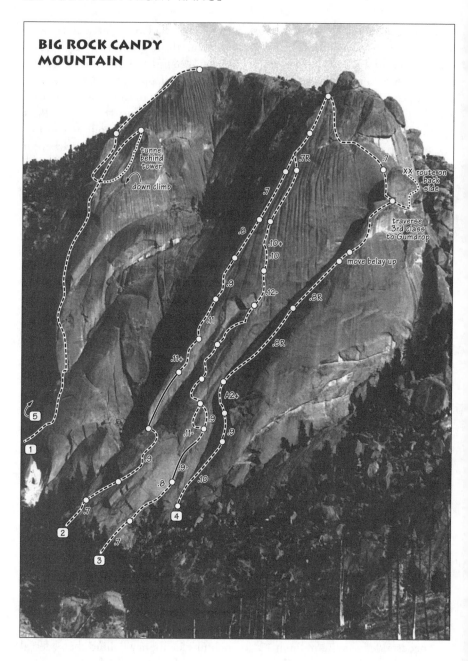

BIG ROCK CANDY
MOUNTAIN

tunnel
behind
tower

down climb

.7R

.7

.7

XX route on
back
side

traverse
3rd class
to Gumdrop

.8

.10+
.10

move belay up

.9

.12-

.8R

.11

.8R

.11+

A2+

.9

.9

.9

.11-

.9

.9-

.8

.10

.7

.7

5

1

2

3

4

2. **Fields of Dreams Growing Wild** (III 5.11+) A long spectacular line that ascends the central buttress in 11 pitches. Begin south of the foot of the buttress. **Pitch 1** jams an easy crack to a runout 5.7 R slab. Angle left up the slab to a ledge below a prominent right-facing dihedral. **Pitch 2** climbs a crack (5.5) up the slab right of the dihedral to a stance up and right below a large roof. **Pitch 3** works out right of the roof and up a crack in a right-facing corner (5.6). At the crack's end climb a short headwall (5.9) to another crack. Work up left from that crack on easy slabs to a spacious ledge with boulders. **Pitch 4** ascends a leaning finger and hand crack (5.10b) up the left wall of a huge right-facing dihedral to a bolted belay on a ramp near the top of the crack. **Pitch 5** face climbs up the steep tongue of rock above (5.11d at the first bolts) past 5 bolts to a bolted belay. **Pitch 6** continues up the steep slab (5.11a) past 5 bolts to a small roof; turn it on the left and finish up 5.9+ rock to a bolted belay stance just below the upper slab. **Pitch 7** frictions up (5.9) past 5 bolts onto "The Fields"— the striped upper slabs. Some of the granite on these upper pitches is loose and flakey. **Pitch 8** continues up the slab (a spot of 5.8) past 2 bolts to a bolted belay. **Pitch 9** edges up easier, low-angle rock (5.7 and 1 bolt) to a bolted stance. **Pitch 10** is a 1-bolt slab pitch with a touch of 5.7 past the bolt. Belay from bolts. **Pitch 11** finishes up easy, unprotected slabs to the large summit ledge. Use caution on the sparsely protected upper pitches. They're relatively easy for slabmasters, but a fall would be painful. All belays on the route are fixed with double bolts. **Rack:** Bring a generous rack of stoppers and Friends to #4.

3. **Childhood's End** (III 5.12-) This parallel line to FIELDS OF DREAMS offers 12 superb pitches of slab and crack climbing, with more bolts and peace of mind than FIELDS. Most bolts are 3/8". Begin just south of FIELDS below a broad slab topped by a right-facing dihedral system. **Pitch 1** follows a wide crack (spot of 5.7) up the lower apron to a stance in the crack. A #2 Friend is useful for the belay, while a #4 Camalot will protect the crack. **Pitch 2** continues up the crack in the large corner (5.8) to a bolted stance. **Pitch 3** works up the chimney above (5.9-) to a slab (5.10) with 5 bolts. Belay from bolts on a ledge. **Pitch 4** can be done two ways. Traverse delicately straight left (5.11-) past 3 bolts to a right-facing corner. Climb the corner to a bolted slab. Angle up left past 4 bolts to a bolted belay ledge. Or climb a crack above the belay and work up left (5.9) onto the bolted slab and the ledge. **Pitch 5** works up a steepening slab tongue right of the huge open dihedral (5.8 and 3 bolts) to a bolted stance. **Pitch 6** frictions up the slab (5.9) past 4 bolts to a ledge up left. **Pitch 7** climbs the 5-bolt slab right of the dihedral (a couple of 5.9 spots) to a bolted stance on the right side of the huge roof that caps the dihedral. **Pitch 8**, the crux lead, climbs a rotten crack on a ramp (#9 stopper) to a ladder of 11 bolts that

works up onto the striped upper slabs. This well-bolted 5.12- pitch is easily aided by pulling on bolts at the dicey sections. Coil your rope at the belay atop this pitch to avoid it hanging up on a huge flake below (which may be gone). **Pitch 9** scales a difficult slab up and left with several 5.10 and 5.9 cruxes and 10 bolts. **Pitch 10** is a long, moderate, unprotected lead to a bolted stance. **Pitch 11** works up left and joins FIELDS OF DREAMS just below the bolt on its tenth pitch. Continue (5.7 R) to a bolted stance. **Pitch 12** climbs an easy slab (no pro) that ends on the summit platform. **Rack:** Carry a small rack with a few medium and large Friends and a #4 Camalot, and 12 to 15 quick draws. All the belays are bolted.

4. **Sweet Catastrophe** (II 5.10 A2+) This 6-pitch route up the south buttress ends below Gumdrop Spire, a huge block adorning the top of the buttress. Continue to the top of Big Rock via 2 pitches up south-facing slabs above the Gumdrop. To start, scramble up big boulders just south of the huge chimney system that separates the central and south buttresses. **Pitch 1** climbs a long 5.10 slab pitch (10 bolts). It's 5.9 R to the first bolt. Belay at a 2-bolt anchor. **Pitch 2** continues up the slab (5.9 and 4 bolts) to a ledge belay at the base of a steep headwall. **Pitch 3,** the crux lead, aids up the headwall above. Face climb up a hard 5.10 seam/crack to the first bolt near the wall's left edge. Hook or tension traverse to another bolt, and aid off an RP in a narrow corner to a flake that takes a #4 Friend with 3 cams in. A #1 RP leads to the lip of the headwall and a bolt. Slab climb to a stance. (Beta from Pete Gallagher 15 years after the fact.) Or climb free (5.12a) up left on lichen face to crux seam. First freed by Charlie Fowler and Dan McGee. **Pitch 4** climbs 165' up the left edge of the slab (5.8 R) past 1 bolt to a bolted belay. **Pitch 5** continues for a full rope length up the lower-angled slab (5.8 R) to a stance below a tree. Little or no pro is encountered. Shift the belay past the tree to the highest possible anchor before leading out to ensure you have enough rope to reach the base of the Gumdrop. **Pitch 6** (165') climbs a steep slab to a left-facing corner (5.9) on a hanging block. Belay on the large ledge below The Gumdrop. **Pitch 7** climbs The Gumdrop via its east face. Traverse around the right side of the spire (3rd class) and aid an A1 bolt ladder to a 5.9 bolt-protected traverse that leads to the summit ridge. Rap 50' back to the ledge from anchors on top. Continue to the summit of Big Rock by climbing 2 pitches up the runout slabs (5.7 and 5.5) north of the Gumdrop.

5. **Shock Treatment** (III 5.12c) This sustained and difficult 6-pitch route offers superb crack climbing and a spectacular bolt-protected face pitch up Big Rock's sheer north face. Find the start by skirting the base of the cliff north from the long slab routes on the west face or descending scree slopes below the north face from behind or east of Big Rock. Either way, find the start below an obvious dihedral. Climb 15' up a 3rd class off-width crack

BIG ROCK CANDY MTN

SHOCK TREATMENT
III 5.12C

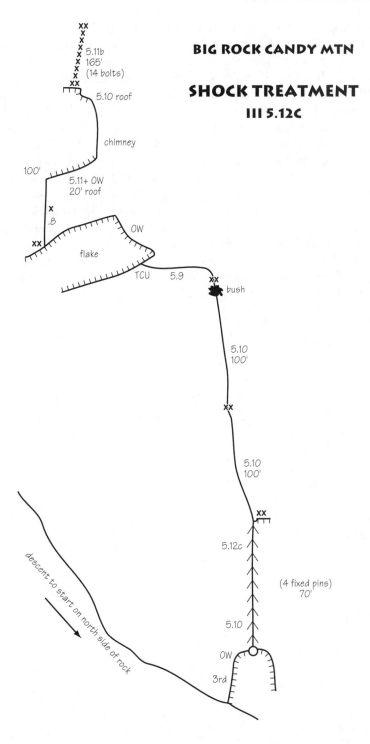

5.11b
165'
(14 bolts)

5.10 roof

chimney

100'

5.11+ OW
20' roof

.8

flake

OW

TCU   5.9

bush

5.10
100'

5.10
100'

5.12c

(4 fixed pins)
70'

5.10

OW

3rd

descent to start on north side of rock

to a large ledge below the dihedral. **Pitch 1** (70') climbs the steep dihedral. It's 5.10 initially and sustained 5.12c up high. 4 Lost Arrow pitons are fixed to protect the crux moves. It can be easily aided with small Friends and TCUs. Belay from 2 bolts on ledge on right. **Pitch 2** angles up a crack (5.10) 100' to 2-bolt stance. **Pitch 3** continues up crack (5.10) 100' to 2-bolt stance above bush. **Pitch 4** hand-traverses straight left along a wide, horizontal crack for 40' or so (5.9). Use #4 Friends and/or Camalots for pro. At crack's junction with large pterodactyl-shaped flake, reach up to perfect TCU placement and layback into off-width crack. Belay from 2 bolts on ledge at far left side of flake. **Pitch 5** (100') climbs a crack with 1 bolt (5.8) to huge roof. Traverse right under 20' roof along off-width crack (5.11+) and move up into chimney. Belay above roof (5.10) on left on ledge with 2 bolts. **Pitch 6** edges directly up the immaculate tombstone-shaped slab above past 14 bolts to 2-bolt anchor atop the buttress. Kevin McLaughlin calls this one of Colorado's best face pitches with its line of crisp 1/4" edges. **Descent:** Rap off the back side from anchors (1 double-rope rappel or 2 single-rope rappels).

JACKSON CREEK DOME

OVERVIEW

Jackson Creek Dome, sitting atop an airy ridge above a shallow valley just east of Jackson Creek, is one of Colorado's rare hidden gems. The 300-foot dome conceals its bulky profile until the access road is almost beneath the granite mantle. Your first glimpse of the dome as you bump down the rough, one-lane road is of an immense white slab glaring in the sun. The dome cannot be otherwise seen, except from atop bulky Devils Head to the immediate west.

Climbing history: This and the surrounding domes and cliffs lie in the backwater of Colorado climbing. Few climbers are aware of the area and its still vast potential for new slab routes of all grades, especially on the abrupt crags littering the eastern flank of Devils Head. The Taj Mahal, across the valley west of Jackson Creek Dome, hosts what was probably the area's first recorded technical rock climb—the classic 5.8 *Ouellette-Woodford Route* done in 1957 up the northwest face. Jackson Creek Dome's first known line is *Living in Sin,* an obvious, slashing 5.7 crack that bisects the south face's left edge and was first ascended by Alan Mosiman and Bill Coffin in 1978. Denver climbers later began exploiting the dome's potential in the late 1980s, drilling bold new lines up the steep slabs.

The slab, creased by dark water grooves, lifts an almost featureless countenance above the surrounding tangle of broken domes, boulders, and forest. Both the southwest and south faces yield a selection of great bolted slab routes that range in difficulty from 5.7 to 5.11. The routes are generally protected with 3/8-inch bolts and good hangers—a far cry from some of the manky hardware found on other South Platte area domes. Expect runouts, some as long as 30 or 40 feet, on the easier climbing. Most routes scale the dome in 2 pitches, with established anchors or chains at the belay stations. **Descent** is best accomplished by rappelling the routes or downclimbing a rocky gully east of the dome. *Consenting Adults* makes a good rappel route, with chained anchors at the belay station in the middle of the broad south slab. The rappels require two ropes. **Rack:** Most routes are done with a handful of quick draws and a couple of extra runners. Some, however, require additional protection from small wired nuts to large Friends and Camalots.

Trip Planning Information

General description: A 300-foot granite dome with excellent bolted routes on a wide, south-facing slab.

Location: South of Denver in the eastern Front Range west of Sedalia.

Camping: Jackson Creek Campground, open through the summer only, lies 1.6 miles down the Jackson Creek Road. Otherwise lots of free campsites line the road in the lower valley near Jackson Creek Dome. The area is popular in

JACKSON CREEK DOME

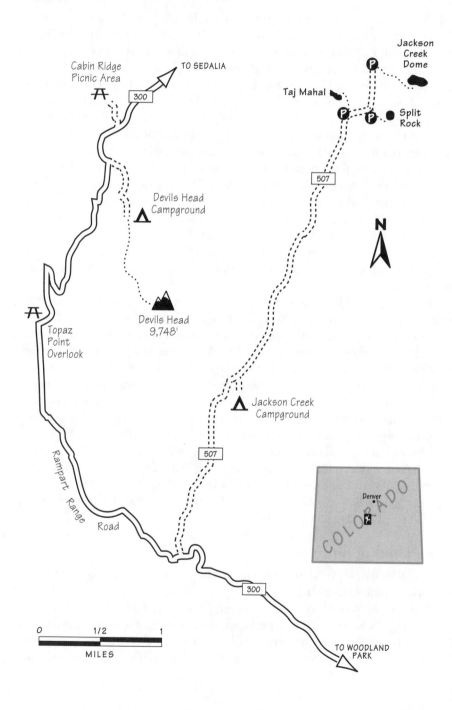

Ian Spencer-Green frictions up *Consenting Adults* on the smooth flanks of Jackson Creek Dome. *Photo by Stewart M. Green.*

summer and on fall weekends with motorcyclists. Two other national forest campgrounds—Devils Head and Flat Rocks—are north along the Rampart Range Road.

Climbing season: Year-round. April through October is the best season. The road may still be closed by snow or mud in April. Expect warm days on the south-facing slabs, particularly in summer. Heavy thunderstorms accompanied by lightning regularly occur on summer afternoons. Autumn brings excellent weather, with warm days and cool nights. Snow usually closes the access roads, including the middle section of Rampart Range Road, by early November. Use the alternate access route in winter to reach the cliff. Winter days can be very warm on the south-facing slabs.

Restrictions and access issues: None; Jackson Creek Dome sits on Pike National Forest land.

Guidebooks: *Front Range Crags* by Peter Hubbel, Chockstone Press, 1994, offers a complete topo guide to Jackson Creek Dome and the surrounding domes and slabs, including Mega Dome, Split Rock, the excellent North Face routes on Taj Mahal, and selected routes on Devils Head.

Nearby mountain shops, guide services, and gyms: Grand West Outfitters, The North Face, Paradise Rock Gym (Denver).

Services: All services in Castle Rock and Denver. Limited services, including gas, in Sedalia.

Emergency services: Dial 911. St. Anthony Hospital, 4231 W. 16th Ave., Denver, CO 80204, (303) 629-3511.

Nearby climbing areas: Devils Head, Mega Dome, Taj Mahal, Turkey Rock and Turkey Tail, Dome Rock, Atlantis Slab, Scorpio Dome, Woodland Park boulders, Mount Evans, Lover's Leap, North Table Mountain, Morrison bouldering, Castlewood Canyon.

Nearby attractions: Devils Head Lookout and National Recreation Trail, Rampart Range Road, Lost Creek Wilderness Area, South Platte River canyons, Mueller State Park, Florissant Fossil Beds National Monument, Castlewood Canyon State Park, Chatfield State Recreation Area.

Finding the crag: This remote dome is reached by several dirt roads in the northern Rampart Range. From Denver drive south on U.S. Highway 85 to Sedalia or west from Interstate 25 and Castle Rock to Sedalia. Turn south on Colorado Highway 67 in Sedalia and drive 10 miles to Rampart Range Road (Forest Road 300). Turn south on Rampart Range Road and drive south almost 14 miles to Jackson Creek Road (FR 507). Drive north on this one-lane, rough dirt road 4.5 miles to its washed-out end. Park in the small lot here. Cross the creek at the wash-out and immediately head southeast along the east creek shore along a rough trail. The path contours southeast and east up a steepening gravel hillside and reaches the southwest flank of Jackson Creek

Dome after about 10 minutes of hiking. Scramble up a short gully below the face past several routes, cut through a notch, and drop east along the edge of the dome's south face. The dome can be approached in winter and spring when Jackson Creek Road is closed by driving south from Sedalia on Colorado 105 6.3 miles to Douglas County Road 38, which becomes FR 507 upon entering Pike National Forest. Follow the paved and gravel road into the mountains for 7.2 miles and its intersection with FR 502. Park here and continue on foot or mountain bike down FR 507 for a couple of miles to the parking lot. FR 502 also continues west 2 miles to Rampart Range Road.

JACKSON CREEK DOME - SOUTHEAST FACE

The southeast face is the first large face encountered along the access trail. Routes are listed from west to east. They all end on a low-angle slab mid-way up the face. **Descend** by rappelling the routes or continuing to the broad summit on easy, but mostly unprotected rock.

1. **Nervous Disorder** (5.11c) This route begins on the far west side of the southwest face near a group of large boulders and below a gravel gully. Climb a steep, smooth slab just left of a blunt, angled arete past 7 bolts to a steeper headwall and anchors.

2. **Hot Rize** (5.10a) A very good climb up the right side of the angled arete. Climb past several bolts onto the dull arete, continue up and over the promi-

nent roof to another bolt, and head up left to the NERVOUS DISORDER anchors. **Rack:** Some wired stoppers and small Friends provide additional pro.

3. **Cold Frize** (5.8) Ascend an obvious open corner, turn the roof on its right side, and finish at the NERVOUS DISORDER anchors. **Rack:** Bring a small rack to supplement the route's couple bolts.

4. **Alien Elite** (5.10a) Climb a shallow, right-facing corner (5 bolts) to anchors. **Rack** to #3 Friend.

5. **Mythical Kings and Iguanas** (5.9) A good line up the slab's steep center. Scamper up easy rock from the access gully and thread through several overlaps. **Rack:** Some wired nuts provide additional protection. 5 bolts.

6. **One Track Pony** (5.8) Clip the first couple bolts of MYTHICAL KINGS AND IGUANAS before striking out right and climbing a slab and an overlap (3 bolts) to anchors.

7. **D Winger** (5.7+) A fine moderate line up the face's east edge. Begin near the top of the access gully and arch up and left past 3 bolts to anchors.

SOUTH FACE

Continue up the access trail around a detached buttress and scramble up to the south face base or third class up below the southwest face to a shallow notch and drop down and east among scrub oak below the south face. A crude trail follows the face for a short distance before wandering out atop the boulder field below the smooth slab. Most of the routes on the east side of the face begin on top of the boulders. The routes are listed from west to east (left to right).

8. **Face the Face** (5.11a) Begin by a large tree just right of a west-leaning ramp system immediately past the notch. Climb the steep 5.11a face above past 3 bolts, continue up easier rock past 2 more bolts to anchors.

9. **Flaming Monkey** (5.7) Follow a broken, right-angling crack system to the crux exit onto a slab above and 1 bolt. **Rack:** Bring stoppers and Friends to 3".

10. **Energy Vortex Direct** (5.9) Climb past a dike and several bolts to a belay stance atop a prominent crack. The second pitch (2 bolts) climbs up 5.6 rock, passes a small roof, and ends on the summit slabs.

11. **Living in Sin** (5.7 R) This route ascends a wide grooved crack to a belay. Continue up unprotected slabs with occasional 5.6 and 5.7 moves to the summit. This was the dome's first route.

12. **Mr. Chips** (5.9-) Begin just right of a large flake leaning against the face.

Pitch 1 follows 5 widely spaced bolts up the slab to belay anchors. The route crux is thin face moves by the first bolt. **Pitch 2** (5.7) has 3 bolts. **Rack:** Some medium pro is useful on the upper part of the 2nd pitch.

13. **Consenting Adults** (5.10a) An excellent 2-pitch line up the left side of the white slab. **Pitch 1** begins by the first large boulders. Climb to a bolt, edge up the 5.10a crux moves, and waltz upwards past 6 more bolts to a chained anchor. **Pitch 2** (5.8) follows 4 bolts up the steepening headwall to anchors on the summit.

14. **Snail Trail** (5.9) Scramble across the boulder tops and find the obvious right-angling crack below a short headwall. Climb the crack, step right to a bolt, and continue up CREATURISTIC to belay bolts. **Rack:** Bring Friends to 3" for pro.

15. **Creaturistic** (5.11b) **Pitch 1** face climbs up the steep slab side of a chimney at the face's base. The hard climbing is past the second bolt. Continue up the open slab with bolt-protected 5.9 and 5.8 moves to a belay stance. 7 bolts. **Pitch 2** follows 3 bolts up 5.8 rock to the summit.

16. **Wild Thing** (5.9+) A very good route up the central slab. Begin atop boulders and climb past 3 bolts then run it out on 5.5 climbing to belay anchors. The superb 2nd pitch, capped by a prominent roof turned on its right, offers 5.9 climbing and enough bolts to feel secure.

17. **Lego Land** (5.9 R) Another great climb on the central slab. Begin on boulders. Climb up along a 5.8 water streak past a couple bolts and run it out on easier climbing to the belay anchor. The steeper upper slab is well-bolted (5 bolts) and has a spot of 5.9 friction up high.

18. **Hang Ten** (5.7+ R) Begin just up from the face's low point. Ascend the lower slab past 2 bolts to anchors and slings. The 2nd 5.7 pitch climbs the upper wall (2 bolts) to anchors.

19. **Time Out** (5.8) An excellent route up the right side of the central slab. Climb 5.8 rock past a bolt and follow a water groove (1 bolt) to anchors. The steeper 2nd pitch follows a line of 6 bolts up 5.8 rock to summit anchors.

20. **Tease** (5.8) A good moderate 1-pitch route. Scramble up a ramp system in the gully on the face's east flank to a boulder-top belay stance. Climb to a cold-shut hanger and follow 3 more bolts to anchors on the lower-angle slab above.

21. **Crispy Critters** (5.10a) The middle route up the dome's southeast side. Climb 1 pitch up grooves in the slab past 4 bolts to the anchors.

22. **Nipple Flipper** (5.10b) Begin high in the gully, climb up left past 2 bolts to anchors.

NEW AGE SLAB

This short slab sits just east of the gully that separates it from Jackson Creek Dome. Scramble up through the boulder field to the slab's base. All 4 routes have runouts on moderate climbing. Rappel from anchors atop the slab. A few more good routes lie on the Winger Wall, a broken slab immediately east of New Age Slab, including a good 2-pitch 5.7 up the slab's longest section.

23. **Psychic Intuition** (5.8 R) Climb left near the slab's west edge past 2 bolts to anchors.

24. **Astral Projection** (5.7 R) Straight up the middle of the slab. 2 bolts.

25. **Out of Body Experience** (5.8) Smear up to ASTRAL PROJECTION'S first bolt, traverse right to a bolt and head up past 3 more bolts. The crux is past the third bolt where the slab steepens.

26. **Out of Mind Experience** (5.9) Climb to ASTRAL PROJECTION'S first bolt, make a longer traverse right to a bolt on the slab's far right edge. Edge up and left to the anchors. 6 bolts total.

SCORPIO DOME

OVERVIEW

Scorpio Dome, perched high above North Monument Creek in the Rampart Range, is a little-known crag visited mostly by Colorado Springs locals. Few routes ascend the rock's abrupt 250-foot south face, but a couple superb lines grace its western flank. The remote granite dome, offering distant views of the high plains to the east and snow-capped Pikes Peak to the southwest, hides among forested ridges east of the Rampart Range Road. Scorpio is reached via rough forest roads that traverse ridgelines north of the crag. The south-facing dome gives good cool weather climbing, and is even climbable in winter, although access can be a problem if deep snowfall lingers on the roads.

Several multi-pitch crack and face routes climb Scorpio Dome's steep south face, jamming intermittent cracks and delicately edging up thin crystals. But the dome's best climb ascends a prominent 80-foot block below and west of the main rock. *Scorpio Crack,* one of the Front Range's finest finger and hand cracks, splits the vertical south face of the block. Bob Robertson discovered the crack and did the first ascent of it and *The Sting,* a 165-foot slab pitch below the crack.

The dome's large south face routes include one that follows an obvious squeeze chimney and off-width crack to a sling belay/rappel station on the right side of the face. Another climbs a chimney for 50 feet, traverses right onto a steep slab, and edges up past a half-dozen bolts to a belay/rappel point.

Bulldog Dome, a low-browed rock 0.2 mile west up the road and ridge from Scorpio Dome, has several 5.10 crack routes done by Bob D'Antonio as well as an easy slab below and to the south with toprope anchors. Another good slab sits at the bottom of the steep draw that drops west below Bulldog Dome. Scramble down the draw to an aspen grove at the slab's base. Several good bolted, 1-pitch routes with rappel anchors climb the south-facing slab.

Trip Planning Information

General description: A large granite massif with several excellent routes, including the three-star classic *Scorpio Crack.*

Location: Northwest of Colorado Springs in the Rampart Range.

Camping: Primitive camping is found along Forest Road 323. A good spot is on the north side of Bulldog Dome 0.2 mile up the road from Scorpio Dome.

Climbing season: Scorpio Crack can be climbed year-round, but April through October offers the best weather. Winter access is problematic, particularly if much snow falls.

Restrictions and access issues: None. The crag is on Pike National Forest.

Guidebooks: No other guidebook includes Scorpio Dome or other Rampart Range crags.

Ian Spencer-Green hand-jams *Scorpio Crack* on Scorpio Dome. *Photo by Stewart M. Green.*

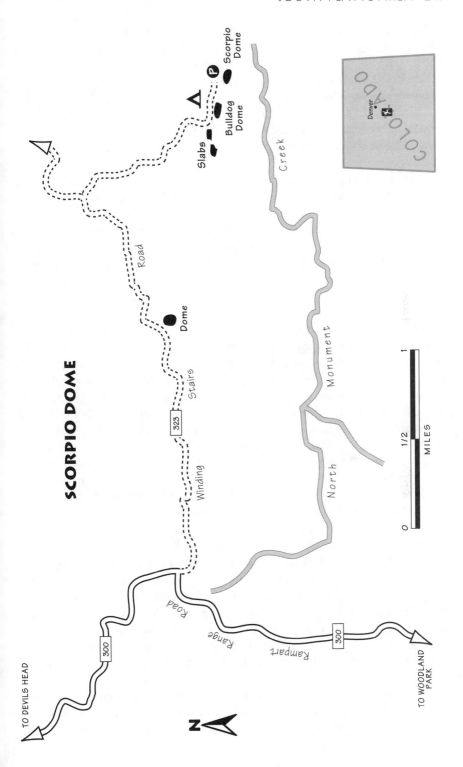

SCORPIO DOME

Nearby mountain shops, guide services, and gyms: 8th Street Climbing Club, Sport Climbing Center of Colorado Springs, Mountain Chalet, Grand West Outfitters, Pikes Peak Mountain Sports (Colorado Springs).

Services: All services in Woodland Park.

Emergency services: Call 911. Memorial Hospital, 1400 E. Boulder, Colorado Springs, CO 80909, (719) 475-5000. Penrose-St. Francis Healthcare System, 2215 N. Cascade, Colorado Springs, CO 80907, (719) 630-5000. Langstaff-Brown Medical Center, Hwy. 67 at Hwy. 24, Woodland Park, CO, (719) 687-6022.

Nearby climbing areas: South Platte domes and crags, Sheeps Nose, Turkey Rocks, Jackson Creek Dome, Elevenmile Canyon, Pikes Peak crags, Garden of the Gods.

Nearby attractions: Devils Head National Recreation Trail, Rampart Range Road, Lost Creek Wilderness Area, South Platte River, Florissant Fossil Beds National Monument, Pikes Peak, Elevenmile State Recreation Area, Garden of the Gods, Pikes Peak Highway, Cripple Creek-Victor National Historic District.

Finding the crag: Scorpio Dome sits above North Monument Creek in the Rampart Range almost mid-way between Colorado Springs and Denver. The crag is reached by a series of dirt roads that are generally passable in a 2-wheel-drive vehicle. Wet weather or snow on the roads might require 4-wheel-drive. The dome is best accessed from Woodland Park. Turn northeast off U.S. Highway 24 onto Baldwin Street at the McDonald's Restaurant on the east side of Woodland Park. Baldwin runs northeast from town. After 3 miles, keep left at the Y-junction on Lloyd Creek Road (FR 393). The paved road winds up a shallow canyon, passing the Woodland Park Bouldering Area at 3.6 miles. The road reaches the gravel Rampart Range Road (FR 300) at 4.2 miles. Head north up the Rampart Range Road. The Mount Herman Road, which drops east to Monument and Interstate 25, is reached at 6.8 miles. Continue north to FR 323 at 10.3 miles. Turn east on this rough, one-lane, dirt road and follow it 2.7 miles to a road junction. A small dome with 3 good cracks on its south flank sits just south of the road at 2.3 miles. At the road junction, turn right and follow the deteriorating road for 1.2 miles to a parking area just north of Scorpio Dome. The road becomes a rocky jeep trail below the pulloff. Walk down the old road and drop south to a gravel saddle behind Scorpio Dome, the prominent, broken outcrop immediately to the south. Turn west at the rock and follow a short trail down a gully to the west side of an immense block. Drop down and crawl under the block's corner to a gravel ledge. *Scorpio Crack* looms above.

1. **Scorpio Crack** (5.10+) Reach the crack by descending a shallow gully on the north and west side of the block. Crawl under the overhanging southwest corner of the block and onto a large gravel ledge. The south-facing

SCORPIO DOME

crack cleaves the steep face above. Climb the 1" to 3" crack 80' to the block's flat summit. Belay from a couple of bolts on the lip above the crack. Tape your hands well—the granite is somewhat coarse. **Descend** via a couple of eyebolts and 5.7 moves on the northeast corner. **Rack:** Bring double Friends from #1 to #4. Stoppers are also useful down low. The shorter right-leaning hand crack on the right side of the block goes at 5.8.

2. **The Sting** (5.11- R) This excellent pitch climbs the steep slab below SCOR-PIO CRACK and makes a great 1st pitch to the crack. Scramble around the west flank of the dome to the base of the slab. The obvious route climbs the rock between two water streaks. Follow 6, 1/4" bolts up the slab and then run it out up easy climbing over a couple of big flakes. **Rack:** Bring some medium Friends for extra pro on the flakes and a full 165' rope. Better yet, use a 200' rope to make sure you don't run out of cord on this long pitch. Belay on the gravel ledge below SCORPIO CRACK.

3. **Arcturus** (5.11+) A good 1-pitch route up the south side of Scorpio Dome just east of the gravel ledge below SCORPIO CRACK. The climb ascends an obvious shallow, right-leaning corner capped by a triangular roof. The route begins on a ledge 40' down and right of the crack ledge. It's a tricky downclimb to the ledge. Face climb into the thin crack system. Stem the corner and jam the strenuous fingertip crack up and right for 75'. Finish with 60' of gravelly 5.8 climbing to the top. **Rack:** Bring thin pro for the crack.

ELEVENMILE CANYON

OVERVIEW

The South Platte River twists across South Park, a wide inter-montane basin, from its headwaters on the Continental Divide to Elevenmile Reservoir on the park's far southeastern corner. Below the reservoir's dam the river plunges into Elevenmile Canyon, a narrow steep-walled gorge on the southern edge of the Puma Hills. Numerous granite crags ranging from 50 to 500 feet high line the 9-mile canyon, their bold outcrops etched against the sky. More than 250 routes thread the canyon's cliffs, ascending thin cracks, bald slabs, detached flakes, meandering dikes, in-cut holds, and sharp crystals. The canyon's sweeping, light-hearted slabs offer some of Colorado's best beginner and moderate routes, while it's steep walls yield some hard crack and face climbs.

Climbing history: Climbers long ignored Elevenmile Canyon's potential, their attention given to nearby South Platte domes and Turkey Rock. A few ascents were made in the 1950s and 1960s, but it wasn't until the Pikes Peak Group of the Colorado Mountain Club and the Colorado College Mountain Club used the canyon for annual rock climbing schools in the 1970s that the canyon attained popularity. Brian Teale and Dan Morrison ascended many of today's classic moderates in the mid-70s while working for Turret Dome Climbing School. The area's standards jumped in 1979 with the free ascent of the *Teale Tower Route,* the canyon's first 5.11 route, and again in 1982 when Australian Chris Peisker scaled *Peisker Crack,* an overhanging 5.12d finger slit on Sports Crag. Through the mid-1980s numerous climbers, including Bob D'Antonio, Dale Goddard, Richard Aschert, and Mark Milligan, established a host of extreme sport routes on newly discovered crags. Local activists continue to find exciting new lines in this superb crag-infested canyon.

Descent: Most routes have walk-offs, although lowering or rappel stations are found on some modern lines.

Rack: Many bolted routes ascend the canyon's cliffs, as do numerous traditional lines that require a standard rack with sets of wired stoppers and Friends, as well as a few RPs and an occasional large Camalot or Big Bro for off-widths.

Trip Planning Information

General description: Some of Colorado's best beginner and moderate routes, with excellent granite climbing on domes, slabs, and steep faces that range from 50 to 500 feet high.

Location: West of Colorado Springs.

Camping: Elevenmile Canyon is an excellent camp and climb area. Camping is restricted to 6 Pike National Forest campgrounds that sit on or just off the canyon road, including 21-site Blue Mountain, 19-site Riverside, 15-site Springer Gulch, 7-site Wagon Tongue, 5-site Cove, and 24-site Spillway campgrounds. Springer Gulch, Cove, and Spillway campgrounds are best for climbers, with

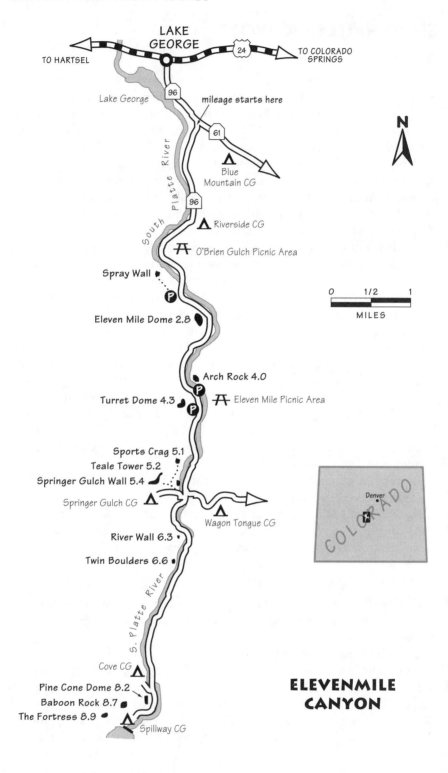

LAKE GEORGE

TO HARTSEL

TO COLORADO SPRINGS

96

Lake George

mileage starts here

61

Blue Mountain CG

N

96

Riverside CG

O'Brien Gulch Picnic Area

Spray Wall

P

Eleven Mile Dome 2.8

Arch Rock 4.0

Turret Dome 4.3

Eleven Mile Picnic Area

0   1/2   1

MILES

Sports Crag 5.1
Teale Tower 5.2
Springer Gulch Wall 5.4

Springer Gulch CG

Wagon Tongue CG

River Wall 6.3

Twin Boulders 6.6

Denver

COLORADO

S. Platte River

Cove CG

Pine Cone Dome 8.2
Baboon Rock 8.7
The Fortress 8.9

Spillway CG

South Platte River

ELEVENMILE CANYON

Ian Spencer-Green on *Randy Speaks Farsi* on the Spray Wall in Elevenmile Canyon. *Photo by Stewart M. Green.*

nearby crags and bouldering. Campgrounds, available on a first-come, first-served basis, tend to fill up early during the busy summer months, particularly on weekends. A daily fee is charged. All campgrounds offer toilets, water, tables, and fire grates. Limited off-season camping is free. All campgrounds will be moved out of the canyon by 1997.

Climbing season: Year-round. May through October offers the best climbing weather. Days are generally warm with highs ranging between 50 and 80 degrees, with cool nights. Expect regular afternoon thunderstorms in summer. Winters tend to be cold, although occasional days offer good climbing on south-facing crags. Snow covers the cooler slopes from November through March. Spring brings cool, breezy days. The canyon is above 8,000 feet in elevation.

Restrictions and access issues: The canyon, also popular with fishermen, campers, and bikers, is in Pike National Forest. No restrictions on climbing are currently in place, but climbers need to be sensitive to other canyon users. Avoid climbing or bolting routes near the road. Use webbing that matches the rock color on rappel anchors and remove unsightly slings from routes. Use existing footpaths to the base of the crags and park well off the road at pulloffs and picnic areas. Do not park in campgrounds unless you are staying there. A $3 per car daily fee is charged at the canyon entrance. A $15 annual pass is available.

Guidebooks: No current guidebook. A complete canyon guide will appear in a Pikes Peak select book by Bob D'Antonio in late 1995.

Nearby mountain shops, guide services, and gyms: 8th Street Climbing Club, Sport Climbing Center of Colorado Springs, Mountain Chalet, Grand West Outfitters, Pikes Peak Mountain Sports (Colorado Springs).

Services: All services are found in Colorado Springs and Woodland Park. Limited services are in Lake George and Divide.

Emergency services: Call 911. Memorial Hospital, 1400 E. Boulder, Colorado Springs, CO 80909, (719) 475-5000. Penrose-St. Francis Healthcare System, 2215 N. Cascade, Colorado Springs, CO 80907, (719) 630-5000.

Nearby climbing areas: South Platte domes and crags, Turkey Rock, The Crags, Pikes Peak, Shelf Road, Garden of the Gods, North Cheyenne Canyon, Scorpio Dome, Mueller State Park.

Nearby attractions: Lost Creek Wilderness Area, Florissant Fossil Beds National Monument, Cripple Creek-Victor National Historic District, Gold Belt Tour Back Country Byway, Pikes Peak, Elevenmile State Recreation Area, South Park.

Finding the canyon: Elevenmile Canyon lies 45 miles west of Colorado Springs south of U.S. Highway 24. Turn south in Lake George at the service station/store onto Park County Road 96. After 1 mile the road turns west into the canyon at an obvious, marked intersection. Drive 0.4 mile to the entrance station and continue down the narrow gravel road to the crags. Mileages for each crag are: Spray Wall, 2.5 miles; Elevenmile Dome, 2.8 miles; Arch Rock, 4 miles; Turret Dome, 4.3 miles; Teale Tower, 5.2 miles; River Wall, 6.3 miles; and Pine Cone Dome, 8.2 miles. The road deadends at the dam just past Pine Cone Dome.

SPRAY WALL

The Spray Wall, the newest sport crag in Elevenmile Canyon, was developed in 1993 and 1994. The cliff offers several 5.13 and 5.12 routes on steep, overhanging faces, as well as some 5.10s. All of the routes are bolted with lowering anchors. Bring 10 quick draws. This small crag sits across the river from the road. Park in a small pulloff just past the first bridge 2.5 miles from the canyon entrance and walk east on a climber's access path across the bouldery slope north of the river. The crag is reached after about a 0.25-mile hike. The severely overhanging wall on the left offers three routes—all with manufactured holds. These routes are not included in this guide. Every hold on one route is chipped, and an undercling flake was epoxied on at the crux. Remember—chipping destroys the future of climbing. If you can't do it as is, it's better to leave it for a better climber to ascend the rock in better style.

1. **Spew** (5.12c) Follow overhanging arete that climbs onto headwall. 7 cold shuts to a 2-cold-shut anchor.

2. **Rapture** (5.13a) A good route with long reaches and dynos. 5 cold shuts to 2-cold-shut anchor.

SPRAY WALL

3. **New Dawn Fades** (5.13+) A project up the white wall and roof.

4. **Pagan Wisdom** (5.12b/c) An excellent route that swings up and left above roof's lip on small incuts to a hand-jam in finishing crack. 4 bolts to anchors over lip.

5. **Only Entertainment** (5.12c) This superb line ascends 6 bolts up a leaning wall to cold-shut anchors above.

6. **Unknown** (5.12a/b) Follow line of 6 black cold shuts to anchors on right side of main shield. Not the greatest line on the cliff.

7. **Randy Speaks Farsi** (5.10d) A very good, pumpy line up steep right wall to anchors. 5 bolts and 2 cold shuts at lowering station.

8. **Unknown** (5.11a) Follow a shallow dihedral and pull overhanging wall. 5 cold shuts to anchors.

ELEVENMILE DOME

This 250' dome sits beside the road just up-canyon from the Spray Wall at 2.8 miles. The long south-facing crag offers moderate slab and crack routes up to 3 pitches long, and almost no approach. The 1st pitch on most routes is the most difficult. A good parking area sits on the west end of the dome below the *Overleaf* route. Pull well off the road. **Descent:** To descend from the routes, traverse southwest below the dome's headwall into a bouldery gully that leads southeast to the road or trend north down forested slopes to the road. **Rack:** Bring an assortment of wired stoppers, TCUs, Friends, and quick draws for the crack routes. All of the climbs listed can end on the low-angle slabs below the summit's overhanging brow. Avoid trundling or knocking boulders off the crag as the road is directly below. Routes are listed from left to right when facing the dome.

9. **Kathy's Crack** (5.4) Follow the low-angle 80' hand and fist crack that arches up dome's west slab.

10. **Stone Groove** (5.6) A moderate pitch up an off-size crack in a right-facing corner. Carry a couple of large Friends or Camalots for security.

11. **The Overleaf** (5.8) This fine 2-pitch route ascends a right-facing crack system using finger-locks, hand jams, and laybacks above the road on dome's western flank.

12. **South Face Direct** (5.10b) A fine 4-pitch outing up steep water-worn slabs and grooves. **Pitch 1** is steep 5.10 bolted slab to a 2-bolt belay. **Pitch 2** moves up slab (spot of 5.8) and ends 80' higher at 2-bolt belay. **Pitch 3** is easy 5.0 rock to belay ledge under prominent summit roof. Walk left to descend here if you don't do the roof pitch above. **Pitch 4** is an excellent bolted 5.11 pitch over the roof; Bring a few wires for upper crack.

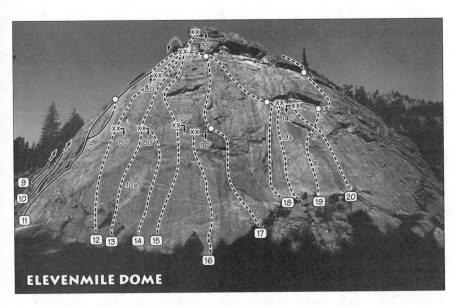

ELEVENMILE DOME

13. **Unnamed** (5.10a) Climb an 80' 5.10 pitch right of SOUTH FACE DIRECT to anchors. **Pitch 2** continues up left on 5.6 rock to a bolted belay. Rap the route.

14. **Face Value** (5.8+ R) A runout, 2-bolt slab route to a 2-bolt anchor.

15. **Cheryl's Peril** (5.9) A fine bolted route that face climbs 140' over some dikes to a 2-bolt rappel ledge or continues upwards on easy rock.

16. **Unnamed** (5.9) Scale bolted slab broken by occasional grooves for 140' to a 2-bolt anchor.

17. **Phantom Pinnacle** (5.7) 2 pitches climb up through weathered hollows and thin discontinuous cracks to ledges below summit overhangs. **Rack:** Bring small and medium pro.

18. **Moby Grape** (5.7) **Pitch 1** ascends prominent right-facing dihedral (5.7). A bolted belay/rap stance is on right. **Pitch 2** scampers upwards on easy slabs. **Rack:** Carry some small and medium pro for corner's thin crack system.

19. **Jet Setter** (5.7 R) This classic traditional route climbs the steep slab right of MOBY GRAPE. **Pitch 1** edges up 40' of unprotected slab climbing. Put small gear in and scale a small overhang. Move up and right over another roof (5.7-) to slab that leads to a stance under large roof. Bring a large sling to tie off a block at belay. **Pitch 2** traverses right past the roof's right edge (5.6) and up easy climbing through tinajas to the right side of the summit overhangs. **Pitch 3** is a short, 5.4 pitch to summit. **Rack:** Bring an assortment of small wires and a few small to medium Friends.

20. **Happy Trails** (5.6) Climb straight up slab to a small nose. Surmount it and continue to a 2-bolt belay under the obvious roof. Rappel with 2 ropes. First ascent party led the general line in 1979 with scant protection, but it now has 6 bolts.

ARCH ROCK

Arch Rock offers some of Colorado's finest moderate routes on its slabby west face. Two- and 3-pitch routes ascend corners, cracks, and slabs to the crag's broken summit. Arch Rock is 4 miles in, above the east side of the road. Park at one of several pulloffs or at Elevenmile Picnic Area just up the road. Several trails wind up steep but short slopes to the crag base.

Descend from Arch Rock's summit by heading south on a rough trail around the rock's south end. **Rack:** Carry a standard rack with stoppers, TCUs, and Friends. Routes are listed from left to right.

21. **The Staircase** (5.5) One of the best 5.5s anywhere. This popular route offers 2 pitches of crack climbing, with spacious belay ledges and numerous nut placements. **Pitch 1** Climb obvious right-facing dihedral (5.4) on the crag's left side with great hand jams and face holds. **Pitch 2** stems up deep corner (5.5). A direct 5.8 finish squeezes up short off-width at top of pitch, otherwise step left to easy rock. Bring standard rack.

22. **Kansas Honey** (5.9) A 3-pitch route. **Pitch 1** Climbs steep slab past 5 bolts to a belay under an obvious arch. **Pitch 2** Traverse left on unprotected 5.9, turn arch, and head right to another belay under main summit arch. **Pitch 3** A hand crack just north of the belay leads to the top.

23. **Hollow Flake** (5.6) A large flake leans against the face right of STAIRCASE. Scale center of flake or its right side to a belay ledge and tree. Rappel to ground. The 5.11b R SPROUT ROUTE face climbs straight up through overlaps past 1 bolt to Arch Rock summit.

24. **Death by Drowning** (5.10c/d) A 3-pitch route. **Pitch 1** Climb a short easy pitch up right side of HOLLOW FLAKE to a small pine tree and belay. **Pitch 2** The bolt-protected 2nd pitch goes up right to a quartz dike and continues right up steep face climbing (5.10+) to a belay with bolts on a lower angle slab. **Pitch 3** Surmount the arch above (5.8) and belay in the water-worn tinajas.

25. **Captain Fist** (5.8) Climb the left side of Tilted Tower via hand jams, laybacks, and stems. A 5.6 center route also scales the tower; and the three 25' Meanie Cracks (5.7) at the tower's base make good practice for beginner crack climbers.

26. **Arch Rock Direct** (5.7 R) This excellent route, beginning atop Tilted Tower, ascends up and right via unprotected slab climbing (5.7-) to a belay stance under the arch. Turn roof on face holds, belay, and walk off right.

ARCH ROCK

27. **Village Idiot** (5.9) Begin on a grassy ledge just left of the Tilted Tower's south-facing dihedral. **Pitch 1** Climb directly up, placing wired nuts and RPs for pro to a bolt 40' up. Continue on excellent face climbing past 3 more bolts and belay at a stance with 2 cold-shut anchors. Rappel 100' or do **Pitch 2** straight up and over arch above (5.7). **Rack:** Bring a couple of medium-to-large Friends to protect move over the arch.

28. **Zendance** (5.7-) A superb face route. Climb straight up steep bucketed slab past 2 bolts to a bolt at a left-angling quartz dike. Continue up the dike to another bolt and end at the 2 cold-shut anchors of VILLAGE IDIOT. Rap 100' or do second lead. Some runouts on this climb can be protected with small to medium wired stoppers, including an easy crack in a dike below anchors.

29. **Obscura Direct** (5.7) Another great climb up steep slab. Begin on ledge right of Tilted Tower. **Pitch 1** jams an easy hand crack (5.5) to small belay stance below a right-facing corner. **Pitch 2** edges up narrow, right-facing corner (5.7-) above using a thin crack. Step left onto unprotected slab, and climb up and over the arch (5.7) to belay ledges. Bring assortment of stoppers and a large Friend or Camalot to protect arch moves. The regular OBSCURA route climbs right above first belay stance and joins ARCH ROCK REGULAR ROUTE.

30. **Arch Rock Regular Route** (5.8) Climbs a crack and chimney system just right of OBSCURA in 2 pitches.

TURRET DOME

Turret Dome, rising 450' above the South Platte River, forms Elevenmile's highest crag. Its long south face yields excellent beginner and intermediate routes up both cracks and slabs. Park at Elevenmile Picnic Area at 4.3 miles, cross the river via a foot bridge, and head west 0.25 mile along a narrow trail to the dome's base. **Descend** from the rounded summit by downclimbing north to a shallow saddle, then east through thick forest to the picnic area. **Rack:** Carry a standard rack for most climbs and watch for long, unprotected runouts on easy slab routes. Numerous holds allow a plethora of routes, both named and un-named, to thread across the dome's south slabs. Routes are listed from right to left.

31. **Sunshine Slab** (5.0) This long, low-angle slab makes for good beginner toproped and multi-pitch routes. Climb anywhere on the slab—the difficulty never rises much beyond 5.0.

32. **Jaws** (5.5) **Pitch 1** ascends the right side of large prominent River Arch atop lower slab using hand jams, chimneying, and face climbing. Turn arch on its left side and belay on a small ledge. **Pitch 2** is easy climbing through bathtubs to the summit overhang. **Pitch 3** finishs up a right-leaning 5.4 hand crack or up UPPER LIP, an overhanging 5.7 finger crack, to summit.

33. **Schooldaze** (5.5) Climb an excellent wide crack via laybacks and fist jams to west end of River Arch. Watch that the belay rope doesn't snag in wide crack below. Climb tubs and finish on JAWS.

34. **Guide's Route** (5.6) A superb 3-pitch line up a crack system just west of River Arch. **Pitch 1** climbs a 5.6 hand and finger crack to a good belay ledge. **Pitch 2** moves up easy rock and shallow cracks to belay stance under the summit roofs on turret's southwest corner. **Pitch 3** works up 5.6 rock over overhangs to summit.

35. **Aid Route** (5.10a) Climb an 80' finger crack to rappel anchors around corner from the GUIDE'S ROUTE on the dome's west face. Bring small wires and Friends to protect it. Other routes on this wall include WHITE STRESS, a 5.12a thin face pitch with 5 bolts (bring TCUs and wires), and INNER SPACE ARCH, a 5.9 face climb with 3 bolts and rappel anchors. Both are just left of Aid Route.

TEALE TOWER

Teale Tower looms across the South Platte River from the road at 5.2 miles. This imposing south-facing crag is best accessed from the Springer Gulch Campground area just up the road. Park at a small pulloff just inside the campground and hike east over a couple of ridges to the cliff base. Several excellent routes scale cracks that split the steep granite shield. **Descend** by down-climbing easy rock on the crag's north side.

36. **Unnamed** (5.11) A fist-to-off-width crack on shield's left side.

37. **Teale Tower Route** (5.11a) A great 2-pitch route up striking, Yosemite-type dihedral in center of face. It was Elevenmile Canyon's first 5.11 after Brian Teale's 1979 ascent.

38. **Run for Your Life** (5.11a R) This hazardous route laybacks a thin crack just right of TEALE TOWER ROUTE. Pro includes 3 bolts, RPs, small wires.

39. **Reality Check** (5.10d) Climbs overhanging hand jams to exposed finger crack in a corner system on crag's right side.

TEALE TOWER

RIVER WALL

The River Wall, sitting at 6.3 miles, is a long, somewhat discontinuous wall along the river's north bank. Several excellent bolted and traditional routes up to 80' long grace its steep faces, following pebbled slabs, vertical finger cracks, and aretes. Approach the cliff by parking opposite it in a wide pulloff above the river. Walk east on the road and over the bridge. Follow a trail along the north river bank to the base of the wall. Routes are listed from west to east.

40. **Captain Cod Piece** (5.11c) This excellent line jams a thin finger crack directly behind some big fir trees. **Descent:** Walk west to ledges to descend. **Rack:** Bring some wired nuts and TCUs.

41. **Simple Minds** (5.12b) Begin right of CAPTAIN COD PIECE. Scale steep wall to finger crack in thin corner. Climb past 2 bolts above to anchors.

42. **Darylect** (5.12c) A superb bolted line up a leaning wall just east of trees. Lower from anchors.

43. **Loaf and Jug** (5.7-) Begin on vertical wall below left-leaning slab. Swing up on fun jugs to slab and follow its left edge up to high-step crux at top. Belay from a tree and walk off.

44. **Life on the Run** (5.10a) Start right of wide dihedral that leads to huge roof. Finger jam up right-angling crack system to high crux. **Rack:** Bring wired stoppers, TCUs, and small Friends.

RIVER WALL

45. **Blood Brothers** (5.12a) A bolted route up a slab to steep headwall. 1 anchor.

46. **Flat Earth Society** (5.11c) A fine line left of large left-facing dihedral. Edge up thin slab past 2 bolts (5.11a) to left-diagonaling crack. Hand traverse left then work up right on thin face climbing past 2 more bolts to 2 cold-shut anchors. Go right at last bolt for easier finish.

47. **Skid Marks** (5.11c) A superb arete climb with great position above river. Begin on west side of obvious arete. Climb onto arete and pass 5 bolts to double anchors on top.

PINE CONE DOME

Pine Cone Dome, at 8.2 miles, gives several fine moderate gear and sport routes up its grooved roadside face. **Descent** is a walk-off to the north and east down a gully.

48. **Pine Away** (5.8) Climb up and left via overlaps and cracks.

49. **Parr Four** (5.10a) Discontinuous cracks and slabs to obvious tree just below summit.

50. **Armaj Das** (5.5) Good 2-pitch beginner route up slabs and flakes. **Rack:** Bring wires and small to medium Friends.

51. **Stone Age** (5.5) Follows long, obvious crack system. A small rack of Friends and wired stoppers suffices. 2 pitches.

52. **Ben Dover** (5.9+) A short bolted slab route to lowering anchors. 5 bolts and anchors.

53. **Lichen or Leave It** (5.8) Climbs a long crack system in 2 pitches.

54. **Roof By-Pass** (5.7) A long crack system that edges by large roof midway up. 2 pitches.

55. **Anorexic Lycra Dog** (5.12a) Thin edging and smearing up bolted slab to a lowering anchor below roof. 6 bolts and anchors.

OTHER CANYON CRAGS

Many other cliffs line the canyon, offering excellent climbing. Springer Gulch Wall, perched on the ridgetop behind Teale Tower, yields many quality lines. A couple of the best include *Here's to Future Ways* (5.12b/c) on the crag's west face, and the exhilarating *Surfing With the Alien,* a 9-bolt, 80', 5.11d pitch with thin edging and stemming up a bulging arete on the cliff's southwest corner to a 2-bolt belay stance. Sports Crag, 0.1 mile east of Teale Tower on the north slope above the river, concentrates several 5.11 and 5.12 overhanging cracks including *Peisker Crack,* the area's thin-crack testpiece with sustained 5.12d finger jamming. Baboon Rock at 8.7 miles and The Fortress at 8.9 miles sit above the Spillway Campground. Both offer superb rock and sustained crack climbing. Good bouldering is also found at the campground. The best boulders are in the first four campsites. The canyon's best bouldering is found on the East and West Twin Boulders across the river from a parking area at 6.6 miles. Wade the river and crank. The East Twin offers the *Triangle Face* (V2+) on its river side and *Bob's Face,* an excellent V5+ done by Bob D'Antonio and Harrison Dekker, on its steep west wall. The West Twin has some good problems on its shaded north wall.

COLORADO SPRINGS AREA

GARDEN OF THE GODS

OVERVIEW

The Garden of the Gods, a Colorado Springs city park since 1910, nestles in a broad valley against the forested Rampart Range. The rocks here are part of a long series of uplifted sandstone hogbacks swept up against the Front Range from Wyoming to Canon City. The ruddy sandstone layers at the Garden are the dramatic remains of the Rocky Mountain's uplift some 25 million years ago. The exposed rocks, scattered like an immense outdoor sculpture garden, were originally deposited in Paleozoic times as sand dunes, ancient marshes, and alluvial aprons below long-eroded mountains. Today the rock formations are a geologic marvel and a popular attraction for tourists, hikers, bikers, horseback riders, and rock climbers.

Climbing history: The Garden of the Gods is one of the oldest technical climbing areas in the United States. The area's first climbers were undoubtedly the Ute Indians who frequently camped among the rocks. Technical climbing, however, began in 1914 when Colorado College professor Albert Ellingwood returned from a three-year Rhodes Scholar visit to England and brought back English climbing and rope techniques. Ellingwood applied his skills to local rock faces and ascended a few Garden routes including *Lance* on Gray Rock's west face and *Ellingwood Chimney* on the summit block of Keyhole Rock. Robert Ormes, an Ellingwood protégé, continued the tradition with other Garden ascents in the 1920s and 1930s. Stanley Boucher and Vernon Twombly, using better equipment including homemade pitons and sisal ropes, climbed several classics in the 1940s such as the ever-popular *Practice Slab* on South Gateway Rock. U.S. Army climbers also left their mark with first ascents of *Montezuma Tower, The Three Graces,* and *West Point Crack.* Later climbers placed permanently drilled soft-iron pitons, precursors to today's bolted sport routes, on the Garden's crackless rock faces for protection. This innovation allowed the creation of most of today's classic climbs. The late 1960s and 1970s brought free climbing to the Garden of the Gods, with numerous climbers including Layton Kor, Jim Dunn, Earl Wiggins, Ed Webster, and Leonard Coyne ascending new and difficult lines. After a long hiatus, a 1990s resurgence in new routes has resulted in several excellent lines including *Diesel and Dust* on Gray Rock.

The Garden of the Gods is not a typical sandstone climbing area. Its different rock strata and their varying qualities and diverse character make for a unique climbing experience. The sandstone varies from being compact and reliable to friable sections more akin to dried brown sugar than rock. The novice Garden climber generally remembers loose dinner plate-sized flakes and sandy footholds rather than the crisp edges, smooth friction smears, sharp ribs, rounded solution pockets, and large potholes found on the more well-traveled routes. The routes, generally ascending steep faces and slabs, vary in height from 40 to 350 feet and from 1 to 5 pitches. Most climbs are protected by soft-iron pitons drilled up to three or four inches deep in the sandstone. Bear in mind that many of these pitons are over 30 years old, are rusted, and have seen many leader falls. The ring eyes on many of the older pitons also exhibit signs of metal fatigue. Do not lower or rappel off a single anchor here. Some 3/8" and 1/4" bolts are also found on routes. Do not rely solely on any of these bolts for your protection. They have, on occasion, sheared off or pulled out with body weight. Larger expoxied expansion bolts and forged eye-bolts are slowly replacing the Garden's decaying anchors.

South Gateway Rock and Gray Rock offer some of the Garden of the God's best rock climbing adventures. *Photo by Stewart M. Green.*

Rack: Most routes are climbed with a rack of quick draws, although the occasional pothole thread requires a sling, and some routes are protected with a small rack of stoppers, nuts, and Friends.

A number of city regulations need to be adhered to by Garden of the Gods climbers. All climbers must register annually at park headquarters. Climbing is prohibited on North Gateway Rock's south face beside the large plaque and on the fragile Kissing Camels formation atop North Gateway Rock. No one is allowed to climb higher than 10 feet above the ground without registering and without proper climbing equipment. This regulation keeps scramblers from venturing into dangerous zones. Solo climbing, sport rappelling, and the use of white chalk is banned. Some Garden areas, including the Tower of Babel and the upper southeast face of Gray Rock, are seasonally closed for bird nesting. Check at park headquarters for closure info and dates. Climbing is discouraged after heavy rains or snowfall to protect the rock surface. The soft rock absorbs and holds moisture after extended bad weather periods, making the rock crumbly and sandy.

Trip Planning Information

General Description: A Colorado Springs city park that offers more than 225 climbing routes of all grades on a spectacular series of upturned sandstone hogbacks and spires.

Location: Immediately west of Colorado Springs.

Camping: No public camping in the immediate area. Private campgrounds sit just south of the Garden of the Gods off U.S. Highway 24. The nearest Pike National Forest campgrounds are north of Woodland Park, about 25 miles northwest of the Garden via U.S. 24 and Colorado Highway 67.

Climbing Season: Year-round. Summers are often hot in the afternoon, with daily highs in the 80s. Shady routes are easily found, including the Drug Wall on South Gateway Rock and the southeast buttress of Gray Rock in the afternoon and evening. Spring brings warm, windy days. Autumn days in October and November offer good climbing weather with warm afternoons and only occasional rain or snow showers. Colorado Springs's mild winters yield excellent afternoon adventures on the sandstone cliffs.

Restrictions and access issues: This city park is a fragile and beautiful area. Rock climbers need to be sensitive to other park users. Climbing access is an ongoing challenge, with some local residents against continued climbing in the park. The city Park and Recreation Department, however, recognizes rock climbing as both a legitimate and historical use of the Garden. Climbers in turn need to recognize climbing here as a privilege and act accordingly. All climbers must register annually at the park visitor center and agree to follow all park climbing rules. These include the use of proper equipment when climbing above 10 feet; no bouldering on the bases of Sentinel Rock and the Twin Spires; no sport

GARDEN OF THE GODS

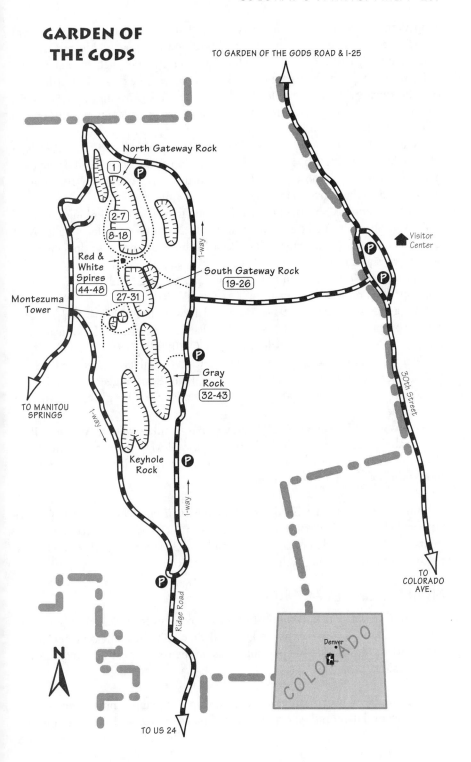

TO GARDEN OF THE GODS ROAD & I-25

North Gateway Rock

1

2-7

8-18

Red & White Spires

44-48

South Gateway Rock

19-26

Montezuma Tower

27-31

TO MANITOU SPRINGS

1-way

Gray Rock

32-43

Keyhole Rock

1-way

Ridge Road

Visitor Center

30th Street

TO COLORADO AVE.

Denver

COLORADO

N

TO US 24

rappelling; no white chalk; only rust-colored slings used for semi-permanent rappel anchors; no climbing on sensitive bird nesting areas on North Gateway Rock and Gray Rock; no additional fixed protection unless necessary; climbing only during daylight hours; and no climbing after rain or snow storms. The rock becomes brittle and fragile after heavy thunderstorms and wet snowfalls. Climbers should wait until the rock surface dries completely, usually one to three days after a storm.

Guidebooks: *South Platte Rock Climbs* by Peter Hubbell and Mark Rolofson offers a fairly complete but dated 37-page section at the book's end. It includes maps and topos to almost all of the rock formations. A few new routes have been added to the Garden since the book's 1988 publication.

Nearby mountain shops, guide services, and gyms: Sport Climbing Center of Colorado Springs, 8th Street Climbing Club, Mountain Chalet, Grand West Outfitters, (Colorado Springs). Pikes Peak Mountain Sports also does climbing shoe repairs and resoling.

Services: All services, including gas, food, restaurants, and lodging, in Colorado Springs and Manitou Springs.

Emergency services: Call 911. Memorial Hospital, 1400 E. Boulder, Colorado Springs, CO 80909, (719) 475-5000. Penrose-St. Francis Healthcare System, 2215 N. Cascade, Colorado Springs, CO 80907, (719) 630-5000.

Nearby climbing areas: North Cheyenne Canyon, Silver Cascade Slab, Shelf Road, Aiguille de St. Peter, Mount Big Chief, Pikes Peak, Bigger Bagger, Pericle Rock, The Crags, South Platte domes, Turkey Rocks, Sheep's Nose, Mueller State Park.

Nearby attractions: Pikes Peak Highway, Barr Trail, Air Force Academy, Pike National Forest, Cripple Creek, Beaver Creek BLM Wilderness Study Area, Royal Gorge, Arkansas River State Recreation Area, Mueller State Park, Florissant Fossil Beds National Monument.

Finding the crags: The Garden of the Gods is on the west side of Colorado Springs below the abrupt Front Range escarpment. The area is accessed from Interstate 25 via Garden of the Gods Road and 30th Street, and from U.S. 24 on the south by 31st and 30th streets or Ridge Road.

NORTH GATEWAY ROCK

North Gateway Rock, composed of pink Lyons sandstone, is the largest rock formation in the Garden of the Gods and towers 350' above the central Garden zone. Park at the Hidden Inn parking areas on the rock's west side to access the cliff bases.

1. **Anaconda** (5.11c) A superlative climb up the leaning north edge of the Tower of Babel on the northern end of North Gateway Rock. Layton Kor

aided the route with difficult piton placements, particularly on the initial expanding flake and the wide crack on the 2nd pitch. Jim Dunn and Earl Wiggins freed it in 1975. Many parties climb only the 1st pitch to anchors below the final crux. Begin by scrambling up to the base of the route below an obvious expanding flake. **Pitch 1** works up the flake (5.8), steps left past a drilled piton, and enters a vertical crack system. Jam, stem, and pull up (5.10) to 2 left-leaning thin cracks. Strenuous climbing (5.11c) leads up left to a hanging belay from pitons. **Pitch 2** goes up the obvious funky off-sized cracks above to the tower summit. **Rack:** Fixed pro exists on the entire pitch, although tenuous 5.11 leaders will want to carry some medium-sized stoppers and Friends.

2. **Rainbow Bridge** (5.11a R) Somewhat runout pothole pulling up a steep wall just right of the huge arching overhang east of the parking lot. Do a short 5.6 crack to the top of a flake and crank upward past several fixed pegs. **Descent:** Rappel with 2 ropes from anchors on a ledge with a tree.

3. **Borghoff's Blunder** (5.10a) Begin atop the flake below RAINBOW BRIDGE and climb up and right to a mantle crux. Bring a few large slings for pothole threads. Again rappel from the ledge or climb 2 loose pitches to the rock summit.

4. **Men at Work** (5.11b) This long pitch begins half-way up the slanting crack/flake below BORGHOFF'S BLUNDER. Work up and right to a dyno crux (5.11b). Continue above through potholes and more hard sections. Bring 2 ropes for the rappel from anchors. 8 fixed pitons.

5. **Pete and Bob's** (5.11c) Most only climb the 1st pitch, an excellent 5.9 hand crack to a flake-top belay. **Pitch 2**, a long drilled-piton protected traverse to the right, keeps getting harder as flakes break off, but the peg ladder is easily aided. **Pitch 3** climbs the bulge above the belay ledge at 5.9 and continues up easy but runout slabs (5.6) to the top. **Rack:** Bring a few large Friends or hexes for extra pro.

6. **Amazing Grace** (5.11b) A long pitch up a serious and loose water streak. It's well-bolted but scary nonetheless. Ed Webster wrote in a 1978 issue of *Climbing*: "The climb was named after the religious exclamation of a nearby middle-age woman who saw Earl Wiggins fall to within a foot of the ground when a hold broke." Begin just right of an arching alcove. Crank up right of a large pothole and mantle on a sloping hold (5.11b). Continue up the flakey face above past lots of drilled pitons to chained anchors. Rap with 2 ropes.

7. **The Warren-Johnson Route** (5.10b/c R) A serious lead with only 4 fixed pitons and a potential groundfall at the crux. Usually toproped.

8. **Trigger Finger** (5.9) Begin on a wide ledge below a southwest-facing slab. Move up the slab past a couple of fixed pins to a good ledge belay. Bring a long sling to anchor a rock spike at the belay. **Descent:** Downclimb the gully immediately to the east.

9. **Cowboy Boot Crack** (5.6) A classic finger and hand crack on the right side of the 70' slab. **Descent:** Downclimb the gully to the east. **Rack:** Bring a rack of medium nuts and Friends and a long sling for the belay spike.

10. **Mr. Fred** (5.10d) Approach this route by scrambling up a short gully just right of COWBOY BOOT CRACK or by climbing up wide, rounded TOURIST GULLY (5.2). This 2-pitch route edges up the far north side of the Finger Face slab. Usually only the 1st pitch is done. **Pitch 1** is thin, devious face climbing past 3 drilled angles to anchors. **Pitch 2** works up and right over the steep break past 7 pitons to anchors. **Descent:** 2 rappels with 1 rope from the second belay stance.

11. **Pig Dreams** (5.10b) An excellent 2-pitch friction route just right of MR. FRED. Climb up to a pin, delicately traverse right past 2 more drilled pitons, and then go straight up to the belay. The loose 2nd pitch climbs the prominent bulge with 6 pitons. **Descent:** Rappel the route.

12. **Chatters** (5.9+) A good 1-pitch climb that ends at the first PIG DREAMS belay. 5 pitons.

13. **No Ethics** (5.10d) Ascends a steep headwall (5 drilled pins) out of the gully to a belay stance with anchors. Rap here or follow a variety of 2nd pitches up the wall above. DUST TO DUST (5.10a) is the best 2nd pitch, climbing thin face-holds to an exhilarating bulge above. **Rack:** Carry some Tri-cams

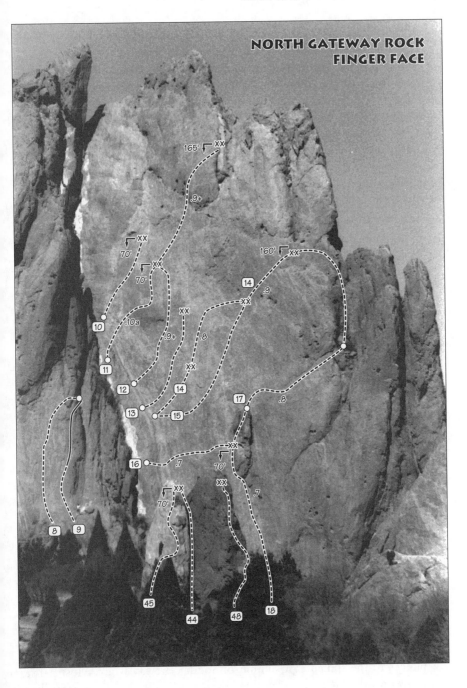

NORTH GATEWAY ROCK
FINGER FACE

and Friends to 3.5" to fit in the numerous potholes and pockets on the bulge on DUST TO DUST. **Descent:** Rappel the route.

14. **Son of Tedricks** (5.8) and **Tedrick's** (5.9) Climb Son of Tedricks and Tedrick's together from the gully for a good 2-pitch voyage to the top of the face. **Pitch 1** begins just above the steep gully section. Face climb up right (5.8-) past 3 pins for 45' to a belay stance. Rap here or continue straight up on thin face climbing (5.8) past 2 pins. Traverse right from the second piton to a small belay stance atop PLACE IN THE SUN. **Pitch 2** traverses up right on loose flakes (3 pitons) to a spacious ledge. **Descent:** Make a long 2-rope rappel from a slinged 2-piton anchor on the ledge to the ground.

15. **Place in the Sun** (5.8) A classic 1-pitch route (5 fixed pins) to a 2-piton rappel station on the face.

16. **Lower Finger Traverse** (5.7) A superb 1-pitch route that traverses (5.7) from a gully belay stance to a small alcove under The Finger, a small buttress perched on the face. **Descent:** Rappel 70' from anchors.

17. **Upper Finger Traverse** (5.8) Continue the traverse from atop The Finger. Work up and right past 5 pitons to a brushy gully. Seconds can take a long fall in mid-traverse after unclipping from a fixed piton and having to downclimb (5.8) to the next one. **Descent:** Rappel 165' from the ledge at the end of TEDRICK'S with 2 ropes.

18. **Finger Ramp** (5.7) This popular route begins below The Finger on the rock's southwest corner. Climb the sloping ramp past 3 fixed pitons. The 5.7 crux is edging around the base of The Finger to a belay alcove. **Descent:** Rap 70' from anchors to the ground.

SOUTH GATEWAY ROCK

This large, complex formation looms south of the Gateway gap. The slabby Drug Wall, facing northeast, offers several excellent friction and thin face-climbing routes. The West Face yields some good beginner topropes and a few decent 1-pitch routes.

19. **Candyman** (5.10a) A short pitch that begins in the deep slice on the east side of the Drug Wall. Ascend a steep wall on sandy pockets to a 2-bolt station. 3 pitons.

20. **The Deal** (5.11c/d) Crank the face just right of CANDYMAN past 4 pins.

21. **Cocaine** (5.10b) This brilliant slab route wanders up the wall for 2 long pitches to the spiked east summit of South Gateway Rock. Most parties climb only the 1st pitch and descend by downclimbing a gully or rappelling. All the hard climbing is well-protected. Bring a long sling for the traverse bolt half-way up the 1st pitch to ease rope drag. A good 5.11 variation,

SOUTH GATEWAY ROCK

NINETY-NINE PERCENT PURE, balances up the steep slab below the 1st pitch traverse. 6 drilled pegs. **Descent:** Rap with 2 ropes from anchors on a ledge atop the 1st pitch.

22. **Cold Turkeys** (5.11b) Ascend COCAINE to a ledge 60' up. Smear up the thin slab to the left, frictioning up shallow ribs past a thin face crux (5.11b). The upper part stays entertaining to a belay ledge. 6 drilled pitons. **Descent:** Rap from COCAINE'S anchors or downclimb the steep gully.

23. **Silver Spoon** (5.5) Probably the most popular pitch in the Garden. A friction slab leads to easy traversing under the prominent roof and a belay stance in the gully. The route was named for a large kitchen spoon wrapped around a scrub oak branch at the base. 4 bolts and pins. **Descent:** Downclimb the shallow gully (5.4 at the bottom).

24. **The Fixer** (5.10b) This good route frictions up a steep slab right of the steep gully. Climb easy rock to a piton about 40' up. Continue up and left past several more pitons on thin friction. Finish above on easy, unprotected rock to a high alcove/ledge. The belay stance and rappel anchors are in the alcove below the headwall. **Descent:** 2 ropes are needed to reach the ground, otherwise a single-rope rappel will reach the gully at the SILVER SPOON belay.

25. **Rocket Fuel** (5.11b) Steep slab climbing with a hard smear move (5.11b) lead to the upper headwall (5.10b) and a narrow belay ledge with anchors. **Descent:** 1 rope will not reach the ground from the belay ledge. Use a 200' rope or rap with 2 ropes to the ground.

26. **Mighty Thor** (5.10b) A popular route up the water groove on the right side of the wall. Climb the groove and upper headwall to a belay ledge. Crux move is a long reach. Lots of drilled piton protection. **Descent:** Rap with 2 ropes from belay ledge.

27. **Practice Slab** (5.4-5.8) This long slab on the north end of the West Face offers many popular beginner topropes above a large ledge. Access the anchors via chopped steps on the right side of the slab.

28. **Kor's Korner** (5.12a) Scale chopped steps below a sharp buttress. The 2-pitch route above is obvious. **Pitch 1** traverses right around the buttress past some fixed pitons (5.11d) and enters a vertical finger crack. Jam the pin-scars to a semi-hanging belay in a shallow dihedral. Lower from here or do a 2nd pitch up and right (5.11a) past many drilled pegs to the pillar's summit. This excellent route, first climbed on aid by Layton Kor in 1965, makes a good, clean aid route (C2). **Rack:** Bring a small rack of medium to large stoppers and small Friends and TCUs for extra pro.

29. **West Point Crack** (5.8) This classic 2-pitch route, pioneered and named by U.S. Army climbers in 1946, ascends the obvious crack south of KOR'S

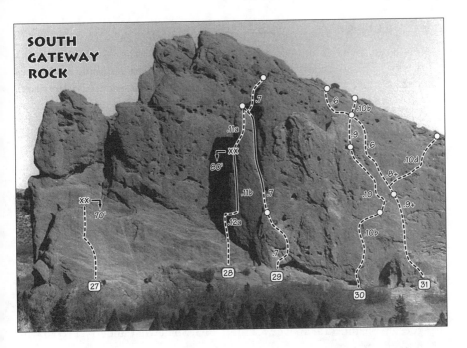

SOUTH
GATEWAY
ROCK

KORNER. **Pitch 1,** climbing above a shallow alcove, is somewhat difficult to protect. **Pitch 2** works up the widening crack to a pillar belay. **Pitch 3** (5.7) goes up right to the summit ridges. **Rack:** Bring a small rack of medium to large stoppers and Friends to supplement the fixed gear.

30. **Pipe Dreams** (5.10c R) A daring, sparsely protected 4-pitch line that weaves its way up a loose intimidating face. Watch for lengthy runouts on hard climbing. **Pitch 1** ascends a hollow flake to a steep face (5.10b) with 3 fixed pins. Traverse right (2 pegs) to a belay stance. **Pitch 2** works up left (5.10c R) to a pothole belay. **Pitch 3** climbs the headwall above (5.9) with 2 fixed pegs to a large ledge behind flake. **Pitch 4** goes up left (5.6) or right (5.10b, 1 pin) to the summit ridge. **Rack:** A selection of large stoppers and medium to large Friends is needed.

31. **Credibility Gap** (5.9+) Most parties climb only the 1st pitch to a belay stance and a threaded pothole anchor. Begin behind a large tombstone rock in front of the main face. **Pitch 1** follows the juncture of the red and white sandstone past a couple of fixed pitons to a steep face (5.9+) with 4 drilled pins. Rap 70' to the ground. **Pitch 2** goes up and left (5.8+) to a ramp to a wide flake. A good 2nd pitch, DOG DAY AFTERNOON (5.10d) is a wild traverse up and right on exposed face climbing (9 drilled pitons).

GRAY ROCK

This large, twin-summited formation towers above the road on the park's south side. The southeast buttress offers the crag's best climbing with steep faces, sharp flakes, and incut hand holds on compact sandstone. Like the rest of the Garden routes, these are mostly bolt-protected lines. Park in pulloffs below the east face and follow a rough trail to its base. Good bouldering is found in the Snake Pit below the road on two large boulders.

32. **Skyline Pig** (5.10b R) This good, steep line climbs up an incipient crack and belays on a small stance. Finish up the obvious right-facing open book to the sloping south face. **Rack:** Carry thin to medium pro and be wary of the funky, existing pitons.

33. **Question Authority** (5.12c) Very thin face climbing past numerous cold-shut bolts to anchors. 2 cruxes—5.12c down low and a 5.12a crux 40' up.

34. **Beat Me Up Scotty** (5.10d) Awesome climbing on thin flakes to a 2-bolt stance.

35. **Black and Blue** (5.8 R) An old 2-pitch route up shallow corners. **Pitch 2** goes up the dihedral above SKYLINE PIG. Somewhat underprotected with funky fixed pins.

36. **Civil Disobedience** (5.12a) A thin bouldery start (5.12a) leads to the 2nd bolt. Continue above on easier climbing past 5 more bolts to 2 lowering anchors.

37. **Alligator Soup** (5.9+ or 5.11a) A superb route since its retrobolting. The one hard move is well-protected. After **Pitch 1**, rappel or lower from anchors. **Pitch 2** climbs up steep headwalls (5.11a) on thin flakes to anchors. **Descent:** Rap with 2 ropes to the ground or one rope to the first belay.

38. **Diesel and Dust** (5.11a) Excellent face climbing on flakes and edges leads to a semi-hanging belay. **Pitch 2** climbs directly up steep, crispy rock to a 2-bolt belay. **Descent:** Rappel the route or downclimb south.

39. **New Era** (5.7) This Garden classic follows the obvious large dihedral for either 2 or 3 pitches. The hard climbing is a layback (5.7) just below the upper belay stance. **Descent:** Downclimb south from the summit of Kindergarten. This route is often closed for raptor nesting in spring and summer. Obey all closures. **Rack:** Bring medium to large pro to supplement the few fixed pins.

40. **End of an Era** (5.8+) Airy face climbing up the aesthetic, sharp, bolted arete right of NEW ERA leads to a lowering station 70' up. **Pitch 2** continues up and left on easier climbing.

41. **End to End** (5.10a) This well-protected, overhanging line ascends the north-facing buttress just right of END OF AN ERA to a belay/lowering stance 70' up. 5 pitons.

42. **Bob's Buttress Crack** (5.8+) Steep face climbing along a crack to a belay station. **Rack:** Bring plenty of medium pro including Friends and hexentrics. 1 bad piton.

43. **Beginning of the End** (5.9+) More face climbing on friendly incut holds to a bolted station next to Ormes Chimney. 4 fixed pitons. Rap or lower 70'.

RED AND WHITE TWIN SPIRES

These twin spires sit in the Gateway area with a paved sidewalk looping around them. Several popular routes ascend the rocks. **Descent** is by rappel from summit anchors.

WHITE TWIN SPIRE

44. **South Ridge** (5.6) An easy classic with 2 fixed pins. Bring a few nuts for extra security. Rap west 60' from summit anchors.

45. **West Face** (5.8+) Begin on the left side of the west face, scale a small overhang to a ledge, traverse right and back left to the summit. 3 fixed pitons. Numerous variations exist on the face, including KOR'S START, a 5.10b move on the face's right side.

46. **North Ridge** (5.7 R) A good but under-protected climb up the ridge's right side. 2 bad fixed pitons.

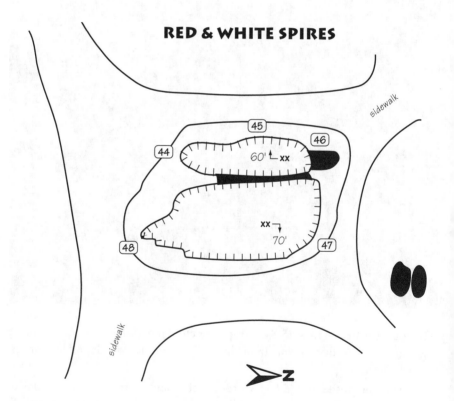

RED & WHITE SPIRES

RED TWIN SPIRE

47. **Potholes** (5.7) A popular line up the elongated potholes on the spire's northeast flank. Well protected, but the top moves are sandy. 4 drilled pitons. Rap northwest 70' from anchors.

48. **South Ridge** (5.8 R) A decent but seldom-climbed route with only 2 old funky pins for protection.

MONTEZUMA'S TOWER

Montezuma's Tower, a thin 140' fin soaring above the central Garden zone west of South Gateway Rock, offers an airy, scary classic 5.7 route up its *North Ridge*. The bolt-protected route begins on the northwest corner of the north ridge. Do a few sandy moves onto the ridge (5.7) and climb upward on thin, unprotected face climbing (5.7) to a narrow ledge with a pothole. Bring a long sling to thread the pothole for protection. Continue up the narrowing ridge (5.5), past 2 fixed pegs, to a flat belay platform. The next pitch heads up the steep ridge (5.6) to the summit. Straddle and belay. Bring 2 ropes for the rappel down the west face. *The South Ridge* goes at 5.8 up a sandy chimney and cracks.

SILVER CASCADE SLAB

OVERVIEW

The narrow gorge of North Cheyenne Canyon slices through rosy Pikes Peak granite in the abrupt Front Range uplift southwest of Colorado Springs. The creek rushes over Helen Hunt Falls (named for 19th-century writer Helen Hunt Jackson), rushes down a twisting canyon, and quietly empties into Fountain Creek in Colorado Springs. Granite precipices and faces adorn the lower canyon, soaring above the road and the canyon floor. The canyon, long a tourist attraction, was praised in an 1893 travel brochure: "This canyon abounds in beautiful waterfalls and cascades.... Beautiful, picturesque, grand, and in places awe-inspiring, are these stupendous gorges, awakening deepest emotions in all beholders."

A few good rock climbs are found on the crumbling towers in the lower canyon, including the *Army Route,* a 3-pitch, 5.5 route up corners and cracks on the north side of The Pinnacle, and *Crack Parallel,* an excellent 5.7 slab route on The Pinnacle's west face. Most of the climbs, however, have little character or charm to recommend them.

The canyon's best rock and climbing routes lie on 165-foot Silver Cascade Slab, a dark granite slab that stretches across the mountainside south of Helen Hunt Falls in the upper canyon. Most of the canyon's granite is heavily jointed, breaking down quickly through erosion into loose, fractured crags and boulders. Silver Cascade Slab, however, lies on a band of hard, erosion-resistant granite that is weathered by exfoliation into a large curving slab.

The slab is reached by a short, steep trail from Helen Hunt Falls. It perches above Silver Cascade Falls and a stone overlook. The low-angled, water-polished slabs below the overlook are unsuited for climbing, although an easy and popular ice climb builds up the central slab in winter. The slick slabs also entice unsuspecting tourists onto them, leading to occasional fatalities from falls. Silver Cascade Slab sits above the overlook, below the old railroad grade and tunnel from the now-abandoned Short Line Railroad to Cripple Creek. This track section, part of the Gold Camp Road, is now closed to auto traffic because of collapsing tunnels.

Scramble up a faint trail through undergrowth to the base of the wall below a large prominent 4th class dihedral that divides the slab in half. The left or south half offers a selection of excellent bolted routes that edge up the polished slab to its treed summit. All are 1-pitch long. The steeper right half is accessed by a wide sloping ramp that divides a lower slab from the upper wall. Several superb lines ascend the upper wall in full-rope pitches. A rack of quick draws and a 165-foot rope suffice for most of the routes. Bring a long sling to tie off a tree for the summit belay. **Descend** by walking south toward the tunnel and dropping down the slab's southern edge. Be careful not to kick gravel or loose rock off the summit on anyone below.

Stewart Green edges up *Reality Check* on Silver Cascade Slab in North Cheyenne Canyon. *Photo by Ian Spencer-Green.*

Trip Planning Information

General description: A selection of good 1- and 2-pitch, bolt-protected slab routes.

Location: On the southwest edge of Colorado Springs in North Cheyenne Canyon.

Camping: No nearby camping. Several private campgrounds scatter across west Colorado Springs. Pike National Forest campgrounds lie north of Woodland Park on Colorado Highway 67.

Climbing season: March through November. Easy ice climbs are found on Silver Cascade Falls below the slab in winter.

Restrictions and access issues: No restrictions or access problems. The slab lies on the edge of North Cheyenne Canyon City Park. Immediately west is Pike National Forest.

Guidebooks: None.

Nearby mountain shops, guide services, and gyms: 8th Street Climbing Club, Sport Climbing Center of Colorado Springs, Mountain Chalet, Grand West Outfitters, Pikes Peak Mountain Sports (Colorado Springs).

Services: All services in Colorado Springs.

Emergency services: Call 911. Memorial Hospital, 1400 E. Boulder, Colorado Springs, CO 80909, (719) 475-5000. Penrose-St. Francis Healthcare System, 2215 N. Cascade, Colorado Springs, CO 80907, (719) 630-5000.

Nearby climbing areas: Garden of the Gods, North Cheyenne Canyon, Specimen Rock, Aiguille de St. Peter, Mount Big Chief, Shelf Road, Pikes Peak crags, Pericle Rock, The Crags, Scorpio Dome, Eleven Mile Canyon.

Nearby attractions: Pikes Peak, High Drive, Gold Camp Road, Broadmoor Hotel, North Cheyenne Canyon Park, Gold Belt Tour Back Country Byway, Garden of the Gods, Barr National Recreation Trail, Air Force Academy.

Finding the crag: From Colorado Springs exit Interstate 25 at Tejon Street and head southwest up Tejon Street and Cheyenne Boulevard. Keep right at the canyon entrance, and head up North Cheyenne Canyon to Helen Hunt Falls. Park in one of the roadside lots by the falls and follow a trail over the waterfall and up a steep eroded hillside to the south. After about 0.5 mile the trail reaches a walled overlook above Silver Cascade Falls. The slab lies above to the west. Scramble up a narrow path through trees to the cliff base.

SILVER CASCADE SLAB

1. **Silver Left** (5.6) Begin on the ledge on the slab's far south side and climb past 1 bolt to a belay stance above.

2. **Tunnel Vision** (5.7) A fun, 140' route that starts on a lower slab. Climb past a bolt to a left-leaning ledge and continue up past 3 bolts to a belay at a large boulder.

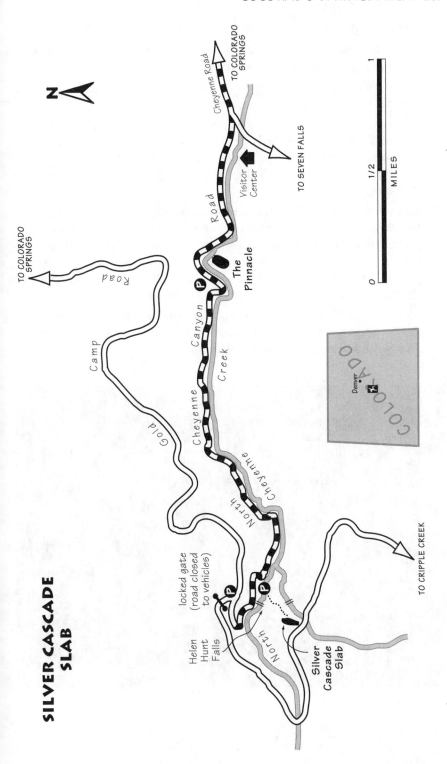

SILVER CASCADE SLAB

3. **Ladder** (5.6) A good bolted route up the center of the left slab.

4. **Robertson Wall** (5.7 R) Ascends the slab above the ledge past a couple of old bolts to the summit. Somewhat runout in places.

5. **Chronic Bedwetter** (5.7) A great moderate, 5-bolt route to the rounded summit. Runout climbing on the easy upper slab.

6. **Reality Check** (5.8) Probably the cliff's best line. Begin on a narrow ledge with no anchor south of the large left-facing corner. Ascend the steep slab on thin edges and smear past 5 bolts. Step right from the 5th bolt onto an upper slab and pass 1 more bolt en route to the summit. This pitch is a full rope-length long. 6 bolts.

7. **Johnson Route** (5.10d) This good route, originally put up by Mike Johnson, begins just north or right of the easy dihedral below the left side of a long prominent roof that divides the lower face. **Pitch 1** climbs a short slab, mantles over the roof by a bolt (5.10d), and scales the dark slab up right past 3 more bolts to a ledge with cold-shut anchors. **Pitch 2** continues up right past 2 more bolts and a couple of 5.8 moves to the top.

8. **Black Science** (5.10b) Pull over the obvious roof on jugs and follow a shallow arch to a steep slab and the ledge on the JOHNSON ROUTE. A medium Friend protects the 5.6 roof move. 4 bolts.

SILVER CASCADE SLAB

9. **Intensive Care** (5.8) Belay in a shallow corner on the wide sloping ramp. Head up easy slabs to a V-shaped break in the long roof. Step left past a bolt and up onto rounded ledges. Climb straight up to the summit past 5 more bolts. Bring a large Friend for the awkward move to the first bolt. Some good runouts, but all the hard moves are protected. Use a 165' rope for this long pitch.

10. **Old Boy's Club** (5.8) Scramble across the sloping ledge below the arched roof to a belay stance with old pitons. Climb the headwall above and follow the slab left of a rotten chimney past 4 bolts.

CANON CITY AREA

SHELF ROAD CLIMBING AREA

OVERVIEW

The Shelf Road, following the original stagecoach route to Cripple Creek's gold fields on the back side of Pikes Peak, threads north along Fourmile Creek through wide valleys and sharp canyons from Canon City. After crossing cattle-studded ranches in broad Garden Park the road dips into rugged Helena Canyon and edges high above the tumbling creek. Long bands of limestone tower above the road and line the rims of shallow nearby canyons forming Shelf Road Climbing Area, one of Colorado's premier sport climbing areas.

The erosion-resistant limestone cliffs, from 60 to 140 feet high, were deposited almost 500 million years ago on an ancient sea floor during the Ordovician Period. The hard limestone, ranging in color from pale white to ebony black, forms abrupt cliffs sculpted with numerous in-cut holds, sharp edges, and pockets. The cliffs offer almost 500 established routes with steep, powerful moves and devious sequences. Almost all of the routes are bolted clip-and-go climbs, although many of the area's cracks are clean-climbed with nuts and Friends. The cliff tops are loose, blocky, and dangerous. Consequently most routes end at lowering stations below the canyon rims.

The climbing area naturally divides itself into five publicly owned crags—The Bank, The Dark Side, Sand Gulch, The Gallery, and The Gym—in four canyons. More cliffs, currently closed because they are on private property, lie both north and south of The Gym in the main canyon. The Bank and Sand Gulch are the most popular cliffs, with numerous classic routes and designated access trails. The Gallery, the westernmost crag, offers superb routes in a quiet and remote setting. The Gym, a sweeping cliff band above the Shelf Road itself, yields the area's hardest lines, notably *The Example,* a sequential 5.13a, and *Deeper Shade of Soul,* a powerful 5.13b.

Climbing history: Shelf Road's climbing history dates back only to the early 1980s. A few mixed free and aid lines went up on several cliffs including *Limestone Cowboy,* the area's first bolted route put up on the lead by Charlie Fowler,

Josh Morris on *Ice Cream Hangover,* one of Shelf Road's classic routes.
Photo by Stewart M. Green.

Maureen Gallagher, Harvey Miller, and Pete Gallagher in 1985. This landmark ascent placed hand-drilled bolts and hooks for pro. In 1986 development began in earnest on Cactus Cliff, a cliff band on private property and unfortunately now closed to climbing. The following year exploration spread onto today's popular crags—The Bank, The Gallery, The Dark Side, and Sand Gulch. A handful of climbers, including Bob D'Antonio, Steve Cheyney, Bob Robertson, Darryl Roth, Dave Dangle, and Richard Aschert, spearheaded the new route frenzy. More routes went up over the next few years by the likes of Dale Goddard, Lou Kalina, Will Gadd, Kevin Gonzales, Colin Lantz, Glen Shuler, Mike Johnson, and Mark Van Horn, the author of the area's comprehensive guidebook. Few routes are currently being established as most of the best lines were climbed by 1990.

Dangers here include loose rock and flakes, particularly along the cliff tops; beehives and wasp nests; and rattlesnakes. Western diamondback rattlesnakes are found in the canyons and along the cliff bases in summer and fall. Use caution when bushwhacking and walking in heavy undergrowth and when crossing boulder fields or along rocks below the cliffs. Watch where you put your hands when scrambling. Rattlers like to sun on ledges or escape from ground heat by climbing into bushes. **Rack:** The only essential equipment needed for a day's fun at Shelf Road is a dozen quick draws and a 165-foot rope. Climbers should not add additional bolts to existing routes. Nobody should chip holds or enlarge pockets to lower a route's standard to their own ability—it's just not necessary. If you can't do the route, save it for someone who can.

Trip Planning Information

General description: One of Colorado's largest sport climbing areas offers almost 500 bolted, established routes on long bands of limestone that reach heights of 140 feet.

Location: West of Colorado Springs, between Canon City and Cripple Creek, on the southwest flank of Pikes Peak.

Camping: Campgrounds are at The Bank and Sand Gulch parking areas. The fee areas ($4 a night) offer pit toilets and tables but no water. Practice no-trace camping by packing out all garbage. Use existing fire rings and bring wood if possible. The lower Sand Gulch campground tends to be warmer and less windy than the higher, Bank site.

Climbing Season: Year-round. Summers tend to be hot, with highs usually in the 80s. Nights are cool. The west-facing cliffs at The Bank and Sand Gulch are hot in the afternoon. Heavy thunderstorms can slicken the roads. Use caution. Autumn brings warm, pleasant days with occasional rainy spells. Winter days are often delightful, with afternoon temperatures climbing into the 50s. Snow melts off quickly on the warmer slopes. Spring arrives in April and offers warm days punctuated by cool weather with rain and sleet. Spring days are often breezy, although most of the crags are sheltered from high winds.

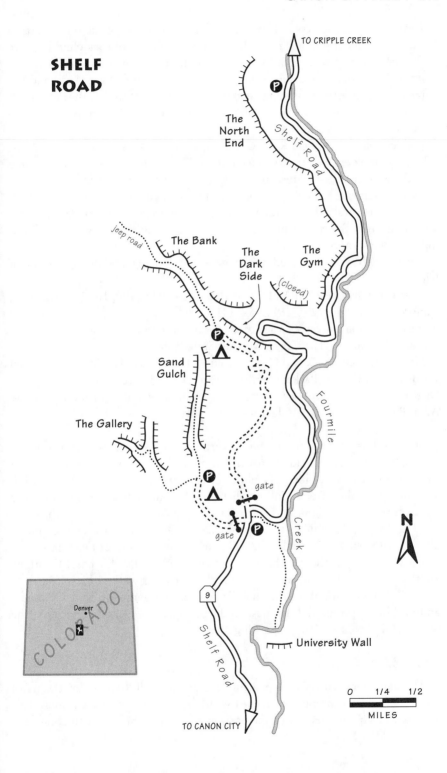

SHELF
ROAD

TO CRIPPLE CREEK

The
North
End

Shelf Road

jeep road

The Bank

The
Dark
Side

The
Gym

(closed)

Sand
Gulch

Fourmile

The Gallery

gate

gate

Creek

9

N

Shelf Road

Denver

COLORADO

University Wall

0   1/4   1/2

MILES

TO CANON CITY

Restrictions and access issues: Most of the climbing crags lie on Bureau of Land Management public lands. The BLM is supportive of rock climbing here and works closely with local activists and climbing organizations to ensure continued open access to the cliffs. Several crags are on private land and are currently off-limits to climbing, including Cactus Cliff and University Wall. Respect the landowner's rights. Some cliffs at Sand Gulch might be seasonally closed for falcon nesting.

Guidebooks: *Shelf Road Rock Guide* by Mark Van Horn, Chockstone Press, 1990. A complete guide to existing climbs at Shelf Road. The easy-to-use guide includes topos of most routes and offers recommendations. Ratings are in both YDS and French grades. An up-coming edition will detail more cliffs.

Nearby mountain shops, guide services, and gyms: Mountain Chalet, Grand West Outfitters, Sport Climbing Center of Colorado Springs, 8th Street Climbing Club (Colorado Springs).

Services: All services, including gas, groceries, lodging, and dining, in Canon City.

Emergency services: Call 911. St. Thomas More Hospital, 1019 Sheridan St., Canon City, CO 81212, (719) 275-3381.

Nearby climbing areas: Garden of the Gods, Hardscrabble Pass, Royal Gorge, Elevenmile Canyon, The Crags, Mueller State Park.

Nearby attractions: Royal Gorge, Gold Belt Tour Back Country Byway, Red Canyon Park, Garden Park paleontology area, Cripple Creek National Historic District, Pikes Peak, Temple Canyon Park, Grape Creek BLM Wilderness Study Area, Beaver Creek BLM Wilderness Study Area.

Finding the crags: From Canon City turn north on Raynolds Avenue off U.S. Highway 50 on the east side of town. Follow Raynolds north for 0.8 mile and bend left on Pear for 1 block to Fields. Turn north on Fields. It climbs a low hill and turns into Shelf Road. Follow Shelf Road 13 miles to the Bank and Sand Gulch turnoffs. The Bank, hidden from view, lies almost 2 miles north, while Sand Gulch sits 0.5 mile to the northeast. The Gym is reached by continuing along Shelf Road for 2.5 miles. A trail marked with a cairn at mile marker 12 threads up through the cliff band above the road to the cliff base. Continue another mile to a parking area alongside the creek and walk or bicycle back to the trail. Do not park along the Shelf Road itself. It's narrow with few pullouts and parking is prohibited. It's best to drop your passengers and packs at the trailhead and continue to the parking area.

THE BANK

The Bank, reached via a steep, 2-mile road from Shelf Road, offers the area's most concentrated number of routes with almost 200 established lines. This area, with its numerous routes and easy access, is the best bet for the first-time visitor. The cliff bands lie north of the parking area along the canyon rim. Hike north on the road as it drops into Trail Canyon. Just after entering the canyon a rough path heads southeast to The Dark Side, the black, north-facing cliff lining the canyon rim east of the parking area. Farther down, a marked trail drops into the canyon and heads up to the 2150 Wall. After reaching the canyon floor, another marked trail heads east to the Surreal Estate Wall. The Bank's cliffs are divided into eight main walls: Cash, Gem, 2150, Back to the Future, Surreal Estate, Peg Leg, and Cactus Rose walls, and the Quarry. The 2150, Back to the Future, Surreal Estate, and Cactus Rose walls offer the best routes.

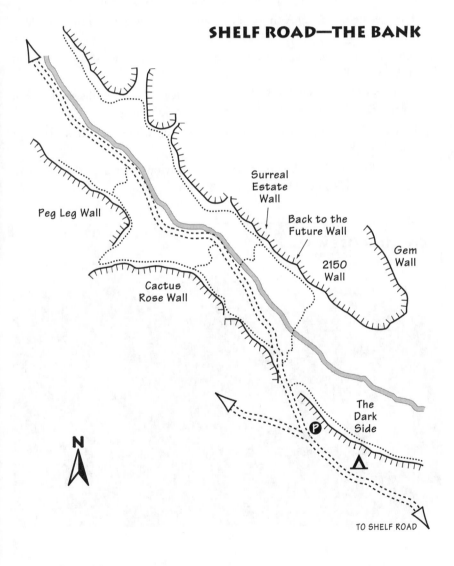

SHELF ROAD—THE BANK

Surreal Estate Wall

Back to the Future Wall

Peg Leg Wall

Gem Wall

2150 Wall

Cactus Rose Wall

The Dark Side

N

TO SHELF ROAD

THE CACTUS ROSE WALL

The Cactus Rose Wall sits on the canyon's west rim about 0.5 mile up the road from the parking lot. This wall offers good, shady climbing on hot summer afternoons. Scramble up a rough trail through pinyon pines to the cliff base. Several good lines punctuate the pale cliff. Routes are listed left to right.

1. **Welcome to the Machine** (5.11c) Thin face route up cliff's left margin. 5 bolts to anchors.

2. **Mark Finds Bob Bolting** (5.10d) Climbs the white face to anchors below obvious horizontal crack; some of clips are awkward. 5 bolts.

3. **The Needle Lies** (5.9) A short, moderate route to ledge in wall's middle. 3 bolts to anchors.

4. **John Wayne Never Wore Boxer Shorts** (5.10d) Another short route that ends by small tree. 2 bolts to a tree anchor.

5. **Back Her Up Against the Wall and Caulk Her** (5.11a) Climbs right side of central face (4 bolts) to 2-bolt anchor on obvious ledge.

6. **E=MC²** (5.11c) A reachy 6-bolt route up steep white face on wall's right side.

7. **Cactus Rose** (5.11d) A good route up an obvious corner to the headwall crux at top. It's somewhat runout with only 5 bolts.

CACTUS ROSE WALL

8. **Barbecuing Traditions** (5.12b) An excellent route on wall's right edge. Follow right-leaning corner past 3 bolts, crank strenuous crux on pockets, and climb past 2 more bolts to anchors.

SURREAL ESTATE WALL

The Surreal Estate Wall is reached from the road on the canyon floor via a short, marked trail that scrambles east. The wall, one of the highest at The Bank, towers above the trail. Routes are listed left to right. *Sparkle in the Rain*, an excellent 5.12b/c route, scales the bulging cliff 35' north of Surreal Estate Wall, while *Ice Cream Hangover* (5.11b) and *Le Pincher* (5.12d) climb the clean wall 30' to the south.

9. **Stormy Weather** (5.11a/b) Ascends left edge/arete of the wall to anchors.

10. **Heavy Weather** (5.12a) A superb 8-bolt route with continuous, strenuous climbing.

11. **Unusual Weather** (5.11c) 6-bolt line up wall's mid-section with stiff climbing up thin crack above scooped-out ledge.

12. **Surreal Estate** (5.12c) This line, one of Shelf Road's best routes, ascends the right side of the white wall with strenuous, technical moves. 7 bolts to double anchors.

SURREAL ESTATE WALL &
BACK TO THE FUTURE WALL

BACK TO THE FUTURE WALL

This wall, reached via the same trail as Surreal Estate Wall, sits just south of *Ice Cream Hangover.* It's a vertical, white cliff laced with numerous bolted routes. All the routes end at 2-bolt lowering stations. 2 good short routes, *Moaner* 5.10c and *Deforestation* 5.10d, begin on a high ledge just north of the Back to the Future Wall. Routes are listed left to right.

13. **Ice Cream Hangover** (5.11a/b) A superb 5-bolt line up left side of narrow white wall.

14. **Le Pincher** (5.12d) Hard, thin climbing up edges and mono-pockets right of ICE CREAM HANGOVER.

15. **Deforestation** (5.10d) Scramble left up chimney onto large ledge that splits cliff left of Back to the Future Wall. This 3-bolt line works up excellent black rock on far left end of ledge. Hard for the grade.

16. **Moaner** (5.10c) Hard face climbing up edges behind the juniper on the big ledge. 3 bolts to anchors. Bouldery start.

17. **Peter Pan** (5.11b) Climb up a steep slab to a roof past 5 bolts above the right side of the ledge.

18. **The Arete** (5.11a) Belay on far left edge of Back to the Future Wall. Climb crack to sharp arete. 6 bolts to anchors.

19. **Suedehead** (5.12d) This excellent, powerful route, first climbed by Colin Lantz in 1988, ascends steep line of 7 bolts near the wall's left margin. The first 5.12 crux, reached just before sloping shelf at half-height, involves a technical pull off mono-pocket. Another 5.12 crux is on the upper wall.

20. **No Rest for the Wicked** (5.12a) Superb route that fingers up thin, bottoming crack past 8 bolts to anchors.

21. **Future Fossil** (5.12b) A strenuous, technical route up a steep white wall to anchors under beetling overhang. 6 bolts to double anchors.

22. **Back to the Future** (5.11b) The climb, a Shelf Road mega-classic, is one of area's most popular routes. Follow the black water streak on the wall's south side past 6 bolts to anchors. First 30' involve powerful pulls on pockets to rest stance. Strenuous moves up incipient crack lead over small overhang to anchors above.

23. **Rock Frog** (5.10c/d) Short, sharp route up black face to tree anchor 10' south of BACK TO THE FUTURE WALL.

24. **B/C** (5.9) This 5-bolt line, one of the area's easier routes, climbs outside edge of a pillar 20' south of ROCK FROG. Watch for some loose rock.

25. **Concentrated Weirdness** (5.8+) A fun, 4-bolt line up a narrow south face around an arete from B/C. Scramble onto brushy ledge to begin.

2150 WALL

The 2150 Wall is reached via a trail that dips into the canyon just north of The Bank's parking area or by continuing south along the cliff-base trail from the Back to the Future Wall to the 2150 Wall's steep, white slab. Eight good bolted routes scale the smooth cliff. Routes are listed left to right.

26. **Primal Scream** (5.9) A 4-bolt route up outside wall of pillar 50' left of 2150 Wall.

27. **Emperor's Robe** (5.11d) A reachy, 7-bolt route up cliff's left edge.

28. **Lime Street** (5.11b/c) A continuous 6-bolt route. A 5.12d variation goes straight up above 3rd bolt.

29. **Oaxamoxa** (5.12b) This over-bolted, 11 cold-shut bolt extravaganza scales steep slab with thin, well-protected climbing. It's a good climb to work for a first 5.12 redpoint.

30. **Ripped** (5.10c) Climbs obvious crack that splits the wall in half. Bring cams to 3". No anchors on top.

31. **Living in America** (5.12a) An excellent route just right of RIPPED. Climb in from crack for 5.12a start, otherwise direct start to first clip is 5.12d. Stick clip first 2 bolts. 6 bolts to anchors.

32. **Taping Tendons** (5.11c/d) Stick-clip high first bolt to begin this continuous feast of pocket-pulling and thin edging. 6 bolts to anchors.

33. **Lost Planet Airmen** (5.11a) A good but strenuous route up the wall's right side. 7 bolts to anchors.

2150 WALL
THE BANK

34. **2150 A.D.** (5.10d) This route ascends leaning crack on 2150 Wall's south edge past a couple of good rest stances. The crux is pulling roof where crack ends.

THE GALLERY

The Gallery lies on the west end of the Shelf Road climbing area. The almost mile-long hike to the crag preserves an aura of solitude and wildness. The cliffs line the rim of a Y-shaped canyon, with routes in both branches. The Gallery is

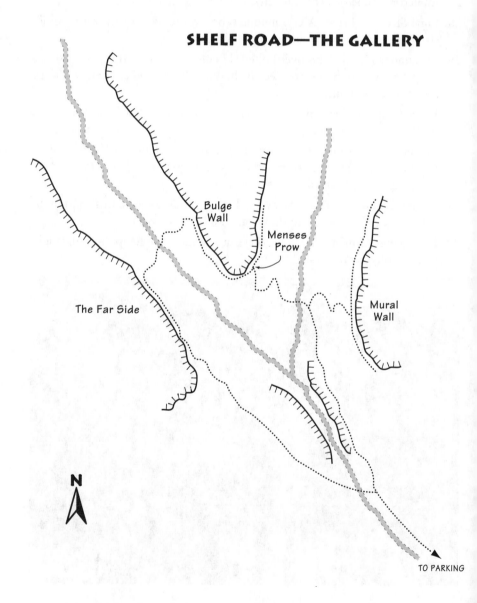

SHELF ROAD—THE GALLERY

Bulge Wall

Menses Prow

The Far Side

Mural Wall

N

TO PARKING

accessed by a trail that begins southwest of the BLM register below Sand Gulch. The trail drops across Sand Gulch and winds west up a canyon into The Gallery. Keep right at the Mural Wall trail junction to reach the Mural Wall and Menses Prow. The Gallery features seven main climbing areas—Mural Wall, Menses Prow, California Ethics Pinnacle, Bulge Wall, Phenomenology Wall, Incredible Hulk Boulder area, and the Far Side.

MURAL WALL

The Mural Wall, a compact whitish wall on the east rim of the east canyon, offers five excellent 5.12 routes. Several more moderate routes lie 100' south of the wall. The access trail leads directly to the cliff. Ten routes ascend the cliff about 150' north of the Mural Wall. The best are *Soluble Fish* (5.11c) and *Tuna, Tuna, Tuna* (5.11b) on the right wall of a large corner; *Happy Nightmare Baby* (5.10b) just left of the corner; and *Have a Blast* (5.12a) up the smooth white wall left of a loose crack. Mural Wall routes are listed left to right.

35. **M&M** (5.12a) A good, strenuous route that's easy for grade. 7 bolts to anchors.

36. **Montage** (5.12b/c) An excellent thin-face route up bulging wall. Finger pockets are hard to find for on-sight flash. 7 bolts to anchors.

37. **Mosaic** (5.12b/c) Another brilliant sustained route up steep rock on the wall's mid-section. 6 bolts to anchors.

38. **The Mural** (5.12b) This classic scales the wall right of a small tree on difficult pocket climbing. 5 bolts to anchors.

39. **Monet** (5.11d) The wall's easiest route scales superb rock on right side. 6 bolts to anchors.

40. **Motif** (5.12a) Climbs wall's far right margin on continuous pocketed rock. 8 bolts to anchors.

41. **Morrocan Roll** (5.10b) Lies 100' south of Mural Wall and scales north edge of the dull arete on a large pillar. Runout start to 1st bolt. 4 bolts to anchors.

42. **Mother of Invention** (5.10d) Around the corner from MORROCAN ROLL up the outside wall of the pillar.

43. **The Bobbit Effect** (5.10a) On opposite wall from MOTHER OF INVENTION.

44. **Pi** (5.12b) A hard route over a roof on jugs. It's hard to clip 3rd bolt. Follows line of red angle-iron hangers.

45. **John Cruiser Melloncrimp** (5.10a) A good moderate up the left edge of an open face.

MENSES PROW

The southeast-facing Menses Prow sits above the canyon's Y junction. Take the Mural Wall trail, but cut off at the dry streambed below the wall and follow a trail west to the prow's base. Routes are listed right to left.

46. **Menses** (5.10d) A sustained line up the right wall of a large dihedral to lowering anchors. 7 bolts to anchors. THE BIG CHILL (5.11c) to right.

47. **Lunch at the Y** (5.11b/c) On dihedral's left wall. 8 bolts to anchors.

48. **No Passion for Fashion** (5.11b/c) Follow 10 bolts up left wall of large corner to anchors.

49. **Sundogs** (5.12a/b) A short, strenuous line up steep prow immediately left of NO PASSION FOR FASHION to anchors. 7 bolts to anchors. Two 6-bolt 5.11 routes climb the arete just left of SUNDOGS.

50. **Unnamed** (5.11d) Follow bolts up arete left of crack to anchors. Watch loose rock. 8 bolts to anchors.

51. **Unnamed** (5.12a) Steep and strenuous. Watch very loose block up high! 5 bolts to slinged anchors.

52. **Period Piece** (5.7+) One of the area's few moderate routes. Climbs a long south-facing slab above boulder to anchors.

MENSES PROW
THE GALLERY

BULGE WALL

This south-facing wall lies around the corner from Menses Prow. Walk west along the cliff base past the California Ethics Pinnacle to the obvious wall. A pillar with a chimney behind it is on the right side of the wall. Scramble up to a long ledge directly below the cliff. The pinnacle has a couple of good 5.7 routes on its northwest corner. Routes are listed right to left.

53. **Dumb Waiter** (5.10a) This fun route ascends the west wall of the pillar right of Bulge Wall. Follow bolts up face right of chimney to anchors.

54. **Love Pump** (5.10b) A great line up the right side of the wall past 5 bolts to anchors.

55. **Liquid Affair** (5.11b) Move up thin rock past 4 bolts then trend right to LOVE PUMP'S anchors or up left to 2 more bolts and anchors.

56. **Thirteen Engines** (5.11c) Follow 8 bolts up the center of the wall to anchors above large white patch.

57. **My What a Big Bulge** (5.11d) Thin, sequential climbing past 7 bolts to anchors.

58. **Stratabulge** (5.12a) A short, fiercely thin route with long reaches between pockets. 5 bolts to anchors.

59. **Pig Dictionary** (5.12a) Another short hard testpiece with 6 bolts.

60. **Turbo Charged, Intercooled, Meat Machine** (5.10a) A decent easier route with 7 bolts and anchors on the far left side of wall.

THE GYM

The Gym lies 2 miles north up Shelf Road from The Bank and Sand Gulch turn-off. Follow the narrow, winding road along steep slopes in Helena Canyon to a climber's access path below The Gym's long east-facing cliff band at mile marker 12. The trail switchbacks up the dry hillside to the cliff base below *The Example*. Parking for The Gym is found another mile farther north where the road dips down to Fourmile Creek. A large parking area is on the north side of the road. Walk or mountain bike back south along the road to the trailhead. It's best to drop your partners and packs at the trailhead and solo drive up to the parking. Do not park along Shelf Road on this long narrow stretch. It's illegal and you might receive a ticket from the sheriff. Not parking on the road helps maintain area access and good relations with local authorities. The Gym is mostly on BLM public land. The south part of the cliff, however, is on private property. There are routes here, but it is currently off limits. Routes are listed left to right.

SHELF ROAD—THE GYM

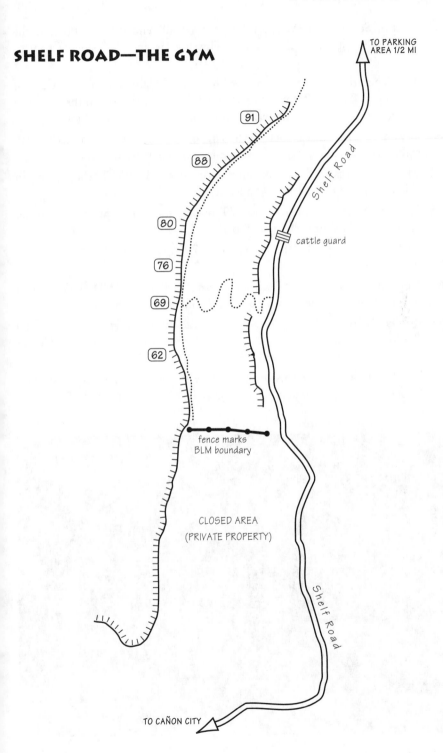

TO PARKING
AREA 1/2 MI

Shelf Road

91

88

80

76

69

62

cattle guard

fence marks
BLM boundary

CLOSED AREA
(PRIVATE PROPERTY)

Shelf Road

TO CAÑON CITY

61. **Ejection Seat** (5.12b) Walk south from the trail's end at the cliff base to the huge roof just above the ground. This line ascends left side of roof to headwall.

62. **My Generation** (5.12c) This 8-bolt line works up and left on jugs over roof to a superb headwall. End at lowering cold-shut anchors. To the right is a project (possible .13+) that was unfortunately chipped in 1994 into a 5.12a.

63. **Crystal** (5.11a) An excellent technical route that works up a steep black slab. 8 bolts (some with funky angle-iron hangers) to anchors.

64. **The Great Escape** (5.11c) A companion route to CRYSTAL up the right side of black slab. 6 bolts and anchors.

65. **Morning Stretch** (5.11a) A good 70' line up the wall right of tight corner system. 8 cold-shut bolts to anchors.

66. **It's OK to Fart** (5.12b) Climb up and left 70' on steep wall past 7 cold shuts to anchors.

67. **No Shelf Control** (5.12c) Begin with same start as MORNING STRETCH but work 50' straight up wall above. 5 cold shuts to anchors.

68. **Bubba's Belly** (5.12c) Begin right of the crack system on the right wall of a shallow dihedral. Climb up pocketed rock, pull over small roof, and lower from anchors. Long reach crux down low.

69. **The Example** (5.13a) This brilliant route is one of Shelf's very best lines. It's a coveted testpiece that was on-sighted by J.B. Tribout in 1995. Sequen-

tial climbing on pockets leads up left on beautiful rock to a shake-out, then moves up right to the crux—a thin sidepull move over a small roof. Above 5.10 climbing leads to chains. 8 Metolius ring bolts.

70. **Gym Arete** (5.12a) A Gym classic up the right side of the blunt arete around the corner from THE EXAMPLE. Traverse up left to the arete. Edge up a seam to anchors. 7 bolts to chains. Direct start with 2 bolts is 5.12c/d.

71. **To Bolt or To Be Bad aka Gym Crack** (5.10a/b) A decent enough layback/jam crack with 6 red angle-iron hangers. Lower from anchors.

72. **Head Cheese** (5.12d) A spectacular and airy line that weaves up and over left side of an immense pointed roof. Start up the shallow corner in a large dihedral, then work up and over a series of overhangs. 9 bolts to cold-shut anchors.

73. **Trout Fishing** (5.10a) A fun 6-bolt pocket climb up a steep slab below the right side of HEAD CHEESE roof. Lower from open cold-shut hooks. If you toprope, leave last draw clipped in for safety.

74. **Arnold Arnold** (5.11b/c) A pumpy route up the left side of a bulging buttress. 6 bolts to anchors.

75. **Solar Flex** (5.11b/c) Another good pump up the right side of black bulge. 6 bolts to anchors.

76. **Five Dollars** (5.11a) A technical 60' route with only one strenuous section on the far left side of jet black slab. 5 bolts to cold-shut hooks.

THE GYM

77. **Hot Rod Lincoln** (5.11b) A devious face route up a black slab. 6 bolts to anchors.

78. **Comin' in Smooth** (5.11c) Another wandering face line on the right side of black slab. 7 bolts to anchors.

79. **Cimarron Lanes** (5.11b) An excellent route up the left side of the Orange Marmalade Wall just right of a small spire. Red angle-iron hanger marks the start. Most people climb only to lowering anchors at 75'. A second section climbs up and over the bulging headwall high above. Long pitch with 14 bolts to anchors.

80. **Orange Marmalade** (5.12a) A superb line that edges up the center of a steep wall. Another red hanger at start. 6 bolts to anchors.

81. **Jane Fonda's Warm-up** (5.10b/c) A fine climb up the right side of wall just left of crack system. 4 cold shuts to 2 cold-shut anchors.

82. **Unnamed** (5.11) A funky, somewhat under-protected route up a steep slab left of the huge left-facing dihedral. It looks better than it is.

83. **Pump Up and Air Out** (5.12c) This very good route ascends the right side of a large south-facing dihedral to anchors.

84. **Unnamed** (5.10) Climb directly up the prow/arete on the outside of the south-facing dihedral.

85. **Unnamed** (5.10) A line up the wall right of the prow.

86. **Needle Haven** (5.10b) Step right few feet from Number 84 for this route.

87. **Prophets of Rage** (5.12d) Climbs the south-facing wall of a huge left-facing dihedral farther north up the cliff. It's long and somewhat loose in parts.

88. **Deeper Shade of Soul** (5.13a/b) Walk north around a corner from PROPHETS to start by a large flat boulder. Powerful climbing leads up and right onto blunt arete. Crux is strenuous cross-over. 8 bolts to anchors.

89. **Bone Daddy** (5.12c) 9-bolt line just right of DEEPER SHADE OF SOUL.

90. **Hammer Therapy** (5.12b) Steep route just right of PROPHETS with lots of cold shuts and good climbing.

91. **Bone 'n Vein** (5.12c) Walk farther north from DEEPER SHADE OF SOUL along the cliff base to a buttress with a large roof. This excellent route follows 7 bolts up a steep wall and over a huge roof to anchors.

Central Colorado

REGION

ASPEN AREA

INDEPENDENCE PASS

OVERVIEW

Colorado Highway 82 crosses the Continental Divide atop 12,095-foot Independence Pass, Colorado's highest paved pass, before plunging west along the Roaring Fork River in a deep glacier-carved valley. The pass straddles the spine of the Sawatch Range, a long, twisting sierra topped by fourteen of Colorado's fifty-four 14,000-foot peaks including Mount Elbert, the state's high point at 14,433 feet above sea level. Numerous small but excellent crags scatter along the highway as it descends 20 miles from the pass to the resort town of Aspen, offering a diverse assortment of superb rock routes from 30 to 200 feet in height. The climbs here are a mixed bag of both clip-and-go sport pitches and traditional, place-your-own-gear routes. The rock lends itself to intimidating climbing, with less-than-obvious sequences and sometimes hard-to-find protection. Michael Kennedy, now publisher of *Climbing* in nearby Carbondale, described pass climbing in 1974: "A good sense of direction and willingness to piece together the various facets of the climb are invaluable. Not all the routes are devious, but one's sense of humor is often as strained as one's body."

Two distinct rock types occur on the pass—quartz monzonite, a resistant, fine-grained granite, and biotite gneiss, a metamorphic rock deposited as horizontal marine sediments and later altered and deformed by extreme heat and pressure within the Earth's crust. The granite forms slabby cliffs such as Wall Walls and Weller Slab, while the twisted metamorphic gneiss patterns upper valley crags including the Grotto Walls and Olympic Crag. Glacial periods, one as recent as 12,000 years ago, excavated the broad U-shaped valleys here. They left behind characteristic traces of glaciation including terminal and lateral moraines of rough, unsorted boulders and glassy surfaces of glacial polish. As the glacier inches across bedrock, it scours and smooths the rock surface leaving a slippery veneer. Good places to see glacial polish include the undulating bedrock at Lincoln Gulch Campground and the lofty aerie of Olympic Crag, where the heavy glacier plucked and polished its vertical face.

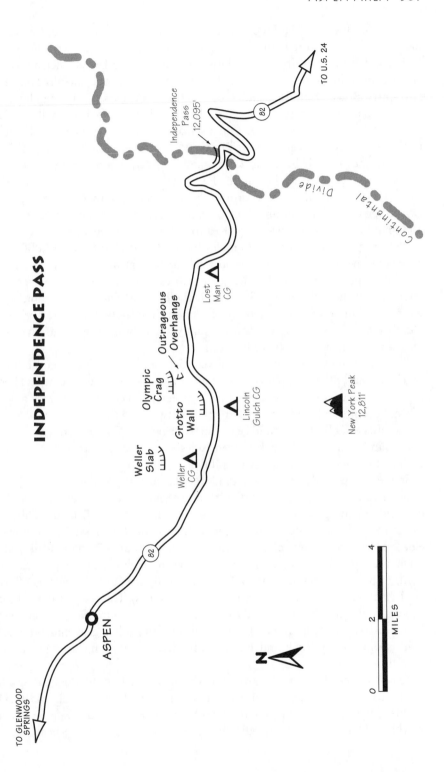

INDEPENDENCE PASS

TO GLENWOOD SPRINGS

ASPEN

82

Weller Slab

Weller CG

Grotto Wall

Olympic Crag

Outrageous Overhangs

Lincoln Gulch CG

Lost Man CG

New York Peak 12,811'

Independence Pass 12,095'

82

TO U.S. 24

Continental Divide

N

0   2   4

MILES

Climbing history: The Independence Pass crags boast a long and colorful history that spans more than 30 years. The classic easier routes went up in the 1950s and 1960s, but first ascents blossomed during the 1970s when a host of activists including Lou Dawson, Michael Kennedy, Steve Shea, Molly Higgens, and Larry Bruce established numerous fierce free climbs. Traveling climbers such as Henry Barber, John Long, and Lynn Hill, also left their chalk marks. The landmark route *Dean's Day Off,* a serious 5.12a testpiece with funky protection on Lincoln Creek Wall, fell to barefooted Henry Barber in 1977. The power of the portable Bosch drill brought a resurgence of new routes and new climbers to Independence Pass in the late 1980s and into the 1990s. Kennedy, Mike Benge, and John Steiger from *Climbing,* along with Kurt Smith, Bob D'Antonio, and Tom Perkins, bolted many excellent routes on vintage crags and on new-found cliffs including D'Antonio's excellent Olympic Crag.

The crags along Colorado 82, at elevations between 8,000 and 12,000 feet, are visited between May and October when the highway is open. The road generally opens in mid- to late-May and closes sometime in early November after the first heavy snowfall. Summer at the high elevations is pleasant, with warm days and cool nights. Expect afternoon thunderstorms. September and October bring a succession of warm, sunny spells broken by occasional unsettled weather that sometimes includes snow.

The pass routes generally range between 5.10 and 5.12, with a sharp fall-off on either end of the scale. This is not a great area for beginner climbers. There are few good, easy or moderate routes. Eighteen main crags, along with a host of smaller cliffs and boulders, sit along the highway or a short walk away. Most of the cliffs offer both sport and gear routes. Bring a rack of quick draws for the sport climbs and a basic rack that includes sets of RPs, wired stoppers, and Friends for the gear or mixed gear and bolt routes.

In the following descriptions, all mileages begin at the White River National Forest entrance sign just past Difficult Campground almost 3 miles east of Aspen. Other good pass crags, besides those included here, are Difficult Cliff (an assortment of gear routes above Difficult Campground), Classy Cliff (a lower elevation crag with several cracks and sport routes at 0.7 mile), Wall Walls (high-angle slab climbing immediately below the highway at 3.6 miles), Pass Walls (a popular roadside crag at 4.7 miles with gear and bolt routes), Whirlpool Rock (steep trad and sport routes at 4.9 miles), Upper Grotto Wall (an exposed wall with numerous hard routes above Lower Grotto Wall at 5.4 miles), Lincoln Creek Cliff (home to Dean's Day Off and other gear climbs at 6.1 miles), and Turkey Rock and Bulldog Cliff (two small crags at 7.4 and 7.6 miles).

Excellent bouldering is also found on the pass. The Jaws Boulder, alongside the Roaring Fork River opposite Weller Campground, offers a classic B5.11 problem over a prominent roof and up a blunt arete on its northeast face. The World of Hurt, an aptly named boulder field strewn across the base of the

Lower Grotto Wall, yields super bouldering on sharp, angular blocks. The area, named by John Sherman for its treacherous landing zones, boasts **Deep Six Holiday,** a serious problem that Sherman assigned an X rating. Several good roadside boulders scatter across the boulder field 7.6 miles from the national forest sign.

The Independence Pass crags, including some of those detailed in this guide, can be hard to spot from the highway or find in the forest. If at first you don't succeed in your search, try again or ask a local at the Lower Grotto Wall—someone is almost always there. Parking is a growing problem on the pass because of increasing numbers of climbers and other visitors. Try to use the larger roadside parking areas and pull well off the highway. Use existing trails to the crags to minimize erosion and damage. Some paths, like the steep trail to Olympic Crag, are in dire need of work. Watch for loose rock, both on the routes and on the access trails.

Trip Planning Information

General description: Numerous sport and traditional routes on small granite and gneiss crags.

Location: Along Colorado 82 between Aspen and the summit of Independence Pass.

Camping: 4 White River National Forest campgrounds— Difficult, Weller, Lincoln Gulch, and Lost Man—sit along CO 82. Portal Campground is a few miles south of the highway on the rough Lincoln Creek road. Weller and Lincoln Creek campgrounds are nearest the cragging areas. All campgrounds have pit toilets, water, tables, grills, and are fee areas. Summer weekends are usually full.

Climbing season: Summer and fall. The highway is usually open from late May until late October, depending on the snow season. Summer highs are in the 60s and 70s, with cool nights. Expect heavy thunderstorms on summer afternoons. Autumn brings cool, dry days, the golden flush of changing aspens, and occasional rain or snow showers.

Restrictions and access issues: The crags are in White River National Forest. No restrictions or access problems exist. Parking is problematic near most of the crags, particularly on weekends. Park well off the highway in wide pullouts and watch for traffic when crossing or walking along the highway.

Guidebooks: *Heinous Cling* by Andre Wille, Quasimoto Enterprises, Basalt, CO, 1994, is a complete guide to all the crags along the Independence Pass highway.

Nearby mountain shops, guide services, and gyms: The Ute Mountaineer, Aspen Athletic Club (Aspen); Summit Canyon Mountaineering (Glenwood Springs).

Services: All services in Aspen.

INDEPENDENCE PASS

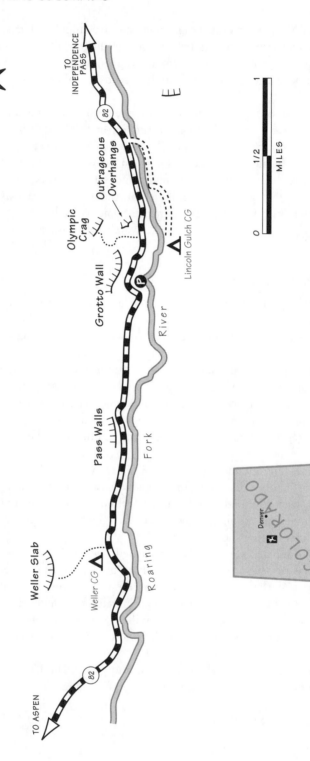

Emergency services: Call 911. Mountain Rescue-Aspen, 630 W. Main St., Aspen, CO 81611, (970) 925-7172. Aspen Valley Hospital, 0200 Castle Creek Rd., Aspen, CO 81611, (970) 925- 1120.

Nearby climbing areas: Maroon Bells, Pyramid Peak, Capitol Peak, Monitor Rock, Redstone sport climbs, Black Canyon of the Gunnison, Rifle Mountain Park, Buena Vista crags.

Nearby attractions: Independence Pass, Mount Massive Wilderness Area, Collegiate Peaks Wilderness Area, Maroon Bells-Snowmass Wilderness Area, Hunter-Fryingpan Wilderness Area, Maroon Lake, Conundrum Hot Springs, Pearl Pass, Aspen, Glenwood Hot Springs.

Finding the crags: From Aspen drive east on CO 82 toward Independence Pass. Mileages for all crags are taken from the White River National Forest sign at the Difficult Campground entrance almost 3 miles east of Aspen on CO 82. Weller Slab is 4.3 miles; Lower Grotto Wall is 5.4 miles; Outrageous Overhangs and Olympic Crag are 5.6 miles.

WELLER SLAB

This excellent granite slab perches high above Weller Campground and the highway on the north side of the valley. Park at or near Weller Campground in pulloffs alongside the highway at 4.3 miles. The 20-minute approach begins on the north side of the campground loop. Walk northwest from the campground through a lush aspen forest and up a steep talus slope to the foot of Weller Slab. The routes are listed left to right or west to east. Descend from the slab's summit by hiking around the west flank. Some routes have lowering or rappel anchors. The crag offers solitude from the highway masses and several superb classic routes.

1. **Low Charge of Stealth Heeled Boys** (5.9) Climb short slab on west flank past 2 bolts to ledge. Anchors are to right.

2. **Three-Eyed Toad** (5.10d) Great slabbing past 3 bolts.

3. **Nickles and Dimes** (5.10d) Thin edging leads up steep, well-protected slab past 6 bolts to 2-bolt anchor on ledge. Continue up and left of roof above, or tackle it direct at 5.12.

4. **Militant** (5.8) An old gear route up cracks and slabs. Go left under roof.

5. **Two Ears** (5.7) This 1-pitch route begins near foot of buttress and climbs up and right past small roof. End on slanting ledge.

6. **Zanzibar Dihedral** (5.7) This classic 2-pitch route, the best of its grade on the pass, was first ascended in 1970. **Pitch 1** scales an easy slab to slanting ledge half-way up wall. **Pitch 2** stems, laybacks, and edges up huge open book 140' to anchors. **Rack:** Bring a basic rack of stoppers and Friends.

**WELLER SLAB
INDEPENDENCE PASS**

7. **Apple Pie** (5.10a) A good route that climbs the slab just right of ZANZI-BAR DIHEDRAL.

8. **Suchness of Now** (5.10d) Climb open slab past 2 bolts. **Rack:** Bring a small rack with some wires and RPs.

9. **Ultra Edge** (5.9) Another excellent classic that edges up sharp right edge of steep slab.

Three more routes lie right of ULTRA EDGE. **Needle Drugs** (5.12a) climbs the right underside of the edge, while the bolted **Generation of Swine** (5.11d) and **Crack City** (5.9) climb the far right side of the slab past a large area of broken rock.

FIRST GROTTO WALL

The Lower Grotto Wall, the most obvious, most visited, and most accessible crag on Independence Pass, lifts its immense looming bulk of twisted rock above a sharp highway turn at 5.4 miles. Park in a pulloff just south of the cliff, cross the highway, and scramble over a blocky boulder field to the base of the crag's south face. The wall offers a selection of varied 1- to 3-pitch routes. **Descend** by rappel from the route or hiking down loose rock on its west flank. Routes are listed from left to right.

10. **Twin Cracks** (5.8) This classic 2-pitch line is probably the most climbed route on the pass as well as the scene of many beginner epics. Scramble up talus below the west buttress to the base of the obvious twin cracks. **Pitch 1** (short) jams the hand cracks to a tricky 5.8 traverse to a ledge. **Pitch 2** climbs the short, broken corner above. **Rack:** Bring a rack of Friends and nuts.

11. **One for the Road** (5.10d) Begin on the face right of TWIN CRACKS. Climb discontinuous cracks past 4 bolts to a chained lowering/rappel anchor. A #2 Friend protects the runout to the 1st bolt.

12. **Under Pressure** (5.10d) Use the same start as ONE FOR THE ROAD only branch right from the 1st bolt and climb upward past 6 more bolts to a ledge and anchors.

13. **Cryogenics** (5.10c) This excellent climb, first ascended by Bill Forrest and Glen Denny, offers perhaps the best crack pitch on the pass. The 1st pitch, following a steep white dihedral, was led free by Duncan Ferguson in 1972, while Mike Kennedy freed the 2nd pitch the following year. **Pitch 1** begins just left of the toe of the central buttress below a striking corner. Layback and jam the thin hand and finger crack, some 5.9+ moves near the top, to a large ledge and anchors. Rappel from here or continue up the shorter **Pitch 2** by traversing left below the steep headwall above and then heading back right above it. The broken overhanging corner directly above the belay goes at 5.11+. **Rack:** Bring a rack of Friends and larger stoppers.

LOWER GROTTO WALL

14. **Bicentennial** (5.10+) A classic 3-pitch line that wanders up the steep wall right of the tree at the foot of the buttress. **Pitch 1** begins just left of the huge fir at the cliff base and takes the easiest line up and right to a belay under the obvious BICENTENNIAL ROOF. **Pitch 2** traverses right on steep rock under the roof (5.10+ crux) and moves up left to a belay ledge. **Pitch 3** goes straight up moderate rock or traverses left up easy ramps to the walk-off. **Rack:** Bring a standard rack along with some long runners to reduce rope drag.

15. **Bicentennial Roof** (5.12a) This long-standing problem finally yielded to Henry Barber in 1977, making what was probably the hardest route on the pass at that time. Instead of following BICENTENNIAL'S right-ward traverse, climb the obvious splitter crack in the horizontal roof above with thin hard moves pulling over the lip.

16. **Victims of Fashion** (5.2b/c) Start up BICENTENNIAL but after 20' follow thin, discontinuous 5.10 cracks right of the buttress's nose to a bolted belay stance. **Pitch 2** climbs the crux 5.12 roof above and finishes up easier rock.

17. **Scene of the Crime** (5.12c/d) The first rap-bolted route on Independence Pass was established by John Steiger in 1986. Climb flakes up the steep white face east of the fir tree, passing 3 bolts and difficult underclings and sidepulls to a double-bolt anchor. Stick clip the 1st bolt to avoid a hard clip.

18. **Pea Brain** (5.12c) Hard climbing down low past 3 bolts, then up a broken corner to BICENTENNIAL.

19. **The Knucklehead** (5.13a) This thin Kurt Smith route climbs past several bolts to a lowering anchor, or continue up GIRLY MANN'S broken corners above. Stick clip the 1st bolt. The route's main difficulties are encountered in its first few feet—thin strenuous moves to a good flake.

20. **Unknown** (5.12) Follow a line of 6 bolts up the steep right side to anchors below the obvious ledge.

21. **Space Sluts in the Slammer** (5.12b) A good 5-bolt route up the right edge of the lower face to anchors.

22. **Grotto Wall Traverse** (5.7) This 1958 classic follows left-leaning ramps and cracks upward in 3 pitches, generally taking the easiest course possible.

23. **Exotic Headache** (5.13a/b) A spectacular and difficult line up the east side of the upper wall. Begin on the east side of the ledge/ramp that divides the upper wall.

The Second Grotto Wall, sitting up and west of the First Grotto Wall, offers an additional selection of good routes. Four good routes scale The Plaque, a smooth slab high on the wall's west margin. Several sport routes, some requiring additional gear, ascend the right wall, including **Might As Well Jump** (5.11d), **Zebra** (5.12a), **Free For All** (5.12a), and **Alison in Wonderland** (5.12c), a long pumpy dihedral that surmounts numerous roofs.

OUTRAGEOUS OVERHANGS

This small cliff, sitting about 200 yards up the road from the First Grotto Wall at 5.6 miles, hides in the woods just north of the highway and a small parking pulloff. Approach the crag via a short trail that begins on the highway's north edge. Several good sport routes climb the steep west-facing cliff. Routes are listed right to left. No cliff topo included.

24. **Motown Philly** (5.13a) A short steep 4-bolt route to 2-bolt anchors. Begin on the south or right end of the obvious ledge approached via an easy right-angling ramp.

25. **Boyz to Men** (5.12c) A good, short 4-bolt route. Scramble onto a ledge on the right side of the cliff via a ramp to the route base.

26. **New Jack City** (5.12b) 2 bolts and a fixed pin to anchors. Begin at the top of the ramp and follow a black streak.

27. **Boyz in the Hood** (5.11d) Begin above and left of the ramp. Follow 4 bolts to anchors.

28. **Thug Route** (5.11c) Start this excellent route, the best on the crag, at the base of the ramp just south of large tree. Power up the 80' overhanging pitch past 6 bolts on good incuts to a last-move dyno and the anchors. **Rack:** Bring a medium Friend to plug the mid-height crack for additional security.

29. **Outrageous Overhang** (5.9) Follow the shallow right-facing corner just left of THUG ROUTE to a tree belay. **Rack:** Bring a small rack with stoppers and small Friends and TCUs.

30. **Walk in Fairmont Park** (5.12c) Begin just left of the prominent roof on the left side of the lower face. Climb left of the roof, then up right across a dark water streak and ledges to a 3-bolt headwall. **Rack:** Bring some small gear to #1.5 Friend.

31. **Walk in Central Park** (5.12a) A good route that also begins left of the roof, but climbs straight up past 5 bolts to an anchor.

32. **Cheap Thrills** (5.10a) A more moderate outing up the lower angle shield on the crag's north or left end.

OLYMPIC CRAG

The Olympic Crag, sitting atop airy ledges high above the valley floor, yields the best sport climbs on Independence Pass. The south-facing cliff, developed by Bob D'Antonio, Pete Heck, and Tom Perkins in 1992, offers a multitude of bolted routes on its smooth, glacier-polished face. The rock, broken by roofs and seamed by shallow cracks and corners, gives excellent incut handholds and sidepulls. Approach the crag via the same trail as Outrageous Overhangs at 5.6 miles. Walk past Outrageous Overhangs and continue left up steepening slopes on a rough, eroded trail. After about 10 minutes of steep walking, cut east or right below some blocky cliffs with several bolted routes. Olympic Crag is just around the corner to the east. The routes are listed from left to right. **Rack:** Bring quick draws and a clip-stick.

33. **50 Yard Dash** (5.10a) This superb route, the crag's easiest, scales the steep slab on the cliff's west end past 6 bolts to anchors. **Rack:** Bring some medium Friends for extra pro.

34. **False Start** (5.12a) Climb the V-shaped roof and follow the left edge of an arete upwards past 8 bolts to anchors.

35. **I Got Skills** (5.12b/c) Climbs the right side of the bulging arete over small roofs to anchors. 7 bolts and a fixed piton to anchors.

36. **Fear of a Punk World** (5.12c) Thin hard moves up burnished rock to a committing mantle onto a small ledge with the anchors. 5 bolts to anchors.

37. **Project** (5.13b) Thin climbing just right of a black water streak to anchors. 5 bolts.

38. **Steroids or Bust** (5.12a/b) A good route up steep rock just left of a wide water streak. Begin on the left side of the obvious lower roof. 5 bolts to chain anchors.

39. **Standing Eight Count** (5.11c) This climb, one of the crag's best, follows the black streak left of a big roof. Pull over the low, blocky roofs with powerful moves and continue above on easier well-protected climbing. 5 bolts.

40. **One Strike, You're Out** (5.12a) Another great route. Pull over the low roofs and head up the rounded arete past a difficult reach move to the final delicate slab and anchors. 5 bolts.

41. **Ball Four** (5.11a/b) Begin on the right side of the blunt arete. Climb up shallow corners past 3 bolts and move left to join ONE STRIKE, YOU'RE OUT.

42. **Len's World** (5.12d/13a) Thin, technical face climbing, long reaches, and 3 bolts ascend the lower slab. Thread through and over the big roofs above on fun, pumpy climbing to cliff-top anchors. Difficult to clean. 7 bolts.

43. **Horny for You** (5.11a) A popular climb right of the obvious chimney. Climb slabby overlaps past 4 bolts to anchors.

44. **For Pete's Sake** (5.11c) A short 4-bolt route on the far right side of the crag.

Continue on the broad ledge east from Olympic Crag to Bedrock just around the corner. Several short bolted lines scale this small crag. From left to right the routes are: **No Fret Arete** (5.11a, 3 bolts); **Anarchy in Bedrock** (5.11a, 4 bolts); a steep 3-bolt project; **Yabba Dabba Doo** (5.11a/b, 5 bolts up a water streak); an overhanging project; **Hostile** (5.12c, 4 bolts); and **Something Smells Fishy** (5.11a/b, 3 bolts and gear).

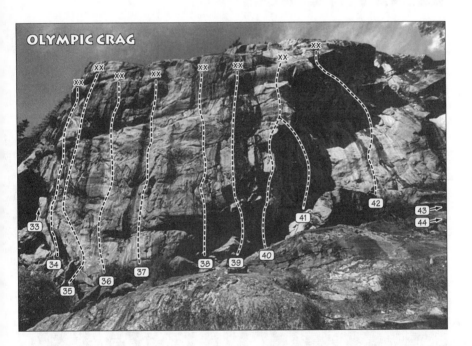

BUENA VISTA AREA

BUENA VISTA CRAGS

OVERVIEW

The small town of Buena Vista nestles along the Arkansas River in the evening shadow of the Sawatch Range, a twisting 100-mile sierra topped by fifteen 14,000-foot peaks including Mount Elbert, Colorado's 14,433-foot high point. The town, originally settled by silver miners in 1879, bills itself today as the "Whitewater Capital of Colorado," a title earned by the superlative rafting and kayaking opportunities on the Arkansas River. East of Buena Vista above the river, however, also hides some excellent climbing and bouldering areas.

Bob D'Antonio rappels off Elephant Rock north of Buena Vista.
Photo by Stewart M. Green.

Several developed crags lie northeast of town off Chaffee County Road 371, including Bob's Rock, Elephant Rock, Turtle Rock, Pump Station Rock, Split Rock, Pleasure Dome, and Davis Face. The highest concentration of quality climbing is found on the roadside cliffs of Bob's Rock and Elephant Rock. A hard, compact granite, studded with crystals, flakes, and incuts and seamed by cracks, forms the short cliffs. Both crags offer numerous routes, traditional and bolted, that range in difficulty from 5.7 to 5.12.

The other area crags also offer routes. Pump Station Rock, a few miles farther north of Bob's Rock alongside road 371, is a 140-foot face scaled by 17 routes and variations ranging from 5.6 to 5.11a. Good routes here include *Don's Delight,* a 5.8+ finger crack on the northwest corner, and *Ruthless People,* a 5.9+ route that climbs the face left of the prominent dihedral and up a strenuous corner crack above. Split Rock, reached by driving 1.3 miles up Forest Road 375, offers 28 routes, mostly bolted sport climbs on coarse pebbled granite. Good bouldering is nearby. Davis Face, a broad, white slab, lies farther east on the southern flank of Marmot Peak. Two 4-pitch routes ascend its face. More information on these crags and climbs can be obtained from the local B.S. (beta sheet) book at The Trailhead outdoor shop in Buena Vista.

Climbing history: The climbing history of these small crags is somewhat nebulous before the late 1980s. Several traditional lines ascended the crags, but little is known of their origin. In the late 1980s, however, local activists including Larry Floyd and Brad Schilling began serious exploration of the cliffs. Superb bolted lines appeared on Bob's Rock including the sustained *Top Dawg* and *Power Pig* lines, while a couple of hard cracks and face routes were completed on Elephant Rock. Bob's Rock, says Larry Floyd, was named for an ex-local named Bob Rember "...who was notorious for taking major, unanticipated whippers while leading cracks that seemed well within his ability. When Brad and I explored the rock, we just settled on the very unimaginative name `Bob's Rock' for reference. And it stuck."

Trip Planning Information

General description: Roadside granite crags with good face climbing.

Location: Midway between Leadville and Salida, in the low mountains east of Buena Vista and the Arkansas River.

Camping: Primitive camping is permitted on BLM public land along the river north of Bob's Rock and in San Isabel National Forest along FR 375. Good spots are found on the east side of Turtle Rock just west of the road. The nearest public campgrounds are west of Buena Vista, including Collegiate Peaks Campground along the Cottonwood Pass Road and three campgrounds along Chalk Creek southwest of Buena Vista.

Climbing season: Year-round. The best time to visit is May through October. Expect warm, sunny days with possible afternoon thunderstorms. Spring days

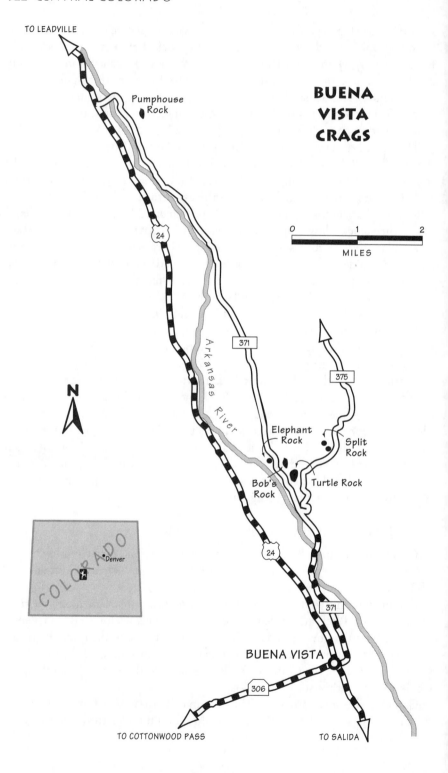

TO LEADVILLE

Pumphouse
Rock

BUENA
VISTA
CRAGS

0   1   2

MILES

24

371

375

N

Elephant
Rock

Split
Rock

Bob's
Rock

Turtle Rock

COLORADO

Denver

24

371

BUENA VISTA

306

TO COTTONWOOD PASS

TO SALIDA

can be very windy with variable weather conditions. Cold winter spells are broken by warmer weather with highs climbing into the 50s. Snowfall is generally light in the lower elevations of the Arkansas Valley.

Restrictions and access issues: No present restrictions. Climbers should present a low profile and pick up their trash. The parking area below Bob's Rock is a popular hangout for Buena Vista teens, who leave trash and build fire rings. Painted graffiti covers the roadside base of Elephant Rock.

Guidebooks: No guidebook is currently available. The Trailhead in Buena Vista maintains a route book that climbers can consult.

Nearby mountain shops, guide services, and gyms: The Trailhead (Buena Vista).

Services: All services, including gas, food, lodging, and dining, in Buena Vista.

Emergency services: Heart of the Rockies Regional Medical Center, First and B Streets, Salida, CO 81201, (719) 539-6661. Buena Vista Medical Clinic, 36 Oak St., Buena Vista, CO 81211, (719) 395-8632.

Nearby climbing areas: Monitor Rock, Independence Pass crags, Arkansas River Canyon crags, Taylor Canyon crags.

Nearby attractions: Collegiate Peaks Wilderness Area, Buffalo Peaks Wilderness Area, South Park, Weston Pass, Mount Princeton Hot Springs, St. Elmo ghost town, Mount Antero, Alpine Tunnel, Mount Princeton, Mount Yale, Cottonwood Pass, Taylor Park, Mount Elbert, Independence Pass, Mount Massive Wilderness Area, Leadville National Historic District.

Finding the crags: From U.S. Highway 24 in Buena Vista, turn east onto Main Street at the traffic light. Go east 0.1 mile and turn north or left on North Colorado Street (Chaffee County Road 371). Go north on County 371 out of Buena Vista. Past the Arkansas River, the pavement ends at 2.1 miles. FR 375 heads east to some small sport climbing crags and good boulders after another 0.5 mile. Continue north on County 371 through a series of old railroad tunnels. The turn-off to Bob's Rock is 3.2 miles north of Main Street. A short dirt road bumps northeast a hundred yards to the rock's base and a large parking area. Elephant Rock sits another 0.1 mile up the road from the Bob's Rock turn. Park at it's base.

BOB'S ROCK

The routes are listed right to left, or south to north.

1. **Air Soles** (5.9+) Begins around the corner on the edge of the rock's south face. Take the first broken crack system to a one-move 5.9+ roof.

2. **Bob's Crack** (5.9) A good finger and hand crack up the vertical to overhanging crack on the southern edge of the face. **Descent:** Rappel from a 2-cold shut anchor on top of the route. **Rack:** Bring an assortment of large wired stoppers and small to medium Friends for protection.

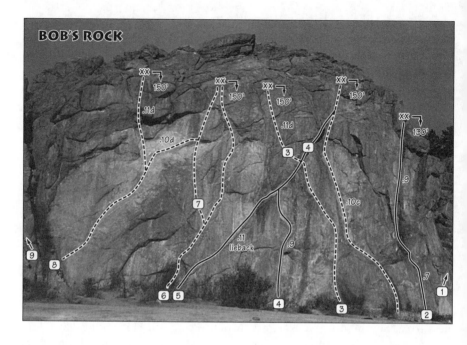

3. **Power Pig** (5.11d) An excellent route up the rock's central shield. Begin below a broken right-facing corner. Climb up and left past 2 ring-type bolts to the prominent right-angling crack system. Continue up and left past 3 more bolts and a steep, thin crux to a 2-bolt anchor. **Rack:** A medium Friend or large wired stopper is useful for placing in the crack below the steep headwall.

4. **Flakes** (5.9) Finger jam and layback the right-facing flakes to WIRE MAN. Continue up and right to anchors. **Rack:** Bring wires and Friends.

5. **Wire Man** (5.11a) Follow the right-trending seam-crack. Crux is the first 20' with thin laybacking and undercling pinches. **Descent:** Rap off 2-bolt anchor atop corner. **Rack:** Bring wired stoppers and RPs for lower crack and Friends for upper section.

6. **Top Dawg** (5.12c/d) A brilliant sustained route up a thin face. Begin just left of WIRE MAN. Climb up and right past 5 bolts to a 2-bolt anchor. Another start underclings up the thin arch to the left.

7. **Lactic Acid Overload** (5.11d) Same start as TOP DAWG, only jog up and left after the first bolt up a steep face with sidepulls and laybacks. Finish up the slab above to TOP DAWG'S anchors. **Rack:** Bring RPs for a placement between the second and third bolts, and wired stoppers for the top.

8. **Twist and Shout** (5.11d) Follow obvious right-leaning seam past 3 bolts to a smooth slab below the roof. Pull over the roof, 5.11d, to a bolt and anchors. An easier 5.11b variation trends right across the slab to TOP DAWG'S anchors. **Rack:** Some thin stoppers and RPs offer additional pro between the second and third bolts and under the roof.

9. **Toprope Slab** (5.6) The lower-angle slab on the rock's northwest corner offers numerous topropes and leads.

ELEPHANT ROCK

Elephant Rock, a squat granite pinnacle, sits 0.2 mile up County 371 from the Bob's Rock turnoff. Park in a pulloff below the rock's east face. **Descent** off the 70' pinnacle is by rappel. Anchors with wired cable sit on the east end of the summit. Route descriptions begin from the southeast corner of Elephant Rock.

10. **South Side Classic** (5.8) Follow a thin crack past 1 fixed piton to the large ledge on the rock's south face. Step right to the southeast corner and climb past another fixed pin to the summit.

11. **Trunk Line** (5.9+) Start on left side of obvious roof on the southeast corner. Climb the shallow crack system and continue to summit on SOUTH SIDE CLASSIC. **Rack:** Bring small wired nuts.

12. **Safari Land** (5.10c) Same start as TRUNK LINE only step right above the roof to a bolt. Two bolted sport routes ascend the short steep south face above the ledge. The right one is 5.11d and the left one is 5.12c/d.

13. **For Boars Only** (5.11) Thrash up the right-leaning, body-sized crack to an overhanging hand crack crux. **Rack:** Bring Friends.

14. **Curve of the Tusk** (5.10b) A 2-bolt slab climb up the tusk's west edge. The upper section is runout, but 5.7.

15. **North Prow** (5.10a) Face-climb the shallow dihedral up and right, pausing to clip nearby bolts. Runout but easier up high.

16. **Three-Ring Circus** (5.10d) Steep pebble-pinching and edging up the 4-bolt slab on the tusk's east side to anchors. Shares the first bolt of NORTH PROW.

17. **Ivory Coast** (5.11+) Follow a dirty right-angling crack up a corner on the east face to the obvious funky roof. Turn on desperate jams. **Rack:** Bring medium to large pro.

18. **In Fear of Fear** (5.13 a/b) Formerly Overhanging Aid (5.10 A3) A beautiful thin crack on the east face. **Rack:** Bring RPs, wired stoppers, TCUs, and a few medium pieces.

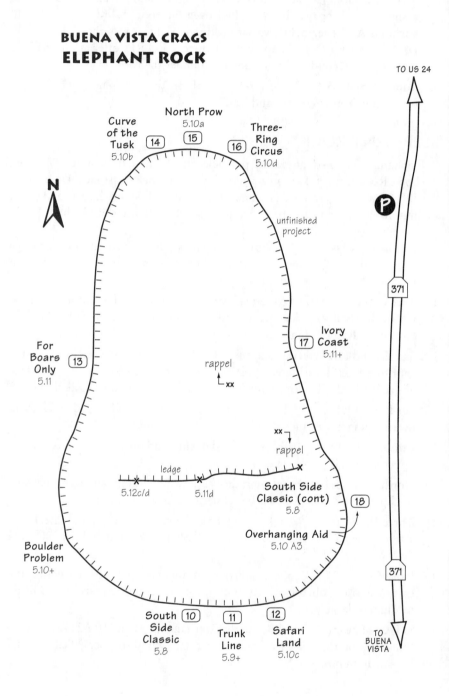

BUENA VISTA CRAGS
ELEPHANT ROCK

SANGRE DE CRISTOAREA

CRESTONE NEEDLE

OVERVIEW

The Sangre de Cristo Range, one of the Rocky Mountain's longest mountain chains, stretches more than 150 miles from its origin at Poncha Pass near Salida to its hilly terminus east of Santa Fe, New Mexico. The range, in Colorado, forms a magnificent escarpment of lofty, sawtoothed peaks that separates the Wet Mountain Valley and the San Luis Valley. This lengthy crest, topped by eight 14,000-foot peaks, is crossed by no highways and is protected by the immense Sangre de Cristo Wilderness Area. The range received its name, according to myth, from the Spanish explorer Valverde who fervently exclaimed *"Sangre de Cristo"* or "Blood of Christ" on viewing the mountain peaks in morning alpenglow.

Four of the range's Fourteeners—Crestone Needle (14,191 feet), Crestone Peak (14,294 feet), Kit Carson Peak (14,165 feet), and Humboldt Peak (14,064 feet)—tower above the verdant Wet Mountain Valley. These remote peaks were among the last of Colorado's high peaks to be ascended, at least by Anglos. Humboldt, a massive anthill of rock chips, was climbed in 1883, but the other three saw no successful ascents until 1916. Crestone Peak and Needle, a pair of twin summits separated by a serrated ridge, are among Colorado's most spectacular and rugged peaks. Both peaks are flanked by looming walls and buttresses of vertical conglomerate and creased by steep snow-filled couloirs. The Needle, a beautifully proportioned alp, lifts its slabby north face above an above-timberline cirque studded with glassy alpine lakes. Several technical climbing routes ascend this classic face, with the elegant line of the Ellingwood Arete being the finest.

Climbing history: The Ellingwood Arete, after its 1925 first ascent, was one of Colorado's first technical rock climbs. The line was initially spied by Albert Ellingwood, a Colorado College political science professor, and Eleanor Davis as they descended the Needle after making its first ascent on July 24, 1916. Ellingwood noted that the northeast flank of Crestone Needle and Peak offered "a superb array of formidable buttresses, seamed by tempting cracks and set off from each other by steep-plunging chimneys that probably have not been free from ice since the glacial era." In the darkening twilight, Ellingwood's eye

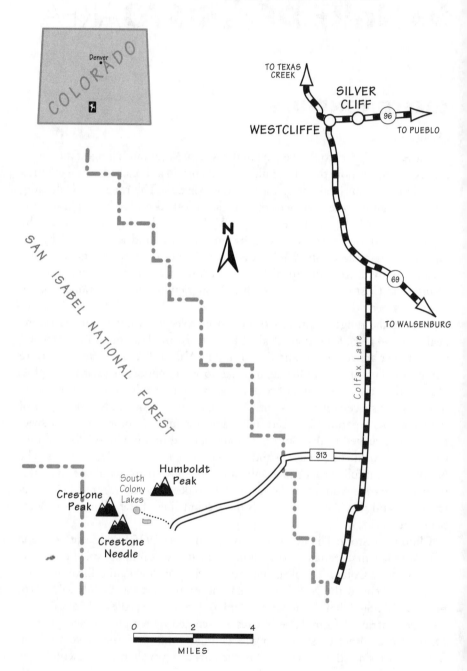

CRESTONE NEEDLE

was drawn to the obvious arete line up the Needle's north wall. He saw no difficulties in the first 1,500 feet up the 55-degree face, but the abrupt cliff below the summit appeared problematic. He wrote that "there were pessimistic doubts expressed as to the last five hundred feet, where the precipice seemed to attain verticality, near the top of which a huge boss of well-polished rock was certain to force us into an enormous overhang from which we could discern no avenue of escape." It was nine years, however, before Ellingwood and Davis returned, with Marion Warner and Stephen Hart, to attempt the line.

The quartet quickly ascended the initial 1,500 feet, following easy cracks and crossing grassy ledges, and after three hours reached the vertical step. During a lunch break, a hailstorm coated the upper route. Ellingwood, however, continued upward along a cold, slippery crack system right of the arete to a ledge. He described the crack as "a diddle-diddle-dumpling sort of climb—one foot in and one foot out, and hands usually clawing at such minute molecules of rock as have survived the process of erosion." The unbroken wall loomed above the ledge and the situation looked bleak. Ellingwood made a tenuous traverse up left on a narrow ledge and found the crucial crux crack—the Head Crack—that led into "an enormous crack almost wide enough to drive a wagon through...but closed in at the top by an impenetrable roof." He stemmed up the chimney and stepped into a hidden crevice that bypassed the roof and landed the party on gentle talus slopes below the summit cairn. Ellingwood died prematurely in 1934 at the age of 46. Robert Ormes, his protege, made the route's second ascent in 1937 and named it *Ellingwood Ledges* in the professor's honor, a name later corrupted to *Ellingwood Arete*. The line didn't see another ascent until the 1950s. After its inclusion in *Fifty Classic Climbs of North America*, the route became extremely popular with numerous parties sharing its ledges on summer mornings.

The superb 2,000-foot *Ellingwood Arete* route ascends a bulging arete along a plumb line directly north of the Needle's summit. Most of the lower climbing is pleasant 4th class scrambling, broken by occasional rock steps. The upper wall, however, yields three sustained and airy pitches below the lofty summit. The unique rock, an ancient Paleozoic conglomerate composed of numerous knobs, cobbles, and boulders firmly cemented in the bedrock matrix, takes some getting used to. It's somewhat disconcerting initially to reach up and grab a jutting knob that appears ready to pull out at the slightest provocation. Ascending these knobs is a joyful experience, one not soon forgotten.

Trip Planning Information

General description: One of Colorado's best alpine rock climbs up a long arete.

Location: Southwest of Westcliffe on the Crestone Needle in the Sangre de Cristo Range.

CRESTONE NEEDLE

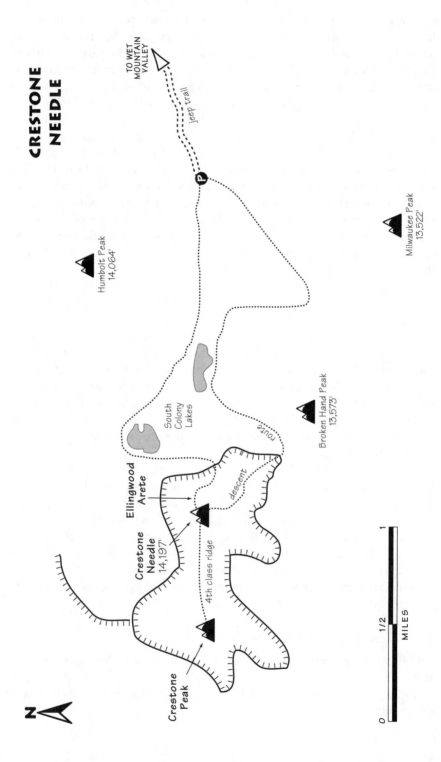

Camping: Primitive camping and bivouacking at South Colony Lakes in the cirque below Crestone Needle.

Climbing Season: June through September. Expect to encounter snow in June, particularly on the descent down the backside. Heavy thunderstorms accompanied by lightning occur on summer afternoons.

Restrictions and access issues: The peak lies in the Sangre de Cristo Wilderness Area in San Isabel National Forest. Wilderness restrictions apply, including no motor vehicles or power drills.

Guidebooks: *Colorado's Fourteeners* by Gerry Roach.

Nearby mountain shops, guide services, and gyms: None.

Services: All services, including gas, groceries, lodging, and dining, in Westcliffe.

Emergency services: St. Thomas More Hospital, 1019 Sheridan St., Canon City, CO 81212, (719) 275-3381.

Nearby climbing areas: Hardscrabble Pass, Royal Gorge, Shelf Road, Arkansas River Canyon, Crestone Peak, Kit Carson Peak, Blanca Peak.

Nearby attractions: Sangre de Cristo Wilderness Area, Wet Mountain Valley, Westcliffe, Great Sand Dunes National Monument, Grape Creek Wilderness Study Area, Wet Mountains.

Finding the crag: Drive to Westcliffe via Colorado Highway 96 or Colorado 69. CO 96 offers the easiest access from the Front Range cities, running over Hardscrabble Pass from Florence and Pueblo. From Westcliffe go south 4.6 miles on CO 69 to Colfax Lane (Custer County Road 119). Go south on Colfax Lane 5.6 miles to South Colony Road (Custer County Road 120). Turn west and follow the road up the mountain flank. After about 3 miles the road turns into a 4-wheel-drive jeep trail. Park here and walk the remaining 5 miles up to South Colony Lakes or jeep up the road as far as possible. Follow a marked trail from the end of the jeep trail up to the basin below the peaks. Camp can be made at either the Upper or Lower South Colony Lakes. The upper lake is directly below the route.

1. **Ellingwood Arete** (III 5.7) This 2,000' route is done in two sections. The lower 1,500' is mostly 3rd and 4th class rock, with a rope only occasionally necessary. The upper headwall is ascended by 3 sustained pitches. Descent is off the back or south side of Crestone Needle. Allow 6 hours for the ascent and 2 to 3 hours for the descent. It's a long day. Get an early start to avoid the regular afternoon thunderstorms.

   Begin by hiking to Upper South Colony Lake directly below the prominent, rounded arete. The initial rock section above the lake can be climbed with several moderate 5th class pitches (one variation follows a large right-facing 5.4 dihedral), but the usual route begins to the left. Hike southeast from the lake up talus slopes and over a few rock steps to the base of a slab below an obvious gully that drops down from a notch on the east ridge high above. Scramble up the slab (3rd class) and begin a long traverse up and right along grassy terraces to the arete. Follow the arete by scrambling over exposed rock steps and grassy benches (4th class) for almost 1,000'. Most parties rope up for part or all of this section. Use your own discretion depending on weather and rock conditions and your party's climbing ability. End at the base of the steep wall. Above lie 3 or 4 pitches of technical climbing and some route-finding problems. **Pitch 1** works up a 200' chimney (5.5) just right of arete. Follow center or righthand chimney of 3 systems. Belay on a convenient ledge. **Pitch 2** continues up chimneys and moves up left in a left-diagonaling gully (5.2) to a spacious ledge on the arete. **Pitch 3**, the crux, begins by climbing onto a narrow ledge that leads left around a corner to the base of a steep crack—the Head Crack. Jam the awkward crack for about 20' (5.7) and move up right on small face holds (5.7) to a wide chimney/crack. Stem up an easy chimney and step right into a crack on right wall. Belay above on talus. This route can be done in 2 shorter pitches. Scramble up to summit. **The descent** down the back or south side of Crestone Needle is complicated. Drop southeast or left from summit down ridge to top of a steep gully. Descend gully 500' to a wide ledge at its base. Contour east or left onto the ridge and follow along to an obvious low point (3rd class) where easy hiking leads back down to lakes. The route is well-traveled in summer. Watch for snow in the steep gully in June.

CRESTONE NEEDLE

SAN LUIS VALLEYAREA

PENITENTE CANYON

Overview

Penitente Canyon, hidden in the low-browed volcanic foothills on the western side of the broad San Luis Valley in south-central Colorado, comprises, along with the Rock Garden, Witches' Canyon, and Sidewinder Canyon, one of Colorado's most unique climbing areas. It's a rough, dry land, seamed by shallow canyons and arroyos, studded with volcanic dikes and broken rock outcrops, and clothed in a dusty forest of pinyon pine and juniper. The San Luis Valley, an immense intermountain basin flanked by serrated mountain ranges, spreads east from Penitente Canyon in a patchwork of green farmland and pastures and windswept sagebrush plains.

Kevin Branford cranks finger pockets on *Sister of Mercy* at Penitente Canyon.
Photo by Stewart M. Green.

PENITENTE CANYON

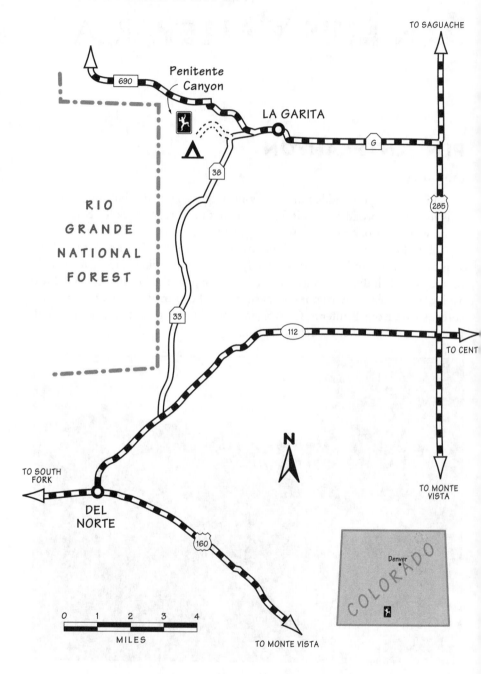

The canyon nestles among dry hills, its sheer flanks hidden from casual passersby. A dusty, rutted one-lane road bumps west from the small town of La Garita up a shallow canyon and after a mile reaches a Bureau of Land Management camping area and parking lot at the canyon's narrow entrance. Dark cliffs of Fish Canyon Tuff, a dark porous rock deposited from nearby volcanic eruptions some 33 million years ago, line the canyon walls and offer a spectacular array of rock climbs on its rough, gritty surface. Most of the canyon's routes scale steep, hueco-pocketed walls that are well-protected with bolts and end at lowering anchors below the cliffed rim. The routes range from 25 to 75 feet long, with most tending toward the short side.

Rack: A rack of quick draws and a rope are all the needed equipment for a day's fun. The canyon's crack routes require wired stoppers and an assortment of cams.

Climbing history: Boulderer Lew Hoffman from the nearby Balloon Ranch found the canyon in the early 1980s and introduced Bob D'Antonio to the area. Bob quickly recognized the canyon's potential and began establishing routes in 1984. More than 100 new routes were climbed by the early 1990s by D'Antonio and a host of other activists including Richard Aschert, Mark Milligan, Mike Kennedy, Mike Benge, and Kevin McLaughlin. *Bullet the Blue Sky* and neighboring *A Virgin No More,* both hard canyon classics, went up in 1987. Reclusive boulderer Bob Murray cranked numerous hard boulder problems at Penitente Canyon and at surrounding bouldering areas.

Penitente Canyon lies on land administered by the Bureau of Land Management. The BLM, a multi-use agency, manages the canyon for recreation and has made many improvements (including the campground, parking areas, and pit toilets) with visiting climbers in mind. Future plans include moving the campground and main parking area farther east and out of the canyon to help preserve the canyon's solitude and ecosystems. The deservedly popular canyon is seeing a lot of use by climbers. In 1993 the BLM estimates there were more than 20,000 user-days. Climbers need to respect the canyon and minimize their impact by staying on established trails when possible, using the trash cans and outhouses at the trailhead, packing out all their trash, not retrobolting routes, and not drilling pockets or chipping holds on any rock or route. Manufactured holds chipped by inconsiderate buffoons on routes including *Bullet the Blue Sky* and *Cassandra* have been patched. Much inconsiderate bolting has also occurred here, with extra bolts being placed on existing climbs and boulder problems. The BLM allows no bolting east of *Mysterious Redhead* in the canyon or along the access road. Watch for rattlesnakes in the warmer months, especially when thrashing through canyon brush or hiking near rocky outcrops.

Trip Planning Information

General description: Numerous short, bolted routes line volcanic canyon walls of one of Colorado's most popular sport climbing venues.

Location: Northwest of Alamosa, about 2 miles west of La Garita on the western edge of the San Luis Valley.

Camping: A primitive BLM campground with designated sites, pit toilets, and garbage cans sits at the canyon entrance. No water is available. Use existing fire rings and bring firewood to avoid scarring the old pinyon pines and junipers surrounding the campground. A new campground will be placed east of the canyon at a later date.

Climbing season: Year-round. Spring and fall are the best months to climb. Summers tend to be hot, with daily highs in the upper 80s and few shaded routes in the canyon. Expect afternoon thunderstorms in July and August. December through February is often very cold, although occasional warm days yield good climbing weather.

Restrictions and access issues: The cliffs in Penitente Canyon and the nearby canyons lie on BLM public land, although some approaches might be on private land. If in doubt, check with the BLM office in Alamosa and ask permission to cross the land. The Rock Garden to the north of Penitente Canyon is closed at its ranch entrance during hunting season from October 15 to November 15. Check at the Spearman Ranch across the road for permission to park and enter the canyon there. Birds of prey often nest in the area's cliffs; respect their rights by not climbing routes near nests. Penitente's growing popularity necessitates a healthy dose of courtesy: park and camp in designated areas; use the public restrooms at the canyon entrance; control your dog; and use existing trails. The BLM prohibits any bolted routes along the short cliffs on the entrance road or anywhere east of *Mysterious Redhead* in the main canyon—control your Bosch.

Guidebooks: *San Luis Valley Rock Climbing and Bouldering Guide* by Bob D'Antonio, Chockstone Press, 1994. This excellent guide lists all the areas and existing routes in the western San Luis Valley area.

Nearby mountain shops, guide services, and gyms: Casa de Madera, run by Alex Colville on Del Norte's Main Street, sells climbing gear.

Services: Limited services in La Garita, including gas, food, and groceries at the Cash Store run by Ed and Ele Lambert. The store offers good breakfasts and lunches at reasonable prices, and is a good place to hang out, drink coffee, read the latest climbing mags, and visit with the locals. Complete services, including motels and private campgrounds, in Center, Del Norte, Monte Vista, and Alamosa.

Emergency services: St. Joseph Hospital, 1280 Grande Ave, Del Norte, CO 81132, (719) 657-3311. San Luis Valley Regional Medical Center, 106 Blanca Ave., Alamosa, CO 81101, (719) 589-2511.

Nearby climbing areas: Rock Garden, Sidewinder Canyon, Witches Canyon, Eagle Rock Boulders, Elephant Rocks, South Fork canyon.

Nearby attractions: Rio Grande National Forest, Wheeler Geologic Area, La Ventana, Silver Thread Scenic Byway, Creede National Historic District, Rio

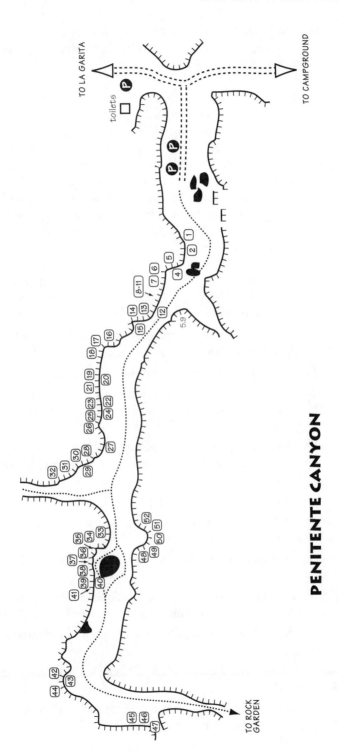

TO LA GARITA

TO CAMPGROUND

toilets

TO ROCK GARDEN

PENITENTE CANYON

Grande, La Garita Wilderness Area, Weminuche Wilderness Area, Monte Vista National Wildlife Refuge, Alamosa National Wildlife Refuge, Great Sand Dunes National Monument, Sangre de Cristo Wilderness Area.

Finding the canyon: Head west from La Garita on County Road 38 for a short mile. Look for a sign on the north side of the road marking the rough dirt track that leads into the canyon. Bump west just over a mile to the canyon entrance. La Garita is 7 miles west of U.S. Highway 285 via G Road, or 12 miles north of Del Norte via Colorado 112 and County 38A.

Most of Penitente Canyon's routes lie on the sunny north side of the canyon. Park in designated areas near the canyon mouth and hike northwest up the canyon. New parking areas will be installed outside the canyon in the future.

Routes are listed from east to west. Route 1, *Mysterious Redhead*, is found on the first vertical cliff encountered.

1. **Mysterious Redhead** (5.11a) The first route in the canyon on vertical buttress on the right side. It's a good 4-bolt warm-up or a first 5.11 lead. **Descent:** Lower from anchors.

2. **Nature of the Beast** (5.12a) Shares start of MYSTERIOUS REDHEAD. Short, sharp, and continuous. 4 bolts to anchors.

3. **Twist of Fate** (5.11d) Left edge of buttress. 4 bolts to anchors.

4. **The Color of Devotion** (5.13a) On pretty west-facing wall left of a wide crack. A boulder problem start (5.13a) leads to hard cranking. Stick-clip first bolt. 4 bolts to anchors.

5. **The Color of Emotion** (5.13a/b) Sequential climbing on small pockets up a colored vertical wall. Beautiful climbing, but finger-injury potential. This classic sports 6 bolts and anchors.

6. **To Error is Human** (5.11d) A 3-bolt corner.

7. **Tangerine Dream** (5.11d) Good route up corners. 3 bolts and anchors. **Rack:** Bring medium Friends.

8. **Mission in the Rain** (5.12b/c) A technical, steep-slab route with 5 bolts and anchors.

9. **No Regrets** (5.11c) Just right of obvious black water groove. Stick-clip first bolt to protect bouldery start. Thin edging past 4 bolts to anchors.

10. **Whipping Post** (5.11a) A good but runout route up black streak. 2 bolts, no anchors.

11. **Forbidden Fruits** (5.12a) Excellent face climbing left of grooved streak with 5 bolts and anchors.

12. **French Lesson** (5.11d) Up a short corner, turn the small roof on left, and climb past 3 bolts to slab anchors.

PENITENTE CANYON

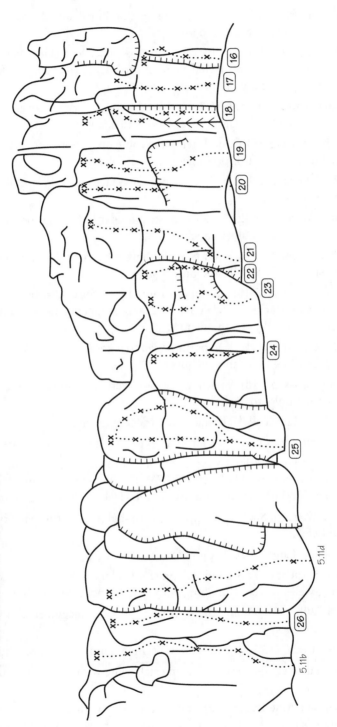

13. **Cassandra** (5.12d) A steep, sustained, and brilliant Christian Griffith line up a steep face. 8 bolts to anchors.

14. **Sitting in Limbo** (5.13b/c) A sequential, excellent Dan Michael line up a thin crack system protected by 7 bolts to anchors just left of CASSANDRA. Probably the canyon's hardest route.

15. **The Art of Suffering** (5.12c) A bouldering start pulls over roof on small pockets; ends on ledge above. 4 bolts to anchors.

16. **Lovesnake** (5.10b) Good stemming route up a steep, left-facing corner to a chain anchor left of prominent roof. 3 bolts.

17. **Prick Pocket** (5.12b/c) A steep, pocketed face route on left dihedral wall. 5 bolts to anchors.

18. **Stemmoroids** (5.12c/d) Difficult stemming up a leaning corner for very limber climbers. 6 bolts to anchors.

19. **Rocketman** (5.11c) Thin face climbing to a ledge then pockets and edges up steep wall. 5 bolts and anchors.

20. **Bucket Slave** (5.10b) A superb route up a short 5.8+ crack and huecoed headwall. **Rack:** Carry a couple of large stoppers and medium Friends for lower crack. 4 bolts to anchors.

21. **Dyno-Soar** (5.12b/c) A soaring dyno to a good hold then up right on technical rock. 4 bolts and anchors.

22. **Iron Cross** (5.11d) An iron cross move across a corner, over a roof, and up a slab. 4 bolts to anchors.

23. **OPS** (5.12a) Thin slabbing past 4 bolts to anchors.

24. **Dos Hombres** (5.11b) A short 4-bolt line left of grooved water pour-off.

25. **Yah-Ta-Hei** (5.10c) An excellent route up a steep slab right of a chimney. 7 bolts to anchors. THIS IS THE WAY (5.10b) goes up right edge of the slab after Yah-Ta-Hei's first 3 bolts. Yah-Ta-Hei is a Navajo greeting.

26. **The Wages of Sin** (5.10b) Good line up shallow, intermittent cracks. 4 bolts and anchors.

27. **Looney Tunes** (5.10c) A good route up buttress with 6 bolts and anchors.

28. **The Serpent** (5.7) A good slab line for beginners. Start is a hard move, then easy, well-protected climbing with 6 bolts and 2-bolt anchor.

29. **Mr. Wind** (5.6) Again, the start is tricky. Good beginner lead with 6 bolts and anchors.

30. **Mr. Breeze** (5.2) An over-bolted beginner climb up a slabby buttress.

31. **Unnamed** (5.8) Steep west-facing slab route with 5 bolts and anchors atop a pillar.

32. **Captain America** (5.10a) Start off a ledge with a hard move then great hueco climbing. 3 bolts to 2 anchors. Up the shallow canyon just left is a

good bolted hueco arete HOW THE WEST WAS WON (5.8+).

33. **Passion Play** (5.11c) Boulder problem start (harder for short folks) to steep pocketed wall above a rounded ledge. 5 bolts to anchors.

34. **Breakdown Dead Ahead** (5.11b) This good hueco climb lies on right side of tall pillar right of Virgin painting. Crank an awkward 5.10 corner with 1 bolt and pull huecos up right side of pillar above. 5 bolts to chains.

35. **Tanks for the Huecos** (5.10c/d) The canyon's must-do route—simply superb. Goes directly up center of pillar. The first hard moves up a leaning, wet dihedral (5.10) are out of character, with overhanging 5.9 hueco climbing on headwall above. 6 bolts to chains.

36. **Bullet the Blue Sky** (5.12c) This mega-classic arete climb, put up by Bob D'Antonio, offers spectacular positions and excellent climbing. One of the best 5.12s anywhere. Climb sharp arete left of TANKS. The long dyno to jug after first bolt is committing, but not as bad as it looks. 8 bolts to chained anchors.

37. **Not My Cross to Bear** (5.11a) A continuous and excellent stemming route up a classic dihedral. 5 bolts to anchors.

PENITENTE CANYON

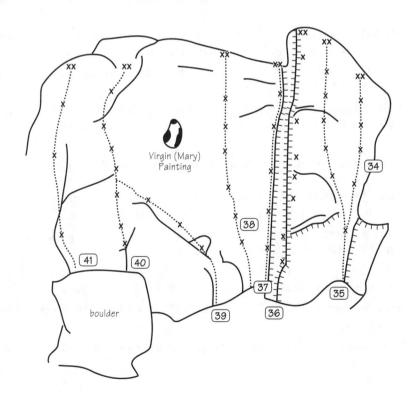

Virgin (Mary) Painting

boulder

38. **A Virgin No More** (5.12d) Steep, continuous, and technical climbing on small pockets and edges just right of Virgin painting. Some idiot enlarged a few finger pockets, but they've since been returned to their original condition. 6 bolts to anchors on this D'Antonio classic.

39. **Los Hermanos de la Weenie Way** (5.11c) A great, athletic line that traverses below Virgin painting. Begin below A VIRGIN NO MORE and follow line of holds up left. Continue up devious face climbing to anchors. 7 bolts to anchors.

40. **Los Hermanos de la Penitente** (5.12c) One of the canyon's early routes by D'Antonio and Richard Aschert in 1986. Climb a thin, entertaining crack to upper headwall. A couple of small wired nuts help protect lower moves. Follow a shallow corner to top. 6 bolts to anchors.

41. **Morada** (5.12a) Technical climbing up incipient cracks past 3 bolts to anchors. A few small Friends add additional security.

42. **Ordinary People** (5.9) Find a streaked, west-facing slab 100 hundred or so yards up canyon. This 2-bolt route climbs up smooth water groove then angles left to anchors.

43. **Children of a Lessor Grade** (5.10c) Delicate and fun slab climbing on this Kevin McLaughlin route. 4 bolts to anchors.

44. **Jewel of the Mild** (5.10c) More graceful climbing up a 4-bolt slab to anchors.

45. **10,000 Maniacs** (5.11c) A brown, south-facing cliff where canyon divides. Steep and devious face climbing past 5 bolts to anchors.

46. **Brown Sugar** (5.11a) A brilliant route that wanders up brown wall left of 10,000 MANIACS. 4 bolts to anchors.

47. **Candy Apple Grey** (5.10c) On the slabby ridge left of BROWN SUGAR. Dicey boulder problem start to a good slab. 4 bolts to anchors.

The following routes lie downcanyon and across from the Virgin wall.

48. **Black Jesus** (5.12c/d) This line pulls up right side of a pretty wall past 5 bolts to anchors. The ending pull onto slab on right is tricky.

49. **Sister of Mercy** (5.12b) Good sequential route up smooth pocketed wall left of BLACK JESUS. 6 bolts to anchors.

50. **Dazed and Confused** (5.12a) Ascends the right edge of a smooth wall in a box recess. Thin face climbing to roof pull. 4 bolts to anchors.

51. **Shear Strength** (5.11c) Delicate climbing up recessed wall's left side. 5 bolts to anchors.

52. **Shear Lunacy** (5.12a) A superb, thuggish arete climb on left side of the cliff. 5 bolts to anchors.

Western Colorado

REGION

Mia Axon on *Cryptic Egyptian* at The Wicked Cave in Rifle Mountain Park.
Photo by Stewart M. Green.

RIFLEAREA

RIFLE MOUNTAIN PARK

Overview

Climbers consider Rifle Mountain Park, 13 miles north of Rifle on Colorado's Western Slope, as America's premier sport climbing area. More hard routes scale the overhanging limestone walls here than at any other comparable American area. The park's narrow 2.5-mile canyon, lined with sheer, blue and grey cliffs, was chiseled by relentless East Rifle Creek. The sound of the tumbling creek fills the canyon, drowning out the calls of belayers and muting traffic. A leafy canopy of trees, broken by grassy meadows, shades the verdant canyon floor.

Climbing history: Rifle Mountain Park is a relative newcomer to Colorado's climbing scene. It wasn't until the early 1990s that the first routes went in after a few climbers checked out rumors of a spectacular limestone canyon north of Rifle. *Never Believe,* one of the canyon's first established routes, went in an area of the wall known as *The Wasteland* thanks to Pete Zoeller, Kurt Smith, and Mike Pont. A host of other activists, including Colin Lantz, Phil Benningfield, Christian Griffith, and Bret and Stuart Ruckman, quickly joined the bandwagon, bolted many superb lines, and began developing the numerous caves and walls.

Almost all of the lines at Rifle can be climbed with a rack of quick draws and a 165-foot rope. Some routes, including *Slice of Life,* require a full-length rope, while others like *Beer Run* need a 200-foot rope or a trail rope for the descent. Cliff access is usually measured in minutes from car to cliff.

Descent: All routes have lowering anchors, some with quick-clips.

The canyon is an active climbing area, with new routes and projects going in every season. Ask around for what's new and respect other people's projects. Quick draws are often left on routes while they are being worked. Respect their owners and leave the draws hanging. Thieves, using the Old West code of honor, will probably be stripped and hung for stealing quick draws or other gear. Loose rock and rubble covers the canyon walls. Route pioneers often clean a ton of rock off new routes, but chunks still work loose. Keep your head up and don't belay or sit under a climber. Numerous accidents have occurred due to rockfall. Watch for loose rock early in the season after the spring thaw has loosened flakes and blocks.

Rifle Mountain Park has several climbing rules. Avoid climbing above the popular lower section of Koper Trail. Ropes and belayers are not allowed on the road; take note at the roadside Project Wall. Avoid climbing on cliffs that overhang roads and trails. Several areas along the road are clearly marked with "No Climbing" signs. Placement of hardware, including bolts, requires a permit. Use only designated parking areas. Do not park along the road. If the parking lot at your crag is full, park at the next lot and walk. Parking tickets can be given for illegal parking. To avoid the hassle, leave your car at the campsite and bicycle to the crag. Park visitors are required to purchase a day-use pass. The Rifle police and campground host regularly check cars for an up-to-date permit. The fragile riparian zone along the creek and canyon floor is easily damaged by overuse. Use established trails to reach the walls and pick up all your trash, including tape scraps. Remember that you're a visitor at Rifle Mountain Park and that climbing in this marvelous canyon is a privilege, not your right. Demonstrate to other park users and the park staff that rock climbers are a polite, friendly, and caring user group.

Trip Planning Information

General description: Colorado's premier sport climbing area boasts numerous difficult, overhanging limestone routes on steep walls along Rifle Creek.

Location: 25 miles west of Glenwood Springs; 13 miles north of Rifle and Interstate 70.

Camping: Campsites at Rifle Mountain Park are just north of the canyon along the creek. A fee is charged. Camping is found at Three Forks Campground a few miles farther north in the national forest. This small, popular area is often crowded. Camping is also found at Rifle Falls State Park and Rifle Gap State Recreation Area down canyon from the climbing area. Rifle Gap is warmer and drier than the upper canyon campgrounds, particularly in late September and October. Water is available at the lower campground.

Climbing season: Mid-April through October. The rock seeps in April and May and may be wet. Summer days are generally warm with highs in the 80s and regular afternoon thunderstorms. September and October bring warm days and chilly nights. Sunny or shaded routes are easily found in the narrow canyon, and the overhanging walls are usually dry during and after rain. Excellent ice climbs form up between December and March.

Restrictions and access issues: Rifle Mountain Park is owned and operated by the city of Rifle. A number of climbing rules are in effect: avoid climbing on the lower half of Koper Trail; ropes and belayers are not allowed on roads; avoid climbing on areas that overhang the park road and trails; camp and park only in designated areas; placement of hardware requires a permit. A $3 daily use fee is charged. Pay at the entrance kiosk or at the campground. Remember that climbing at Rifle is a privilege, not a right. Be courteous to other park users. Avoid polluting the stream, which runs into the State Fish Hatchery

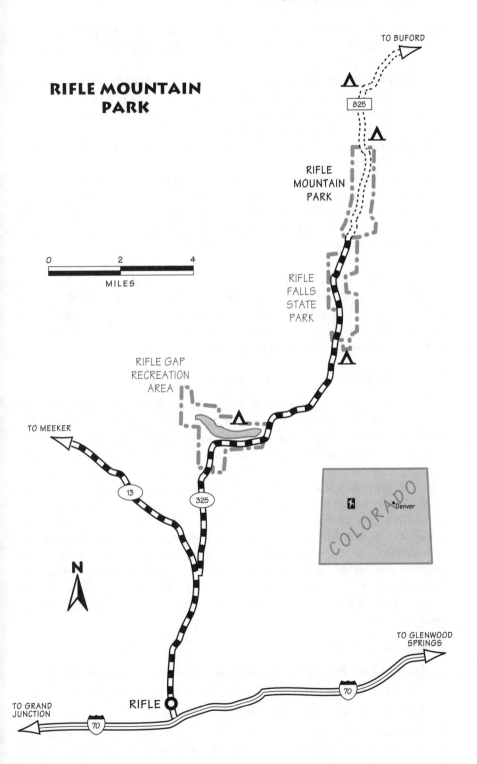

at the canyon entrance; use the outhouses provided at various parking areas.

Guidebooks: *Rifle: Climber's Guide to Rifle Mountain Park* by Hassan Saab, King Coal West, 1995..

Nearby mountain shops, guide services, and gyms: Nothing in the immediate area. Nearest shops are in Glenwood Springs and Grand Junction.

Services: All services, including gas, groceries, dining, and lodging, in Rifle. Showers are available at the public swimming pool.

Emergency services: Clagett Memorial Hospital, 701 E. Fifth St., Rifle, CO 81650, (970) 625-1510.

Nearby climbing areas: Colorado National Monument, Glenwood Springs area, Independence Pass, Redstone, Capitol Peak, Glenwood Canyon.

Nearby attractions: Rifle Gap and Harvey Gap state recreation areas, White River National Forest, Flat Tops Wilderness Area, Trappers Lake, Rifle Falls State Park, Glenwood Hot Springs, Grand Mesa.

Finding the canyon: From Exit 90 on I-70, drive north to the town of Rifle on Colorado Highway 13. Continue north on CO 13, then north 11 miles on Colorado 325, passing Rifle Gap Reservoir and heading up the narrowing canyon past Rifle Falls State Park. Rifle Mountain Park and its climbing begin just past the fish hatchery where the pavement ends.

THE ARSENAL AND WICKED CAVE

The Arsenal and Wicked Cave are the park's southernmost developed climbing areas, although other routes lie farther south toward the entrance. The Wicked Cave, an immense roofed amphitheater, sits just west of the road 0.6 mile from the cattle guard at the park's entrance. Park in the picnic area east of the road. A short trail winds through the trees to the cliff base. This excellent wall is home to *Cryptic Egyptian* and *Slice of Life,* one of Colorado's hardest rock climbs. A couple of projects next to *Slice of Life* promise to raise the standards higher. *Fluff Boy,* an excellent 5.13c, is east of the picnic area in Sno-Cone Cave. Reach it by crossing Rifle Creek via logs and following a trail east and south to the steep, shallow cave. The Arsenal, a long, overhanging wall, stretches west of the road just upcanyon. Park at the wall's base at 0.8 mile. Most of the routes lie within 30 seconds of the parking area. Routes at Wicked Cave and the Arsenal are listed south to north. Bolt counts do not include anchors.

WICKED CAVE

1. **Deity** (5.13b) A steep route up the cave's south side. Above is a project.
2. **The Crew** (5.14b) Difficult Chris Knuth route. Lots of kneebars.
3. **Zulu** (5.14a/b) Long-time project freed by Chris Sharma in 1996. Very dynamic.
4. **Slice of Life** (5.13d) Kurt Smith finally fired the Slice, one of Colorado's hardest routes, after more than 50 falls at dyno crux. It's a long, pumpy

RIFLE MOUNTAIN PARK
THE ARSENAL & WICKED CAVE

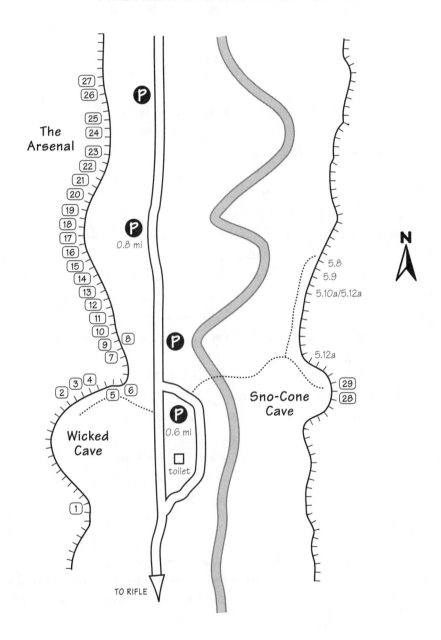

The
Arsenal

27
26
25
24
23
22
21
20
19
18
17
16
15
14
13
12
11
10
9
8
7
6
5
4
3
2
1

P

P
0.8 mi

P

P
0.6 mi

toilet

Wicked
Cave

5.8
5.9
5.10a/5.12a

5.12a

Sno-Cone
Cave

29
28

N

TO RIFLE

pitch with several hard cruxes, including a traverse above the dyno. Look for kneebars. The last 30' after the crux is sustained and strenuous.

5. **Cryptic Egyptian** (5.13b) An excellent long pitch. Many redpoint attempts fail on final moves to anchors.

6. **Atheist Mass** (5.12c) Sharp, dynamic, continuous pitch.

THE ARSENAL

7. **Bissell Missile** (5.12b) Loose and somewhat funky. 7 bolts.

8. **Plastic Orgasmic** (5.13) Project.

9. **Pretty Hate Machine** (5.12b/c) Classic route. 8 bolts.

10. **Matador Pants** (5.12d) Dirty with crux at the top. 9 bolts.

11. **Piletronix** (5.12d) A pile! 9 bolts.

12. **Slagissimo** (5.12d) A superb, classic route. 8 bolts.

13. **Spurtatron** (5.13a) Sustained. 11 bolts.

14. **Path** (5.13b) Excellent. Sustained headwall. 11 bolts.

15. **Jambor-Knee** (5.13b) Two cruxes separated by rests. 11 bolts.

16. **Sprayathon** (5.13c) A Rifle mega-classic. Excellent rock at top. 10 bolts.

17. **Colinator** (5.13d) Long route. Three difficult cruxes. 14 bolts.

18. **Pump-o-Rama** (5.12d) Excellent route. 10 bolts.

19. **Doctor Epic** (5.13c) A difficult, rarely climbed route. 10 bolts.

20. **Rendezspew** (5.13a/b) Kneebar crux followed by sustained headwall. 12 bolts.

21. **Vitamin H** (5.12c/d) A superb pumpy classic. 11 bolts.

22. **Debaser** (5.12d) Classic. 8 bolts.

23. **Dope Party** (5.12d) Hard under roof. 7 grey cold-shuts.

24. **Bruit de Cochon** (5.12c/d) 7 bolts.

25. **Black Caesar** (5.12c) A short route left of tree. 6 bolts.

26. **Smarmicus Maximus** (5.12b) Good line right of tree. 7 bolts.

27. **Pollinator** (5.12a) Slopey and polished. 8 bolts.

SNO-CONE CAVE

28. **Fluff Boy** (5.13b/c) An excellent bouldery route up the cave's center.

29. **Dry Doctor** (5.13a) A Steve Hong line up the left side. Incredibly sustained pitch. Just up the wall from Sno-Cone Cave are a couple of multi-pitch 5.12a's, and a 5.9 and 5.8 up a slab to a long prominent roof.

THE WASTELAND

This area, the first to be developed at Rifle, is 1 mile from the canyon entrance. Park in a large pullout on the west side of the road immediately after crossing the creek. Toilets are at the north end of the parking area. Cross the road and walk to the base of the wall. The cave on the left is The Wasteland, while The Nappy Dugout is reached by a short trail to the south. Routes are listed from south to north. Bolt counts do not include anchors.

30. **Drunken Monkey** (5.12c) One hard move. 5 bolts. CANTINA BOY (5.12d) to right.

31. **Lung Fish** (5.14a) Hard and bouldery. 10 bolts.

32. **Fringe Dweller** (5.13a) Bouldery and steep. 6 bolts.

33. **Frizzle Fry** (5.12d) A left-to-right traverse up the crack/break. 7 bolts.

34. **Fossil Family** (5.12a) Go left part-way up for a good 5.11. Right is .12a. 7 bolts.

35. **Family Unit** (5.12d) Continues through difficult roof above 1st anchors. 10 bolts.

36. **Cappucino** (5.12c) A 2nd pitch, CAPPUCINO CORNER (5.11b), goes up hanging dihedral above. Done in 1 pitch with CAPPACINO, this becomes one of Rifle's longest routes. 20 bolts.

37. **Espresso** (5.12c) Up 7 bolts of #36, then past 3 more bolts to anchors.

38. **Gunshy** (5.12c) Continuous and excellent. Hard start. 8 bolts.

39. **Thieves** (5.13a) Slab crux. Classic route. End at #38 anchors. 5 bolts.

40. **The Beast** (5.12d/.13a) A classic. 6 bolts.

41. **Never Believe** (5.12d) Excellent. End at BEAST'S anchors. 5 bolts.

42. **Vision Thing** (5.13a) Classic Kurt Smith route. Rest on ledge below roof. 14 bolts.

43. **Slacker** (5.12d) Long dyno to hole. 2nd crux is deadpoint. 4 bolts.

44. **Ruckus** (5.12b) A good short warm-up. End at #43 anchors. 5 bolts.

45. **Guilt Parade** (5.12c) Long and vertical. Good rock. 11 bolts.

46. **Lady Luck** (5.12c) Good, long line over small roofs. 9 bolts.

47. **Public Service** (5.11d) Long and excellent. Popular. 9 bolts.

48. **Popular Demand** (5.10c) Somewhat loose, but one of the easier routes here. 8 bolts.

Across the creek and up Koper Trail past the First Ice Cave are some popular warm-up and easier routes on the Good Moanin' Wall. From left to right: **Bumblebee** (5.9); **Smell the Coffee** (5.11c); **Good Moanin'** (5.11a); **Wake Up Call** (5.10a); **Continental Breakfast** (5.10b); **Mel's Diner** (5.11a); and **Plastic**

Prince (5.11b). Keep a low profile here and don't hog the routes or the trail—it's a popular hiking path and complaints have been lodged about the climbers here.

RIFLE MOUNTAIN PARK
THE WASTELAND & FIRST ICE CAVE

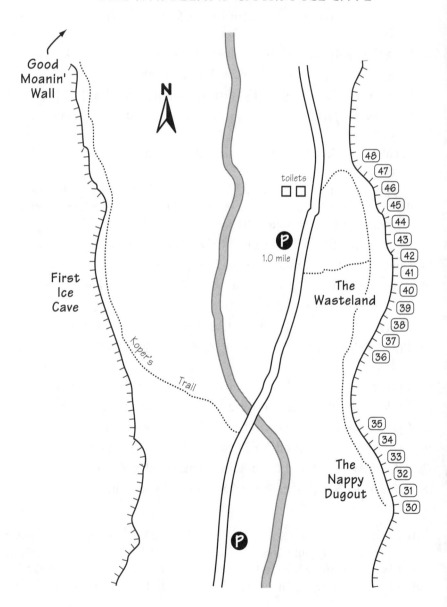

THE ANTI-PHIL WALL AND WINCHESTER CAVE

These two walls rise on the west side of the canyon. Park in a pullout on the left side of the road at 1.7 miles. Cross the stream on a log bridge and turn south or left along Koper Trail. The Anti-Phil Wall is a short hike west from the trail, while Winchester Cave lies just down-canyon. Routes are listed from south to north starting with Winchester Cave. Bolt counts do not include anchors.

WINCHESTER CAVE

49. **Ricochet** (5.12a) Sustained and slabby. Excellent. 11 bolts.

50. **Puppy Love** (5.12a) Poorly bolted. 8 bolts.

51. **Project.** 3 bolt project joins #52.

52. **Unknown.** (5.13+) 6 bolts.

53. **Truth or Lies.** (5.13a) 10 bolts. 8 bolt project to right.

54. **Lung Biscuit.** (5.12d) 4 bolts to anchors.

55. **Unknown.** 6 bolts.

56. **Kill for a Thrill** (5.13a) Good steep line. 7 bolts.

57. **Fully Automatic** (5.12c) Over left-angling corners. 9 bolts.

58. **Quick Draws** (5.12c) Pumpy crux down low. Easier uphigh. 9 bolts.

59. **Guns 'n' Posers** (5.11d) 8 bolts.

THE ANTI-PHIL WALL

A bunch of new routes have gone in left of **Sing It in Russian.** From left to right—**Philandery** (5.12b), **Land Phil** (5.12a), **Fullphilment** (5.11c), and **Philanthropy** (5.11b).

60. **Sing It in Russian** (5.12b) Left of main wall. 6 bolts.

61. **Serpentine** (5.12c) Left side of wall. 6 bolts.

62. **Movement of Fear** (5.12c) Classic. Over inverted-V roof. 8 bolts.

63. **Easy Skanking** (5.12b) Excellent route. Need a 200' rope to lower from the anchors. 11 bolts.—**Philosophy** (5.12d) is just right. 11 bolts.

64. **I'm Not Worthy** (5.13a) Sustained. Begins at bottom of ramp. 9 bolts. **Philistine** (5.13b/c) to right. 10 bolts.

65. **The Anti-Phil** (5.13a) Excellent. Crimpy and continuous. Alternate finish (5.13b/c). 14 bolts.

66. **Poetic Justice** (5.12d) Hard roof and headwall. 8 bolts.

67. **Eurotrash** (5.13b) Sustained. 7 bolts.

68. **Philibuster** (5.12c/d) Good and sustained. Up arete. 7 bolts.

69. **Def Jam** (5.12d) Hard clips. 8 bolts.

Up the hill to the right are four new routes—**Purple and Green** (5.10d), **Quasimodo** (5.11b), **The Dancing Pickle** (5.11c), and **Bong 30** (5.13a).

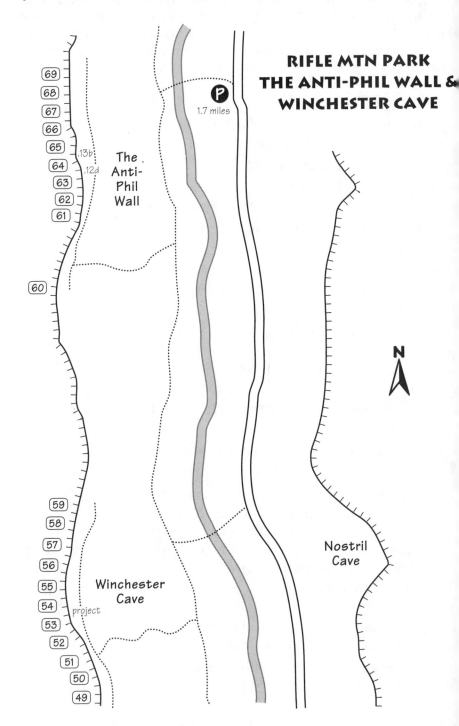

PROJECT WALL

The Project Wall, towering east of the road on a bend, offers long and difficult routes up a vertical to overhanging wall. The parking area, at 1.8 miles, is small and cramped, with room for only three cars. If the parking lot is full, park just up the road at the Firing Chamber and walk down. Do not park on the road itself. Violators will be ticketed. Also do not belay or stand on the road and obstruct traffic. Bolt counts do not include anchors.

70. **Eighth Day** (5.13a) Long and excellent. Need two ropes to get off. 22 bolts.

71. **Bottom Feeder** (5.11c) Up trough to anchors below slab. 7 bolts.

72. **Irie Meditation** (5.11d) Begin right of pedestal. End below corner. 11 bolts.

73. **Physical Therapy** (5.11c) Up right side of pillar to anchors on ledge. 11 bolts.

74. **Fist Full o' Dollars** (5.11c) Left side of pillar. Good warm-up. 12 bolts.

75. **Hang 'em High** (5.12b) Sustained and technical. Begin below X-cracks. 12 bolts.

76. **Defenseless Betty** (5.11d) Excellent. 2 roofs to corners and groove. 13 bolts.

77. **Mousetrap** (5.12d) Very long route. 2 pitches. Up-angling groove. **Pitch 1** is 13 bolts. **Pitch 2** is 3 bolts.

78. **Apocalypse '91** (5.13a/b) A long, pumpy, endurance route. Crux is clipping 15 bolts.

79. **Gay Science** (5.13c) Lots of kneebars. Bouldery. Very overhung. 10 bolts.

80. **Simply Read** (5.13d) An excellent route. A boulder problem start followed by crux at the lip. 11 bolts.

(Three bolted projects are between SIMPLY READ and SOMETIMES ALWAYS.)

81. **Sometimes Always** (5.13b) Sustained to dihedral. 16 bolts.

82. **Living in Fear** (5.13c/d) Super route. Very continuous. 15 bolts.

(Three bolted projects are between LIVING IN FEAR and LESS THAN ZERO.

83. **Less Than Zero** (5.12c) On streaked wall left of Project Wall. Begin on pedestal. 10 bolts.

84. **Rumor Has It** (5.11a\b) Long and good route. 125' pitch. Use two ropes to rap off. 1st route in canyon. 11 bolts.

85. **Cool World** (5.11d) 10 bolts.

86. **Handi Boy** (5.12b) Rated to first anchors; project above. Good short route up shallow cave. 8 bolt project left of cave.

87. **Right El Sapper** (5.12a) Good and pumpy. 7 bolts.

88. **Left El Sapper** (5.11d) One tough move. Finish at #87 anchors. 5 bolts.

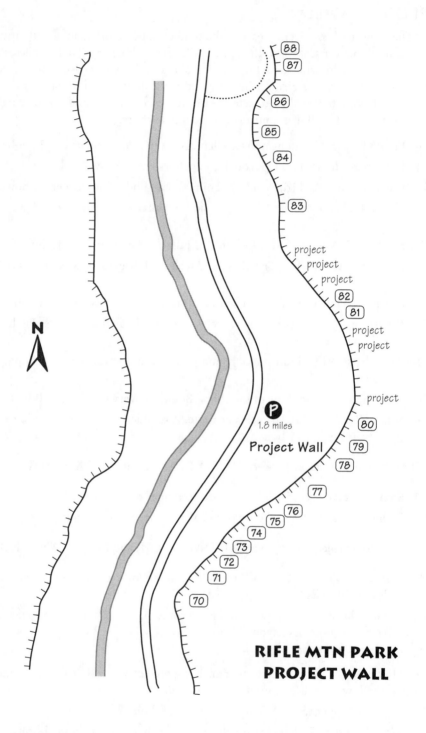

N

88
87
86
85
84
83
project
project
project
82
81
project
project
project
P
1.8 miles
Project Wall
80
79
78
77
76
75
74
73
72
71
70

**RIFLE MTN PARK
PROJECT WALL**

THE FIRING CHAMBER AND THE MEAT WALL

These two walls, on opposites sides of the canyon, are the most popular crags in the canyon. Both offer excellent routes with a wide range of difficulty. The large parking area is 1.9 miles from the cattle guard at the canyon entrance. Park close together so others have room to park. Two pit-toilets are at the north end of the parking lot. The Firing Chamber, on the canyon's west side, is accessed via a log-jam footbridge. Bring a rope tarp; it's awfully dusty at the cliff base now. The Meat Wall lies east of the road. Approach via a short trail just north of the parking area. Routes are listed from south to north beginning with The Firing Chamber. Bolt counts do not include anchors.

THE FIRING CHAMBER

89. **Shiboomi** (5.12d) Stems and pulls over left-angling corners. 12 bolts.

90. **Promise** (5.12c) 3rd class to start. 200' rope. 10 bolts.

91. **Beer Run** (5.13a). Long pitch. 200' rope. Difficult crux up high. 11 bolts.

92. **Choss Family Robinson** (5.11b). Somewhat blocky. On left side of cave. 9 bolts.

93. **Head Full of Lead** (5.11d) Loose and dangerous. No hanger on 2nd bolt.

94. **Street Knowledge** (5.12b) Sustained pocket and edge route. 5 bolts.

95. **Bolt Action** (5.11d) Great warm-up to first anchors under roof. 7 bolts. Continue above roof past 7 more bolts in a long pitch (5.13a) to upper anchors. Two ropes off.

96. **Pump Action** (5.12b) Good route. 6 bolts.

97. **In Your Face** (5.12d) Sustained line up right side of cave. 7 bolts.

98. **Unknown** (5.12c) A pile of loose tottering rubble.

99. **Firearms** (5.12a) Quality, technical climbing to dihedral. First bolt on #100, then left. 10 bolts.

100. **Primer** (5.11a). A good warm-up route. 9 bolts.

101. **Pellet Gun** (5.10c). An easier warm-up. Popular and polished. 5 bolts.

THE MEAT WALL

102. **Cardinal Sin** (5.12a) Right side above trail. Angle-iron hangers. 7 bolts.

103. **Steroid Power** (5.11d) Fun line up a bulge to a slab. 10 bolts.

104. **Sex Machine** (5.11c) Good and popular. 7 bolts.

105. **James Brown's Wild Ride** (5.11d) Good rock. Fine line. 7 bolts.

106. **Project.** Hangers are gone.

107. **Cold Cuts** (5.11a) Popular and good. Right of path. 9 cold-shuts to open-shuts.

108. **80 Feet of Meat** (5.11a) Popular and pumpy. Hard at top. 9 bolts.

109. **Dirt** (5.12d) Right side of bulge. Wet until late in season. 7 bolts.

110. **Le Specimen** (5.12c) Up middle of bulge. Technical. 7 bolts.

111. **Bulges of Munge** (5.10d) Follow trail upstream from bridge. Excellent rock. Sharp. 7 bolts.

RIFLE MOUNTAIN PARK
THE FIRING CHAMBER & THE MEAT WALL

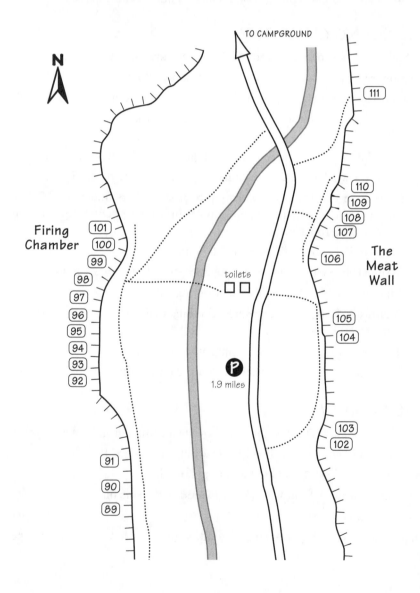

GRAND JUNCTIONAREA

COLORADO NATIONAL MONUMENT

OVERVIEW

West of the Continental Divide, Colorado's geography and climate abruptly change on the edge of the Colorado Plateau. The dark evergreen forests and green alpine meadows vanish. Instead the air becomes bone dry, with the hot sun beating down and desiccating the land. Bare rock is the defining element of the Colorado Plateau, a vast upland desert province that encompasses western Colorado, most of Utah, and northern New Mexico and Arizona. Rimrock escarpments, slickrock pavements, sandstone pinnacles, and rock-walled canyons are everywhere on the plateau. It's a sharp angular landscape, composed of a distinctive rock architecture that forms mesas, buttes, cuestas, spires, buttresses, pillars, cliffs, and headlands; all fantastically shaped by sun, wind, and water.

Colorado National Monument, a 32-square-mile parkland, protects a spectacular slice of the Colorado Plateau just outside Grand Junction near the Utah border. Here, on the northern edge of the Uncompahgre Plateau's great rounded hump, hide deep canyons carved into dipping sandstone layers. The monument's rock landscape lies open like a giant geologic book. Each rock formation is a chapter that tells ancient tales of long-ago swamps populated by dinosaurs, immense wind-swept dune fields, mountain ranges poking above sluggish seas, and beaches washed with emerald tides. The dark basement rock that carpets the canyon floors at the monument formed some 1.5 billion years ago in a lifeless, barren world. Above lie sandstone layers deposited much later during the Mesozoic Era beginning 200 million years ago. The Chinle, Wingate, Kayenta, Entrada, Morrison, Burro Canyon, and Dakota formations all form distinctive natural features.

Rock climbers are most interested in the Wingate and Kayenta formations, the two dominant rocks at the monument. The fine-grained, buff-colored Wingate sandstone, forming the monument's cliffs and spires, tells a story of deserts, wind, and shifting sand. Look closely at the rock and notice the clues that point to its sand dune origin—long, curving striations; thin layers of frosted sand; and cross-bedded layers that mirror a dune's shape. Atop the Wingate lies a thin, coarse layer of stream-deposited Kayenta sandstone, a hard erosion-resistant rock that protects the softer, under-lying Wingate from eroding away. A good example is Independence Monument. The white Kayenta caprock forms the spire's huge flat summit and slows erosion below. In contrast, the nearby Coke Ovens have lost their protective cap, leaving small, pointed summits atop their rounded spires.

Colorado National Monument offers some of Colorado's most unusual rock climbing adventures on its unique sandstone spires and cliffs. This special place, more akin to Utah's canyon country than anything else in Colorado, leaves the climber in awe at the beauty and serenity of these high desert canyons. Excellent Wingate sandstone, superb crack systems, and numerous spires attract climbers to the monument. Spires here include Independence Monument, Sentinel Spire, Pipe Organ Spire, Kissing Couple, Egypt Rock, Pharaoh Point, Clueless Tower, and Cleopatra's Couch.

Independence Monument, the tallest at 350 feet high, is the monument's most popular climb. The huge, fin-like pinnacle, perched between Monument and Wedding canyons, boasts a long and colorful climbing history that began with its first ascent by eccentric John Otto on July 4, 1911, to celebrate Independence Day. Otto, a trailblazer, promoter, outdoorsman, patriot, and rock

Independence Monument separates Wedding and Monument canyons below Rim Rock Drive in Colorado National Monument. *Photo by Stewart M. Green.*

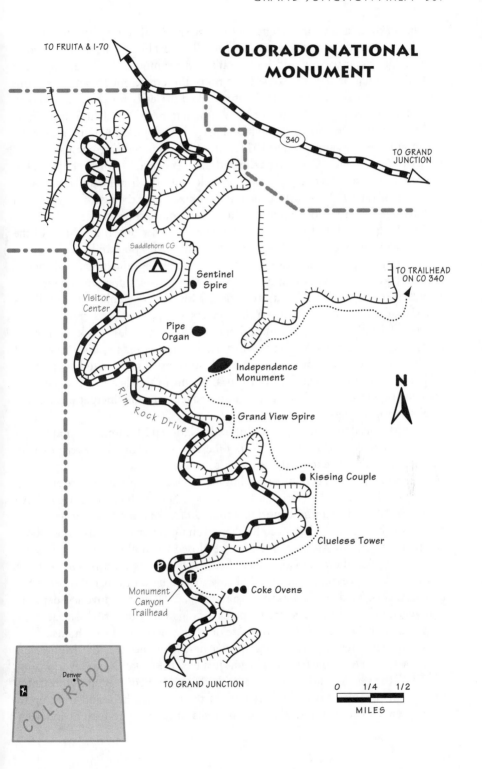

COLORADO NATIONAL MONUMENT

TO FRUITA & I-70

340

TO GRAND JUNCTION

TO TRAILHEAD ON CO 340

Saddlehorn CG

Sentinel Spire

Visitor Center

Pipe Organ

Independence Monument

Rim Rock Drive

N

Grand View Spire

Kissing Couple

Clueless Tower

P
T

Monument Canyon Trailhead

Coke Ovens

Denver

COLORADO

TO GRAND JUNCTION

0   1/4   1/2

MILES

climber, moved into a canvas tent beneath the spire in 1906. He wrote, "I came here last year and found these canyons, and they feel like the heart of the world to me. I'm going to stay and build trails and promote this place, because it should be a national park. Some folks think I'm crazy, but I want to see this scenery opened up to all people." Otto worked tirelessly for the establishment of Colorado National Monument by writing letters to President Taft, guiding tourists through the canyons, and building trails with pick and dynamite. After the monument was approved in 1911, Otto was appointed custodian at a grand salary of $1 a month. Otto first ascended Independence Monument after laboriously drilling a ladder of pipes and footholds into the friable sandstone. Atop the spire he raised Old Glory, a custom he followed for the next few years. All of Otto's hardware is long gone, but his classic route still remains.

Climbing at Colorado National Monument is a serious affair. Most of the routes range from 1 to 6 pitches in length, with fixed rappel and belay anchors on the more popular lines. Use care when climbing on sandstone. Bad rock—fragile flakes, loose blocks, and soft, sandy sections—is often encountered. A helmet provides essential head protection. Most of the climbing here follows cracks, including everything from thin fingers and perfect hand cracks to desperate off-widths and super-wide chimneys. Bring a standard rack with wired stoppers, nuts, and extra Friends for most ascents. Tri-cams, Big Dudes, and Big Bros are necessary on many off-width sections. Use your judgment as to what's needed. Bring two 165-foot ropes for most rappels and extra slings to rethread rappel anchors. The extreme heat and temperature fluctuations quickly weaken rappel slings.

Climbers need to be sensitive to Colorado National Monument's unique ecological and geological resources. Walk on established trails wherever possible. The desert soils are extremely sensitive to human impacts and take years to recover from damage. A number of climbing rules and regulations are enforced at the monument by the National Park Service. No climbing is allowed above or within 100 feet of a tunnel portal, within 50 feet of a roadway, or within 50 feet of any rock art site. Balanced Rock in Fruita Canyon and Mushroom Rock on the north end of Monument Mesa are closed to climbing. Some areas are temporarily closed on a seasonal basis because of nesting raptors. No portable power drills are permitted. Use only brown webbing on rappel and belay anchors. Anchor hardware needs to be camouflaged. Do not remove soil deposits and vegetation from cracks, attach precast holds to natural rock surfaces, or chip and alter the rock surface to create or enlarge hand and foot holds.

All of the spires require hiking approaches. Most lie near the Monument Canyon Trail, a 6.3-mile trail that begins just past the Coke Ovens Overlook on the Rim Rock Road and ends just outside the monument boundary on Colorado Highway 340. Most climbers park at the trailhead here and walk up to their intended route. Allow about 45 minutes to hike to the base of Independence Monument. Some bolted slab routes on Lower Monument Canyon Slabs lie off the trail about 0.5 mile up. The Kissing Couple is best reached from the upper trailhead in the monument. Sentinel Spire is accessed via a rappel from the canyon rim. Either leave the rope fixed and jumar out or hike north from Wedding Canyon to the lower park road or Colorado 340.

Colorado National Monument, like the Black Canyon of the Gunnison, is an excellent adventure climbing arena. The routes listed here are only a few of the many routes that ascend the monument's cliffs and spires. Numerous opportunities exist in all the major canyons for excellent first ascents. Eric Bjornstad's, updated *Desert Rock* guidebook includes numerous new routes in the Monument.

Trip Planning Information

General description: Abrupt sandstone canyons offer rock climbs on numerous towers, including Independence Monument and Sentinel Spire.

Location: Immediately southwest of Grand Junction near the Utah border.

Camping: Saddlehorn Campground is near the visitor center a few miles up Rim Rock Drive from the west entrance. Sites are available on a first-come, first-served basis. The campground is open year-round, with a fee collected in the warmer months, usually May through September. No wood fires are permitted in the campground.

Climbing season: Year-round. Best climbing is during spring and fall months. Expect variable spring weather, with wind and occasional rain showers. Fall days are generally warm and pleasant. Summers can be prohibitively hot, although climbing is possible on many days. Winter days can be warm in the sun or cold and blustery. Snowfall is generally light on this high desert.

Restrictions and access issues: Climbing is not permitted above or within 100 feet of a tunnel portal, above or within 50 feet of a roadway, or above or within 50 feet of a rock art site. Climbing is prohibited on Balanced Rock in Fruita Canyon and Mushroom Rock on the north end of Monument Mesa. Some areas near active raptor nests are temporarily closed and clearly posted with closure signs. Portable power tools and drills are not permitted. Webbing left on routes at rappel stations or anchors should be brown to match the rock color. All anchor hardware including bolts or rappel anchors should be camouflaged. It is illegal to remove soil deposits and vegetation from cracks, to fasten precast holds to natural surfaces (it's happened on boulders just east of the monument boundary), or to chip rock surfaces to create or enlarge hand and foot holds.

Guidebooks: The only guide to the monument is Eric Bjornstad's out-of-print *Desert Rock* from Chockstone Press. A photo-copy in a notebook is kept in the monument visitor center. An updated release of *Desert Rock,* available by 1996, includes numerous new routes in Colorado National Monument.

Nearby mountain shops, guide services, and gyms: Vertical Works Climbing

Ed Webster jams the first pitch of *Fast Draw* on Sentinel Spire in Colorado National Monument. *Photo by Stewart M. Green.*

Gym and Pro Shop, Summit Canyon Mountaineering, Tower Guides/Andy Petefish, Natural Progression Rock Guides (Grand Junction).

Services: All services in Grand Junction and Fruita.

Emergency services: Call 911. Community Hospital, 2021 N. 12th St., Grand Junction, CO 81501, (970) 242-0920. St. Mary's Hospital and Medical Center, Seventh St. and Patterson Road, Grand Junction, CO 81501, (970) 244-2273.

Nearby climbing areas: Unaweep Canyon, Rifle Mountain Park, Escalante Canyon, Black Canyon of the Gunnison, Naturita crags, Fisher Towers (Utah), Castleton Tower (Utah), Wall Street (Utah).

Nearby attractions: Grand Mesa Scenic Byway, Land's End Road, Unaweep Canyon, Unaweep-Tabeguache Scenic Byway, Dolores River Canyon, Rattlesnake Canyon, Black Ridge Canyons BLM Wilderness Study Area, Dominguez Canyons BLM Wilderness Study Area, Ruby and Horsethief Canyons, Colorado River, Rabbit Valley Paleontological Area, Fruita Paleontological Area, Highline State Recreation Area, Grand Junction attractions and Museum of Western Colorado, Mount Garfield, Island Acres State Recreation Area, Dynamations Dinosaur Museum in Fruita.

Finding the crags: Leave Interstate 70 at the Fruita exit (Exit 19) west of Grand Junction. Turn south on Colorado 340 and drive a couple of miles to the monument's west entrance. The 35-mile Rim Rock Drive, beginning here, traverses the high rims of several canyons before dropping down to the monument's east entrance south of Grand Junction. This road allows access via trail to several canyons and climbing sites. Write to the Superintendent, Colorado National Monument, Fruita, CO 81521 for more information on the monument.

INDEPENDENCE MONUMENT

Independence Monument, the monument's most frequented summit, towers 350' above its talus cone between Monument and Wedding canyons. The spire is best approached via the lower Monument Canyon Trail. From the west entrance, continue 2 miles on Colorado 340 to the lower trailhead on the south side of the highway beside a subdivision. Follow the trail for about 45 minutes to the base of Independence Monument's southeast face. Contour around the tower to its northwest flank and *Otto's Route*.

1. **Otto's Route** (II 5.8+) This classic route up the spire's northwest face and upper south ridge is generally climbed in 4 pitches. **Pitch 1** follows an easy, right-angling, 4th class ramp to a chockstone. Above jam a 5.5 crack past some chopped holds 70' to a bolted belay/rappel ledge. **Pitch 2** continues up the widening crack and through a 5.8 squeeze slot with drilled 1" holes from Otto's pipe ladder for 60' to a belay/rappel stance. A large Friend provides security. It's 3rd class through an easy slot—the Time Tunnel—

behind a block up and right to a large ledge. **Pitch 3** offers 5.8 face climb-ing—a relative desert rarity—up the face 80' to a 5.8 mantle onto Lunch Box Ledge on the tower's south ridge. Fixed pitons protect the pitch. Lots of drilled pockets and steps are found. **Pitch 4** (80') is spectacular. It fol-lows chopped steps up the runout, airy prow to some fixed pitons on the final overhanging caprock. A large belay ledge hides above the overhang. Use a 1.5 or 2.0 Tri-cam in a drilled hole for some psychological protection on the runout ridge. The final 10' to the summit itself can be bouldered at 5.8 or aided by standing on a vertical pipe (an old flag pole base), and step up to rappel/anchor slings. **Descend** the route in 3 double-rope rappels. First rappel is a 150' double-rope rappel off the north side of the ledge to the ledge below the 3rd pitch. Second rappel is found by downclimbing (3rd class) through the Time Tunnel to the top of Pitch 2. Rap 60' to a big ledge. Third rappel starts on the east end of the ledge with a 3-bolt chain anchor. Rap 140' with double ropes to the ground. **Rack:** Bring a standard rack along with several large pieces like a #4 Friend or Camalot and double ropes for the descent.

2. **Independence Chimney** (III 5.8 A1) This good chimney route, put up by Mike Dudley and Fletcher Smith in 1970, climbs the left side of the south-east face for 4 pitches to Lunch Box Ledge. Continue to the summit on the last pitch of OTTO'S ROUTE. Begin below a vertical crack to the right of an overhanging corner. **Pitch 1** uses 5 points of aid up the vertical crack;

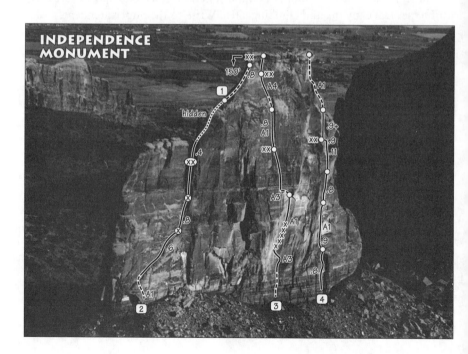

use large wired stoppers, TCUs, and small Friends. Continue past a drilled piton onto a right-leaning ramp. Follow to a fixed pin anchor. **Pitch 2** climbs the obvious wide crack system above. The difficulty eases to 5.6 after a lower 5.8 off-width section. Belay on a sandy stance with a fixed piton in the chimney. **Pitch 3** scales the large chimney to a 2-bolt belay inside the chimney. A 1" to 2" crack inside the chimney provides good protection. **Pitch 4** heads up the 5.4 chimney to Lunch Box Ledge. Continue to the summit on OTTO'S ROUTE and descend from its rappel stations. **Rack:** Bring a standard rack with an emphasis on medium and large Friends; include some off-width protection.

3. **South Face Direct** (IV 5.8 A4) This challenging aid route, first ascended by Mike Dudley, Don Doucette, and Art Howells in 1971, follows a dramatic line up thin cracks in the center of the southeast face. The first ascent party used many pitons from knifeblades to 3" bongs. The line has had few ascents. **Pitch 1** begins directly below the summit near a couple of large boulders. The long 1st pitch, climbing an obvious thin crack system up fractured rock, follows an A3 crack to a bolt ladder and an A1 crack. **Pitch 2** (A3) nails left over roofs to thin cracks and ends at a 2-piton hanging belay. **Pitch 3** nails and free climbs a crack in the Sun Dihedral, a pronounced thin, left-facing corner, to a stance. **Pitch 4** aids thin cracks and flakes, some A4 up high, to a sling belay at drilled pitons. The short **5th pitch** climbs a broken 5.8 A2 crack over the caprock to the summit. **Descend** via OTTO'S ROUTE. **Rack:** Bring a large rack with some thin blades and angles, birdbeaks, sliding nuts, a couple sets of TCUs and Friends, and a lot of free carabiners.

4. **Sundial Dihedral** (III 5.11 A1) This excellent 6-pitch route, put up in 1986 by Ed Webster and Pete Athens, offers superb climbing on clean rock and minimal easy aid on pitches 2 and 6. The route ascends the obvious dihedral system on the right side of the southeast face to the upper north ridge. Webster compares the route's quality and character to THE PRIMROSE DIHEDRALS on Moses in Utah. The route starts below a large 60' pillar that leans against the face. **Pitch 1** climbs the pillar to a ledge. The left side is 5.8 and the right side is a wide 5.10- crack. **Pitch 2** ascends a vertical finger crack with a drilled angle to a small shelf. Climb thin cracks up a white, slightly overhanging 95-degree headwall; a couple moves of A1 here. Above the angle and difficulty ease and the 100' pitch ends on a ledge. **Pitch 3** follows a 5.8 chimney up the corner system 60' to a spacious belay ledge. **Pitch 4** (90') jams and laybacks up a wide, strenuous crack. Use your large gear for pro. Surmount a 5.11 overhang via a fist crack and hand jam to a 5.9 roof. Traverse left under the roof and climb onto a good, airy belay ledge with 2 drilled pitons. **Pitch 5** laybacks and stems 80' up a shallow 5.9+ corner/flake system in a wide slot to a large ledge with a drilled pin

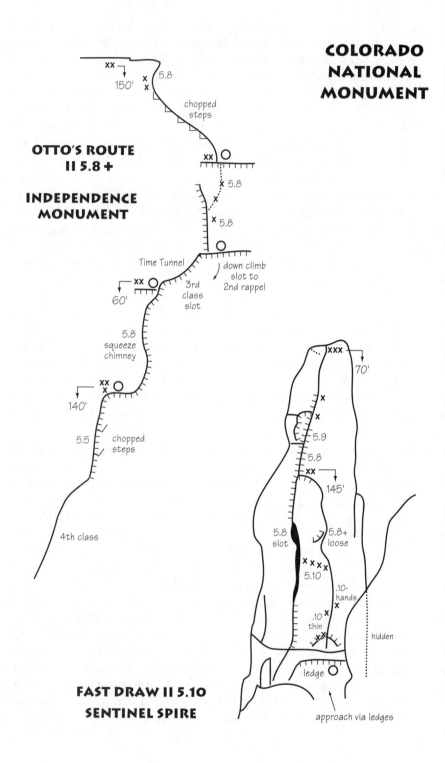

COLORADO NATIONAL MONUMENT

150'

5.8

chopped steps

OTTO'S ROUTE II 5.8 +

INDEPENDENCE MONUMENT

5.8

5.8

Time Tunnel

down climb slot to 2nd rappel

60'

3rd class slot

5.8 squeeze chimney

140'

5.5

chopped steps

4th class

70'

5.9

5.8

145'

5.8 slot

5.8+ loose

5.10

.10- hands

.10 thin

hidden

ledge

FAST DRAW II 5.10 SENTINEL SPIRE

approach via ledges

perched on the north ridge. **Pitch 6** (100') aids up an A1 13-bolt ladder on a steep, blank prow to the summit. **Descend** via OTTO'S ROUTE in 4 double-rope rappels. Rack: **Rack:** Bring a good assortment of large wired stoppers, nuts, a full set of Friends, and a #7 Tri-cam or other large crack pro.

SENTINEL SPIRE

This spectacular finger sits below the west rim of Wedding Canyon just past the Book Cliff View Point on the campground loop road. Two good routes ascend crack systems on the spire. The best approach is via rappel. Park at the overlook parking area and walk south to a point overlooking the pinnacle. A rope can be fixed here for an 80' rappel down a cliff just west of the point. Scramble down slabs to a bench that leads south to the spire's northwest corner. Use ascenders to return to the rim or hike north from the spire to the park road where you can be picked up. If you leave a fixed rope, it's a good idea to have someone on the rim to pull it up or remove it to avoid any tourist problems. The spire can also be approached by walking down Monument Canyon Trail from its start at Coke Ovens Overlook and scrambling up scree slopes to its base. Allow about an hour for this hike.

5. **Fast Draw** (II 5.10) This is an excellent 2-pitch outing to a small, exposed summit. The route, first climbed in 1960, was named for Layton Kor's quick draw and placement of a piton when the bong he was aiding on began to shift out of the crack. The route ascends a prominent crack system on the shaded north side of the tower. Begin from the wide slickrock ledge between Sentinel Spire and the main cliff on the spire's northwest side. **Pitch 1** climbs the obvious finger to hand crack on the right side of the face. Thin finger jams, the route's crux, lead past several old bolts to a 5.9+ hand crack. Use some #2-3 Friends for protection. Near the end of the hand crack a piton-protected 5.10 face traverse leads left to another crack system. Squeeze up the awkward 5.8 crack to a good belay ledge with 2 bolts. Instead of traversing the face, the crack above also goes at 5.8+ to the belay ledge. Watch for some loose rocks in the crack on this section. **Pitch 2** stems the obvious chimney/off-width crack above the belay to the summit anchors. **Descent:** Rappel the route—70' to the belay ledge and 140' to the ground. **Rack:** Bring Friends with some extra #2, 2.5, and 3 Friends, as well as a #4 Friend and/or Camalot for the 2nd pitch.

6. **Medicine Man** (III 5.12c) A brilliant, exposed, and difficult route up the sheer southeast face of Sentinel Spire. It was first climbed in 1986 with some aid, and finally free-climbed by Alan Lester and Pete Takeda in 1994. The 4-pitch route climbs the only crack system on the spire's side that faces Independence Monument. **Pitch 1** jams a 5.10- hand crack and ends at a

MEDICINE MAN
SENTINEL SPIRE

.8

.10d

.11

.12c

.11

.10d

.10a

6

belay ledge. **Pitch 2** climbs a grooved 5.10+ corner then steps left into a 5.11 crack. **Pitch 3**, the crux lead, jams a thin, overhanging crack over a roof to a belay stance in a shallow alcove. **Pitch 4** climbs a corner to a small roof, traverses left under the roof at 5.10+, and jams to the summit. **Descent:** Rappel down FAST DRAW from the summit. **Rack:** Include a set of stoppers and a double set of Friends with several extra #1.5, 2, and 2.5 Friends.

GRAND VIEW SPIRE

This large tower, sitting below Grand View Point, offers a short 2-pitch route to its rubble-strewn summit. The *Southwest Defile Route*, climbing broken crack systems on the southwest side of the monument, is 5 pitches long. The last 2 pitches, easily approached from the rim above, are the best. The seldom-ascended spire was first climbed in 1961. Watch for loose rock on this seldom-climbed route. The saddle can also be reached by climbing a couple of moderate chimney/crack pitches below and to the west.

7.   **Southwest Defile Route** (II 5.8 A2) Approach the route by parking at Grand View Point on Rim Rock Drive and hiking the short trail to the overlook. The route's upper pitches are readily visible on the spire's southwest corner above the narrow saddle that separates Grand View Spire from Monument Canyon's south rim. Scramble down onto ledges south of the spire and fix a rappel rope from several trees. Rappel down into the notch. Bring ascenders to jug back out the fixed rope to the rim. **Pitch 1** begins from the saddle at the tower's upper southwest corner. Climb up past 2 old bolts (A0 or 5.9) and over a couple of small ledges to the base of a prominent, shallow right-facing corner that forms the right side of a pillar. Aid up seams on the left wall of the corner to a small belay stance with an old drilled piton. This goes clean with beaks, ball-nuts, RPs, and small stoppers placed in pin scars. This section would go free with a couple of bolts for protection. **Pitch 2** climb up and right above the belay past a fixed piton to a crack/flake. Layback up the crack to another drilled piton and mantle onto a large ledge on the southeast side of the summit. A short crack leads to the summit itself. **Descent:** A 2-rope rappel descends back to the saddle.

KISSING COUPLE

The Kissing Couple, towering above Monument Canyon, is a 400' semi-detached spire. The rock, first ascended by Layton Kor and party in 1960, offers a very good 5-pitch route up its southern flank. The Kissing Couple is best approached via the Monument Canyon Trail. Drive east on Rim Rock Drive from the visitor center to the Monument Canyon Trailhead just past

Coke Ovens Overlook. The trail, built by John Otto in 1910, descends 600' to the canyon floor. Follow the trail around the Kissing Couple, the large obvious spire split by a chimney below the summit, to its northwest flank. Scramble up scree to the tower's base.

8. **Long Dong Wall Route** (III 5.11a) This spectacular route begins below the notch between the Kissing Couple and the smaller tower to its south. **Pitch 1** jams a 5.10+ finger and hand crack to a drilled piton. Traverse left on 5.11 face climbing (the route's hardest moves) to a belay stance with anchored chains. **Pitch 2** scales the obvious chimney, a couple of 5.7 sections, to another belay ledge with fixed anchors. **Pitch 3** climbs easy blocks into a gully with a belay stance. **Pitch 4** jams the awkward 5.8 off-width above and enters another chimney. Continue up the exposed chimney to The Belfry, the prominent see-through opening, and a belay inside the chimney. **Pitch 5** heads up the huge chimney with spread-eagled stemming and full-body bridging, some 5.10 but harder for short people, past 2 bolts to a belay ledge with rappel chains. A short **Pitch 5** tunnels up through the rock to the summit from here. **Descent:** Rappel the route in 4 double-rope rappels. **Rack:** Bring large stoppers, a few hexes, and a complete set of Friends.

CLUELESS TOWER

This semi-detached spire perches above the Monument Canyon Trail and below the Cleopatra's Couch formation. The only route on the pillar, first ascended in 1993 by Fred Knapp and Bret Ruckman, is a superb, 5-pitch, 450' climb up the south face. Knapp calls it "exceptional, continuous, and exposed...one of the better hard routes in the desert."

9. **Get a Life** (III 5.12c) Approach the route by hiking down Monument Canyon Trail from the rim trailhead near the Coke Ovens Overlook. After switchbacking down through the Wingate sandstone, look up left and locate the obvious crack system up the pillar's south face. **Pitch 1** climbs a loose chimney/groove to a left-facing dihedral. Stem and jam up the corner to a 2" crack (5.11-). Belay above in a niche. **Pitch 2** works up the left-facing dihedral (5.10+) to a spacious ledge with 2 bolts. **Pitch 3**, the crux lead, jams a thin, overhanging finger crack (5.12c) up a right-facing corner above the ledge. This short 40' pitch is difficult and strenuous. Belay on a sloping ledge. **Pitch 4** jams an exposed crack up an arete up and left of the belay ledge. Traverse right under a large roof (5.10d) to a belay ledge with 2 bolts atop a hanging boulder. **Pitch 5** face climbs up left past 2 bolts (5.11-) and makes a scary traverse left (5.8 R) to a drilled piton. Continue up on 5.10 face climbing to anchors beneath the summit. **Descend** the route in 3 double-rope rappels. **Rack:** Bring a standard rack with extra #1.5 and #2 Friends and 2 ropes.

UNAWEEP CANYON

OVERVIEW

The Uncompahgre Plateau, stretching northwest 100 miles from the snowcapped San Juan Mountains to the Grand Valley and the Colorado River, is a humpbacked highland crested with fir, pine, and aspen forests and open meadows. Numerous abrupt canyons carved by quick streams crease the rounded plateau. The canyons slice through ruddy sandstone layers draped over the plateau's ancient bedrock. The plateau's most dramatic canyons lie in Colorado National Monument on its tilted northern flank and in Unaweep Canyon on it's upper mid-section. Unaweep Canyon's steel gray cliffs, ranging in height from 150 to 1,500 feet, are banded with dikes, split by cracks and fissures, and broken into buttresses, castles, and promontories. These numerous walls, lining 25 miles of the canyon, offer an excellent variety of climbing routes that include some of Colorado's best crack lines.

Unaweep Canyon is one of western Colorado's most spectacular but least known natural wonders. The broad U-shaped canyon, its sides walled by towering cliffs, is a unique geologic anomaly. This east-west trending canyon is supposedly the only canyon in the world drained by two creeks that flow in opposite directions from a central divide. Indeed, its Ute Indian name, *Unaweep*, means "Canyon with Two Mouths." The ponderous geologic events that led to the canyon's formation have long puzzled geologists. They agree that the two small creeks that flow in today's canyon could never have excavated this immense chasm. One theory postulates that a deep fault line underlies the canyon, while another credits glaciation with the canyon's formation. The most plausible explanation, based on studies of river gravel deposits at the Gunnison Gravels Natural Research Area in Cactus Park, a half-mile south of the highway, concludes that the canyon was the riverbed of the ancestral Colorado and Gunnison rivers. The Colorado River once ran south from Debeque Canyon and east of Grand Junction before bending west through Unaweep Canyon, while the Gunnison River joined waters with the Colorado just east of today's canyon. The deep river, undoubtedly swollen with glacial meltwater, chiseled down through the plateau's erosion-resistant bedrock and formed this splendid gorge. An eroding tributary creek, however, breached a divide northwest of the plateau and diverted the river's entire flow into the Grand Valley. This erosive action, termed stream piracy, made Unaweep Canyon into a river canyon without a river.

Some of Colorado's oldest exposed rocks are found on the Uncompahgre Plateau and Unaweep Canyon. The canyon's ancient granite and metamorphic rocks date between 1.4 and 1.7 billion years ago from the Precambrian Period. The rocks, similar to those found in the Black Canyon of the Gunnison, include gneiss and granite. The gneiss began as a thick layer of sand, silt, and mud

The Quarry Wall towers above the floor of Unaweep Canyon in western Colorado. *Photo by Stewart M. Green.*

deposited on the floor of a primeval ocean. The sediment hardened into sedimentary rock, which was later drastically altered by heat and pressure into metamorphic rock. Molten magma, intruded into fractures in the buckled metamorphic bedrock, formed coarse dikes and solidified into localized bodies of quartz monzonite, a type of granite. The plateau was uplifted some 300 million years ago forming "Uncompahgria," an ancestral Rocky Mountain range surrounded by seas. Over the next 200 million years the range eroded down to its bedrock roots, with swift streams and rivers depositing layers of silt, sand, and cobbles to the west in today's Utah canyonlands. Later, sandstone strata was deposited atop the ancient bedrock, forming the "Great Unconformity" with almost 500 million years of geologic history missing from the canyon's rock record.

Unaweep Canyon boasts a long, colorful history. The Ute Indians frequented the canyon, using its lush meadows as a summer camp and hunting game on the plateau above. Two abandoned towns flourished on the east end of the canyon in the late 1890s. Copper City and Pearl City arose in 1897 with the discovery of gold, silver, and copper. Copper City became something of a thriving community with two schools, general stores, saloons, brothels, and cabins until it folded in 1914. Pearl City, however, kept the rustic "Camp Four" look until its 1912 demise. In that period no permanent buildings were ever erected. The town remained a village of canvas tents. The Pearl City Hotel offered deluxe accommodations with its three tents joined together. Another historical site is the Driggs Mansion, a stone ruin below Thimble Rock. New York lawyer Lawrence K. Driggs erected the eight-room house between 1914 and 1918. Carved stone mantles over the fireplaces and crystal chandeliers graced its decor. Despite its expensive opulence, the house was probably never occupied until it changed hands and became the Chateau Thimblerock, a hunting lodge. It now sits on the Craig Ranch, one of the canyon's largest ranches.

Climbing history: The canyon's climbing history is brief. Although various parties made forays onto the canyon's cliffs, little is known or recorded of early ascents. K.C. Baum, author of the area guidebook, reports finding some old rusted pitons and hemp rope on the north face of Thimble Rock. Unaweep's modern climbing history begins in the mid-1980s with the systematic exploration and naming of the canyon cliffs by a group of determined Grand Junction locals. Most of the routes were established by local guide K.C. Baum with a variety of ropemates including Andy Petefish, Tom Archibeque, and Jeff Hollenbaugh. Local climbers also purchased, with a generous grant from The Access Fund, some canyon acreage that protected climbing and access to the popular Hidden Valley, Fortress, and Sunday walls. The Quarry Wall offers many excellent and classic 2-pitch crack routes, some of Colorado's very best. At the west end of Unaweep Canyon 9 miles east of Gateway, 1,500-foot Unaweep Wall offers only one route—*Ancient Wisdom* (V/VI 5.11a A3+). This

10-pitch route, soloed by K.C. Baum, is similar in size and quality to The Diamond on Longs Peak. The climbing potential of Unaweep Canyon is only beginning to be recognized. This off-the-beaten-track canyon still offers numerous first ascents for intrepid parties.

Unaweep Canyon is a mixture of both public and private land. Almost all of the valley floor is privately owned by either large ranches or small sub-divided 40-acre land parcels. Most of the canyon cliffs are on private property, with the crag approaches also via private property. The best cliffs to climb on are those owned by The Access Fund or on BLM land. The Access Fund owns Hidden Valley, Fortress, and Sunday walls on the north side of the canyon. An approach trail crosses this Access Fund property. The Quarry Wall, a long southside cliff above the highway, is on BLM land and is easily approached from public land on Divide Road above the cliff or from several small corners of BLM land below the cliff. The potential exists for severe access problems in the canyon. Climbers should keep a low profile and maintain a responsible user ethic that includes carrying out all trash, burying human waste, not damaging fences or scaring livestock, using trails for approaches and pullouts for parking, and not camping anywhere on the valley floor. Be courteous and cooperate with local landowners, ask permission whenever possible to cross their land and climb on their cliffs, and abide by whatever decision they make. Remember, as always, that rock climbing is a privilege, not a right.

Unaweep is a traditional climbing area. Most of the canyon routes follow excellent crack systems. Bolted sport-type routes are also found on several cliffs. Gear is often used to supplement the fixed protection on many of these lines. Local ethics stress preserving the rock resource. Routes have been established from the ground-up and via rappel. Remember, it's the final route that counts, not necessarily the style it was put up in. Place bolts only for free-climbing protection where necessary, not next to protectable cracks. Do not chip or glue holds. Use colored webbing or painted chains at anchors.

Most routes require a rack of some sort. Use your judgment by scoping the line beforehand. A standard rack should include sets of RPs, wired stoppers, and Friends. A selection of TCUs and some off-width pro is advisable on many of the longer routes. Use a 165-foot rope. Most of the fixed rappel stations require double ropes to get down.

The canyon, like most adventure climbing arenas, has objective dangers. Watch for loose rock on ledges and loose flakes. Many routes have not had a lot of ascents and still harbor loose areas. Watch for poison ivy in places. Walk-offs and descents can be tricky and involve some downclimbing and route finding. Err on the side of caution. As K.C. Baum says, "This ain't no sport area, pilgrim!"

Trip Planning Information

General description: A remote and little-known canyon on the Uncompahgre Plateau offers a selection of crack and face routes on granite and gneiss cliffs that range from 150 to 1,500-feet.

Location: 24 miles south of Grand Junction near the Utah border.

Camping: Public camping is available near the canyon on BLM lands. Many good primitive campsites are found along the 6-mile Nine Mile Hill highway section between Whitewater and Unaweep Canyon. Campsites among fine boulders are found between 1.5 miles and 6.5 miles from Whitewater on the north side of the highway. Better camping that is closer to the cliffs is found by turning south on Divide Road 14 miles from Whitewater. Drive 2 miles up the road to the top of the Quarry Wall and cross a cattle guard onto public lands. Several campsites are just west of the road among junipers atop the cliff here. More primitive camping is found farther south along Divide Road as well as at the BLM's Dominguez Campground on the rim above Big Dominguez Creek. All sites are primitive with no facilities or water. Practice no-trace/no-impact camping by using existing fire rings, bringing your own firewood, packing out all trash, and burying all human waste.

Climbing season: Year-round. April through October offers the best weather here, with generally warm days and cool nights. Summer days on the south-facing crags can be hot with temperatures up to 90 degrees. Occasional thunderstorms occur on summer afternoons. Winter brings climbable weather, although heavy snows can fall and linger in the canyon through the winter. The south-facing cliffs dry quickly after snowfall with sunny days.

Restrictions and access issues: Unaweep Canyon is a mixture of BLM public lands and private land. Most of the canyon floor as well as several of the northside crags are privately owned. Most of the area's routes are on private land or are approached on private land. A great increase in climber traffic or climber irresponsibility and misuse could lead to cliff closures. Remember that climbing here, as in other Colorado areas, is a privilege, not a right. Behave accordingly by respecting landowner's rights and concerns. Be courteous and ask permission whenever possible.

Guidebooks: *Grand Junction Rock: Rock Climbs of Unaweep Canyon and Adjacent Areas* by K.C. Baum, 1992. This self-published book is available at climbing shops in Grand Junction. It's a complete guide to Unaweep's many cliffs with excellent topos and gear lists and comprehensive descriptions by the area's most prolific pioneer. An updated version will be available in the near future.

Nearby mountain shops, guide services, and gyms: Vertical Works Climbing Gym and Pro Shop, Summit Canyon Mountaineering, Tower Guides/Andy Petefish, Natural Progression Rock Guides (Grand Junction).

Services: All services in Grand Junction.

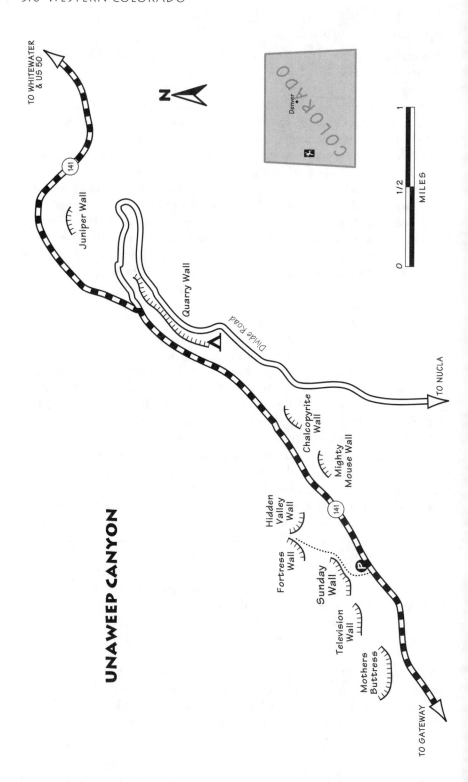

UNAWEEP CANYON

TO WHITEWATER
& US 50

COLORADO

Denver

N

MILES
0   1/2   1

Juniper Wall

Quarry Wall

Divide Road

TO NUCLA

Chalcopyrite Wall

Mighty Mouse Wall

Hidden Valley Wall

Fortress Wall

Sunday Wall

Television Wall

Mothers Buttress

TO GATEWAY

Emergency services: Call 911. Community Hospital, 2021 N. 12th St., Grand Junction, CO 81501, (970) 242-0920. St. Mary's Hospital and Medical Center, Seventh St. and Patterson Road, Grand Junction, CO 81501, (970) 244-2273.

Nearby climbing areas: Colorado National Monument, Dolores River Canyon, Rifle Mountain Park, Escalante Canyon, Black Canyon of the Gunnison, Naturita crags, Fisher Towers (Utah), Castleton Tower (Utah), Wall Street (Utah).

Nearby attractions: Grand Mesa Scenic Byway, Land's End Road, Unaweep Canyon, Unaweep-Tabeguache Scenic Byway, Dolores River Canyon, Rattlesnake Canyon, Black Ridge Canyons BLM Wilderness Study Area, Dominguez Canyons BLM Wilderness Study Area, Ruby and Horsethief canyons, Colorado River, Museum of Western Colorado (Grand Junction), Dynamations Dinosaur Museum (Fruita).

Finding the crags: From Grand Junction drive south about 8 miles on U.S. Highway 50 (or drive north from Montrose and Delta on US 50) to Whitewater. Turn west here on Colorado Highway 141 and continue up into the canyon.

The highway climbs Nine Mile Hill in the lower east section of the canyon and passes through bands of Dakota sandstone and an excellent array of large sandstone blocks for bouldering. About 13.5 miles from Whitewater the highway reaches the Divide Road below the east end of The Quarry Wall. The Divide Road runs south along the crest of the Uncompahgre Plateau for more than 100 miles.

The Fortress, Hidden Valley, and Sunday walls lie 2 miles farther west up the canyon on Colorado 141. Park in a designated pulloff on the north side of the highway and follow the marked access trail northeast to the crags. Unaweep Divide, a broad 7,048-foot saddle that separates East and West creeks, is 5.5 miles west of Divide Road. Beyond this divide the highway dips west past more crags including landmark Thimble Rock and 1,500-foot Unaweep Wall. The road continues west down the narrowing scenic canyon to Gateway and the Dolores River near the Utah border.

SUNDAY WALL

The Sunday Wall, one of the most popular crags, is a long wall on the north side of the canyon. The cliff, reaching heights of 600', lies 2 miles west of Divide Road. Park at a designated roadside pulloff below the wall and follow a marked trail to the base of the rock. Total walking time is about 10 minutes. Sunday Wall is a huge, complicated cliff with numerous corners, dihedrals, crack systems, and ledges. Routes are listed from left to right.

1. **Napa Valley (III 5.11)** This good 4-pitch route jams crack systems up the tallest part of the cliff. Begin about 50' up and left of the toe of a large pillar in the middle of the wall. Bring pro to 4". **Pitch 1** climbs a large left-facing

SUNDAY WALL
WEST SIDE

dihedral via a 5.9 hand crack and chimney. Pass a large chockstone and work up left to a belay shelf beneath a small roof after 110'. **Pitch 2** works left and jams a steep hand crack 100' to a belay ledge atop a pillar. **Pitch 3** moves up left (some 5.11) 50' to a belay in a notch. **Pitch 4** jams a finger and hand crack (5.10) in a corner 110' to a good ledge. **Pitch 5** climbs easy rock 80' to the top of the wall.

2.   **Don Juan** (5.6) This 1-pitch, 55' line climbs the bottom of the prominent buttress in the wall's mid-section. Begin at the toe of the buttress. Jam a hand crack (5.6 at the start) to a ledge. Jam up right in another crack to a large terrace below a wide white dike. **Descend** by scrambling west down 3rd-class rock to a boulder with rappel slings. Rap 35' to the ground.

3.   **Bandito** (5.8+) Begin 15' right of DON JUAN. This 1-pitch route follows a finger crack 50' to the large terrace. The first few feet are 5.8+ and difficult to protect. **Descend** via DON JUAN'S rap route to the left. **Rack:** Bring a selection of small wired nuts, TCUs, and medium Friends.

4.   **Three's Company** (5.7+) This 60' crack route begins about 40' right and uphill from BANDITO below a left-facing corner. Jam a finger (5.7) and hand crack up right to an awkward off-width (5.7+). Chimney above to a ledge. **Descend** 3rd-class ledges left and down to the rap station.

5.   **Bridge of Air** (5.12b) This brilliant classic route offers airy positions, strenuous climbing, great protection, and superb rock. The route climbs the left side of a beautiful face streaked with white dikes. Begin atop a block below the face and right of a large right-facing corner system. Face climb up left to a small roof. Undercling right under the roof and layback to a stance below a shallow right-facing corner. Face climb up the corner (5.12b) and work left into a finger crack. Belay from bolts after 130' on a ledge. 11 bolts and double anchors. **Descent:** Rappel the route with 2 ropes. **Rack:** Bring some TCUs and small cams for the upper crack.

6.   **Simple Mind** (5.11a) A short sport route right of BRIDGE OF AIR. Start atop the square block and face climb up right past 5 bolts to a stance with a 2-bolt anchor. **Descent:** Rappel 35' to the ground.

7.   **Optical Illusions** (5.11b A0) Begin just right of the block. Face climb up right past 6 bolts (5.11b just before the last bolt) and work left onto the SIMPLE MIND ledge. Belay from 2 bolts. Climb good rock above past 3 bolts (A0 at first) to a finger crack. Jam to a ledge with double bolts. **Descent:** Rap 75' to the ground. **Rack:** Bring TCUs and small Friends for the upper crack.

8.   **Monkey Gone To Heaven** (5.12+) Start behind a dead tree below a white dike X. Climb straight up the steepening wall 75' to a good ledge with 1 bolt. 9 bolts. **Descent:** Rap with 1 rope.

9. **Burnt Beautician** (5.12b) This 9-bolt line works straight up a seam on the vertical wall past 9 bolts to a stance with 2 bolts. **Descent:** Rap 140' to the ground.

10. **Hairdresser on Fire** (5.13 project) Climb past 3 bolts on steep, streaked rock 50' to a double anchor. Continue up right 25' past another bolt to a ledge.

11. **Antlers on Sunday** (5.10) This 1-pitch route begins behind a small tree and below an obvious roof. Jam a crack—fingers and off-width—to the roof. Turn it on the left (5.10) and work up a left-facing corner to a ledge. **Descent:** Rap 60' from a tree. **Rack:** Bring small to medium-sized pro.

12. **People Are Poodles Too** (III 5.10a A0) This 5-pitch route follows cracks, ramps, and corners to the top of the wall. Begin some 40' right of ANT-LERS ON SUNDAY below a narrow, right-facing corner. **Pitch 1** climbs the corner (5.10 or A0) in a finger and hand crack to a ledge with a large, prominent pine tree. **Pitch 2** moves up and left on a broken, left-diagonaling ramp system to a good ledge. **Pitch 3** face climbs up to a large right-facing dihedral. Jam and stem the dihedral (5.10) to a long ledge. **Pitch 4** begins by walking left on the ledge for about 100' and setting up a belay below a right-facing, right-leaning dihedral. Climb cracks in the dihedral (5.8) up right past an obvious large roof to a good ledge atop a pillar. **Pitch 5** climbs a prominent series of right-facing dihedrals up and left to the top. **Descend** by walking about 150 paces east to the belay/rappel station on top of SUN DANCER. Downclimb 25' to the Metolius bolts and rap 155' to Sundeck Ledge. A 135' rappel from there will deposit you at a notch. Scramble east to the ground. **Rack:** Bring a standard rack with at least 1, 4" piece and 2 ropes for the rappels.

13. **Standard Route** (5.7) This 150' 1-pitch route is farther east on the face from the preceding routes. Walk east along the cliff base to a blocky gully below a left-facing dihedral and just uphill from a small tree. Climb a hand crack (5.6) just right of a chimney 40' to a ledge. Step left and continue up a crack system (5.7) in a left-facing corner to another ledge below a dike. Continue above up a chimney (5.7) to a belay on a long, large ledge. Walk east 30' and make a 4th-class move up to a ledge with belay/rappel anchors for SATISFACTION GUARANTEED'S pitch below Sundeck Ledge. **Descent:** Rappel 150' with double ropes from 2 Metolius eye bolts. **Rack:** Bring 2 ropes and a rack of small to medium nuts and Friends.

14. **Black Dynamite** (5.10) A good 40' variation start to the STANDARD ROUTE. Start right of the STANDARD ROUTE and jam a left-leaning finger crack (5.10) over a bulge on a streaked wall. Continue up left in a hand crack, and finish up a 5.9+ finger crack to a ledge. Continue up the STANDARD ROUTE.

15. **Sweet Sunday Serenade** (III 5.9) This classic 3-pitch route scales the right side of the cliff. Begin just right of an alcove below a left-facing dihedral. **Pitch 1** (135') stems up the dihedral (5.8-) and into a good hand crack (5.7). Continue up the finger and hand crack past a dike to a spacious ledge with 2 bolts. **Pitch 2** scales the crack (5.9) for 20'. Step left to a finger crack and climb up and left 75' to a ledge in a dike just below Sundeck Ledge. An excellent alternate pitch is SATISFACTION GUARANTEED (5.9). Climb the obvious crack in a left-facing corner to a right-arching flake. Layback, heel hook, and face climb up right to a finger slot. Continue laybacking and face climbing up a seam to a finger crack and ledge. Finish up a 5.8 crack 15' to a belay ledge with 2 bolts. **Pitch 3** begins on Sundeck Ledge. Work up a crack and over a chockstone to a ledge. Move left and jam and face climb a left-angling crack (5.7) to a flake. Work right and into a long finger and hand crack (5.8 and 5.9). **Descent:** Just below the top traverse up and right (5.7) on a face to an alcove with 2 belay/rappel bolts. Rappel 155' back to Sundeck Ledge. Locate 2 more bolts just below the ledge and rappel 135' to a notch. Scramble east to the ground. **Rack:** Bring a standard rack with an emphasis on small to medium pro and 2 ropes for the rappels.

16. **Catch a Wave** (5.11a) This very good, bolted 130' route climbs the steep face right of the first lead of SWEET SUNDAY SERENADE. Begin right of the face below a chimney. Jam a 5.7 crack to a shelf. Work up and left along a dike to the first bolt on the face. Continue up the face past more

bolts to a small roof. Pull over and make a precarious mantle (5.11a), cross a dike, and head up left to the belay platform on SWEET SUNDAY SERENADE. **Descent:** Rap 140' to the ground with double ropes or 60' off right to the walk-off notch. **Rack:** Bring some TCUs for the upper face. 7 bolts.

17. **Motion Fascination** (5.11b/c) Begin 30' right of CATCH A WAVE below an alcove. Climb into the base of the alcove and work right to a bolt. Continue up through a finger crack in a dike and up the face above to a mantle onto a black dike (5.11b). Go left at the last bolt into a notch and belay after 65'. **Descend** 3rd-class ledges east from the notch. **Rack:** Bring a selection of small and medium TCUs for additional pro. 6 bolts.

18. **High Exposure** (III 5.8+) 2 crack pitches above Sundeck Ledge to the top of the wall. Climb one of the lower wall routes to the ledge. Begin below a prominent left-angling crack about 20' left of the ledge rap station. **Pitch 1** jams the hand and fist crack (5.8) to a short off-width section (5.7) and a ledge. Continue up the hand crack in a right-facing dihedral to a harder off-width. Belay after 150' on the left on a large belay shelf. **Pitch 2** goes up a short right-facing corner (5.7) to easy rock. Find the upper rappel station about 40' east and 20' below the top in an alcove. **Descent:** Rap 155' from 2 bolts to Sundeck Ledge. **Rack:** Bring a selection of cams from medium to large including a #4 Friend or Camalot and 2 ropes for the rappels.

19. **Sun Dancer** (III 5.8) A 155' 1-pitch crack route from Sundeck Ledge to the wall summit. Climb one of the lower routes to Sundeck Ledge. Sun Dancer begins above the rap station on the east side of the ledge. Jam a short crack and wrestle over a chockstone to a ledge. Follow double cracks (5.6-5.8) up the obvious left-facing dihedral above for a long lead to the belay/rappel station just below the top. **Descent:** Rap 155' with 2 ropes back to Sundeck Ledge. **Rack:** Bring a generous assortment of small to large pro including a few hexes and a set of Friends.

20. **The Gargoyle** (III 5.10b) 3 short pitches lead up a series of cracks from Sundeck Ledge to the wall's top. Climb any lower routes to Sundeck Ledge. **Pitch 1** begins as for SUN DANCER by climbing the short crack to a ledge. Face climb straight right around a corner and mantle onto a small shelf. Continue right a few feet to a short finger crack. Thrutch up an off-width (5.8) in a right-facing corner to a good belay ledge. **Pitch 2** jams a hand crack (5.8) to an obvious triangular roof. Traverse left under the roof (5.10) and climb a crack up left to an alcove belay stance. **Pitch 3** works up an easy ramp to a squeeze chimney (5.8) and finishes by traversing up left to a spacious alcove. **Descent:** Belay and rappel from 2 bolts. First rappel is 155' to Sundeck Ledge. **Rack:** Bring small to large pro, including TCUs and hand crack-sized pro.

THE FORTRESS

This 250' south-facing wall is directly east of Sunday Wall on the north side of a spacious, cul-de-sac amphitheater. Hidden Valley Wall flanks the east side of the amphitheater. Park at the pulloff below Sunday Wall and approach via the marked access trail. Follow the path east to the base of the cliff. This crag offers excellent rock and superb crack routes. All the routes lie on the east half of the wall.

21. **Nimbasus** (5.10a) A good 2-pitch line up the wall's mid-section. **Pitch 1** begins just left a deep chimney. Climb flakes up and right to an off-width (5.8). Step right and work up a hand crack (5.8) to a belay stance in an alcove. **Pitch 2** stems up the alcove to a hand crack (5.9) over a small roof. Continue up another hand crack in a narrow left-facing corner (5.10a) to a ledge above the prominent dike. Finish up a 5.8 hand crack; belay after 140' on a ledge. Scramble up easy rock to the top. **Descent:** The rappels begin just to the east. Look for double bolts about 30' below the rim. Scramble down and rappel 65' to anchors in a white dike. Make a second 155' rappel to the ground. **Rack:** Bring 2 ropes and a selection of gear that includes 1, 4" piece.

22. **The Emerald Orb** (5.10c) **Pitch 1** begins right of NIMBASUS. Stem up the obvious chimney to a bolt on a ledge on the left. Move up an off-width (5.8) to a hand crack (5.9). Work right out a roof (5.10c) below the dike

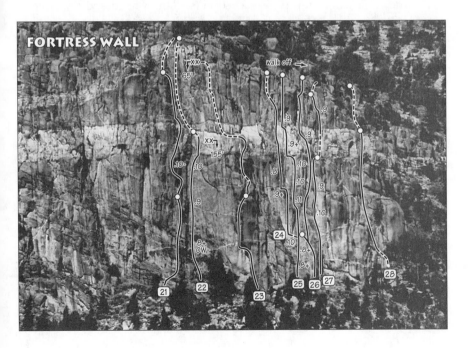

and belay above on a ledge after 155'. **Pitch 2** jams a left-facing corner (5.9) 70' to the summit.

23. **Renaissance** (5.10d) Locate a juniper skeleton below an obvious chimney capped by a large roof. **Pitch 1** climbs the flared chimney/crack (5.9) to the roof. Move left under the roof (5.10) into a flared hand and off-width crack. Hard jamming (5.10d) leads to a ledge. Continue up a pillar and belay after 65'. **Pitch 2** goes right up the left side of the pillar. Work left above around a bulge into a hand crack. Continue up (5.8) and across the dike past a loose flake, make a 5.9 face move onto a good ledge. Traverse left to a right-facing corner. Jam over a small roof, pass a ledge, and end at the rap station bolts. **Rack:** Bring 2 ropes for the 2 rappels and a standard rack. **Descent:** 2 rappels from bolts. 65' and 155'.

24. **Dual Reality** (5.10b/c) Locate a large detached flake right of RENAIS-SANCE. **Pitch 1** jams a left-facing corner up the left side of the flake (off-width and 5.8 hands). At the top of the flake step left to a bolt and work (5.10) into a hand crack. Jam upwards (5.9+) to double cracks (5.8) and belay on a ledge at the bottom of the wide dike. **Pitch 2** stems right up a finger crack (5.9) in the dike and moves up to an alcove. A hard exit move (5.9) from the alcove leads to a good belay ledge. Finish up easy 4th-class rock to the rimrock. **Descent:** Make 2 double-rope rappels from the rap station to the west.

25. **Flashback** (5.11b) Same start as DUAL REALITY. **Pitch 1** works up the 5.8 corner to a ledge atop the detached pillar. Jam a hand and finger crack (5.10) above the left side of the ledge until it ends. Step left to a bolt and face climb left (5.11b) into a finger crack. Jam it (5.10) to a roof just below the obvious white dike above. Move up left and belay at DUAL REALITY'S stance after 120'. Finish with its **2nd pitch. Rack:** Bring a selection of wires and TCUs, and 2 or 3 hand-crack-sized Friends.

26. **Verachocha** (5.10a) Begin on the right side of the large detached flake. **Pitch 1** jams a hand crack to a bulge. Pull over (5.8+) past a small tree and belay on a good ledge after 50'. **Pitch 2** follows a right-angling hand crack to a roof. Turn it on the right and continue up a steep finger crack (5.10a) in a right-facing corner to a finger crack (5.9) over the dike. Work left on steep slabs onto a ramp capped by a roof. A double hand crack (5.8) pulls the roof on the left. Belay on a good ledge after 150' just below the top. Scramble up easy rock to the rim and walk west to the first rappel station. **Rack:** Bring 2 ropes for the descent and a standard rack.

27. **Luxor** (5.10b/c) Begin below a wide flared chimney. Guidebook author K.C. Baum says, "Don't let this one scare you off! Lots of good pro and every climber needs to grapple with a good squeeze chimney!" **Pitch 1** climbs a devious 5.9+ body wedge to a small stance. Climb past a chockstone and

follow finger cracks up the flared chimney to a resting stance under the top of the flare. Thrash up the squeeze chimney and out the upper flare into a good hand crack (5.9). Belay after 100' on a good ledge. **Pitch 2** jams a short crack (5.9) up the dike above and enters a shallow left-facing corner (5.9). Belay after 100' on a spacious platform on the left. Climb easy rock to the rim and walk west to the first rappel station. **Rack:** Bring 2 ropes and a good assortment of gear from wires and TCUs to large cams.

28. **Kachina** (5.10a/b) Begin about 50' east and uphill from the LUXOR chimney at a large mountain mahogany shrub. **Pitch 1** (100') climbs broken rock up left past a small pine tree and steps left into an excellent finger crack. Jam the crack (5.9) past a dike and over a bulge (5.10). Continue up to the prominent horizontal dike and follow a hand crack (5.9-) up a right-leaning roof to a good belay ledge above the dike. **Pitch 2** scampers up easy rock to the summit. **Rack:** Bring a selection of wired stoppers and TCUs, as well as a couple of #3-sized pieces for the roof.

MONTROSEAREA

BLACK CANYON OF THE GUNNISON NATIONAL MONUMENT

OVERVIEW

The Black Canyon of the Gunnison stretches for more than 50 miles across western Colorado from its head, now buried under Blue Mesa Lake, to its confluence with the North Fork just east of Delta. The deepest and most spectacular canyon section is preserved in Black Canyon of the Gunnison National Monument, a 20,763-acre national parkland set aside in 1933 to protect this stunning geological marvel. "Several western canyons exceed the Black Canyon in overall size," writes geologist Wallace Hansen. "Some are longer; some are deeper; some are narrower; and a few have walls as steep. But no other canyon in North America combines the depth, narrowness, sheerness, and somber countenance of the Black Canyon of the Gunnison."

The abrupt defile, reaching depths of 2,500 feet below its rim, was carved by the Gunnison River, Colorado's fourth longest river, over the last three million years. The river's extremely steep gradient and tumbling riverbed boulders continue to chisel the canyon downward. The Gunnison drops 2,150 feet through the canyon's 50-mile length for an average descent of 43 feet per mile. Compare that with the Green River's 12-feet-per-mile drop in Dinosaur National Monument. Even more astounding is the 95-feet-per-mile average gradient in the monument's 12 canyon miles. Geologists estimate that the canyon deepens about one inch annually.

The Black Canyon, hacked out of ancient bedrock, is a beautiful but intimidating place. When approaching either canyon rim, the road swings around low pinyon-clad mesas and through shallow canyons filled with scrub oak and sagebrush. Distant snowcapped peaks poke above the horizon. The first view of the canyon depths is not found until the road reaches the rim's sheer edge. Here the stupendous chasm falls away below. Gullies choked with boulders flank immense rock buttresses. Occasional ledges and shaded side canyons are darkened with hanging forests of fir and pine. And the ever-present roar of the relentless river drifts up on dry breezes.

Pete Williams leads the dicey first pitch of *Journey Home* on North Chasm View Wall in the Black Canyon. *Photo by Peter Gallagher.*

The canyon, called *Tomichi* or "Land of cliffs and water" by the Ute Indians, is composed of both igneous and metamorphic rocks. The metamorphic rock, found in much of the upper canyon, began as sand, silt, and mud deposits on the floor of a primordial sea more than two billion years ago. Heat and pressure later deformed and metamorphosed the sandstone deposits into gneiss and schist. Molten magma or underground lava, injected into cracks and crevices in the metamorphic rocks, cooled into pegmatite, a coarse-grained igneous rock that forms striking pink bands and dikes on canyon cliffs such as the Painted Wall. Large bodies of magma were later intruded into the metamorphic bedrock, forming Chasm View's erosion-resistant walls of quartz monzonite.

The Black Canyon is a forbidding arena for the rock climber. This is not a place for the novice or beginner nor the safety-conscious, bolt-every-four-feet sport climber. No, the Black, as climbers call it, is a place to experience all the adventures, thrills, and chills that climbing offers. This is Colorado's version of Yosemite Valley, a place of utmost seriousness and objective danger. Hazards abound in the canyon, from dense thickets of poison ivy and rattlesnakes on the approach march to loose, Volkswagon-sized flakes poised to spill at the slightest nudge, crumbling pegmatite bands, and imaginary protection on desperate face pitches. "Rockaneering" is what Leonard Coyne, a Black Canyon free-climbing pioneer, calls the climbing here. In an old *Rock & Ice* magazine, Coyne wrote, "...rockaneering is an alternative avenue for expression and exploration that individuals may find lacking in the modern crag scene."

Rockaneering is a combination of rock climbing and mountaineering on big, remote walls. To climb successfully and safely at the Black Canyon the climber needs to be competent. Competent at leading pitches and placing gear. Competent at setting up equalized belays on both ledges and small stances. Competent at finding the right way up the inevitable maze of roofs, corners, dihedrals, aretes, and crack systems that typify the canyon cliffs. Competent at evaluating both objective and subjective dangers, at knowing when to say when, at knowing when to use boldness and when to sound retreat. Competent at setting rappel anchors or enduring a forced, autumn bivouac.

To climb the canyon walls also requires a high level of commitment. Most of the routes are long and complicated. Rock quality varies dramatically on every route from excellent to terrifyingly poor. The canyon's remoteness and complete lack of any rescue facilities or possibilities require every climber to ask hard questions of themselves and their partners. And don't be fooled into thinking that the "easier" routes at the Black Canyon are any easier than the hard ones. They're not. Everyone who has climbed much at the Black has a horror story from so-called moderate routes like the *Russian Arete*. Remember that every Black Canyon climb can quickly escalate from being an enjoyable day's outing to a full-blown epic. But for those up to the task, the Black Canyon offers an array of splendid adventurous rock routes in a wild and rugged setting that epitomize the essence, purity, and joy of rock climbing.

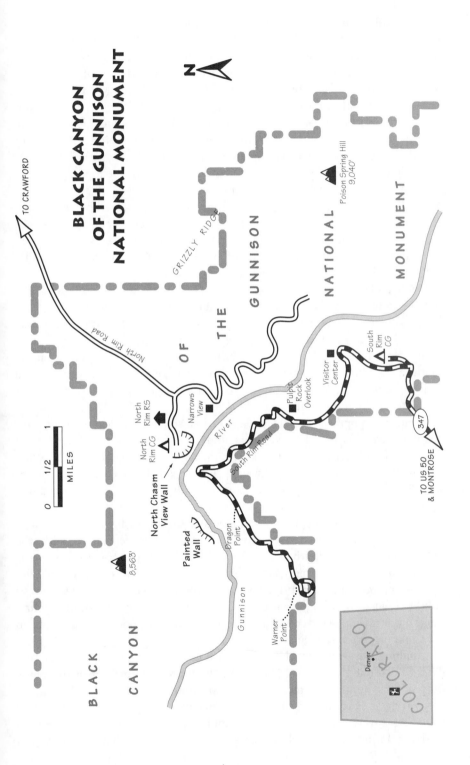

BLACK CANYON
OF THE GUNNISON
NATIONAL MONUMENT

N

TO CRAWFORD

North Rim Road

GRIZZLY RIDGE

BLACK

CANYON

OF

THE

GUNNISON

NATIONAL

MONUMENT

Poison Spring Hill
9,040'

8,563'

North Rim RS

North Rim CG

Narrows View

North Chasm
View Wall

Painted
Wall

River

Dragon
Point

Gunnison

Warner
Point

Pulpit
Rock
Overlook

South Rim Road

Visitor
Center

South
Rim
CG

347

TO US 50
& MONTROSE

0   1/2   1
MILES

COLORADO

Denver

Many routes ascend the Black Canyon's sheer walls, including the Painted Wall, Colorado's highest cliff with a 2,240-foot vertical rise from base to rim, and North Chasm View Wall, an immense granite buttress that offers the canyon's best rock and routes. This guide gives brief descriptions to some of the canyon's best routes, along with approach directions and needed gear. Most active Black Canyon climbers feel the canyon is one of America's best adventure and traditional climbing areas, and as such, a complete beta or topo guidebook is not needed or necessary. A climber's notebook is kept in the North Rim visitor station. Topos can be sketched from this book's first-hand information. Be aware, however, that glaring inaccuracies are found on many of the topos. Use them but don't always believe them. Use your own judgment.

Black Canyon routes are generally approached via steep, boulder-strewn, poison ivy-filled gullies. Use care on the descent and be careful not to knock rocks down. Rappels are necessary on several of the gully descents. Retreat up the gullies is not great fun. Ticks are often found on underbrush in the gullies and on the rim in April and May. Use insect repellent.

Don't underestimate your projected route. Most of the canyon's long free climbs are traditionally done in a day to minimize hauling. All the long ones take a full day for a competent party. Go light if you can and know the route. Otherwise, it's a good idea to bring bivy gear. Many parties are benighted on trade routes like *The Scenic Cruise*. Bring plenty of water, especially on the south-facing cliffs. It gets very hot on these walls, even in the cooler autumn and spring months. As a rule bring two quarts per person per day. In summer it's advisable to bring more.

Standard equipment for Black Canyon free routes includes two ropes (for possible retreat), sets of RPs, stoppers, and TCUs, double sets of Friends, and possible off-width pro like a large Tri-cam, Big Bro, or Big Dude. It's a good idea to bring rain gear, especially in spring or fall. Cooler weather requires warm clothes. Bring enough to stay warm and dry during possible forced bivouacs.

The North Rim Campground, minutes away from the lip of North Chasm View Wall, is the usual climber's campground. A small fee is charged in the busy months at the primitive campground. It's free in the off-season. Water is trucked in, so use it sparingly, or better yet, bring a generous supply with you. Fires are permitted. Again, bring your own wood. Don't tear limbs off trees or collect downed wood in the national monument. The South Rim Campground offers more amenities and costs a little more, but makes a good summer basecamp for climbing on the shaded south-side walls.

Climbing History: The Black Canyon boasts a long, colorful history that dates back to the Ute Indians. These nomadic hunters camped seasonally on the canyon rims, hunting the plentiful game and collecting acorns. The Utes probably rarely, if ever, entered the canyon's precipitous depths. The canyon rims were first traversed by Captain John Gunnison, whose name is now affixed to the river, during an 1853 railroad survey. The canyon's climbing history begins in the 1930s when the San Juan Mountaineers climbed several routes in the canyon including *Curecanti Needle* in the upper canyon. Mel Griffiths, one of those early pioneers, noted the terror of a typical descent into the Black Canyon in 1932: "On such a descent, one leaves a bright, sunny world behind and climbs down into a rocky, forbidding hole eighteen hundred feet below the warm, inviting soil above, a hole which is filled with the terrifying aspects of water-worn rock. One comes away with an overwhelming realization of the titanic forces of nature."

The canyon walls remained dormant until the early 1960s when a lanky climbing whirlwind named Layton Kor took the canyon by storm. Kor climbed his first canyon route, a 1,700-foot route up to the South Rim, in 1960 with Bob LaGrange. During the following years he did first ascents of the *Southern* and *Northern Aretes* of the Painted Wall, *Porcelain Arete, Diagonal Will, South Face of Chasm View,* and had a couple epic attempts on the Painted Wall. Kor compared the superb *Chasm View* route done with Larry Dalke in 1964 with the *Steck-Salathe Route* on Yosemite's Sentinel Rock. The route, done over two days, was rated 5.9 A4.

The second ascent of that route ten years later ushered in a new era and ethic to Black Canyon climbing. Jim Dunn and Earl Wiggins free-climbed the line in impeccable style using the Spartan motto "a rope, a rack, and the shirt on your back." The pair, doing the route in one day from rim to rim, dubbed the free line *The Cruise* and rated it 5.10+. The Painted Wall itself, Colorado's highest wall, was first climbed by Bill Forrest and Kris Walker over eight days in late spring of 1972. An Arizona team of Rusty Baille, Karl Karlstrom, David Lovejoy, and Scott Baxter snared the wall's second ascent a couple months later via *The Dragon Route,* a 20-pitch line up the wall's central section. Numerous long free routes as well as several big aid lines went up in the 1970s; their first ascents falling to a handful of climbers that included Jim Dunn, Earl Wiggins, Bryan Becker, Ed Webster, Ken Simms, and Leonard Coyne. The 1980s brought more boldness to the canyon, particularly with the first free ascent of the Painted Wall via a link-up of the *Forrest-Walker* and *Dragon* routes by Coyne and Randy Leavitt in 1984. This 30-pitch route, named *Stratosfear* and rated 5.11+, offers wild climbing on loose rock with suspect belay anchors. Shorter five- to ten-pitch routes were also established on the smaller cliffs like the Checkerboard Wall and the Cimarron Slabs.

Trip Planning Information

General description: A deep gorge lined with soaring rock walls offers wild adventure climbing opportunities on long free and aid routes on Colorado's tallest cliffs.

Location: Northeast of Montrose and the junction of U.S. Highway 50 and US 550.

Camping: The South Rim Campground, just inside the monument's southern boundary, has 102 campsites in a scrub oak forest. It operates on a first-come, first-served basis, is closed in winter, and is a fee area. The small, primitive North Rim Campground, sitting atop North Chasm View Wall, makes a good basecamp for climbers. The campground is open spring through autumn on a first-come, first-served basis.

Climbing season: April through November. Expect variable weather in April and May with possible wind, rain, and even snow showers. Summer days can be hot, especially on south-facing cliffs, but the shady south-side walls offer excellent summer climbing. Bring plenty of water on routes. Autumn is the best climbing season in the canyon, with pleasant warm days and cool nights. Expect occasional rain and snow storms in October and November.

Restrictions and access issues: The Black Canyon of the Gunnison National Monument is administered by the National Park Service. Much of the Black Canyon is also a designated federal wilderness area. Climbing restrictions include a ban on the use of power drills.

Guidebooks: No guidebook is currently available for any of the Black Canyon's routes. A climber's notebook is kept in the monument visitor center. Be somewhat wary of the topos and descriptions in the book; not all are accurate.

Nearby mountain shops, guide services, and gyms: The closest mountain shops are in Grand Junction, Telluride, and Gunnison. Fantasy Ridge Mountain Guides, in Telluride, operates a climbing school and guide service at the Black Canyon under a concession permit from the National Park Service. Contact Mike Covington at Fantasy Ridge Mountain Guides.

Services: All services in Montrose, Hotchkiss, and Paonia. Limited services in Crawford and Cimarron.

Emergency services: Call 911. Montrose Memorial Hospital, 800 S. Third St., Montrose, CO 81401, (970) 249-2211.

Nearby climbing areas: Curecanti Needle, Needle Rock, Redstone, Chimney Peak, Unaweep Canyon, Rifle Mountain Park, Escalante Canyon, Naturita crags, Ophir Wall, Mount Sneffels, Lizard Head, Taylor River Canyon crags.

Nearby attractions: Curecanti National Recreation Area, Gunnison Gorge, Ute Indian Museum and Ouray Memorial Park, Uncompahgre National Forest, Big Blue Wilderness Area, San Juan Scenic Skyway, Ouray National Historic District, Ouray hot springs, West Elk Wilderness Area, Grand Mesa Scenic Byway, Land's End Road, Unaweep Canyon, Unaweep-Tabeguache Scenic Byway, Dolores River Canyon, Dominguez Canyons BLM Wilderness Study Area.

Finding the canyon: The South Rim is accessed via US 50 and Colorado Highway 347 just east of Montrose. The North Rim is reached via Black Canyon Road from Colorado 92. To reach the turnoff head south on CO 92 from Hotchkiss to Crawford State Recreation Area. Turn on the marked road on the south end of Crawford Reservoir and follow the gravel road to the North Rim. This same turn is reached from the south by turning onto Colorado 92 from US 50 at Blue Mesa Dam. The North Rim Road is closed in winter, while the South Rim Road is open only to Gunnison Point. Contact the monument at 2233 East Main, Suite A, Montrose, CO 81401, (970) 249-7036.

NORTH CHASM VIEW WALL

North Chasm View Wall on the North Rim offers the most routes and best rock of any cliff at the Black. It's easily accessed from the road and the walk-off to the campground and parking lot is only minutes from the rim. The wall's east and south faces are approached via the Cruise Gully, a steep, boulder-filled gully that drops down the flank of the east face. Find the gully by walking east on the North Rim road from the cattle guard at the campground's entrance. Find a trail about 200 hundred feet down the road on the south side. This trail may be marked by a cairn. Follow the path through brush into the Cruise Gully. The gully quickly steepens and downclimbing is necessary in spots. Make two 120' rappels from anchors or downclimb easy 5th-class rock to gain the lower gully. Three routes—*Leisure Climb, Midsummer Night's Dream,* and *Musical Partners*—ascend three prominent crack systems on Chasm View Wall's East Face near the rappels. Continue down the widening gully to *Journey Home, The Cruise, The Scenic Cruise, The Goss-Logan, The Nose,* and the routes on the South Face.

1. **Leisure Climb** (III 5.9-) First ascent by Ed Webster and Chester Dreiman, 1982. This excellent route, one of the canyon's better moderate lines, follows a prominent crack system with good rock and adequate protection. At the bottom of the second rappel in the Cruise Gully, look for an obvious right-facing corner system on the right wall of the East Face of North Chasm View. This is Leisure Climb's start. Scramble up 30' of 3rd class rock to a large grassy ledge below the corner. **Pitch 1** face climbs right of the brushy corner above the ledge on 5.7 rock, then steps left and continues up a 5.8 off-width/layback crack in the corner on the left side of a pillar to the right end of a long, bushy ledge. **Pitch 2** follows a long left-facing corner (some 5.8 hand jamming). Work right higher to easier rock and a small belay stance. **Pitch 3,** the crux lead, traverses left from the belay on narrow ledges, then face climbs up and right to a 5.7 finger crack up the left side of a thin flake. Above the flake use a thin crack for protection to the right, but climb the face left of the crack over a 5.9- overlap and continue up unprotected 5.6 to a sloping ledge. **Pitch 4** climbs a long, broken 5.5 right-facing groove/ dihedral to a pedestal. Face climb up and right (unprotected 5.4) to a belay stance. **Pitch 5** follows a 5.5 groove to a large ledge. Climb easy rock from the right side of the ledge and enter a 5.4 chimney. Belay on the large ter-

race (Grand Traverse Ledge). **Pitch 6** is found by walking left on the terrace past many pinyon pines to an easy 5th class slab that ends minutes from the campground. **Rack:** Bring a standard rack of stoppers and Friends.

2. **A Midsummer Night's Dream** (III 5.11-) First ascent by Ed Webster and Lauren Husted, 1983. First free ascent by Ed Webster and Chester Dreiman, 1983. This good 5-pitch line joins the last 2 leads of LEISURE CLIMB. Find a steep crack system just left of LEISURE CLIMB. It follows this line for 5 pitches up excellent cracks and corners to LEISURE CLIMB. A finger crack on the second pitch is the technical crux. **Pitch 1,** starting in the middle of the grassy ledge, jams a finger crack to a thin, right-facing corner. A 5.9 move pulls over a roof above. Belay on a narrow ledge after 120'. **Pitch 2** (75') wedges up a shallow chimney (5.9) to a bulge. A continuous and difficult finger and hand crack (5.11-) jams over the bulge to a small stance. **Pitch 3** ascends a right-facing 5.7 corner 60' to a ledge on the right. **Pitch 4** stems and jams up a shallow right-facing dihedral, over a bulge, and swings through a roof (5.10-) to a belay ledge 30' above. **Pitch 5** works right (5.5) into the left-angling groove dihedral on LEISURE CLIMB'S fourth pitch. **Pitches 6** and **7** are the same as LEISURE'S CLIMB'S fifth and sixth leads. **Rack:** Bring a standard rack of stoppers and Friends.

3. **Musical Partners** (III 5.9+ R) First ascent by Ed Webster and Paul Scannell, 1983. This good Webster route, following the left-hand crack on the upper East Face, offers 7 pitches of cracks and grooves from gully to summit. Begin below the second crack system left of LEISURE CLIMB on the far left side of the grassy ledge. **Pitch 1** diagonals up left on a slab to an intermittent finger crack (5.8). Follow easier rock above to a belay stance on the left side of a long, narrow shelf. **Pitch 2** jams an obvious finger and hand crack (sustained but excellent 5.9+) for 120' above the belay ledge to a small alcove. **Pitch 3** works into a chimney (5.8) and up a hard-to-protect bombay chimney slot. An awkward exit up high leaves the chimney and edges left on runout 5.9 face climbing to a belay stance. Some poor rock is encountered on this pitch. **Pitch 4** climbs up and right on steep, broken, and bushy rock (5.7 and 5.8 moves) for a long pitch to your choice of belay ledges. **Pitch 5** works right into the left-angling, grooved dihedral on LEISURE CLIMB'S fourth pitch. Belay at the top of the corner or up right depending on rope length. **Pitches 6** and **7** follow LEISURE CLIMB'S fifth and sixth leads to the summit.

4. **Journey Home** (IV 5.10b R) First ascent by Ed Webster and Bryan Becker, 1977. A superb 8-pitch route up the sunny and exposed East Wall of North Chasm View. Continue down the Cruise Gully below LEISURE CLIMB. The gully broadens here and passes a huge boulder. Locate a large right-facing corner about 250' past the boulder. This corner is KACHINA WINGS, a loose, unpleasant 5.10 route. JOURNEY HOME, named for the Ed Ab-

NORTH CHASM VIEW WALL EAST FACE

Cruise Gully

1

6

4

5

Goss-Logan
V 5.11-

Hallucinogen Wall
VI 5.11 A4+

bey book, climbs a left-facing corner system left of KACHINA WINGS. Scramble up broken, blocky 4th class rock on the right side of a small buttress to a large ledge. Go left on the ledge past a rotten crack in the left-facing corner to a large block. Begin here. **Pitch 1,** the psychological crux, begins with a serious and scary runout on 5.9 face climbing. Above a flake follow thin cracks, some 5.10, around a small roof and onto a belay ledge. **Pitch 2** climbs a 5.9 chimney in the corner to a stance. **Pitch 3** continues up the chimney and over a roof to another stance. **Pitch 4** climbs the 5.9 corner to a finger crack up an obvious pink pegmatite band. **Pitch 5,** the technical crux, follows 5.10 cracks in a shallow corner to a good ledge. **Pitch 6** goes off the right side of the ledge into a 5.9 off-width crack and ends on a small ledge. **Pitch 7** heads up cracks and faces with occasional 5.8 moves to a spacious ledge. **Pitch 8** goes up easy rock on the left side of the ledge system to the summit. **Rack:** Bring a rack with sets of RPs and stoppers, a double set of Friends to #3, and 1 #4 Friend.

5. **The Cruise** (V 5.10+) First ascent by Layton Kor and Larry Dalke, 1964. First free ascent by Jim Dunn and Earl Wiggins, 1976. This great 15-pitch free route, probably the most climbed route in the Black, offers steep, exposed climbing on excellent rock. It and the SCENIC CRUISE variant, are among Colorado's best long free climbs. Find the start of the route by hiking down the Cruise Gully to a large boulder below a long right-facing dihedral near the foot of the East Face. THE CRUISE begins here. **Pitch 1** follows the moderate corner for a long pitch to a belay in a V-shaped groove beneath a small roof. Start the pitch by climbing the 5.9 face left of the corner and then stepping into the dihedral. **Pitch 2** climbs easy rock to a large ledge. **Pitch 3** face climbs off right and follows a 5.9 crack for 155' to an alcove belay stance below a chimney. The SCENIC CRUISE leaves THE CRUISE here. **Pitch 4** works up a strenuous off-width and squeeze chimney (5.10) 130' to a stance. **Pitch 5** continues up the crack system, beginning with runout 5.8 climbing off the belay. Continuous stems and liebacks (5.10) lead up the thin right-facing corner 155' to a belay ledge with a bolt above a 5.8 pegmatite band. **Pitch 6** climbs a right-facing corner (5.9) to the well-protected 5.10+ crux thin crack. Belay above on the right on a sloping ledge. **Pitch 7** follows a steep hand crack on the right side of a pillar (5.8) and angles up left on a 4th class ramp to a bivy ledge at the route's junction with the GOSS-LOGAN. A long 160' pitch. **Pitch 8** chimneys 60' up the left side of a huge flake to a 2-bolt belay ledge. **Pitch 9,** the Pegmatite Traverse, traverses right (5.7) past some fixed protection and up across a 5.8+ face to a belay stance. Almost 150' long. **Pitch 10** liebacks up and left over a bulge above the belay (5.9) and past some loose blocks to a ledge. It's possible to belay here. Continue up a poorly protected 5.9- face to a ledge. **Pitch 11** jams a hand crack in a slanting orange corner (5.9), works

NORTH CHASM VIEW WALL
SOUTH FACE

7

7

The Diagonal

Hallucinogen Wall
VI 5.11 A4+

9

8

7

left past a possible belay stance, and back right into a left-facing 5.7 corner. Belay above on a big ledge. Continue up and right on 3rd and 4th class rock to the summit. **Rack:** Bring some #4 Friends and Camalots for pro.

6. **Scenic Cruise** (V 5.10+) First ascent by Ed Webster and Joe Kaelin, 1979. THE SCENIC CRUISE variant avoids the notorious off-width pitch on THE CRUISE, but compensates with a hard, tricky traverse. Climb the first 3 pitches of THE CRUISE. **Pitch 1** angles right into a crack system with thin jamming (5.10-); continue to a belay on the right. **Pitch 2** heads up a left-facing corner above the belay to a 5.10 hand crack. **Pitch 3** is the crux. Work up and left to a short 5.9+ finger crack and make a devious traverse left out of the crack system (5.10-) and up a sloping ramp and rejoin THE CRUISE below its hard fifth pitch. Continue up THE CRUISE to the summit.

7. **Air Voyage** (5.12a) First ascent by Jim Dunn and Dean Tschappet in 1975. First free ascent by Ken Simms and Leonard Coyne in 1978. A superb and airy 13-pitch route up the South Face of Chasm View Wall. It's a fairly serious line with lots of hard crack climbing. Begin by descending Cruise Gully all the way to the base of the Nose of Chasm View. Hike west along the base to THE DIAGONAL, a large, right-angling ramp system. Climb 3rd class rock up THE DIAGONAL for about 300' where the climbing becomes technical. Belay here. Climb 13 pitches from here to the top of the wall. The crux is a menacing 5.12a off-width crack with possible fixed tube chocks on Pitch 10. Pitch 11 gives serious and scary 5.11 face climbing with pro from an old bolt. **Rack:** Bring a generous rack that includes sets of RPs, Rocks or stoppers, and double sets of Friends to #4. Include 3 #4s. Also carry some off-width pro—large Tri-cams, tube chocks, or Big Bros. A knifeblade or thin Lost Arrow piton may be needed on Pitch 12.

8. **8th Voyage** (V 5.12a) First ascent by Jim Dunn and Dean Tschappet in 1975. First free ascent by Jim Dunn and Leonard Coyne in 1981. A long and serious 17-pitch line up the intimidating South Face of Chasm View Wall left of AIR VOYAGE. It shares AIR VOYAGE'S crux 11th pitch, a 5.12a off-width crack. Begin 100' left of THE DIAGONAL below another right-angling ramp that's a couple of pitches up and at the top of a hill at the wall base. The route follows corners and dihedrals left of AIR VOYAGE for 12 pitches to a large ledge shared with AIR VOYAGE. Pitch 13 jams the 5.12a off-width above and then works up right for 3 more pitches to the top. **Rack:** Bring pro for the crack if the fixed tubes are gone. Otherwise, bring a standard rack with doubles of Friends through #3.

9. **The Stoned Oven** (V 5.11d) First ascent by Jim Dunn and partner in 1975. First free ascent by Mark Sonnenfeld and Eric Winkleman in 1985. This sustained and serious line on the South Wall of North Chasm View Wall

offers airy situations, lots of hard cracks, and problematic route finding in parts. Begin below a black crack topped by a roof (5.10d) atop a small 3rd class buttress about 200' left of THE DIAGONAL. The 14-pitch route climbs corners and dihedrals up the wall left of 8TH VOYAGE. **Pitches 1 to 3** work up and right from the crack to a pillar. **Pitches 4 to 7** jam assorted corners to a cramped belay above a pegmatite band. **Pitches 8 and 9** work up a sustained and difficult right-arching corner, with Pitch 9 offering sustained 5.11d hands, fist, and off-width climbing before cutting over the arch to a ledge. **Pitches 10 to 14** work up and right through corners and cracks to the summit. **Pitch 13,** nicknamed The Womb Fight, is a horizontal slither also called The World's Hardest 5.7. **Rack:** Bring a generous rack that includes a set of stoppers; 2 sets of RPs with triples of #4 and #5; doubles sets of Friends with 3-4 #4, 3-4 #3, 3 #2, and 3 #1; and a couple of large Tri-cams or other off-width pro.

10. **The Casual Route** (II 5.8) This casual route, put up by local Jim Newberry in the late 1970s, is a good introduction to Black Canyon climbing and route finding. The moderate line lies on the first buttress on the left in SOB Gully. The gully is a slicing defile that separates the west flank of Chasm View Wall from the western canyon walls, allowing relatively easy access from the North Rim to the canyon bottom. Reach the gully by walking east from the campground entrance to the first cattle guard. Take a left here and follow a trail west to the top of the gully. Descend southwest down the gully. Watch for loose talus and thickets of poison ivy. THE CASUAL ROUTE ascends cracks and corners up the first buttress on the left. The route wanders over the buttress with numerous variations. Follow whatever looks reasonable for 4 to 5 pitches to the rim. The crack systems don't exceed 5.8 and are generally well-protected. Some are bushy. Carry a standard rack.

11. **Debutante's Ball** (V 5.11) This 13-pitch route scales the right side of the Casual Buttress, the first buttress on the left in upper SOB Gully. It's one of the easier Grade Vs in the canyon, with good rock, adequate protection, and short cruxes. Begin by hiking down SOB to the first buttress on the left. Scramble up to the right side of the buttress about 75' left of the huge, black gully that separates the Casual Buttress from Escape Artist Buttress. Begin below a pair of double finger cracks. **Pitches 1 and 2** have some difficult route finding. **Pitches 1 through 6** go up and left through corners and cracks to a large sloping ramp. **Pitches 4 and 5** offer excellent climbing up cracks and over roofs. **Pitches 7 through 13** continue up the steep wall above to the buttress summit. **Pitch 7** begins right on the ramp below a left-arching corner topped by a roof and black streak. **Pitch 12** jams a huge, excellent dihedral (5.10).

12. **Escape Artist** (III 5.9+) (or 5.11 LIGHTNING BOLT CRACK variation) First ascent by Ed Webster and Chester Dreiman in 1982. ESCAPE ART-IST is an excellent 9-pitch route up the second buttress, Escape Artist Buttress, on the left in SOB Gully. The route offers varied climbing with superb cracks, a long traverse pitch, good belay ledges, and fun face climbing. The LIGHTNING BOLT CRACK, a superb finger crack, makes a great variation for 5.11 leaders. Begin the route by hiking down SOB Gully from the campground area to the obvious second buttress on the left. It is separated from the Casual Buttress by a deep gully/chimney. Total walking time is about 20 minutes. Take a minute to scope the route—ESCAPE ARTIST follows a long left-angling crack system to a prominent left-facing dihedral on the left side of the buttress. Begin by scrambling up 3rd class rock to the top of a broken pedestal on the right. **Pitch 1** steps left from the pedestal onto the main buttress face below the long left-diagonaling crack. Jam 5.7 cracks to a belay atop 2 large boulders on a ledge. **Pitch 2** jams the right of 2 finger cracks (5.9) into an left-arching corner. Belay on a shelf above and left after 90'. **Pitch 3** is the elegant Vector Traverse. Traverse up and left, underclinging along the long angling crack (5.9) 100' to a good belay platform beneath the prominent long, left-facing dihedral. Good pro with wired stoppers and Friends on the traverse. **Pitch 4** follows the long strenuous dihedral (5.9+ jams and stems) 175' to a belay with a piton up and left of the corner. This long pitch requires 10' or so of simul-climbing for the leader to reach the belay stance. The last 10' to the belay traverses up left across a slab. Use a 200' rope to avoid the simul-climb. **Pitch 5** climbs twin finger cracks up right (5.8). Work right above to a ramp/ledge (100') beneath the LIGHTNING BOLT CRACK that zigzags up the right wall of an overhanging dihedral. **Pitch 6** jams cracks in a black dihedral (5.9+) left of the LIGHTNING BOLT CRACK for 140' to a stance on the upper slab. Or jam the LIGHTNING BOLT CRACK (5.11 strenuous finger jams) up the right-hand wall to a rest stance. Wrestle up over a bulge to a belay stance after 75' or continue onto the upper slab. **Pitch 7** face climbs up and left on good holds (5.4) on a broad slab for 150'. **Pitch 8** continues up the slab (5.4) another 150' to your choice of belay shelves. **Pitch 9** climbs easy rock up left to the summit of the buttress. Move left to a good belay. **Descent:** From the buttress, find rappel anchors on the left side of the summit and rappel 140' into a steep gully. Scramble up a loose 3rd class gully behind the Casual Buttress to the rim. The campground is a short walk to the east. **Rack:** Bring a standard rack and 2 ropes. A 200' rope is useful for the long pitch.

13. **Comic Relief** (III 5.10-) First ascent by Ed Webster and Chester Dreiman in 1983. Another great route with lots of sustained 5.9 climbing up the buttress face right of ESCAPE ARTIST. Use the same approach as ESCAPE

ARTIST. Scramble up and right to a flat ledge atop a huge block just right of ESCAPE ARTIST'S start. Set up the first belay here. **Pitch 1** (80') jams an obvious finger crack (5.9) just right of ESCAPE ARTIST'S 5.7 corner crack. Traverse right (5.9) at a fixed pin and follow flakes up and left to a small shelf below a right-trending finger crack. **Pitch 2** climbs the well-protected crux finger crack (5.10-) with strenuous jams and laybacks to a stance atop a large block after 120'. **Pitch 3** continues up a crack (5.6) and traverses 50' right around a corner. Work back left on easier rock above to a dark, left-angling slabby ramp. Friction up the ramp (sparse pro) to a good ledge. **Pitch 4** traverses left (5.7) around an edge for almost 100' to a flake belay stance on the left side of a narrow ledge. **Pitch 5** jams 65' up a superb hand and fist crack in a groove (5.9) to a spacious ledge. **Pitch 6** (a long 140') works up left in a short finger crack (5.9) to a chimney behind a flake. Above, friction up right along a ramp to a orange-colored, left-facing dihedral. Strenuous jams and stems up the dihedral (5.9+) lead to the ledge below the LIGHTNING BOLT CRACK. **Pitch 7**, shared with ESCAPE ARTIST, climbs the dark corner left of the LIGHTNING BOLT CRACK to the upper slab. **Pitch 8** continues up the slab (5.4) 150' to a small shelf. **Pitch 9** diagonals right up the easy slab to a fun hand crack (5.4) over a bulge. End on the top of the island buttress. **Descent:** Same as for ESCAPE ARTIST. Scramble down left to rap anchors. Rappel 140' into a steep gully and hike up a narrow scree gully behind the first buttress to the rim. **Rack:** Bring a standard rack and 2 ropes.

THE CHECKERBOARD WALL

This small wall, criss-crossed by pink pegmatite bands, is a semi-detached buttress/island that sits just below the rim on the east side of the Cruise Gully. It was first climbed by Layton Kor and named The Red Wall. Now it's commonly called The Checkerboard Wall. Approach via the Cruise Gully by walking east from the North Rim Campground along the road. Past the cattle guard, turn right or south on a small trail that leads into the woods and down the gully. Follow the gully to the first of 2 sets of rappel anchors. Make 2 120' rappels (or 5.5 downclimb) down the gully. From the base of the last rappel, scramble left or east up a short gully to the base of the wall. Three good routes ascend the wall: *The Monkey and the Engineer* on the left; *Maiden Voyage* in the center; and *The Checkerboard Wall* on the right.

14. **The Monkey and The Engineer** (II 5.10) This 4-pitch route lies on the left side of The Checkerboard Wall. **Pitch 1** works up a left-angling crack on the right side of a small pedestal. When the crack starts getting hard, face climb up and right (5.8) and work back left up a flake. Above, traverse left from a crack to more cracks. Belay on a ledge. **Pitch 2** jams a long 5.8 crack

CHECKERBOARD
WALL

Descent:
Cruise Gully

80'

walk off

14

15

begin around
corner

16

to a wide sloping ledge. **Pitch 3** works up into a crack/corner left of some black streaks. Ascend the corner (5.10) and keep right up a crack to an alcove belay. **Pitch 4** heads up left in a crack that becomes a 5.8 off-width up high. Belay on a huge terrace. Traverse on ledges around the left side of the summit pyramid and follow scree gullies and oak thickets up to the rim.

15. **Maiden Voyage** (II 5.9+) First ascent by Layton Kor and Bob Culp in the mid-1960s. This 6-pitch route, originally called RED WALL, follows cracks and corners up the left-hand side of the wall. The line, with only one 5.9 move, is moderate in difficulty. It's not the best route in the canyon, but is certainly worth doing as one of the canyon's easier lines. Expect bushes and occasional dirty cracks, and some suspect rock. Begin by descending the Cruise Gully to the bottom of the second rappel. Hike east and up a gully to the base of the obvious wall. The route begins a few feet left of a left-leaning wide crack. **Pitch 1** face climbs up into a crack, continues up and right into a short right-facing corner, pulls a 5.7+ bulge, and moves right around a large block into a right-facing corner and a hanging belay. **Pitch 2** works up the corner to an overhang. Chimney and stem over and follow a hand and finger crack up the dihedral (5.9+) to a bush. Face climb up left into a short chimney and belay on broken ledges. **Pitch 3** climbs an off-width (5.7) to a roof. Undercling and layback right around the roof (5.7) to a belay stance just right of another large roof. **Pitch 4** traverses left under the roof (5.8) to a long, arching dihedral. Climb double cracks up the right face (5.7) for a long pitch to a stance. **Pitch 5** continues up the corner (5.4) to a 5.6 move near the top. End on a large terrace with scrub oaks. **Pitch 6** climbs a crack up left (one 5.7 move) to the left ridge of the summit tower. Follow 4th class rock to the summit. **Descent:** Rappel 80' from blocks just below the summit back to the terrace. Walk left on the terrace and contour northwest on ledges around the corner. Bushwhack up oak-filled gullies to the rim.

16. **The Checkerboard Wall** (III 5.10+ R) First ascent by Ed Webster and Chester Dreiman in 1982. This excellent route ascends the wall's midsection, following a devious line up a seemingly blank face. The route offers more face climbing than most of the other routes in The Black. Ed Webster call it "some of the most aesthetic and exhilarating face climbing I've encountered in the canyon." Be prepared to work at route finding and to dice it up on parts. Approach the base of the wall via the Cruise Gully. Walk along the wall's foot to the base of an obvious right-angling ramp. **Pitch 1** ascends the slabby ramp (5.7) for 140'. Belay on a ledge to the left. **Pitch 2** (150') climbs corners and cracks (5.7) up left to a higher right-angling ramp. Continue up the ramp to a belay niche under a roof. **Pitch 3** works straight right around an edge to a slab. Jam a thin, vertical finger crack (5.9) up the steep slab to a large ledge. **Pitch 4** (50') climbs easily (5.3) up to a stance atop a

flake, the Postage Stamp Belay. **Pitch 5** begins the hard climbing. Climb the strenuous arch above with underclings and laybacks (5.10+ with some flaky rock). Move left into a thin, right-facing corner and follow it (5.10) past a fixed piton to a finger crack. Set a hanging belay in the crack after 140'. Watch that you don't knock any rock onto your belayer below. Some runouts are encountered on this pitch. **Pitch 6** (100') continues up the finger crack to a fixed piton. Above the crack climb the runout crux face moves (5.9+ R) to a narrow arch. Underclings and laybacks lead up right along the crumbly arch (5.10-) to a tiny belay alcove. **Pitch 7** makes an exposed hand traverse left (5.8) above the arch and heads up a steep airy face (5.8) to the large terrace across the top of the wall. Do the last pitch of MAIDEN VOYAGE from the left side of the ledge and rap 80' back to the terrace, or traverse left on broken ledges into brushy gullies that lead to the canyon rim. **Rack:** Bring a standard rack, including full sets of TCUs and Friends, as well as a comfortable harness or belay seat for sling belays.

NORTH RIM ROUTES

17. **Lauren's Arete** (III 5.7) First ascent by Ed Webster and Lauren Husted 1984. This is one of the canyon's better arete routes, with decent route finding, generally good rock, and an easy approach. The upper part of the ridge was first climbed by Bob LaGrange and Jim Disney in the 1960s. Ed Webster and Lauren Husted made the first complete ascent of the arete. Lauren tragically fell while unroped on 3rd class rock just below the route's finish. The 12-pitch arete is a long, knife-edge ridge that borders the western side of SOB Gully. Bring a standard rack and some long runners. To reach the start of the route, drop down SOB Gully almost to the river. Walk west around the base of the ridge to its western flank. Hike up a loose, tree-choked gully and follow an easy ramp system back right to the crest of the ridge. Belay on a spacious ledge directly beneath a pegmatite band. The route follows cracks and corners up the arete itself or the walls on either side. The harder climbing is found on pitches 2 and 6. The final lead works straight up corners on the arete or traverses right on an exposed narrow ledge into SOB Gully. Watch for loose rock.

18. **The Russian Arete** (III 5.9) First ascent by Layton Kor and Larry Dalke in 1962. Another long arete route with 8 hard pitches and a few more easy ones near the top. It climbs the prominent crack system up the prow of the first arete west of the base of SOB Gully. Approach by descending all the way down SOB Gully to the river. Hike west a short distance over talus slopes and locate the obvious crack line up the arete. Start from a ledge on the left side of the arete. **Pitch 1** works up and right into a 5.8 dihedral. **Pitch 3** has 5.9 jamming in double cracks up a left-facing dihedral. **Pitch 4** continues up double cracks (5.9) in the corner. **Pitch 7** is the crux lead with

Descent:
SOB Gully

12
13

17

16

**LAUREN'S ARETE
& WEST CHASM VIEW**

DIAGONAL WALL & GOTHIC PILLAR

23

22

21

The Hooker

a 5.9 chimney in a pegmatite band. The first 9 pitches are fairly continuous with lots of 5.7 to 5.9 climbing. Above, continue up several more pitches on easier but loose rock (4th class) as the angle eases back. Follow the broken steep gully system to the rim. Hike along the mostly level rimrock back to the campground. **Rack:** Bring a standard rack with a couple of large cams for big cracks.

19. **Ghost Dancer** (IV 5.10) This route climbs the right-hand side of the steep wall on the right side of THE RUSSIAN ARETE. The line offers 6 pitches of hard climbing and a few more easier ones to the rim. Begin below a tongue of easy slabs and climb up and right in corners, cracks, and slabs.

20. **Ripe Stuff** (IV 5.11) First ascent by Earl Wiggins and Katy Cassidy in the mid-1980s. A companion route to GHOST DANCER on the right wall of THE RUSSIAN ARETE. Begin at the same place as GHOST DANCER only face climb out left (5.9) after the first slab pitch and follow cracks and dihedrals upwards for a total of 7 pitches. The crux lead is an overhanging 5.11 corner on pitch 5. Continue to the rim with several easy 4th class pitches. Watch for loose rock.

21. **Gothic Pillar** (V 5.10 A3) First ascent by Layton Kor and Ed Webster in the mid-1980s. This route lies on the blunt arete right of a deep gully and left of a huge sweeping wall decorated with 3 wide left-diagonaling bands of pegmatite. Approach by descending SOB Gully to the river and hiking downstream past THE RUSSIAN ARETE. The route climbs the face of an obvious pillar just right of a huge gully. Begin by climbing several hundred feet up 3rd and 4th class ledges and easy rock up and left to the foot of the steeper wall. From here climb up 10 or 11 pitches to the summit of the pillar/island. **Pitch 1** ends at a bolt. **Pitch 2,** going over the first pegmatite band, has some A3 nailing. **Pitch 3,** over the other white bands, is also A3. **Pitch 4** (5.9 A2) ends at a good bivy ledge. **Pitch 5** is a 5.8 traverse right. **Pitch 6** is exposed 5.9 up and right. The remainder of the route works up and right on face and crack climbing to the summit. Make a rappel into the notch behind and climb back to the rim.

22. **Pathfinder** (V 5.11-) Pathfinder is a long 18-pitch route up the right side of the Diagonal Will Buttress, the large buttress left of the GOTHIC PILLAR and a deep, dark gully. It begins about 100 yards right of an obvious scree cone below the DIAGONAL WILL route. Locate a right-leaning finger crack (5.10-). Jam the crack to a terrace. Climb 3 pitches up a right-facing corner system (5.8 to sustained 5.10+). Work up and right on broken rock for 2 pitches and enter another dihedral system. Climb 4 pitches up the dihedrals (5.8 to sustained 5.11-) to a terrace. Climb assorted cracks, chimneys, slabs, and ramps for another 8 pitches to the rim. A good bivy ledge is atop pitch 11. Pitch 15 has a 5.9 traverse up and left to a chimney.

23. **Diagonal Will** (V 5.11+ R/X) An excellent 17-pitch route up the center of the Diagonal Will Buttress, the large rectangular face left of a deep gully and 2 buttresses right of The Painted Wall. Approach via SOB Gully and hike downstream to the base of the buttress. The route follows an obvious hook-shaped, left-leaning dihedral to a large roof and continues up the wall above to the rim. Begin atop a prominent talus cone directly below the dihedral system. **Pitches 1 to 3** are easy 5th class and 4th class scrambling to the base of the steeper wall. **Pitches 4** through **9** climb the prominent hook to a ledge up left of its top. Expect cracks and chimneys from 5.7 to 5.9 and rotten rock. A large rockfall here has also created a 5.11+ R/X section. Expect route finding difficulties. **Pitch 11** leaves the crack system and moves up right across an unprotected 5.9/5.10 pegmatite band. Continue up corners above for 6 more pitches to the summit.

24. **Stratosfear** (VI 5.11+ R) First ascent of the lower part of the route (to pitch 19) by Bill Forrest and Kris Walker, 1972. First free ascent by Leonard Coyne and Randy Leavitt, 1984. STRATOSFEAR, the longest free climb in Colorado, wanders up The Painted Wall, Colorado's tallest cliff, in 30 pitches. This bold, audacious route is reserved only for the very competent. It offers almost 3,000' of serious, runout climbing on loose rock and looser pegmatite bands. Belay anchors are somewhat questionable; protection is often marginal; and route finding is devious. If this kind of masochism appeals to you, beg or borrow a copy of *Rock & Ice* #54 and photocopy the good topo inside. Approach The Painted Wall, an immense pegmatite-striped, southeast-facing cliff, by descending SOB Gully. Follow the Gunnison River downstream almost a mile to the scree slopes below the wall. Allow about 2 hours to hike to the base from the campground. Most parties bivouac on the sandy riverbank below the route, which necessitates going light or having a good friend carry your bivy gear out.

    The route ascends the left side of the wall for 19 pitches. The next 6 pitches traverse up and right into the Dragon Chimneys. The last 5 pitches work up these loose chimneys to the rim. The traversing pitches are all serious, with runouts on difficult and loose climbing, and funky belay anchors. The 25th pitch is the crux lead with downward traversing to a 5.11 corner edge. Some of the fixed pro—old copperheads, pitons, and 1/4" bolts—is dubious. Use caution and back up whenever possible. The Painted Wall may be closed to climbing from February through June for nesting raptors. Check with a ranger for more info on cliff closures. **Rack:** Bring a rack with sets of RPs, wired stoppers, TCUs, and Friends. Bring double Friends #1, #2, and #3. Also bring pro (3-5 pieces) to fit 6" cracks on the upper exit pitches—Big Bros, large Tri-cams, or tube chocks. Use 2 ropes (9mm or 10mm) for leading to alleviate severe rope drag, especially on the traverses.

25. **The Southern Arete** (IV 5.10) First ascent by Layton Kor, Larry Dalke, and Wayne Goss, 1962. This long route climbs The Southern Arete of The Painted Wall for about 25 pitches of crack and face climbing. This spectacular arete forms the left boundary of the wall. The lower pitches climb cracks and chimneys up the narrow buttress. The upper pitches ascend the steep headwall of the arete. The route tends to wander so pick the best-looking line and have at it. Bring a standard rack along with a piece or two for some off-width cracks.

SOUTH RIM ROUTES

The South Rim of the Black Canyon of the Gunnison National Monument offers some excellent routes on shaded buttresses on the south side of the canyon. These cliffs include the Cimarron Slabs, South Chasm View Wall, and the short Alimony Wall. These routes make good summer excursions. Access the South Rim by driving 6 miles east from Montrose on US 50 to Colorado 347. Turn north on Colorado 347. Follow the highway 5 miles to the entrance to the national monument. Continue along South Rim Road to the cliffs. The road deadends at Warner Point after 8 miles.

Access the Cimarron Slabs via Old Headquarter's Draw, a deep ravine nicknamed the Chillumstone Gully for a huge chockstone wedged part-way down. To reach the gully park at Devil's Overlook and walk about 0.25 mile west along the road to the first major gully. It sits below a guardrail as the road bends left. Descend the loose scree gully to the Chillumstone. Rappel 150' from fixed anchors with double ropes to the base of the drop-off. If you have to climb out the gully, this section has some 5.9 moves. *The Cimarron Slabs* and *Mirror Wall* are right of the gully. *Black Jack* and South Chasm View Wall are on the left. To reach South Chasm View, descend all the way to the river and follow its south bank downstream. A couple of river crossings are necessary. Use extreme caution when crossing because of high, swift water. Another way to the wall base that does not require river crossings is to drop down the first gully past The Painted Wall Overlook. About 200' of 3rd class rock are near the gully's bottom. Below this rock work up and right to a saddle behind a large pinnacle. Drop down a gully from the saddle to the river and the wall base.

26. **Cimarron Slabs** (III 5.7 R) First ascent by Ed Webster and Susan Patenaude in 1979. This moderate 9-pitch route ascends the Cimarron Slabs on the east flank of Headquarters Draw or Chillumstone Gully. The line requires some route finding and is bushy and loose in a few spots. Approach by dropping down the gully from the paved road and rappelling 150' off the Chillumstone. Continue down the gully to a prominent grass and bush-covered ramp that slants upwards to the right. The large slab above the ramp is the Cimarron Slab. The route begins on the upper end of the ramp

just right of a large block. **Pitch 1** climbs a broken groove to a traverse right onto a ledge dotted with scrub oak. **Pitch 2** continues up a clean crack system (5.6) 140' to a ledge left of the crack. **Pitch 3** works up the face (5.4) above to several belay shelves. Keep to the right of the broken, lower-angle rock to the left. **Pitch 4** pulls over an easy bulge and continues straight up easy rock to a stance. **Pitch 5** moves up the left side of a rectangular shaped block/flake above to a spacious ledge atop the block. **Pitch 6,** the crux lead, edges up the slab via a long, right-diagonaling crystal dike on somewhat runout climbing (some 5.7) for a long pitch to an alcove belay under a headwall. A bolt protects the lower section, while the 5.7 is protected by stoppers and small Friends. **Pitch 7** jams an easy crack above the alcove onto easy but loose and bushy rock above. Continue up to a large tree that leans over the wall. **Pitch 8** works up and left on easy, loose rock to the top of the buttress. **Pitch 9** downclimbs into a notch between 2 steep gullies, then climbs cracks, flakes, and headwalls interspersed with grassy and brushy ledges (some 5.6 and 5.7 moves). Belay wherever and continue up broken rock to the summit of the island behind the buttress. Competent parties might dispense with a rope on this section, but there are occasional 5.7 moves, loose rock, the potential for serious falls, and exposure. From the top of the island, walk south through scrub oak to its southernmost point. Rap about 50' or carefully downclimb loose blocks into another notch and scramble and bushwhack south to the road. **Rack:** Bring a standard rack along with 2 ropes.

27. **Ground Control to Major Tom** (III 5.8) First ascent by Stewart Green, Dennis Jackson, and Major Tom Lumen in 1980. This route, joining the CIMARRON SLABS for its crux pitch, offers better climbing on its lower pitches and is less brushy. Begin by descending Headquarters Draw and rapping off The Chillumstone (150'). Drop down the gully to an obvious grassy ramp on the right. Scramble up the ramp a short distance and rope up below a prominent right-angling crack. **Pitch 1** jams the hand and finger crack (5.8) to a small stance. **Pitch 2** works right up the crack and face climbs (5.7) to a belay shelf below some prominent down-facing flakes. **Pitch 3** climbs carefully up through the loose flakes (5.7) and left to a belay ledge. Be careful not to pull any of these giant flakes off—they'll mince your belayer for sure. **Pitch 4** is a fun face traverse up and left (5.7) with wires for pro. Belay on a ledge below some cracks. **Pitch 5** climbs the crack system on the left (5.7) to a brushy ledge. **Pitch 6** continues up the dirty, bushy crack (5.8) to a good ledge below the crux lead of the CIMARRON SLABS. **Pitch 7** face climbs up right on a marvelous crystal-studded dike (5.7 and run-out) to a belay alcove directly below a huge pine tree that leans over the face. **Pitch 8** jams an easy crack and broken rock up to the tree. **Pitch 9** works up left on a broken, loose ridge to the top of the but-

tress. **Pitches 10** and **11** drop into a notch and climb cracks and headwalls (occasional 5.7 moves) to the summit of the rock island. Walk south along the flat top and rap 50' or downclimb to a notch. Scramble south 100 yards to the road. **Rack:** Bring a standard rack and 2 ropes.

28. **Mirror Wall** (IV 5.10) First ascent by Pat Ament and Roger Briggs in the 1960s. First free ascent by Ed Webster and Bryan Becker in 1979. This long 20-pitch route scales the huge, slabby wall left of the CIMARRON SLABS. Most parties only climb the excellent first few crack pitches and rappel off. To find the start descend down Headquarters Draw, rappel 150' off The Chillumstone, and continue down past the CIMARRON SLABS ramp to the foot of the wall on the right. The MIRROR WALL climbs the obvious crack system up the wall. Jam superb finger cracks for several pitches and rap off, or continue up easier slabs above for many pitches to the summit of the buttress where the CIMARRON SLABS route ends. **Rack:** Bring plenty of pro for finger cracks and 2 ropes.

29. **Black Shadow Arete** (IV 5.10d) First ascent by Harvey Miller and Brian Teale in 1982. First free ascent by Harvey Miller and Reggie Slavens in 1987. This 7-pitch line jams the crack system left of the MIRROR WALL, joining it at a huge ledge partway up the wall. Begin left of the MIRROR WALL and follow cracks for 4 pitches (5.10d) to the top of large flake. Walk across the flake and drop down to the base of another crack system. Follow the cracks (5.10d) for 3 more pitches to the large ledge. Continue up the MIRROR WALL'S upper slab pitches. **Rack:** Bring a standard rack along with some off-width pro and 2 ropes.

30. **Blackjack** (III 5.10-) First ascent by Leonard Coyne and Dennis Jackson in 1978. This excellent and sustained route jams a huge open dihedral just east of South Chasm View Wall to the canyon's south rim. Begin by descending Headquarters Draw and rappelling off The Chillumstone (150'). Below the chockstone descend a short way down the gully to the base of long brushy ramp on the left. Scramble up this ramp (3rd class and some exposure) to the base of a huge yellow and green north-facing dihedral. Traverse right on 3rd class rock from the open book to a chimney behind a huge block and set up the first belay. **Pitch 1** liebacks and hand jams up a flake system (5.9) above the block and right of the dihedral to a belay stance near the top of the flake. **Pitch 2** continues up the flake and enters the dihedral. Climb a squeeze chimney (5.8) and thrash over some bushes to a semi-hanging belay. **Pitch 3** climbs double cracks (5.7) up the corner past bushes and a 5.9 overhang to a small platform. **Pitch 4** works up pink rock through a loose off-width and squeeze chimney (5.8) to a semi-hanging belay stance. **Pitch 5** jams up to an obvious roof, turns it via a slot (5.10-) on the left, and moves up and right to a small ledge. **Pitch 6** continues up the dihedral or angles up left on the face via cracks and face moves

(5.8) to a ledge. Continue on easier 4th and 5th class rock to the summit of the buttress. Walk south to the road. **Rack:** Bring a standard rack that includes RPs and plenty of medium to large pro (include some off-width pro), and 2 ropes.

SOUTH CHASM VIEW WALL AND OTHER AREAS

The huge South Chasm View Wall lies on the shady south side of the Black Canyon opposite Chasm View Wall. A good view of the wall's steepness and seriousness is apparent by stopping at Chasm View overlook atop the wall and peering directly over the cliff edge behind the tourist safety railings. Several excellent Grade V routes ascend the wall. Info and topos on these are available in the climber's logbook in the monument visitor center. Routes include **The Flakes** (V 5.10+) up obvious flake systems on the left-center of the wall; **Astro Dog** (V 5.11+), an excellent 14-pitch route that begins 50' west of **The Flakes** and ends just east of South Chasm overlook; **The Goldberg Special** (V 5.10 A3), a 17-pitch line directly up the center of the wall; **The Bushmeister** (IV 5.10), a 10-pitch free route on the right central wall; and **Falcon Wall** (V 5.11), a 16-pitch line left of **The Bushmeister.**

Some short, stiff free climbs are found on the Alimony Wall. Approach it by driving to the Painted Wall Overlook trail. To scope it out follow the trail west 200 hundred yards and walk over to the north side of a deep, slicing gully. The short wall lies opposite. It's a steep, north-facing buttress flanked on its left by a deep chimney. **Alimony** (II 5.9) climbs the wall left of the chimney in 3 short pitches via an off-width up the left side of a pillar and cracks above. **Last Payment** (II 5.9 or 5.11) climbs a crack system on the right side of the buttress right of the chimney in 4 short pitches. The third pitch above a ledge is either a 5.11 off-width or a 5.8 face pitch right of the crack. **Steppin' Out** (II 5.9) jams the first 2 pitches of **Last Payment,** then traverses off left under the obvious roofs to the chimney.

TELLURIDEAREA

OPHIR WALL

OVERVIEW

The Ophir Wall towers above Colorado Highway 145 west of Telluride. The highway here makes a wide bend, following an old spiraling railroad grade dubbed the Ophir Loop a century ago. Wide ledges and sloping ramps divide the 1,000-foot cliff into a many-faceted wall. Steep, water-streaked slabs mark the Ophir Wall's western flank. A roughly diamond-shaped vertical wall seamed with incipient cracks and beetled with overhangs graces the crag's torso. The eastern half is a mixture of slabs, steep smooth cliffs, and loose, broken sections. A wide evergreen-studded ledge separates the lower East Buttress from the shiny, glacier-polished Mirror Wall on the crag's far right side, while Cracked Canyon, home to a brilliant collection of crack routes, splits the wall's east flank.

The Ophir Wall offers one of Colorado's unique climbing experiences. It's a lovely place hidden below ragged alpine ridges. The sun bakes its lofty granite face on summer mornings. Dramatic afternoon thunderstorms roll across the high ridges above the wall, darkening the sky and pelting the cliff flanks with rain and hail. Autumn brings peaceful, warm days, colored by the flutter of golden aspen trees on the valley floor. The views from airy belay stances are breathtaking with snowcapped Sunshine Peak above evergreen-clad slopes and the Ames Wall down-valley. And after a long day of cranking the rads or one shortened by the usual afternoon downpour, solace and company is traditionally found at Telluride's Last Dollar Saloon.

Climbing history: Climbing on the wall began in the 1970s with the growth of Telluride as a destination ski resort. Newcomers soon discovered this hidden granite gem and began scaling the obvious lines up its abrupt faces. Bill Kees, author of the wall's first guide and founder of the acclaimed MountainFilm Festival, put up numerous routes, while Henry Barber, a summer instructor at a local climbing school, established classics including *Hot Wee Wee* and *Honey Pot*. First ascents reached a fever pitch in 1978 when Californians Royal Robbins

Antoine Savelli scales granite edges on *White Salamander* on lower Ophir Wall. *Photo by Stewart M. Green.*

and Chris Vandiver, while teaching at Robbins's Telluride-based Rockcraft School, began systematically ticking off a list of now-classic lines that include *Javelin* and *Cello*. A handful of locals—Kees, Allen Pattie, Dan Langmade, Tim Kudo, Dave Bell, and Kevin Cooney—jumped into the action lest the west coast invaders grab all the plums. A couple of years later two more Californians, John Long and Lynn Hill, visited the wall and established several superb routes including *Dr. Gizmo, Reptilicus,* and *Black Magic,* as well as leading *Ophir Broke,* an overhanging hand crack that was one of Colorado's first 5.12s.

By the 1980s all the obvious lines on the Ophir Wall had been climbed, and it was left to a new generation of Telluride climbers to explore the blank spaces. Antoine Savelli, a French climber and guide who settled in the area, established a number of superb, difficult climbs on the wall in the company of Teri Kane and Ace Kvale. These routes include *Morning Glory, Dingo Maniaque, Weaving Through Golden Waves,* and the mega-classic 5.10d *Powder in the Sky.* Besides bringing bolt protection to the crag, Savelli firmly established the 5.13 grade on the Ophir Wall. Charlie Fowler also was very active through the 1980s, pioneering new routes of all grades on the Ophir Wall, Cracked Canyon, and the shaded cliffs of the Dark Side on the canyon's opposite wall.

The south-facing Ophir Wall, its base lying at an elevation of 9,500 feet, is one of Colorado's highest developed climbing areas. This relatively high elevation and the sometimes harsh mountain weather allows a short June through October climbing season. The superb rock and easy access provides an excellent collection of routes of varying difficulties. Almost 200 routes criss-cross the Ophir Wall and Cracked Canyon. Most are traditional lines requiring a standard rack of Friends, TCUs, RPs, and stoppers. Others are brilliant bolted lines with occasional gear placements. Some are bold, runout climbs established in impeccable ground-up style, while others are extremely technical, pre-protected routes of exceptional merit. That these differing styles of ascent can co-exist side-by-side is testament to local appreciation for rock and route. As Charlie Fowler notes, "In the long run few people remember who or how a route was done, but everyone remembers a good climb."

With routes ranging from 1 to 6 pitches, this is a serious place to climb. Use extreme caution on the fractured wall. Unstable and loose rock is found on many routes and on walk-off descents. Guidebook author Allen Pattie says, "Be very aware when people are climbing above you, either on a climb or descent. The Ophir Wall is not a real user-friendly place. Although it is safer now with fixed rappel stations and belays." Be cautious here in May and June, especially on Memorial Day weekend when the MountainFilm Festival is held and hordes of visiting climbers head for the wall. The melting snowpack atop the Ophir Wall creates an extreme rockfall hazard during this period. Wear a helmet, or better yet, go climbing elsewhere. Serious injuries have occurred here due to rockfall. Also use care when hiking up the steep boulder field to Cracked

Canyon and in the canyon itself. The talus is unstable and easily sent rolling down onto hapless parties below.

The Ophir Wall is divided into five sections—The Slabs, Ophir Wall, Mirror Wall, East Buttress, and Cracked Canyon. Each is unique and offers its own distinct climbing experience. The Slabs offer slabby routes that sweep up the crag's west side. The Ophir Wall, the highest cliff section, yields numerous quality outings up the steep water-streaked face. The Mirror Wall rises above an obvious tree-covered ledge on the cliff's east flank, harboring some of the wall's best and most dramatic lines. The East Buttress is a somewhat broken and blocky buttress below the Mirror Wall. It's popularity is due to easy access and many routes of varying difficulty and character. Cracked Canyon, a narrow rock-walled canyon lining the Ophir Wall's eastern flank, is a spectacular climbing area of short routes that range from pleasant slabs to fierce overhanging cracks. Its myriad classic routes are reason enough to spend a few days at Ophir.

Trip Planning Information

General description: Numerous superb routes scale a tall granite cliff.

Location: 8 miles west of Telluride on Colorado 145.

Camping: Free camping is available in the small roadside meadow west of the Ophir Post Office and in the San Miguel Canyon below Ilium along Forest Road 625. Otherwise, head a few miles north on Colorado 145 to Sunshine Campground or south to Matterhorn Campground. Bring your own water if you camp at the wall base. The river water is contaminated with mine tailings.

Climbing season: June through October.

Restrictions and access issues: On national forest land, no current access problems.

Guidebooks: *A Climber's Guide to the Ophir Wall* by Allen Pattie, Chockstone Press, 1988, is a good guide to the wall's classic routes. *Telluride Rock* by Charlie Fowler, 1990, updates the Ophir Wall with newer lines.

Nearby mountain shops, guide services, and gyms: Telluride Mountaineer, Telluride Sports, Fantasy Ridge Mountain Guides, Charlie Fowler (Telluride); Antoine Savelli (located on the road below the wall near Ophir).

Services: All services in Telluride.

Emergency services: Telluride Medical Center, (970) 728-3848. Montrose Memorial Hospital, 800 S. Third St., Montrose, CO 81401, (970) 249-2211. For emergency assistance call (970) 728-3081.

Nearby climbing areas: The Jungle Gym, Ames Wall, Lizard Head, Naturita crags, Slick Rock bouldering, Paradox Divide, Dolores River Canyon, Unaweep Canyon, Colorado National Monument, Escalante Canyon, Indian Creek Canyon (Utah), Canyonlands National Park (Utah).

Nearby attractions: Uncompahgre Plateau, Divide Road, Paradox Valley, Dolores River Canyon, Hanging Flume, Unaweep-Tabeguache Scenic Byway,

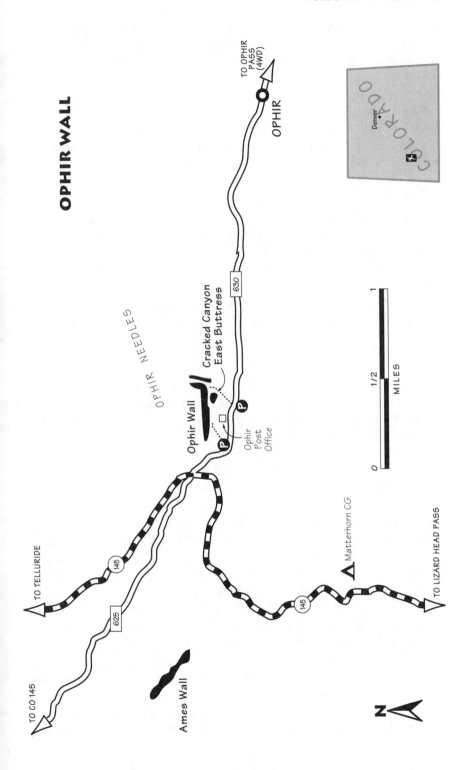

OPHIR WALL

Sewemup Mesa BLM Wilderness Study Area, Palisade BLM Wilderness Study Area, Unaweep Canyon, Mount Sneffels Wilderness Area, Telluride, Imogene Pass, Bridalveil Falls, Lizard Head Wilderness Area, Canyonlands National Park (Utah).

Finding the crag: From Telluride drive 8 miles west to the Ophir Pass turnoff at Ophir Loop. Turn east here, drive just past the Ophir Post Office, and park at a roadside pulloff. The wall towers to the north. Approach the crag via rough access trails that climb steep talus slopes north of the road.

OPHIR WALL

The cliff's mid-section is commonly called the Ophir Wall. Routes on here, accessed via a short, steep hike up broken talus slopes, range from single-pitch to long 5- and 6-pitch affairs. This wall section is defined by the large right-facing open book of *Undecided* on the west and the *Post Office Crack's* long crack system on the east. A wide, east-angling ledge/ramp, the *Tennis Shoe Traverse,* splits the lower wall and allows easy access to routes on the right side including *Honey Pot* and *Morning Glory.* Beware of climbing above or below other parties. Loose rock abounds on the cliff. Routes are listed from west to east.

1. **Undecided** (5.8) This good 2-pitch line scales an obvious right-facing dihedral on left side of wall. Begin at highest talus point below western wall. **Pitch 1** scrambles up and left up an easy ramp 100' to belay ledge below the corner. **Pitch 2** climbs corner for 20', traverses right toward an arete, then follows corner above to a belay ledge. **Descend** by following ramps and slabs westward around wall or rappel 150' from conifer above the practice slabs on west.

2. **Dr. Gizmo** (5.10d) A superb 3-pitch line that was first freed completely by John Long and Lynn Hill in 1980. The route climbs cracks up the steep, water-streaked wall right of UNDECIDED'S dihedral. **Pitch 1** follows UNDECIDED'S easy but loose first lead to a belay. **Pitch 2** jams fingers to hands crack just left of black streak to a stance below a small tree. **Pitch 3** goes up and right toward a small roof. Turn it on left and continue onto easier broken rock above. Rappel route with 2 ropes.

3. **Dingo Maniaque** (5.13b) This difficult 3-pitch route edges up the smooth wall right of DR. GIZMO. Begin below a smooth slab capped by a roof at highest talus point below west wall. **Pitch 1** zigzags up slab past 3 bolts (5.11c) to the roof. Turn roof via an obvious break and climb up past 3 bolts and fixed peg (some 5.11d) to 5.9 face climbing. Belay from 2 bolts. **Pitch 2,** the crux lead, heads up left on very thin edges and sidepulls (5.13b) past 4 bolts. This section can be aided by pulling on bolts. Another 4 bolts

OPHIR WALL

and a second 5.12b/c crux lies above. Belay from a 2-bolt rap anchor. **Pitch 3** traverses right on 5.10a climbing to right side of an arch. Climb past arch (5.11a, 2 bolts), and traverse left into right-facing corner. Above lies steep, exposed face climbing (5.11c). Belay from 2 bolts on a ledge. **Descent:** Rappel route with 2 ropes. First rappel is 130' to anchors. Second rappel is 160' to ground. **Rack:** Bring 10 quick draws, sets of RPs and Tri-cams, and #1 and #3 Friends.

4. **Hot Wee Wee** (5.9) Allen Pattie calls this 1973 Henry Barber route "A full rack classic, not to be missed." The 4-pitch route follows the obvious left-facing dihedral that splits the wall. Climb a 4th class ramp below the steep dihedral to a ledge. The next 3 pitches wander up the corner or on neighboring walls with ledge belays. **Pitch 1** (40') climbs the steep wall left of the dihedral to an alcove. **Pitch 2** (100') climbs the dihedral or the left wall to a ledge. **Pitch 3** follows the large open-book. **Pitch 4** wanders up broken headwalls and gullies. **Descent:** 4 or 5 rappels down route.

5. **White Salamander** (5.12a) An excellent Savelli sport route up a short wall around the corner from HOT WEE WEE'S ramp. 7 bolts and fingery face climbing lead to a 2-bolt anchor 60' up.

6. **Tennis Shoe Traverse** (4th class) This traverse follows a ramp and ledge system that angles right across the wall and allows easy access to routes above the Big Ledge including HONEY POT and MORNING GLORY. It begins right of WHITE SALAMANDER. Take the easiest course. A rope and a couple of nuts might ease the mind on the more exposed sections. Take care with the loose rock and don't trundle it off onto people below.

7. **Horse Chaser Direct** (5.9) and **Hidden Secrets** (5.9) Combine these two routes for a great 3-pitch outing. Find a large A-shaped corner/roof with a slab below it. HORSE CHASER DIRECT climbs the black-streaked wall left of the right-facing corner. **Pitch 1** face climbs up and right to a bolt, then up left to a belay ledge with pitons. This pitch is somewhat underprotected. HIDDEN SECRETS climbs the slab above in 2 leads. **Pitch 2** goes up the slab (1 bolt) to a leaning groove and a belay stance. **Pitch 3** works up obvious holds to a fixed belay with rap anchors. **Descent:** Rappel the route with two 2-rope rappels.

8. **Total Recall** (5.11c/d) A 70' Doug Berry sport route with 5 bolts. Start right of rockfall from the NEANDERTHAL WALL'S fallen-down 1st pitch. The line face climbs around and up an arete to a 2-bolt anchor.

9. **Morning Glory** (5.12d) This great 1-pitch route, aided by Henry Barber in 1973 and freed by Antoine Savelli in 1985, climbs a smooth wall of immaculate granite. Access the route's start on the Big Ledge via the TENNIS SHOE TRAVERSE. The route jams and stems up the obvious crack system left of a large boulder in a long 150' pitch. Five 5.12 cruxes and seven 5.11 cruxes are found along the way. Double rope technique will cut down on

rope drag. **Descent:** Rappel the route with 2 ropes from the belay anchors. **Rack:** 7 bolts and several fixed pins offer protection, but bring a rack with sets of RPs and wired stoppers as well as double Friends from #.5 to #3.

10. **Honey Pot** (5.10b) HONEY POT, or the Y-CRACK, is the Ophir Wall's mega-classic line. This brilliant, aesthetic crack up a vertical, burnished cliff on the right side of the wall is the crag's must-do route. The easiest approach is via TENNIS SHOE TRAVERSE from the west. Follow the Big Ledge to the base of the obvious hand and fist crack. The difficulties are immediately obvious. **Pitch 1** jams upwards 140' to a belay stance below a large corner above the Y. **Pitch 2** climbs the corner 100' to another belay. Continue upward for a couple more pitches on rock broken into headwalls and gullies. **Descent:** Most parties rappel with 2 ropes from anchors atop the 1st pitch. The left Y-Crack is 5.10.

11. **Golddigger's Corner** (5.11) Climb cracks up a right-facing corner via hand and finger jams and stemming to HONEY POT'S first belay ledge. Make a 130' rappel back to the Big Ledge.

12. **Post Office Crack** (5.8) This classic line, following what Pattie in his book calls "a vertical version of the San Andreas Fault," ascends the long crack system on the right margin of the wall for 5 or 6 pitches. Aim for the large tree on the skyline above the system, carry a standard rack, and watch for loose rock. Walk east along the cliff top for a descent gully (Bowling Alley) onto the East Buttress. Look for the obvious rap gully (1 rope rap) into Cracked Canyon.

13. **Raindance Direct** (5.9) **Pitch 1** begin by climbing the 1st pitch of POST OFFICE CRACK to the Big Ledge. **Pitch 2** scales right-leaning cracks and corners for a long lead to a stance below several roofs. **Pitch 3** heads up and left of the roofs on flakes to a ledge. **Pitch 4** continues up broken headwalls to the forest above.

MIRROR WALL

This smooth cliff towers above a wide forest ledge and the East Buttress on the right or east side of the Ophir Wall. **Descend** from these routes by walking eastward along the broken cliff top to an obvious gully called the Bowling Alley that drops onto the main ledge atop the East Buttress or rappel the route to the ledge. Find the obvious rappel gully on the east that descends into Cracked Canyon.

14. **Weaving Through Golden Waves** (5.13a) This terrific 2-pitch line edges up the west side of the Mirror Wall. The route ascends the left side of a prominent water streak. **Pitch 1** is short. Climb a left-leaning ramp (a spot of 5.6) to a 2-bolt belay. **Pitch 2** follows the ladder of 23 bolts above for 150' to

anchors on a ledge. Several very difficult face-climbing cruxes are encountered. **Rack:** Use double rope technique to minimize drag and carry at least 25 quick draws. **Descent:** Do 2 double-rope rappels back to ledge.

15. **Queasy Street** (5.7 A3) A 2-pitch aid line up the wall right of WEAVING THROUGH GOLDEN WAVES. **Pitch 1** starts below the crescent moon arch. Free climb to a belay ledge. **Pitch 2** frees and aids up the arch to a sling belay. **Pitch 3** hooks out of the arch and follows seams to a belay stance. Rap the route. **Rack:** Bring lots of thin aid gear, including crack'n ups, bird beaks, RPs, and hooks. Hammers are barely useful.

16. **Powder in the Sky** (5.10d) Another Ophir Wall classic route. Find the obvious scalloped wall east of QUEASY STREET. **Pitch 1** is 60' of mostly unprotected face climbing with some 5.10b moves near top. Belay from bolts. **Pitch 2** goes up left past 4 bolts toward an obvious roof. Crux is at 4th bolt. Turn the roof on left and end on ledge with anchors. **Descent:** Rappel route with 2 ropes.

17. **Northern Lights** (5.11c) This is the companion route to POWDER IN THE SKY. **Pitch 1** starts up POWDER but deviates right past 4 bolts to the POWDER belay stance. **Pitch 2** heads up and right into an 5.11c finger crack (some fixed pro) and goes right of a roof to a 2-bolt belay ledge. **Descent:** Rappel the route with 2 ropes. First rappel is 170'; be sure to knot the ends of your rope.

18. **Batman's Delight** (5.9) A delightful 2-pitch line up the prominent left-facing corner system on wall's right margin. **Descent:** Walk off eastward to Bowling Alley.

19. **Ophir Broke** (5.12c) Another Hill/Long route that was one of Colorado's first 5.12s. The route climbs a strenuous, overhanging crack on east side of the Mirror Wall. **Rack:** Bring a rack with double sets of Friends. It's also a good C1 aid route.

CRACKED CANYON

The deep cliff-lined cleft of Cracked Canyon, the Ophir Wall's most popular section, slices down the east side of the wall. Almost 100, 1-pitch routes line its abrupt sidewalls. Its climbs, ranging in difficulty from 5.0 to 5.13, are mostly crack routes or mixed crack and face climbing lines protected by traditional means. The few bolted lines usually require additional gear placements. **Descent** from all routes is via rappel from slings around trees or fixed rap anchors. Most descents are with a single rope. Bring a standard rack with sets of RPs, stoppers, and Friends. Some routes might require a piece of off-width gear.

Approach Cracked Canyon by parking in roadside pullouts directly below the canyon. A rough access trail walks up through the forest and onto the steep talus slope below the canyon. Take care not to tumble unstable talus onto those below. More loose talus fills the steeply angled canyon floor. Again, use caution not to avalanche boulders down and be careful of loose holds and blocks on the climbs or atop the cliffs. Many routes lie in Cracked Canyon. This guide samples a few of the best lines near the canyon entrance.

CRACKED CANYON WEST WALL

20. **First Step** (5.10) Follow a left-leaning corner/crack system.

21. **Cello** (5.10) Climb steep rock into a narrow corner. Belay or rappel from ledge with bolt or continue up easier rock to cliff-top.

22. **Javelin** (5.11-) This strenuous 1978 Royal Robbins route uses finger and hand jams to surmount pronounced overhanging crack right of CELLO. Again, belay and rappel from fixed anchors at crack's end or climb up and left to tree belay.

23. **Secrets of Nature** (5.13-) A difficult 3-bolt line up vertical face right of JAVELIN. Stick-clip first bolt and bring small pro for upper section. Belay on JAVELIN ledge.

24. **Reptilicus** (5.10+) This long pitch begins in striking left-facing corner. Follow twin cracks up corner, climb right onto face above, and continue up incipient cracks to top. Rappel from anchors above the gully immediately north or downclimb 4th class gully.

**CRACKED CANYON
WEST WALL**

4th class gully

25. **Where Eagles Dare** (5.11+) A brilliant, sustained line up steep wall right of REPTILICUS. Scramble onto a ledge to start. Clip bolt above and climb thin slashing cracks to bolt on upper slab. Finish atop the cliff. Antoine Savelli first climbed it in 1986 with pre-placed protection. Rap from anchors above the gully to the right. Route has been chopped twice and rebolted twice. **Rack:** Bring RPs and other thin crack pro.

26. **Synchronicity** (5.11+) This climbs steep slab right of WHERE EAGLES DARE. Face climb up thin, broken crack systems past 3 bolts. Rap from anchors to right.

CRACKED CANYON EAST WALL

27. **Entrance Exam** (5.3) An easy slab right of big dihedral. Rap from a tree down cliff-top.

28. **Fox Trot** (5.3) Climbs low-angle right-facing corner system.

29. **Pirouette** (5.8) A great must-do route. Jam a finger/hand crack that splits slab right of a corner. Continue up the V-shaped slot above.

30. **Air Arete** (5.10) Begin right of PIROUETTE and below narrow roof 15' above. Climb up to roof, traverse right to obvious slabby arete and waltz upward to a belay ledge with rap anchors. No real pro is found and 3 protection bolts have been chopped. This is a good toprope problem. WHERE ARE YOUR FRIENDS, thin slab left of arete goes at 5.10+ and again offers marginal pro possibilities.

CRACKED CANYON EAST WALL

31. **Sizzler** (5.11) A steep, strenuous route up slightly overhanging, thin finger cracks around outside corner from AIR ARETE. Use a variety of insecure finger jams and stems to reach belay ledge.

32. **Breakfast of Champions** (5.6) Climbs a right-facing dihedral to tree belay. Rap from a tree downhill.

33. **Tintinnabulation** (5.4) An overgrown, funky, left-facing corner.

34. **Teacher's Pet** (5.8) A fine pitch up a long, bottoming, flared crack system to belay/rappel tree perched on cliff edge. Bring thin pro.

35. **Third Grade** (5.8) Follows good finger cracks up shallow right-facing corners.

36. **Beginner's Luck** (5.6) A superb beginner's climb up an obvious wide crack. Bring some wide pro and small wires.

37. **Exodus** (5.8) Use crack and face moves up right-facing corner and blunt arete. Two good 5.3 routes—GENESIS and MARGIN—climb easy corners right of EXODUS.

38. **Easy Money** (5.8) Jam an excellent hand crack near the outside edge of the canyon to a belay ledge.

LIZARD HEAD

OVERVIEW

Lizard Head lifts its ragged spire above surrounding ridges and forested valleys high in the San Miguel Range in southwestern Colorado's 41,000-acre Lizard Head Wilderness Area. The 13,113-foot volcanic neck, rising 350 feet above the ridge below, is Colorado's most difficult mountain summit to reach. Those who climb it either love it or hate it, calling it a "classic climb" or a "tottering pile of rubble." Both opinions ring true. While Lizard Head boasts a long, colorful climbing history, it is also a rotten tower storied with epics of leader falls, rockfall, bad pro, and jammed rappel ropes.

Climbing history: When first climbed in 1920 by Albert Ellingwood and Barton Hoag, Lizard Head was probably America's most difficult rock climbing route. Ellingwood, the driving force behind the ascent, is Colorado's first famed rock jock. As a Rhodes Scholar in England between 1910 and 1913, Ellingwood learned English rope and protection techniques while climbing in Wales, the Lake District, and the Alps. Upon returning to Colorado Springs in 1914, he brought English techniques and ethics with him. The first ascents of Lizard Head and the Ellingwood Arete on Crestone Needle were his crowning achievements.

The pair of climbers tackled Lizard Head with three soft iron pitons, a length of hemp rope, and nailed boots. After reconnoitering the peak's north and east face, Ellingwood picked a line up the southwest corner and started up at noon. He led two pitches up the crumbling lower face, placing two pitons for protection. He later noted that "most of the enticing small holds crumbled at a touch, and large masses of the loosely compacted pebbles would topple dangerously at a slight pull." Easier climbing above led to the summit. After a half-hour rest on top, they downclimbed to the steep lower cliff and fixed the doubled rope around a spike for the first rappel. The rope, however, would not pull down. While trying to loosen it, a fist-sized cobble dislodged and struck Ellingwood on the head, almost knocking him from his precarious perch. After recovering he climbed back up and reset the rope to make a single-line rappel to the ground. Darkness had fallen by the time Hoag reached the end of the rope almost 20 feet above the cliff base. Groping for holds in the dark, he lost his balance. Ellingwood reported later that Hoag "slipped and, leaving a section of his pants behind, drifted relentlessly downward until the wall became vertical and then jumped (perhaps fifteen feet) to the rocks below. I followed with more caution, regretfully saying goodbye to my rope that had served me well for five good seasons." The second ascent party retrieved Ellingwood's tattered rope in 1929.

Lizard Head is quite a bit easier and safer to climb today with modern gear. It is still, however, a serious outing and demands respect. Its harsh reputation is due mostly to the tower's general looseness. A helmet is the most essential piece

LIZARD HEAD

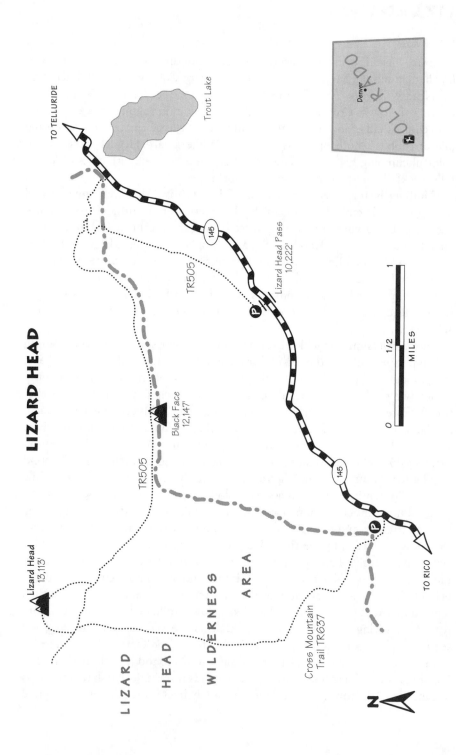

TO TELLURIDE

Trout Lake

COLORADO

Denver

145

Lizard Head Pass
10,222'

P

TR505

Black Face
12,147'

TR505

Lizard Head
13,113'

L I Z A R D

H E A D

W I L D E R N E S S

A R E A

145

P

Cross Mountain
Trail TR637

TO RICO

N

1

1/2

MILES

0

of equipment—loose rocks are everywhere and it doesn't take much to dislodge a volcanic missile that can maim or kill. Bring a small rack with medium to large wired stoppers and a set of Friends including a #4. Plan on an early morning start to hike in and complete the climb before the usual round of afternoon thunderstorms.

Trip Planning Information

General description: A 13,113-foot volcanic plug forms Colorado's most difficult mountain summit.

Location: In the San Miguel Mountains southwest of Telluride.

Camping: Several national forest campgrounds lie along Colorado Highway 145 near Lizard Head. Matterhorn and Sunshine campgrounds are found along the highway in Uncompahgre National Forest north of Lizard Head Pass. Cayton Campground is along the Dolores River in San Juan National Forest southwest of the pass.

Climbing season: Spring through fall. The peak and its approach are locked in snow from late October until sometime in May. It's a fast approach on skis in April and early May. The south-facing wall is usually snow-free in early spring. July through September is the usual time to climb Lizard Head. Watch for afternoon thunderstorms and lightning.

Restrictions and access issues: The peak is in the Lizard Head Wilderness Area, straddling the border between Uncompahgre and San Juan national forests. Wilderness rules apply, including prohibition of motorized vehicles and power drills.

Guidebooks: *The San Juan Mountains* by Robert F. Rosebrough, Cordillera Press, 1986; *Guide to the Colorado Mountains* by Robert Ormes; and *Telluride Rock* by Charlie Fowler, 1990.

Nearby mountain shops, guide services, and gyms: Olympic Sports, Telluride Sports, Fantasy Ridge Mountain Guides, Charlie Fowler (Telluride); Antoine Savelli (Ophir).

Services: All services in Telluride, including gas, dining, groceries, lodging, and camping.

Emergency services: Mountain Medical (970) 728-3848. Montrose Memorial Hospital, 800 S. Third St., Montrose, CO 81401 (970) 249-2211. Southwest Memorial Hospital, 1311 N. Mildred Rd., Cortez, CO 81321 (970) 565-6666.

Nearby climbing areas: Ophir Wall, Naturita crags, Dolores River Canyon, Unaweep Canyon, Mount Sneffels Wilderness Area, Ouray ice climbs, Golf Wall, Durango crags, Canyonlands National Park (Utah).

Nearby attractions: Mount Sneffels Wilderness Area, Telluride, Ophir Pass, Imogene Pass, Dallas Divide, Mesa Verde National Park, Hovenweep National

Monument, Dolores River Canyon, Weminuche Wilderness Area, Ophir Pass, San Juan Scenic Skyway.

Finding the crag: Two trails approach Lizard Head. The first is Lizard Head Trail (Forest Trail 505). From Telluride drive 16 miles southwest on Colorado Highway 145 to the summit of Lizard Head Pass. The trail, beginning at the parking area, climbs east and north onto a high ridge. Follow the trail for a couple of miles until you are below the tower's southwest corner. Scramble up scree slopes to the cliff base.

An easier approach is via the Cross Mountain Trail (Forest Trail 637). Drive 2 miles west of the Lizard Head Pass summit to the 10,000-foot elevation marker. Pull north on a forest road and park in a designated area. Follow the trail 1.5 miles to its junction with Lizard Head Trail under the tower. Again, scramble to the cliff base.

1. **Southwest Chimney** (II 5.7+) This, the best of 3 lines up the south face's lower wall, follows a wide crack/chimney system on the right side of the south face. **Pitch 1** (155') climbs cracks up a prominent left-facing corner, some 5.7+ (couple of fixed pitons) and ends in a notch. A narrow mid-way ledge can break it into 2 shorter pitches. **Pitch 2** scrambles up and left across 3rd class scree and terraces to the base of the upper headwall. Belay below a chimney/crack system. **Pitch 3** passes a small roof protected by a #4 Friend and follows the squeeze chimney above for 50' to the loose summit or climbs the face left of the chimney. **Descend** by making 2 rappels. Rappel 80' from anchors below the summit to anchors below the loose scree section on the southwest corner. Some downclimbing might be necessary to reach the anchors. The second rappel drops 160' back to the tower's base. Bring extra webbing in case the existing rappel slings are weathered and worn.

NATURITA CRAGS

OVERVIEW

Southwestern Colorado is a wild, rugged landscape creased by deep, sinuous river canyons; lorded over by snowcapped peaks and abrupt sandstone palisades, mesas, and buttes; and sparsely populated by cowboys, miners, loggers, and a surprising number of rock climbers. At one time the area's climbing populace congregated in Telluride to sample the Ophir Wall's delights. Now many have moved away from its glitz and expense to real western towns like Norwood, a small community atop grassy Wrights Mesa between the San Miguel River canyon and Uncompahgre National Forest. Numerous climbing and bouldering areas have been developed northwest of Norwood and Naturita along the northeastern edge of the Paradox Valley and in the canyons of the San Miguel and Dolores rivers.

The best climbing is found on small outcrops of Dakota sandstone that line the rims of cuestas or gently tilted mesas and shallow canyons. The Dakota Formation, deposited during Late Cretaceous times some 70 million years ago as dunes and shoreline, is one of Colorado's most widespread rock formations. It's also a formation that climbers, and in particular boulderers, are intimately acquainted with. This generally fine-grained tan sandstone—studded with flakes, edges, and pockets—occurs atop uplifted hogbacks along the base of the Front Range at Horsetooth Reservoir, Carter Lake, and the Morrison bouldering area.

The Dakota sandstone at the Naturita area crags varies in quality and character. Some exposures like Atomic Energy Crag are formed by a thick, fine-grained sandstone replete with pockets and edges, while other cliffs including Lost World Crag are somewhat chossier, with stream-deposited pebbles and cobbles making a rough texture. Climbing on these cliffs can be unnerving, at least until you're used to the rock. Most of the pebbles seem fairly well-cemented in place, but it's hard not to be cautious when cranking off a polished two-finger pebble poking an inch out from the surface. The rock is also very abrasive. Tape up when venturing up the cracks and run an extra length of rope out to the cliff edge for toproping. It's a good idea to pad the rope where it rubs against the cliff top with a piece of ensolite or length of garden hose.

Climbing at Naturita is generally laid back and quiet, with free desert camping near the crags. The cliffs lie well off the beaten track and it's a rare day when you'll encounter another party—except in winter when the local climbing fraternity beats a path to these crags every warm weekend. The cliff bands form small crags reminiscent of England's gritstone edges, with short, fierce bolted climbs and a multitude of good crack climbs. This is the place to go to bone up on your off-width technique, especially at Lost World Crag. Many crags dot the region. The two best and most developed cliffs are Atomic Energy Crag and Lost World Crag. Both are northwest of Naturita on Colorado Highway 141.

Charlie Fowler provided the main impetus in the development of the Naturita crags beginning in 1989, with Doug Berry, Bill Kees, and Steve Johnson helping out.

Numerous excellent boulders also scatter across the slopes below the cliffs. Charlie Fowler, a Norwood local, calls this "perhaps the best bouldering area in the state." One of the best and most accessible collections of boulders lies on a small flat below the Atomic Energy Crag. Other good bouldering areas include the Dead Log Area near Bitter Creek, The Ozone Layer south of Lost World Crag, and the Speedway Crags a couple of miles north of Vancorum on the slopes west of CO 141.

The climbs here are generally short, 30 to 80 feet in height. Bolts provide free climbing protection on the steep faces and slabs, with new routes established both on the lead and on rappel. The use of power drills is strongly discouraged by local ethics. A few routes lack hangers so a selection of keyhole hangers or wired nuts is necessary to tick them. Bring a rack of Friends, Tricams, and wired stoppers to climb the cracks or add additional pro to face routes. Otherwise a rack of 10 quick draws will suffice. **Descent:** No anchors are atop the routes. Scramble over the lip and find a convenient tree to tie off. Descent is accomplished by searching for a suitable downclimb route. The harder routes are generally the better climbs with cleaner rock and bolt protection.

Bob D'Antonio solos *Whispering Wind,* the best 5.6 at Lost World Crag near Naturita. *Photo by Stewart M. Green.*

Trip Planning Information

General description: Abrupt edges of Dakota sandstone offer numerous cracks and bolted face routes, rim canyons, mesas, and tilted cuestas along the northeastern edge of the Paradox Valley.

Location: Northwest of Naturita and Telluride near the Utah border.

Camping: Plenty of free campsites are found along or off the road below the crags. A quiet, off-the-beaten-track campsite is at the boulders below Lost World Crag. Excellent camping among superb boulders is on the flat bench below Atomic Energy Crag. Bring water and use existing sites and fire rings to minimize impact. Pack out all your trash.

Climbing season: Best from October through May. Autumn days can be hot in this high desert. Winter offers excellent climbing weather, with a mild desert climate. Expect warm temperatures on the south-facing walls during sunny days. Snowfall is usually sparse and short-lived. The roads, however, can be difficult to impassable after winter and spring snowstorms with serious mud. Spring brings variable weather, with both warm and cool days, occasional rain showers, and wind. It is possible to climb here in summer, but most days are unbearably hot with highs regularly in the upper 90s. Biting gnats can make climbing difficult in May.

Restrictions and access issues: The cliffs and their access routes are on BLM public lands. No current restrictions, but the possibility of future restrictions exists. The BLM strongly encourages all climbers to minimize their impact as much as is safely possible. Practice low-impact use to keep climbing freedoms intact. Use only existing roads, trails, and campsites. Bring your own firewood to avoid destroying trees. The canyons and cliffs north of Atomic Energy Crag are closed to all activities between May 1 and September 1 to protect nesting peregrine falcons and golden eagles, as well as the endangered Paradox Valley lupine. Avoid climbing on the sandstone crags for at least 24 hours after rain or snow or until the rock is dry. The wet rock is friable and holds often break.

Guidebooks: *Naturita and Paradox Valley Rock Climbs* by Charlie Fowler. Available from Bear Paw Books in Norwood or the Telluride Mountaineer.

Nearby mountain shops, guide services, and gyms: Telluride Mountaineer, Telluride Sports, Fantasy Ridge Mountain Guides, Charlie Fowler (Telluride); Antoine Savelli (Ophir).

Services: All services in Naturita, Nucla, and Norwood.

Emergency services: Montrose Memorial Hospital, 800 S. Third St., Montrose, CO 81401, (970) 249-2211. For the county sheriff or ambulance call (970) 864-7333.

Nearby climbing areas: Ophir Wall, The Jungle Gym, Ames Wall, Lizard Head, Slick Rock bouldering, Paradox Divide, Dolores River Canyon, Unaweep Canyon, Colorado National Monument, Escalante Canyon, Indian Creek Canyon (Utah), Canyonlands National Park (Utah).

Nearby attractions: Uncompahgre Plateau, Divide Road, Paradox Valley, Dolores River Canyon, Hanging Flume, Unaweep-Tabeguache Scenic Byway, Sewemup Mesa BLM Wilderness Study Area, Palisade BLM Wilderness Study Area, Unaweep Canyon, Mount Sneffels Wilderness Area, Telluride, Imogene Pass, Bridalveil Falls, Lizard Head Wilderness Area, La Sal Mountains (Utah), Canyonlands National Park (Utah).

Finding the crags: From Naturita drive west 2 miles on CO 141 to the abandoned site of Vancorum. Turn west here on Colorado 90 and drive 5.2 miles to EE22 Road. Turn northwest on gravel EE22 Road. The road slowly climbs through strike valleys and various rock formations. Lost World Crag, hidden from the road, is reached by turning east on a rough track at 1.8 miles, before the main road reaches Antenna Crag. Atomic Energy Crag, an obvious escarpment east of the road, sits another 4 miles up EE22 Road. Continue north another 12 miles to Uravan and Colorado 141.

LOST WORLD CRAG

Lost World Crag perches atop a high bluff overlooking the Paradox Valley to the west. It's a thin cliff band that reaches up to 50' high and offers more than 80 routes of all grades. The rock is pebbly and takes some getting used to. The Shady Side routes, not covered here, lie on the north-facing shady side of the bluff. The Sunny Side routes scale the west and south-facing cliffs.

To reach Lost World, turn north from Colorado 90 on EE22 Road. After 1.8 miles turn east onto a rough dirt track and follow it for 0.5 mile to a junction. Continue east from the junction a few hundred yards to the mesa base. Parts of this road section may be washed out and inaccessible without a 4x4 vehicle. Don't attempt to drive a regular car if the road's bad. Just park and walk. Otherwise it's a long walk back to get an expensive tow-truck. A short scramble up slopes leads to the cliff base. Route descriptions begin on the west end of the crag beside a large boulder broken away from the prow of the mesa. The slab in a small corridor east of the boulder offers three routes—*Countdown to Kickoff* 5.7 (a 25' seam best bouldered), *Save the Children* 5.8 (2 bolts), and *Positively 4th Street* 5.8 (2 bolts).

1. **Whispering Wind** (5.6) A superb 3-bolt route up an arete just right of a chimney.
2. **Hendrix in the West** (5.11-) 4 bolts up a steep wall to a finishing pull over a roof.
3. **Psychedelic Hangover** (5.12-) 4 bolts up a sheer, south-facing red wall. Don't blow the second clip.
4. **Cowgirls from Hell** (5.10) A short finger-crack that becomes a seam.

5. **Trigger Happy** (5.9+) Good finger and hand crack in a left-facing corner to an overhang.

6. **Natty Rita Goes Shopping** (5.10) Good hand crack in corner leads to face climbing and 1 bolt.

7. **The Big Shot** (5.9) A squeeze chimney to flared off-width.

8. **Frontier Days** (5.12) One of the crag's best with 4 bolts and pockets up a red wall.

ATOMIC ENERGY CRAG & LOST WORLD CRAG NATURITA AREA

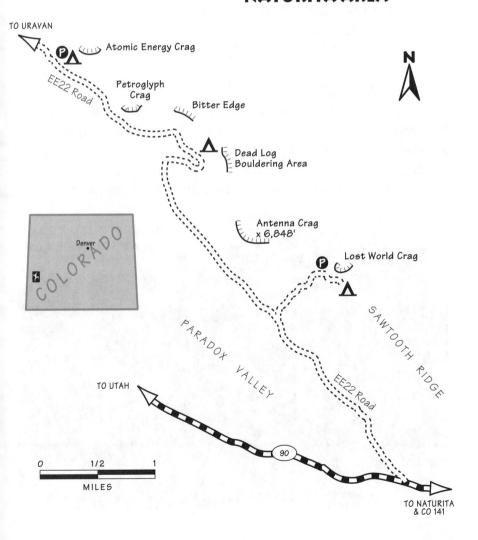

9. **On the Border** (5.10) Finger crack up an arete.

10. **Way Out West** (5.11) Good finger crack with 2 bolts.

11. **Silver Spurs** (5.9) Two bolts on a southwest-facing pebbled wall.

12. **Make it Snappy** (5.7) Short finger to hand crack.

13. **Lowe Route** (5.9) Hand crack—tape up.

14. **Hole in the Wall** (5.11) A good 3-bolt face route.

15. **Big Brother** (5.8) Off-width crack.

16. **The Dove** (5.11) A hand crack and 2-bolt face.

17. **One of Those Daze** (5.10) Pretty good 3-bolt route up a pebbled face.

18. **High Noon** (5.12) Steep wall right of arete.

19. **Sand Creek Massacre** (5.12+) Steep bolted face.

20. **Round Up** (5.9) Off-width crack.

21. **Have Gun Will Travel** (5.12+) Excellent pockets up a smooth face with 3 bolts.

22. **Wounded Knee** (5.10) Aptly named off-width crack.

23. **Hands Up** (5.8) Hand crack up obvious left-facing dihedral.

24. **Spaghetti Western** (5.11) Good 2-bolt route up right wall of open book.

25. **Hang 'em High** (5.12) 3-bolt face route.

26. **Purple Daze** (5.8) 2-bolt route up the west face of a large detached boulder that has fallen away from the cliff. **Descent:** Rap from anchors on top.

LOST WORLD CRAG
NATURITA CRAGS

27. **Desert Rose** (5.11-) 2 bolts up the right side of the boulder's west wall. Rap off.

28. **Do the Right Thing** (5.11-) Begin in the corridor between the boulder and the cliff. This is a good face climb past 4 bolts. Crux is getting to the first one—best to stick-clip it if possible. Above are good pockets and edges.

29. **Hanging Judge** (5.8) Good hand and fist crack right of DO THE RIGHT THING. Flared up high. **Rack:** Bring some 4" pro.

ATOMIC ENERGY CRAG

   This offers the best climbing in the Naturita area with more than 40 routes on steep faces, sharp aretes, and excellent cracks. Good camping and superb bouldering is found among the large boulders scattered across a flat area between the road and the slopes below the crag. Access the crag by continuing up EE22 Road another 4 miles from the Lost World turnoff. The road meanders along, dipping into the Bitter Creek drainage and passing numerous cliff edges. Atomic Energy Crag is most prominent. Park at a pulloff on either the west or east side of the road and scamper up the shale slopes to the cliff base. Route descriptions begin at the north end of the cliff.

30. **Born to be Mild** (5.7) Good 3-bolt slab warm-up.

31. **Fried Chicken** (5.10) 4 bolts up the steep west-facing wall right of a sloped arete. Climb crack up left side of a flake and crank upward.

ATOMIC ENERGY CRAG
NATURITA CRAGS

32. **Fail Safe** (5.11) A good route with 3 bolts up steep rock right of FRIED CHICKEN.

33. **Coyote Corner** (5.9) Indian Creek-style off-width and fist crack in huge corner.

34. **Finger Fusion** (5.10) One of the area's best finger cracks. Climbs the steep wall right of COYOTE CORNER.

35. **Guns or Butter** (5.12-) Spectacular route up a prow behind a dead tree. Thin corner leads to arete and 3 bolts. **Rack:** Bring TCUs for lower crack.

36. **China Syndrome** (5.12) A 3-bolt desert-varnished face.

37. **Mushroom Cloud** (5.8) Jam the obvious hand crack to an easy hand traverse right under the huge roof.

38. **Critical Mass** (5.10) A thin right-facing corner and 2 bolts.

39. **Fallout** (5.10) Another thin corner to a layback on blunt arete.

40. **Covert Action** (5.12) Face climbing to rounded arete with 5 bolts.

41. **Rancho Deluxe** (5.10) A brilliant finger and hand crack up a steep corner to face climbing and 1 bolt.

42. **Firestorm** (5.11) Finger crack to steep face with 3 bolts. **Rack:** Bring small and medium pro.

ATOMIC ENERGY CRAG
NATURITA CRAGS

43. **Off the Beaten Path** (5.9) Obvious off-width and squeeze chimney sliced into wall.

44. **Nuclear Free Zone** (5.12) 7 bolts up the sheer face right of an arete mark this excellent route. Edges, pockets, and the arete offer great cragging.

45. **Unnamed** (5.12) 6 bolts lead up the steep pocketed wall to a 2-bolt lowering anchor almost 50' up.

46. **Enola Gay** (5.12) Another super climb up the blunt arete on the right side of the huge dihedral. Pockets, edges, and 6 bolts.

47. **Jukebox in My Mind** (5.11) 5 bolts up a black face.

48. **It's a Breeze** (5.9) Hand jams and laybacks up a flake crack.

49. **Steep and Deep** (5.8) Undercling to off-size crack.

50. **On the Beach** (5.11) A good climb up the right side of an arete past 5 bolts. More bolted routes and cracks lie on the slabs and walls east from ON THE BEACH.

Mike Clements swings up *Greenkeeper's Playground* on The Back 9 at The Golf Wall. *Photo by Stewart M. Green.*

DURANGOAREA

THE GOLF WALL

OVERVIEW

The Golf Wall, rising just off U.S. Highway 550 north of Durango, offers very good limestone climbing on short, pumpy routes similar to Rifle. The bolted, overhanging routes here, ranging from 5.8 to 5.13, pull over roofs on big jugs and yield to a diversity of techniques including sidepulls, foot cams, and kneebars. The cliff is a thin band of Paleozoic limestone deposited on an ancient sea floor, forming a small escarpment just east of the highway and immediately north of the Tamarron golf course. The wall is easily accessed from a parking area on the west side of the highway via a short trail.

The Golf Wall is divided into three sectors: The Driving Range, The Front 9, and The Back 9. The Driving Range, not included in this guide, offers seven bolted routes that range in difficulty from 5.8 to 5.11a on a short cliff. The Front 9, with 13 separate routes, is the steepest part of the crag. The overhanging mid-section is Country Club Cave. A large dead tree separates the Front 9 from the Back 9. The Back 9, the cliff's southeast sector, offers 12 routes. Variations and uncompleted projects, not included here, also dot the cliff. Needed gear includes 12 quick draws and a rope. All routes end at cold shuts or chain lowering anchors. Loose rock and handholds are found on some routes—belayers and climbers beware.

Trip Planning Information

General description: The Golf Wall offers almost 40 bolted sport routes on a thin limestone band.

Location: In the San Juan Mountains north of Durango.

Camping: Follow Forest Roads 671 and 166 north to Haviland Lake and Chris Park campgrounds.

Climbing season: April through October. The area lies at an elevation of 8,000 feet. Spring can be cool and windy, with rain and snow showers. Summers days are often hot on the south-facing cliff. Expect afternoon thunderstorms. Autumn brings excellent climbing weather, with warm days and crisp nights. Winter begins some time in November with snow piling up until March's spring thaw.

Restrictions and access issues: No current restrictions. The Golf Wall lies on the edge of the San Juan National Forest.

Guidebook: No guidebook is currently available. Information and topos might be found at Pine Needle Mountaineering in Durango.

Nearby mountain shops, guide services, and gyms: Backcountry Experience, Pine Needle Mountaineering, Southwest Adventures (Durango).

Services: All services in Durango.

Emergency services: Call 911. La Plata Community Hospital, 375 E. Main Ave., Durango, CO 81301, (970) 259-1110. Mercy Medical Center, 375 E. Park Ave., Durango, CO 81301, (970) 247-4311.

Nearby climbing areas: X-Rock, The Watchcrystal, Boxcar Boulder, Ophir Wall, Pope's Nose, Needle Range, Ouray ice climbing areas, Lizard Head Peak, Chimney Peak.

Nearby attractions: Durango & Silverton Narrow Gauge Railroad, Weminuche Wilderness Area, Mount Sneffels Wilderness Area, Lizard Head Wilderness Area, Silverton National Historic District, Purgatory Ski Area, Tamarron Resort, Chimney Rock Archeological Area, Navajo State Recreation Area, La Plata Range, Mancos State Recreation Area, Mesa Verde National Park, Escalante and Dominguez Ruins, Hovenweep National Monument, Ute Mountain Tribal Park.

Finding the crag: From the northern edge of Durango drive north 16.5 miles on U.S. 550. Look for a small parking area on the west side of the highway 1.3 miles past Tamarron. The cliff is readily apparent to the southeast. Cross the highway and go through a gate in the fence. Walk east on a path through a meadow and turn south down a shallow valley to a series of switchbacks that lead up to the Golf Wall. The approach takes less than 10 minutes.

THE FRONT 9

1. **Rain Delay** (5.11c) 6 bolts and chains.
2. **The Grip** (5.12c) 7 tan hangers and chains out the left side of the cave.
3. **The Masters** (5.12a/b) Up and over the roof on 5 bolts.
4. **Presidio** (5.13a) Steep route that begins by the Pipe Rock boulder at the cliff base.
5. **Golf War** (5.12b/c) 5 bolts to cold-shuts.
6. **Tamarron Open** (5.13b) 6 black bolts to chains.

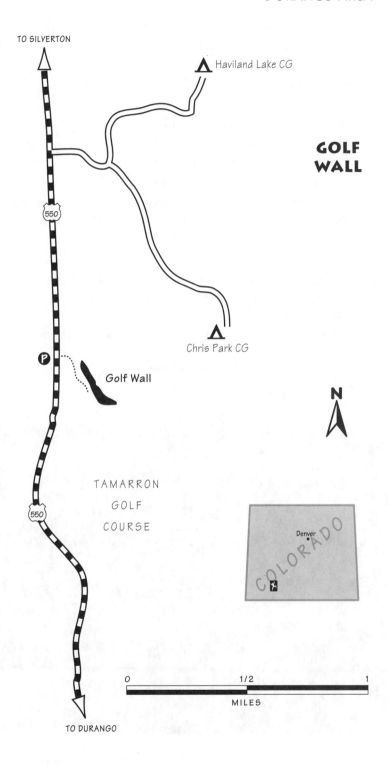

TO SILVERTON

Haviland Lake CG

GOLF WALL

550

Chris Park CG

P

Golf Wall

N

TAMARRON
GOLF
COURSE

Denver
COLORADO

0   1/2   1
MILES

TO DURANGO

7. **Divotator** (5.13a) Start in Country Club Cave and ascend outward past 5 bolts to cold shuts. A variation, LINKS (5.12c), climbs up and right past 3 bolts to BOGEYMAN.

8. **Bogeyman** (5.12a) 5 bolts to chains.

9. **Birdie** (5.10d) 5 bolts.

10. **Double Bogey** (5.11a) 7 bolts to chains up an almost vertical wall.

11. **Hole in One** (5.10d) Begin left of the dead tree. Scramble onto a ledge 10' up and climb up and left past 7 bolts to chains.

12. **Ping** (5.11b) Climb onto the ledge and head straight up past 5 black bolts.

13. **The Gallery** (5.11c) Begin just left of tree and climb past 6 bolts to anchors. Watch when cleaning the route that you don't swing into the tree—ouch!

THE BACK 9

14. **Greenskeeper's Playground** (5.10d) A good route that begins just right of the dead tree. Climb blocky limestone past 1 bolt to a ledge then head up left past 4 more bolts.

15. **Par 6** (5.11b) Excellent jug climbing over a 3-foot roof with good foot cams and a kneebar. Begin as for GREENSKEEPER'S PLAYGROUND only climb right past 5 more bolts to cold-shut anchors.

16. **Gopher Hole** (5.12a) 7 bolts to chains.

THE GOLF WALL

17. **Putt Putt** (5.11b/c) 5 bolts up steep rock left of the hole.

18. **Pebble Beach** (5.12a) A good hard route with a stiff move above the obvious hole. 9 bolts to chains.

19. **In The Rough** (5.10b) A steep but good route up slightly overhanging rock. Slightly loose near the top. 7 bolts to chains.

20. **Fairway Direct** (5.11c) 7 tan bolts to chains.

21. **Get Out of the Cart and Climb** (5.11d/.12a) Climb the "cart," a short ladder, to avoid the blank start and ascend steep rock past 7 bolts to cold shuts.

22. **Top Flight** (5.13 project) 7 black hangers.

23. **Bert and Ernie's Tourney** (5.12c/d) 7 cold shuts to cold-shut anchors.

24. **Cinderella Story** (5.12a) A wandering route on the right side past 8 bolts. Slightly chossy rock.

25. **Tee Off on This** (5.11c) Begin in the brush on the cliff's right side. 6 bolts to chains.

Mac Johnson belays Steve Hong on *Dust to Dust* on The Finger Face in the Garden of the Gods. *Photo by Stewart M. Green.*

APPENDIX A

FURTHER READING

Best of Boulder Climbs, Richard Rossiter, Chockstone Press, 1992.

Boulder Climbs North, Richard Rossiter, Chockstone Press, 1988.

Boulder Climbs South, Richard Rossiter, Chockstone Press, 1989.

Boulder Sport Climber's Guide, Mark Rolofson, 1994.

A Climber's Guide to the Ophir Wall, Allen Pattie, 1988.

Colorado Front Range Crags, Peter Hubbel, Chockstone Press, 1994.

Colorado's Fourteeners: Hikes to Climbs, Gerry Roach, 1992.

50 Select Classic Desert Climbs, Fred Knapp, 1994.

Flatiron Classics: Easy Climbs and Trails, Gerry Roach, Fulcrum Press, 1987.

For Turkeys Only: A Climber's Guide to Turkey Rock, Steve Cheyney and Bob Couchman, 1989.

Front Range Bouldering, Bob Horan, Chockstone Press, 1995.

Grand Junction Rock: Rock Climbs of Unaweep Canyon and Adjacent Areas, K.C. Baum, 1992.

Greyrock, Craig Luebben, 1992.

Heinous Cling: A Climber's Guide to Independence Pass, Andre Wille, 1994.

High Country Stone: Gunnison and Crested Butte Rock, Scott, 1993.

Naturita and Paradox Valley Rock Climbs, Charlie Fowler, 1990.

100 Select Boulder Classic Climbs, Fred Knapp, 1995.

100 Select Rocky Mountain National Park Classic Climbs, Fred Knapp, 1995.

100 Select Shelf Road Classic Climbs, Fred Knapp, 1995.

Rifle: Climber's Guide to Rifle Mountain National Park, by Hassan Saab, 1995.

Rock 'N Road: Rock Climbing Areas of North America, Tim Toula, Chockstone Press, 1995.

Rocky Mountain National Park: The Climber's Guide, Bernard Gillet, Earthbound Sports, 1993.

San Luis Valley: Rock Climbing and Bouldering Guide, Bob D'Antonio, 2nd Edition, Chockstone Press, 1994.

Shelf Road Rock Guide, Mark Van Horn, Chockstone Press, 1990.

South Platte Rock Climbing and the Garden of the Gods, Peter Hubbel and Mark Rolofson, Chockstone Press, 1988.

Telluride Rock, Charlie Fowler, 1990.

The San Juan Mountains, Robert Rosebrough, Cordillera Press, 1986.

APPENDIX B

RATING SYSTEM COMPARISON CHART

YDS	British	French	Australian
5.3	VD 3b	2	11
5.4	HVD 3c	3	12
5.5	MS/S/HS 4a	4a	12/13
5.6	HS/S 4a	4b	13/14
5.7	HS/VS 4b	4c	15-17
5.8	VS 4c/5a	5a	18
5.9	HVS 5a/5b	5b	19
5.10a	E1 5a/5b	5c	20
5.10b	E1 5b/5c	6a	20
5.10c	E2 5b/5c	6a+	21
5.10d	E2/E3 5b/5c	6b	21
5.11a	E3 5c/6a	6b+	22
5.11b	E3/E4 5c/6a	6c	22
5.11c	E4 5c/6a	6c+	23
5.11d	E4 6a/6b	7a	24
5.12a	E5 6a/6b	7a+	25
5.12b	E5/E6 6a/6b	7b	26
5.12c	E6 6b/6c	7b+	27
5.12d	E6 6b/6c	7c	27
5.13a	E6/E7 6b/6c	7c+	28
5.13b	E7 6c/7a	8a	29
5.13c	E7 6c/7a	8a+	30
5.13d	E8 6c/7a	8b	31
5.14a	E8 6c/7a	8b+	32
5.14b	E9 6c/7a	8c	??
5.14c	E9 7b	8c+	??

Sources: *Mountaineering: The Freedom of the Hills*, 5th Edition; *Climbing Magazine*, No. 150, February/March 1995.

APPENDIX C

MOUNTAIN SHOPS, CLIMBING GYMS, AND GUIDE SERVICES

Aspen

Aspen Athletic Club, 720 E. Hyman Ave., Aspen, CO 81611, (970) 925-2531.

The Ute Mountaineer, 308 S. Mill St., Aspen, CO 81611 (970) 925-2849.

Boulder

Basecamp Mountain Sports, 821 Pearl St., Boulder, CO 80302, (303) 443-6770.

Boulder Mountaineer, 1335 Broadway, Boulder, CO 80302, (303) 442-8355.

Boulder Mountaineering Climbing School, 1335 Broadway, Boulder, CO 80302, (303) 442-8355.

Boulder Rock Club, 2952 Baseline Road, Boulder, CO 80303, (303) 447-2804.

Mountain Sports, 821 Pearl St., Boulder, CO 80302, (303) 443-6770.

Neptune Mountaineering, 627 S. Broadway, Boulder, CO 80303, (303) 499-8866.

Buena Vista

The Trailhead, 707 Hwy. 24 North, Buena Vista, CO, 81211, (719) 395-8001.

Colorado Springs

Grand West Outfitters, 3250 N. Academy, Colorado Springs, CO 80917, (719) 596-3031.

Mountain Chalet, 226 N. Tejon, Colorado Springs, CO 80903, (719) 633-0732.

Pikes Peak Mountain Sports, 2111 N. Weber, Colorado Springs, CO 80907, (719) 634-3575.

Sport Climbing Center of Colorado Springs, 4650 Northpark Dr., Colorado Springs, CO 80918, (719) 260-1050.

8th Street Climbing Club, 810 Arcturus Dr., Colorado Springs, CO 80906, (719) 578-5555.

Denver

Grand West Outfitters, 801 Broadway, Denver, CO 80203, (303) 825-0300.

The North Face, 2490 S. Colorado, Denver, CO 80222, (303) 758-6366. Paradise Rock Gym, 6260 W. Washington St., Unit 5, Denver, CO 80216, (303) 286-8168.

Durango

Backcountry Experience, 780 Main Ave., Durango, CO 81301, (800) 648-8519.

Pine Needle Mountaineering, 835 Main Ave. #112, Durango, CO 81301, (303) 247-8728.

Southwest Adventures, P.O. Box 3242, Durango, CO 81302, (800) 642-5389.

Eldorado Springs

Bob Culp Climbing School, 3330 Eldorado Springs Dr., Eldorado Springs, CO 80025, (303) 499-1185 or (800) 993-8355.

International Alpine School, P.O. Box 3037, Eldorado Springs, CO 80025, (303) 494-4904.

Naked Edge Mountaineering, P.O. Box 343, Eldorado Springs, CO 80025 (303) 993-8355.

Estes Park

Colorado Mountain School, 351 Moraine Ave., Estes Park, CO 80517, (970) 586- 5758.
Komito Boots 235 W. Riverside, Estes Park, CO 80517, (970) 586-5391, (800) 422-2668.
Wilderness Sports 358 Elkhorn, Estes Park, CO 80517, (970) 586-6548.

Fort Collins

Adventure Outfitters, 334 E. Mountain Ave., Fort Collins, CO 80524, (970) 224-2460.
Desert Ice Mountain Guides, 1606 Banyan #1, Fort Collins, CO 80526, (970) 493-2849.
Inner Strength Rock Gym, 3713 S. Mason, Fort Collins, CO 80525, (970) 282-8118.
The Mountain Shop, 632 S. Mason, Fort Collins, CO 80524, (970) 493-5720.

Glenwood Springs

Summit Canyon Mountaineering, 1001 Grand Ave., Glenwood Springs, CO 81601, (970) 945-6994.

Golden

Bent Gate Inc., 1300 Washington, Golden, CO 80401, (303) 271-9382.

Grand Junction

Natural Progression Rock Guides, 289 32 1/2 Road, Grand Junction, CO 81503, (970) 434-3955.
Summit Canyon Mountaineering, 549 Main St., Grand Junction, CO 81501, (970) 243-2847.
Tower Guides/Andy Petefish, P.O. Box 3231c, Grand Junction, CO 81502, (970) 245-6992.
Vertical Works Climbing Gym and Pro Shop, 2845 Chipeta Ave., Grand Junction, CO 81501, (970) 245-3610.

Nederland

High Peaks Mountain Shop, 1 West First St., Nederland, CO 80466, (303) 258-7436.

Ophir

Antoine Savelli, P.O. Box 714, Ophir, CO 81426, (970) 728-3705.

Telluride

Charlie Fowler, P.O. Box 2604, Telluride, CO 81435, (970) 327-4192.
Fantasy Ridge Mountain Guides, P.O. Box 1679, Telluride, CO 81435, Phone/Fax (970) 728-3546.
Telluride Mountaineer, 219 E. Colorado Ave., Telluride, CO 81435.
Telluride Sports, 150 W. Colorado Ave., Telluride, CO 81435, (970) 728-4477.

INDEX

456

458

X

Y

Z

ABOUT THE AUTHOR

Stewart M. Green is a freelance photographer and writer living in Colorado Springs. He began climbing 30 years ago and has ascended routes throughout the United States and Europe. His photographs appear in many national publications, including *Climbing, Rock & Ice, Sierra, Outside,* and others. He is the author and photographer of *Pikes Peak Country: The Complete Guide, Colorado Parklands, Back Country Byways, Arizona Scenic Drives, California Scenic Drives,* and is currently working on *New England Scenic Drives.*

Stewart Green photographs on the sheer walls of the Verdon Gorge in France.
Photo by Josh Morris.